DATE DUE

NOV 26 '91			
SDH 5-14-92			

HIGHSMITH   # 45220

THE JAPANESE POWER GAME

THE JAPANESE POWER GAME

What It Means for America

William J. Holstein

CHARLES SCRIBNER'S SONS
New York
COLLIER MACMILLAN CANADA
Toronto
MAXWELL MACMILLAN INTERNATIONAL
New York   Oxford   Singapore   Sydney

Charles Scribner's Sons   Collier Macmillan Canada, Inc.
Macmillan Publishing Company   1200 Eglinton Avenue East, Suite 200
866 Third Avenue, New York, NY 10022   Don Mills, Ontario M3C 3N1

Library of Congress Cataloging-in-Publication Data

Holstein, William J.
    The Japanese power game: what it means for America / William J.
Holstein.
      p.   cm.
    Includes bibliographical references.
    ISBN 0-684-19176-8
    1. Corruption (in politics)—Japan. 2. Political culture—Japan.
3. Japan—Politics and government—1945– 4. Japan—Economic
conditions—1945– 5. Japan—Foreign economic relations—United
States. 6. United States—Foreign economic relations—Japan.
I. Title.
JQ1629.C6H65   1990
306.2'0952—dc20   90-34087

Macmillan books are available at special discounts for bulk purchases
for sales promotions, premiums, fund-raising, or educational use.
For details, contact:

    Special Sales Director
    Macmillan Publishing Company
    866 Third Avenue
    New York, NY 10022

10 9 8 7 6 5 4 3 2 1

Designed by Nancy Sugihara

Printed in the United States of America

To Cathy

Contents

Part Three

INTO THE FUTURE

Part Four

THE AMERICAN RESPONSE

Acknowledgments

I am particularly indebted to *Business Week*. Editor-in-chief Steve She-pard, senior editor Bob Dowling, Tokyo bureau chief Bob Neff, and McGraw-Hill Tokyo bureau chief Toshio Aritake all supported this project. Others who helped educate me about Japan and U.S.-Japanese relations over the years include Larry Armstrong, Amy Borrus, Barbara Buell, Steve Dryden, Neil Gross, Leslie Helm, Ted Holden, Wakako Ishibashi, Paul Magnusson, Sayaka Shinoda, Kyoko Takahashi, and Jim Treece. I have written this book in an individual capacity, however, and the views expressed are mine alone.

I also owe a debt of gratitude to Tomoaki Iwai, a professor and specialist on money politics at Tokiwa and Keio universities, and to Takao To-shikawa, editor of the "Tokyo Insider" newsletter. I have attempted to identify information they provided, whether in the text or by footnote. My assistant, Misako Furukawa, managed my schedule and held the project together.

Tadashi Yamamoto and Hiroshi Peter Kamura of the Japan Center for International Exchange gave generously of their time and insight. Mitsui & Co.'s Jitsuro Terashima and Ichiro Uchida of the Ministry of Foreign Affairs made introductions and offered counsel. I met about two dozen members of both houses of the Diet all together, and I would like to thank all of them for extending that courtesy.

Dewey and Barbara Brackett, Mark Cummings, Fred Franz, Paul Fukuda, Yoichi Funabashi, Kozo Hiramatsu, Rikio Imajo, Masao Kanazashi, Tom Logan, Brad and Hideko Martin, Michiya Matsukawa, Robert and Miyako

Mead, Janet Snyder, Shuntaro Torigoe, Naoaki Usui, Yuki Wakimura, Darrel Whitten, Hiroshi Yamamoto, and others provided either information or moral support or a combination thereof.

Robert Angel at the University of South Carolina, Gerald Curtis of Columbia University, and Chalmers Johnson of the University of California at San Diego read partial drafts or offered their analysis.

At Scribners, Barbara Grossman, John Glusman, and Robert Stewart were instrumental in shaping and guiding my work, as was my agent, Reid Boates.

Unless otherwise noted, all quotes in the book are from my conversations with mentioned sources. Travel and research were independently funded.

My gratitude to neighbors John and Ellen Morehouse for allowing me to move my Macintosh Plus into the quiet room under their porch where the bulk of the book was written. Thanks to Jason and Alison for understanding that Dad was busy and thanks to my parents for just about everything.

THE JAPANESE POWER GAME

Introduction

Today, the eyes of the world are on Japan as never before in the postwar era. It is, therefore, no surprise that attention has been riveted on a remarkable period of scandal and drama that dominated Japanese politics in 1989. At the moment that Japan seemed headed into a critical face-off with the United States over trade and defense issues, Prime Minister Noboru Takeshita was forced to resign as a result of the Recruit insider trading scandal. The high-flying Recruit group published a dozen magazines and had growing real estate and telecommunications businesses with a total of nearly $5 billion in sales. Hiromasa Ezoe, the founder of the rapidly expanding media empire and Japan's answer to Rupert Murdoch, took advantage of the exploding Japanese real estate market and the Tokyo stock market to spread millions of his unlisted shares among the top echelons of Japan's political structure to curry favor—and favors.

The Recruit scandal seemed to discredit nearly the entire top leadership of the Liberal Democratic Party (LDP) by mid-1989. A weak stand-in prime minister, Sosuke Uno, was quickly toppled by a sex scandal and by the party's poor showing in the July 1989 Upper House elections. The career of Yasuhiro Nakasone, the once-proud former prime minister, was prematurely terminated because of his association with Ezoe. The tough Hisashi Shinto, chairman of Nippon Telegraph & Telephone (NTT), at one point the world's largest company in terms of market capitalization, was arrested for accepting Recruit bribes and put on trial, as was Ezoe.

1

Some Japan-watchers believed that the Japanese had risen up and dealt a mighty blow to a corrupt system. They argued that a woman, Takako Doi, and more surprisingly a Socialist woman, appeared headed for real power. Many foreign analysts believed this meant the arrival of a genuine women's movement and the attendant rise of consumerism in producer-oriented Japan, where most consumers are women. Surely, the hope went, the upheaval of 1989 proved that the giant was showing strains after an astonishing postwar economic march. After long decades of discipline and sacrifice, the Japanese were evolving into a more Westernized society. They were becoming "more like us." They would be more willing to open their markets and moderate their external economic drive. To these analysts it seemed as though the very values upon which Japan was built were shifting.

Comforting though it was to a world concerned about Japan's competitive challenge, this analysis was largely wishful thinking. To be sure, the Recruit and Uno scandals offered fascinating glimpses into Japanese society. Combined with discontent over a new 3 percent consumption tax and a farmers' revolt against the import of agricultural goods from the United States, the events of 1989 revealed that the Japanese system had indeed reached a moment of genuine flux.

But it was only temporary. Japan continues on the path it has followed for decades. The scandals did not reveal an outburst of Western-style moralism or a democratic groundswell. Nor were the Japanese suddenly becoming Socialists and throwing monkey wrenches into the workings of their economic machine. In fact, the Recruit group was a minor player in a much larger drama, namely a decade-long bare-knuckled fight for political and economic control of Japan's multibillion-dollar telecommunications kingdom. Shinto, the NTT chairman, and Prime Minister Nakasone were not part of the established order as much as they were challengers. They were using Ezoe to help them assault a telecommunications empire that former Prime Minister Kakuei Tanaka had built. It was the challengers, not members of the inward-looking, structurally corrupt system, who were punished.

Moreover, Uno was not discredited because he maintained mistresses over a period of years. He was humiliated because he didn't manage them properly. It had little to do with the Anglo-American concept of marital fidelity. It is also clear that women will make only fractional gains in this climate, and that any progress they do achieve does not necessarily mean Japan will soften. The pace of social change will be glacially slow, and veer in directions that the outside world scarcely expects.

This is an examination of what really happened and what it means to the outside world. Within a matter of months following the apparent tumult of early and mid-1989, the Liberal Democratic Party blunted the Socialist challenge, and the Recruit and Uno scandals were largely forgotten. The LDP went on to win a thoroughly convincing victory in Lower House elections in February 1990. Powerful bureaucrats and business leaders were scarcely touched by what appeared to be incredible political upheaval. Far from liberalizing, the slightly expanded Socialist role has contributed to a more conservative stance designed to protect the status quo. Rather than suddenly rushing to accommodate external demands, the Japanese political system is now responding to the recognition that Japan has genuine power and does not need to submit so readily to American pressure. The trade accords that the Bush Administration trumpeted in April 1990 had a hollow ring and contained little that would change the direction of the U.S.–Japanese economic relations. In short, the Japanese system is rolling on, and underlying it is a drift to a more nationalistic, assertive mood.

Far from cracking, Japan's economic performance is actually accelerating. With benefit of hindsight, the correction of the Tokyo stock market did not disrupt Japan's overall economic momentum. With each day that passes, its manufacturing and financial prowess yield new gains in world markets. Its trade and investment, aid programs, bank lending, and technological achievements promise to give it a much more powerful and visible role in North America and East Asia, as well as Western Europe and other parts of the globe. Pressure is also building on American auto, machine tools, semiconductor, computer, construction, and other industries in a period that could recall the early 1980s. Tens of billions more dollars are in the investment pipeline in what may be only the early stages of establishing a global presence that will operate on Japanese rules and serve Japanese interests. This will require increasingly deep involvement in shaping American perceptions and American politics.

What's at stake is nothing less than the shape of the twenty-first century. Now that the Japanese have surpassed the Soviets, the United States and Japan are the world's two largest economies. Rarely in history have two societies of such vastly different values allowed themselves to become so interdependent. Although the two have areas of genuine cooperation, they are also engaged in serious confrontation. It is more than an economic contest. It is a question of whose rules and whose values will prevail. Thus, how the power game is played internally and how Japan plays the power game internationally are important questions.

Equally important is how the United States responds, and respond it must. Japan poses a far broader challenge to the U.S. than widely recognized. It is no longer a question of mere trade policy. It has become a question of whether Americans, in areas where the two countries face economic confrontation, can develop systematic responses that also include more effective industrial and investment policies. The greatest challenge is achieving a national strategy that can bridge differences between Republicans and Democrats, between conservatives and liberals, and between Japan-lovers and Japan-haters to achieve a better balance in U.S.-Japanese economic relations.

In the following pages I have attempted to walk a dispassionate path through an increasingly emotional debate about Japan and its role in the world. I have also tried to make the issues accessible. For too long, the debate has been in the hands of a relatively small number of experts. Their deliberations tend to be highly specialized and directed toward a limited audience. This book—which blends culture, politics, business, economics, and governmental policy—attempts to establish a broad framework for understanding. The issues have become so important that everyone deserves an opportunity to explore them.

Part One

THE POWER
SOCIETY

❖ 1 ❖

Change, No Change?

One of my favorite symbols of change in Japan is Harajuku. Every Sunday afternoon, a big four-lane avenue in the Harajuku area of Shibuya-ku is closed to traffic and the teenagers take over. When I first saw this in 1982, I suspected that the youth of Japan were on a straight-line path to ruin. The boys wore dark wraparound sunglasses and had their hair slicked back, Elvis Presley style. They wore white T-shirts with their sleeves rolled up, tight-fitting black jeans, and pointed black boots. The girls wore American-style high school letter sweaters, pleated skirts, and saddle shoes. Groups of eight or ten boys would stand around a radio or a boom box twisting and gyrating. The girls had radios and were also dancing in a circle. Why weren't they home cramming? What was Japan coming to?

My hosts patiently explained to me that it wasn't as bad as it seemed. Sure, the older generation was worried about these youngsters. But in many senses, what they were doing reflected the best of Japanese culture. They were acting as part of small groups. Each group was disciplined and well rehearsed. There was little sign of spontaneity. And everyone was conforming to a certain pattern. Certainly there were no drugs or alcohol. Even though they had to sneak out of their homes to dress and groom themselves in the bushes, I was assured that they would grow to be contributing members of society.

When I went back in 1989 to see the kids in Harajuku, I thought maybe the earlier analysis was all wrong. Things seemed to have gone from bad to worse. A new wave of kids was wearing outrageous clothes, often with the knees ripped out. Some sported painted faces. The fashion this time was punk. Very punk. Eye patches, handcuffs, the works. And the nice well-orchestrated groups standing around their boom boxes had been virtually eliminated by full-fledged punk bands blasting away with electric guitars and amplifiers only thirty yards from each other. The lead singer of the Yellow Duck band was decked out in rings and black leather, and sported long blond hair that must have been a wig. Like a prepubescent Mick Jagger, he pranced in front of a crowd of about a hundred teenage girls and stood up on a box to be better seen. It was a mob scene.

So, was the 1982 interpretation wrong? I pondered it as I shouldered my way through the crowd, feeling overwhelmingly middle-aged. Then it hit me. The kids had moved to a higher level of organization. They now had trucks to deliver all the equipment and managers to better coordinate them. Each band had a big sign hanging behind it in case a big-time agent happened along. But most important, the conformism was still intact. The punk styles were not only very similar, they were thoroughly imitative of what might be seen in New York or London. Westerners associate punkers with various forms of deviancy. But there was no sign of rebellion, or even genuine spontaneity, in Harajuku. The girls who were attracted to Yellow Duck's lead singer were organized in some sort of club. They jumped up and down, threw confetti, and extended their right hands all in unison. Although a handful of the kids might qualify as true dropouts, and some high school kids clearly abuse alcohol, the broader and more important trend was that the youth of Japan were obeying and conforming on a larger scale than ever. It was merely the costumes that had changed.

This is just one snapshot, but it helps explain the difficulty outsiders have had in analyzing change in Japan since the early 1900s when the country first began receiving serious Western attention. Trends or phenomena that have been highly visible to the *gaijin* (foreigner) over the years have suggested that Japan was adopting Christianity on a wholesale basis, that it was moderating its prewar military expansion, that it was shifting course in its economic expansion into the world, or that its society was on the verge of Western-style transformation. Change in Japan! the Westerners proclaimed. In fact, very little of it happened. The reason for the confusion is that Americans and other Westerners tend to grasp at symbols that have echoes in their own culture, and to interpret them in a context that has little bearing on what the Japanese themselves perceive is happening.

For a country that did not have electricity or sophisticated machinery when it opened to the West, Japan has certainly made dramatic changes as it evolved into the industrial powerhouse it is today. It successfully made the transition from an agrarian to a fully industrialized, predominantly urban society—something few peoples in the world have been able to accomplish without a revolution or major dislocation.

But in other respects, Japan staunchly resists change of the sort that the outside world often advocates and then believes it sees. Simply put, the Japanese resist absorbing influences that challenge the notion of who they are as Japanese. If a technology or management practice contributes to Japanese well-being, it can be copied perfectly and perhaps improved upon. But if a notion or a concept is destabilizing or challenges Japan's long-term interests, it is screened out. There is almost always an underlying level of reality that is different from what the *gaijin* sees and hears.

The debate about change versus no change in the early 1900s centered on whether Japan would absorb Christianity and Western ideals of democracy, and how it would conduct itself toward its Asian neighbors. When I used to pass through Shanghai there was a bookstore at the Jinjiang Hotel, where I stayed, that I liked to visit. The Chinese must have been amused that I was willing to spend $15 or $20 in hard currency for musty old books of no apparent value. But I found fascinating tomes with titles like *Democracy and the Eastern Question,* which Thomas F. Millard published in 1919,[1] and *Contemporary Politics in the Far East,* which Stanley K. Hornbeck published in 1916.[2]

These authors were arguing over whether Japan would allow wholesale adoption of American democratic ideals and Christianity or whether it would retain an emperor-based system dominated by conservative elites. One school argued that the progressive and liberal forces were destined to triumph. The other, in language that was perhaps too harsh, wrote that the Japanese were busy copying German authoritarian forms of military and social organization and were clearly bent on a course of expansion in China and throughout Asia. Events in coming years certainly proved that writers looking for Japan to suddenly crack and change course had been deceived.

Years later, in the days prior to World War II, at a time when Japanese armies were on the march throughout Asia, many Westerners tried to find signs of "liberalism" in Japanese society. As a result of boycotts and embargoes imposed on Japan, some outside observers detected great signs of dissatisfaction and discontent in Japan. Living standards were being sacrificed for the war effort. Certainly, the hope went, the strains on the political, economic, and social structure would become so great that the military-dominated system would be overthrown. The forces that stood for democracy, freedom of speech, and representative government would somehow rise up.

Sir George Sansom, a British diplomat, wrote a classic article on the prewar change-versus-no-change debate in April 1941.[3] He argued that Westerners must rid their minds of "misconceptions which arise because we think in terms of our own vocabulary when we discuss Far Eastern affairs. We are inclined to postulate the existence of a numerous class of 'liberals,' and we are misled by our own use of the word 'liberal' into supposing that there is in Japan a school of political thought which approves of democratic institutions and thus somehow corresponds, if only in miniature, to the great majorities in the United States or Great Britain." It was a mistake, Sansom argued, to think that these forces would "by some kind of revolutionary process . . . set up a new, enlightened and prosperous regime with which the democracies can talk business." He added: "Liberalism has never secured a firm foothold in Japan, and it has never, even in its short seasons of success, been a force working against an expansionist foreign policy." Those who had identified dissatisfaction and predicted a sudden softening were proven wrong. Sansom was proven correct.

The current change-versus-no-change debate was foreshadowed in the 1970s, when some Japan-watchers began to express concern about Japan's very stability. In a book published in 1973, Edwin Reischauer, the dean of a generation of Japan-watchers, spoke of sweeping changes in Japanese society.[4] The status of women was rising, religious freedom was expanding, and social relations were becoming more casual. "The pursuit of happiness—or of pleasure—in coffeehouses, movie theaters, and pinball parlors, at symphonies, or on ski slopes, beaches or camping grounds became an accepted goal, especially for youth. These changes . . . created a new social configuration, a new way of life." At the same time, the Japanese were pressing for better housing, health care, public transportation, and sewage facilities. They were upset about money politics, as displayed in the Lockheed scandal, and they had sent a message to the Liberal Democratic Party (LDP) by inflicting losses in the Upper House of the Diet.

Reischauer, who had served as U.S. ambassador to Japan, wrote that in view of the rapid pace of change, one would expect "dislocations" and "strains." The implication was that Japan's external drive had some inherent, built-in limitations.

In fact, Japan's astonishing economic emergence was just beginning in earnest at a time when Reischauer was warning of domestic unrest. It was only a few years later that Ezra Vogel warned, correctly, that Japan was becoming Number 1 in industrial competitiveness.[5] This was the broader, underlying trend during the 1970s. When I first visited Japan in 1979 to cover the economic summit of the seven industrial nations, there was little sense that Japan was struggling for direction. It was patiently putting the building blocks in place for a world emergence.

On the surface, at least, there were signs of genuine change in 1989 and early 1990. More Japanese were working for foreign companies such as IBM and Salomon Brothers. These had become prestigious firms in Japanese eyes and college graduates were willing—and eager—to work for them. Headhunting, or, more politely, executive recruitment, began to make an appearance. Japanese executives in midcareer were beginning to switch jobs, rather than persevering in lifelong commitments to their companies. Women were entering the work force in greater numbers. In many cases, they were holding part-time jobs. A handful even set up their own companies, often in such fields as translation or design. Women were also beginning to recognize that they had a political voice.

Also intriguing was the presence of many more foreigners in central Tokyo than ever before. Not only Americans and Europeans, but also Pakistanis, Filipinos, Chinese, and Koreans. According to the Justice Ministry, nearly a million foreigners now live in Japan, the largest group being the 700,000 second- and third-generation Koreans, who are not considered Japanese citizens. The 37,000 North Americans and 22,000 Europeans are a mere smattering in comparison, but still the number has grown. There were many other signs of increased "internationalization." The number of Mexican, Indian, and Thai restaurants was a surprise. French pastry was in great demand. On pop radio stations, the Japanese were being told: "Get used to the Western life-style. Enjoy your life."

Clearly, there were some new strains as Japan coped with its new wealth. Primary among them was the Japanese perception that the distribution of assets in their society was increasingly unbalanced. The Japanese have traditionally believed in broad equality of wealth, as have the Koreans and Chinese. Some say it is the result of the post-Confucian ethic. But more concretely, in the case of Japan, it is because nearly all Japanese were desperately poor for years after World War II. As they geared up their economic effort, the tendency was to sublimate the pursuit of individual wealth and comfort to the broader national goal of achieving economic parity with the West. To this day, Japan is much more egalitarian in its distribution of wealth than is America. The concern about poor distribution of wealth in Japan must be seen in that context.

The problem, however mild, started in earnest in 1985 when the long-undervalued yen began its astonishing gain in value. The Plaza accords of September 1985, when the major industrial nations agreed that the yen must be higher in value, merely ratified a trend that had started in February of that year. The market had begun to recognize the underlying strength of Japan's economy. The yen was worth more. Over the course of about the next three years, the yen strengthened in value from about 250 to the dollar to as low as 120 before settling in the 140-to-145 range.*

This helped trigger a tripling of real estate prices in Tokyo and a tripling of the Tokyo stock market. Of course, there were other reasons for this boom. An increasing concentration of people and economic activity in Tokyo meant there was greater demand for space, which already was in short supply. The city's population reached 12 million but the greater metropolitan area has more than 30 million people, roughly a quarter of the nation's population. Because of various antiquated land-use and agricultural laws, crowding is particularly acute. With a sudden influx of wealth and a scarcity of available land, values exploded.

The people who most obviously benefited from this explosion in real estate and stock prices were not Japan's traditional elites. This is an essential point to grasp in understanding the roots of the Recruit scandal. Those who flaunted newfound wealth were those who owned real estate or had some connection with construction, retailing chains, or hotels. Even a noodle shop owner in downtown Tokyo who owned the space under his shop could walk away a multimillionaire. *Forbes* magazine, fascinated as ever with rich people, reported that fourteen of the twenty-two Japanese billionaires it identified in 1987 owed the bulk of their fortunes to real estate.[6] These flashy tycoons are the sort that buy Van Goghs and Kentucky racehorses, or snap up big-name, "trophy" buildings in New York and Los Angeles. Recruit's Ezoe, from humble origins in Osaka, fell into the category of someone who took advantage of both real estate and stock explosions to rapidly expand his business and influence.

Unlike old moneyed elites in Japan, the new rich were painfully obvious about displaying their mistresses and Rolls-Royces. To top it off, some of the new rich had underworld associations and relied too heavily on tax evasion and other questionable business practices. "These are not respectable people," sniffed one high-ranking official at the Ministry of Finance.

---

*Note: In converting yen amounts into dollars I have attempted to use conversion rates prevailing at the time. This accounts for the apparent inconsistencies in the yen/dollar relationships throughout the book.

The fast, new money triggered frustration. Tokyo salarymen, or salaried workers, resent having to live in small, expensive homes far from their jobs. When one of the recipients of Recruit funds, Nakasone aide Takao Fujinami, used the proceeds to pay $900,000 for an 1,800-square-foot house, twice the size of the average home, most average Japanese were outraged. This violated the notion that Japanese political leaders should share in the sacrifices that other Japanese people make. Fujinami had broken ranks. His new home was also in a prime area of Tokyo, meaning Fujinami did not need to endure the ninety-minute to two-hour commutes that are routine for many salarymen.

Aside from irritations over wealth distribution, most urban Japanese face other life-style frustrations: the highways are clogged; only a third of Japanese homes are connected to sewers; and having fun is expensive. Membership in a top golf club costs more than $2 million and playing a full round often involves a twenty-four-hour commitment. An avid golfer will rise early in the morning, travel for two to three hours to the golf course, and perhaps get nine holes played in three hours. It takes so long because of congestion on the course. Then he takes a break, eats lunch, and socializes. After the lunch break he plays the next nine holes. It's so late by the time they finish their eighteen holes that many men simply spend the night at the club with their colleagues. "The fruits of our economic activity have not been distributed well," said Takako Doi, the Socialist party chairwoman, in an interview in her cramped Diet office. "We are an economic superpower, they say, but we are not a living-standard superpower." The ruling LDP was clearly out of touch with Japanese voters. On April 1, 1989, at the same time its members were taking advantage of the new money to buy big houses and spend their evenings with their mistresses, the LDP chose to put a 3 percent consumption tax into effect.

So is there a revolt, a kind of "cultural revolution," that challenges the very fabric of Japanese society? Certainly, voters sent a signal of displeasure to the LDP in July 1989. They vented. But politics is a superficial level of analysis in Japan. Some seasoned Japan-watchers in Tokyo liken the importance of politics in Japan to pennant races in baseball, or to soap operas where viewers write in to shape the plot. Business and bureaucratic elites have dominated Japan far more than the politicians. What lay beneath the political show? Would Japanese dissatisfaction suddenly help open up Japan's distribution channels to a flood of foreign products? Was there a crack in the work ethic that would temper Japan's economic machine?

The fact was this: Japanese discontent is actually much more constrained and disciplined than it appears at first glance. The Japanese are hardheaded pragmatists. They know their overall living standards today are far better than ever before. They have efficient trains and socialized medicine. Japan is one of the safest societies in the world, where a person can walk down the streets of the nation's largest city at any hour without the slightest fear of assault. Their system has created tremendous wealth, even if the spoils are not being distributed as quickly or as fairly as some would like. There is no organized consumer movement and the consumer groups that do exist tend to be run by former bureaucrats and supported by major companies. They are not in the business of advocating consumer interests but rather in defusing consumer agitation. In short, very few Japanese feel so dissatisfied about the availability of consumer goods that they want to kill the golden goose. There are certainly no public protests over their quality of life. Just as it may appear that the kids in Harajuku are in sad decline, there's an underlying reality that's different. There was no sudden snapping of the prevailing social and political order.

One reason for this is that there are safety valves. Far from being starved for attractive goods, Japanese consumers are engaged in a veritable orgy of consumerism. The number of Jaguars, Mercedes, and BMWs in the streets of central Tokyo, not to mention the huge Nissan Presidents and Toyota Crowns, is surprising. Many more Japanese than just tycoons and gangsters are able to afford prestige cars.

No consumer goods? Go to Akihabara, which used to be the district where a smart shopper could find reasonably priced consumer electronics goods. It was tucked away in a cramped series of indoor stalls. It still exists, but it's not particularly cheap anymore. More important, the streets around it have been taken over by big, Crazy Eddie–type discount stores for washing machines, refrigerators, personal computers, stereos, air conditioners, lights, and other household items. Amid blaring disco music and neon lights, pretty girls stand out in front on Sunday afternoons with microphones imploring passersby to buy, buy, buy. And buy they do, despite the high prices. A tiny computerized washing machine goes for $700. Virtually everything in these stores is made-in-Japan, and it is all more expensive than it would be in the United States.

At the Mitsukoshi Department Store on the Ginza, the Japanese equivalent of Saks Fifth Avenue, every top Western name in luxury is available: Estée Lauder, Clinique, Tiffany, Pierre Cardin, Norma Kamali, Burberry, Oscar de la Renta. And at the glass-enclosed Nissan showroom across the street, young Japanese are ogling a new Nissan Sports Fairlady Z. This nifty two-seater goes for a mere 4.1 million yen, about $30,000.

Perhaps the most single flagrant display of buying power came when the Japanese took out a sixty-five-day charter of the *Queen Elizabeth II* in the spring of 1989. Japanese tourists paid large sums of money to come aboard and shop or to spend the night, and the ship never went anywhere. It remained docked at Yokohama. Boutiques had trouble keeping enough supplies of $3,360 sapphire, gold, and diamond watches. It cost as much as $2,658 for a top-of-the-line cabin, but guests got the royal treatment, complete with casino gambling.[7]

Tokyo, in a word, is choking on its wealth. It has the best of what the world can offer: French croissants, exotic coffees, and prestigious whiskeys. Goods are more expensive than anywhere else, but the Japanese have little chance of ever cracking the powerful cartels, monopolies, and entrenched distribution systems that dominate many areas of Japan's economy.

Outside of central Tokyo, to be sure, people are less affluent. Many neighborhoods are dreary industrial areas where retirees, shopkeepers, and small subcontractors constitute the fabric of life. In rural areas there is none of Tokyo's glitz, except perhaps in the *pachinko* (pinball) parlors. Still, a rice farmer I visited in rural Niigata Prefecture had three vehicles, three televisions, and at least one VCR. "This may be the only [industrial] country in the world where the losers have Louis Vuitton bags," quips Tadashi Yamamoto, head of the Japan Center for International Exchange (JCIE). "The problem is where can we put all our things?"

There is relatively little that can be done about this space crunch. Some 120 million Japanese live in a country the size of California. Western analysts speculating in the 1930s about Japan's future believed that the nation's maximum population would be 80 million. This is the essential problem. The Japanese can blame local and national governments for failing to create better infrastructures, for restrictive zoning laws, and for laws that keep an enormous amount of land involved in rice production. But there is little prospect of sudden relief. Despite the frustration that Japanese readily demonstrate to foreigners, in many ways the stronger—but silent—force is their acceptance of the inherent limits that being Japanese imposes on them. It cannot be helped, as the Japanese say. *Shikata ga nai.*

If we are probing for change of a sort that would crack the established order, certainly the work ethic should be suffering. While it may be frayed around the edges a bit, it is still far stronger than in the United States. Part of the frustration of the average Japanese may be directed into actually working harder, not relaxing. The evidence is fragmentary, but consider the difficulties the government has had in lowering the number of hours worked. The Ministry of International Trade and Industry (MITI) set a five-year goal in 1986 of reducing the yearly hours that the average Japanese worked from 2,111 (compared with 1,924 in the U.S.) to 1,800 by 1992. That meant they would have to persuade the Japanese to work 60 hours fewer each year, for five consecutive years. But in the first year of the program, the number of hours declined by only 6. At that rate, it would take fifty years to achieve the objective.

The current total is actually higher than in 1983, when the average Japanese worked 2,098 hours a year. Even though more Japanese now have Saturdays off and are being encouraged to take summer vacations, they may put in overtime to compensate for the time they are about to lose. Or else, feeling pressure from colleagues who may resent being left on the job, they resist taking the time because they don't want to be away from their offices or factories when others are working. When they do go on vacations, it is often with fellow workers. "Social change here is glacial," says Ron Napier, an economist with Salomon Brothers in Tokyo. "Don't hold your breath."

Indeed, some younger Japanese, who are supposedly lazy in comparison with their elders, are still working themselves to death. Yoshitake Sajima, a vice president at Mitsui & Co. in New York, once told me, "It is my privilege to work for the everlasting life of my company." I thought he was exaggerating at first, but many Japanese of his generation share an almost mystical reverence for their companies. Sajima did, in fact, give his life for his company. After returning to Tokyo, he died at age fifty-two of throat cancer, in part because he had been too busy working to seek proper medical care. His colleagues were not particularly shocked. "He had no luck," said one. "It was his fate."

Although some younger Japanese are opting out of the "hunger consciousness" that drives corporate Japan, many others continue to give their lives for their company. One young engineer for Isuzu in Tokyo, for example, left his home at 7:00 A.M. and returned at midnight six days a week. That included two hours of commuting time, one hour each way. When he came home, he studied English conversation for an hour because his company ordered him to prepare for an assignment in the United States; he averaged less than six hours of sleep a night. This pattern lasted several years. Finally, in August 1987, at age thirty-five, he died of a stroke, leaving a pregnant wife and two children. Companies rarely offer any benefits to families in this situation, and the Labor Ministry does not recognize death by overwork as grounds for workers' compensation even though there is a Japanese term to describe the syndrome, *karoshi*. Hiroshi Kawahito, an attorney who represents the

families of Japanese men who suffer *karoshi,* says the conditions endured by the thirty-five-year-old engineer are typical of the Japanese
auto industry as a whole. The irony is that Kawahito himself acknowledges working ten hours a day, but probably works longer, on behalf
of the overworked.

It's true that some Japanese are changing jobs in midcareer, but the
more remarkable trend is just how long they endure under punishing
circumstances. That lesson was brought home to me by an old Japanese
friend with whom I had worked many years earlier in Hong Kong and
on several tough assignments elsewhere. At age forty-eight, he was fed
up with the American company for which he worked. But having
always worked for foreign companies, there was no chance that he
could now switch to a Japanese firm. He simply would not be accepted.

"How long will you hang in there?" I asked.

"Maybe only five more years," he replied.

Five more years at a job you can't stand? In the United States, even
at the age of forty-eight, the instinct is to jump if a job situation is
untenable. But it's different in Japan. Although 2.5 million Japanese
now change jobs a year, that's only about 4 percent of the total 59
million employed. The U.S. government does not compile exactly comparable numbers, but 28.8 percent of all Americans have been in their
jobs for one year or less and 17.4 percent of the work force has had more
than two employers in the previous year, according to economists at the
Bureau of Labor Statistics. So, proportionately, somewhere between
four and seven times as many Americans change jobs as Japanese. Many
Japanese stay on their jobs ten to fifteen years, or even twenty, before
it becomes clear whether they are going to be able to achieve their
career objectives.

The Japanese word for describing this kind of perseverance is *gaman.*
It is a cultural force, little recognized by the outside world, that drives
the Japanese forward. We are Japanese, therefore we have *gaman.* Time
and time again, when a foreigner penetrates beneath the surface, the
surprise is not how fast Japanese society is changing, but just how deep
the resistance is to the kinds of change he expects.

To the extent that Japanese frustration can be channeled, the real
target is not the bureaucrats, the banks, or the old-line companies. The
establishment commands far greater resources than such newcomers as
Ezoe. Toyota, for example, is sitting on $11.8 billion in liquid cash
reserves. The major securities houses, like Nomura, are managing hundreds of billions of dollars. I have met portfolio managers who are
individually managing $1 billion. Anger is not directed against these
legitimate guardians of the system but, rather, against the nouveau

riche. It is a question of who has society's mandate to manage wealth. Some holders of wealth are legitimate, others are not. Thus the dissatisfaction that was being expressed and witnessed by the outside world during 1989 was directed not at the system itself as much as it was against the usurpers. "The Japanese . . . can stage revolts against exploitation and injustice without ever becoming revolutionists," one keen observer of Japanese society wrote more than forty years ago. "They do not offer to tear the fabric of their world in pieces."[8]

The Japanese encourage the outside world's confusion about the direction of change in Japan. They send out spokesmen who plead for just a little bit more time. The situation is so complex. Japan is changing so rapidly, they claim, when in fact it is not, at least in the way Westerners expect. This pattern would not repeat itself so many times unless the outside world *wanted* so badly to be reassured and comforted. Outsiders, unwisely, also want to believe that the Japanese will become less Japanese. Isn't it only natural that they will become more "democratic" and "more like us"?

This is analogous to the mistake the Western world made about China. Certainly, in many ways, China and Japan could not be more dissimilar. They are profoundly different societies. What they share, however, is that the Western world tries to interpret them in moral and ideological terms that are often inappropriate. In the case of China, Americans assumed that as the Chinese economy made rapid progress thanks to Western investment, technology, and access to markets, the political system would gradually become less repressive. At a certain point, the Chinese would allow fuller economic progress even if it meant a gradual dismantlement of the Communist system. Americans thought that was logical. That is what they would have done. But it didn't work that way. The Chinese were not American. In the final analysis, the need to maintain the Communist Party's political control, as evidenced by the massacre in Tiananmen Square, was more important than economic progress.

The point is that the Japanese may let off steam by disciplining the LDP and attacking targets of conspicuous consumption, like Recruit's Ezoe. In some respects, it was more an outburst of jealousy than one of moral indignation about leaders who cut deals and bribe each other behind closed doors. But there is little evidence of a broad constituency for dramatic change of the sort that many observers from afar have proclaimed. The Japanese do not like speedy internal change and fight hard to resist it. That is the nature of Japan. It is a difficult culture.

❖ 2 ❖

The Difficult Culture

It's often the tidbits offered in casual conversations with Japanese that are the most thought-provoking. One case in point was a luncheon sponsored by the City of Louisville and Jefferson County, Kentucky, at the swank Union League Club in New York. The purpose of the lunch was to persuade the high-and-mighty to invest in the Louisville area. I was there out of a sense of loyalty to my hometown. Chitoo Bunno, senior vice president of Mitsui Bank, was there because Toyota Motor Company has a major auto plant in Georgetown, Kentucky. Wherever Toyota ventures, Mitsui won't be far behind, because it considers Toyota part of its industrial group. Some of Japan's most powerful corporate entities had, in effect, adopted Kentucky.

Bunno and I were seated next to each other, and we swapped business cards. He was a graduate of the University of Tokyo's Law Faculty, a sign of distinction even among Japan's elite. He had spent time in Germany and spoke some German, which made him trilingual. In addition, he had received a master's degree in economics from Co-lumbia University. His pedigree was completed by the reputation of his bank, which is one of Japan's largest and most prestigious. In his late forties or early fifties, he is just the sort of man who helps run Japan and extend its global reach.

By way of small talk, I mentioned that some Japanese executives in the United States try to immerse their children in American-style edu-cation, whereas others insist on sending their children back to Japan for the more rigorous, distinctively Japanese high school education. The pressure to pass college entrance exams is brutal. What was Bunno doing?

"Both," he said. "I have one child at a university in Virginia and two others back in Japan."

"Why did you organize it that way?" I asked.

"Well, I sent my eldest daughter to Virginia, and my two sons are in high school in Japan."

Why send girls to U.S. schools and sons to Japanese schools? I pressed on.

He replied: "Japanese culture is very difficult. Boys must be very Japanese."

His description of Japanese culture as "difficult" was intriguing. Certainly he didn't mean kabuki theater, tea ceremonies, or flower-arranging. He was using the word *culture* to describe the need to conform, the need to be part of the group, the need to understand all the subtle signals that Japan's behavioral code imposes. In short, the need to be very Japanese. The Japanization process is so thorough that it is difficult to carry out anywhere but in Japan. To some extent, it depends on screening out foreign influences. And it was more important for his sons than his daughter. For Bunno's sons to be able to follow in his footsteps, they must be stamped in the same mold. But it makes perfect sense to educate a daughter in the West—she has a much smaller chance of playing what a Westerner would consider a self-fulfilling role in Japan because of her gender. Many other Japanese families living abroad have made similar decisions.

This difficult culture does not embrace or welcome change when it challenges the Japanese notion of purity. Instead it rewards hierarchy, conformity, order, and acceptance of the group consciousness. Rather than easygoing egalitarianism, the hard, driving force of *gaman* makes it difficult for them as a people to relax. The culture also carries with it a set of values different from the principles prescribed by the Judeo-Christian tradition. Even when the Japanese are out of Japan, they must maintain their inward-looking cultural gaze, or face difficulty reassimilating when they return. In a sense, the boundary between Japan and the rest of the world is not geographic as much as it is cultural.

Far from going soft, this culture still demands a high energy level. Japanese associates or friends expect you to work long and hard, and to accomplish more in a day than the vast majority of Americans would attempt. Even then, a foreigner, particularly a newcomer, may accomplish less than expected. It's not just a question of the linguistic barrier.

It's also difficult for the Japanese themselves. Few traditional Japanese are comfortable discussing business over the telephone, so more time is invested in face-to-face meetings. Getting around Tokyo requires more time and energy than in a major Western city, just as it does in rural areas, where the road systems are surprisingly primitive. It's difficult to simply call someone and get an appointment: the "channel" or the "route" must often be prepared first, usually through a mutual acquaintance. There is detailed preparation for every official encounter. Very little happens that has not been rehearsed or researched.

Foreigners are constantly being told they have to try harder. If you have a 4:00 P.M. appointment, you must move heaven and earth to avoid being a minute late and, as a consequence, insulting your partner. If someone calls you, you must return the call quickly or be considered rude. If someone buys you a lunch or gives you a gift, you must reciprocate as rapidly as possible. In some cases, maintaining one's network of acquaintances and allies—a *jinmyaku*—requires as much effort as one's actual job. It's revealing that the drug most commonly abused by Japanese is not marijuana or cocaine, but amphetamines. Rather than seeking escape, Japanese seek more energy to cope. The streets of Tokyo and other cities also sport vending machines that sell iced coffee and "sports drinks" that give the consumer a quick lift. Pharmacies sell caffeine-packed "health drinks" for an added boost.

Even more than other cultures of Asia, Japanese culture maps out in advance many of the smallest details of human behavior, often on the basis of the hierarchy. One must extend one's name card with the right hand or with both hands, but not with the left. After looking at the card, it is clear to the Japanese whose position is higher. It therefore becomes clear who must bow first and how low. In an elevator, the most powerful or senior person in the group stands in a back corner, and it is clear that this person is to be the first one to get off the elevator. Cultural anthropologist Ruth Benedict, in *The Chrysanthemum and the Sword,* explained the Japanese commitment to hierarchy particularly well. "Every greeting, every contact must indicate the kind and degree of social distance among men," she wrote. "Every time a man says to another 'Eat' or 'Sit down' he uses different words if he is addressing someone familiarly or is speaking to an inferior or to a superior."[1]

Although Japan's commitment to hierarchy has softened slightly, particularly among younger Japanese, it is still starkly at odds with American notions of individualism and egalitarianism. Even in recent years, specialists in Japanese culture continue to be struck by how the individual "is a nobody but becomes a somebody through occupying a fractional place" in the hierarchy, as Takie Sugiyama Lebra wrote in 1976.[2] In his 1983 book, Jared Taylor describes, in slightly less academic terms, how the family and educational system instill an all-encompassing sense of hierarchy. "In a society that values hierarchy so highly, relations of real equality are rare," he wrote.[3]

Most specialists in Japanese culture have also noted the drive for conformity. At a meal, the guest sits in a certain place and should not pour his own beverage. If one sits on a cushion on a tatami mat, there are postures that are considered appropriate and others that are not. While outside of Tokyo, in the countryside, where there are fewer Western-style chairs, I spent several hours sitting cross-legged during interviews. When I arrived at a lunch or dinner and sat on my knees, just to give my Western body a relief from sitting cross-legged, I was invariably told that I should not sit that way. It was too feminine, or else it was not the right way for a guest to sit. The explanations varied and were always polite, but the pressure to sit in a certain way was unrelenting.

I also discovered that I had not been conducting myself properly when I removed my shoes in the entry halls—*genkan*—to restaurants and homes. After taking off one's shoes, the toes should be pointed toward the door. When I asked my assistant, Misako, what it meant if shoes were left pointing in the wrong direction, her reply was simple: "It means you don't understand etiquette." Again and again, the inquisitive foreigner learns that one should not ask why. One simply conforms.

Although difficult to master, the culture offers advantages to those who are part of it. The Japanese have a fascinating concept called *ishin denshin*, which means a form of mental anticipation of what another person is thinking. Because the culture spells out so much in advance, the Japanese are expected to be able to simply know what the other is thinking without having to exchange words. There are signals and postures, perhaps, but more important, the other person simply thinks the same because the culture is so homogeneous. To put it in a popular American context, if a man and woman have been married for twenty years, she simply knows that he wants a beer at halftime when he is watching a football game. He does not need to ask. She anticipates his request.

Sometimes foreigners are confused when dealing with a Japanese company or institution. One informant, an American woman who had worked for a Japanese bank for several years, told me how she had sat in on business negotiations as part of the Japanese side. It is typical for several Japanese bank executives to negotiate or discuss a particular subject with the foreign delegation, but the simple presentation of business cards may not reveal who is really in charge. Among Japanese, it's common for the most powerful individual to engage in the hiding of self.

Foreigners who, like my informant, have spent years in Japan can clearly tell who is who. They can silently read the signals of who is the oldest; they make note of who enters a room first, who speaks first, what tone of voice the Japanese use with each other—whether one is using a polite form of conversation, and therefore speaking up to a superior, or a less polite form, and so speaking down to a subordinate. The Japanese are also likely to sit in order of hierarchy. Even an outsider, if sensitive to the culture, can learn to read the signals. Words are not nearly as important in the Japanese power game.

What drives the Japanese so hard? Why can't they relax now that they have become so successful? One explanation is that their burst of prosperity has come so quickly that the older generation in particular does not believe it is for real. Only a few short decades ago, the Japanese were begging for chewing gum and Hershey chocolate bars from GIs. Catching up with, and surpassing, the West *(Seo ni oitsuki oiksu)* has been a clear national goal since the Meiji era, but military defeat led the Japanese to dedicate themselves to this goal with renewed energy and commitment.

Now, even though they have surpassed the United States in per capita gross national product and control more of the world's assets, it's difficult for them to shift gears. The fear of starvation and poverty is so recent that even very successful Japanese are driven to make extraordinary efforts long after their own financial security has been assured for life and their children are firmly established in the best universities. The notion that "Japan is a small island nation with scarce natural resources" is still deeply ingrained among the majority of adult Japanese who have scant notion of the international power that is concentrated in the hands of their financial institutions and leading companies. Even though a relative handful of Japanese have achieved standards of living on a par with the best in the West, the vast majority have not, and this is also a reason many Japanese are working just as hard as ever.

But underlying all these explanations is the sheer drive embedded in the culture. Japan's feudal history was characterized by centuries of civil conflict among clans and lords. It may have been at a low level, or it may have been subtle, or it may have been temporarily halted by an alliance, but it rarely ended. In societies of great population density, where scarcity is more prevalent than abundance, conflicts may last many generations. It is much the same today except that the struggle is more among ministries, factions, and companies than warlords. A commitment to a common culture does not preclude conflict. Rather, the Japanese are masters of long-term, low-level conflict. Often what the outside world perceives to be harmony or consensus is the result of an intense struggle where many different Japanese interests have competed feverishly against one another. Like a gigantic pressure cooker, these forces may balance against each other so that there is the appearance of nonconflict. But it is often just that, an appearance.

Because of this long history of conflict, the survivors have been those who have never relaxed, or who did so only very gradually. In today's context, there is a huge price to pay for a high school student who does not prepare rigorously for college entrance examinations, for a salary-man who decides to go home at 5:00 P.M., or for a bureaucrat who does not religiously protect his ministry's interests. Hidetoshi Ukawa, Japan's Ambassador for International Economic Relations, says most Japanese cannot relax because of "a sense of anxiety that unless you keep on performing well you will not be accepted or appreciated." That speaks volumes about the force of culture. If a Japanese simply decides that he or she has had enough and wants to coast, that person risks being spurned by the group. The saying is "The nail that sticks up gets hammered down," and it is usually the group that does the hammering.

The culture's drive for order is also strong, as the more perceptive commentators on Japan have long recognized. Nearly every block in Tokyo has a policeman assigned to it. This is convenient for asking directions and it certainly helps prevent crime, but it is also a constant reminder of the control that lies just beneath the surface. At major governmental buildings, far more than in other world capitals, there are guards standing at attention, with riot shields and riot buses nearby. During major events, like an economic summit or the emperor's funeral, these forces of authority bring Tokyo to a screeching halt.

There is also a daily battle for control in the streets. One of my earliest impressions of Tokyo was standing on a streetcorner with no cars in sight, nothing coming in any direction, but the light hadn't actually changed yet. On all sides the Japanese pedestrians stood rigidly still, waiting for the light to change. I was itching to step off the curb and charge across. That was because, in New York, London, Hong Kong, and other major cities of the world, if a pedestrian sees empty pavement and no heavy metallic objects hurtling toward him, it's time to walk.

In certain contexts like this one, however, the Japanese must respect the rules no matter how little sense they make at a particular moment. They stand rigidly at attention waiting for the light to change no matter how long it takes. Foreigners are usually excused if they cross at the wrong time, but occasionally the Japanese attempt to extend the group uniformity to them as well. Bob Neff, the *Business Week* bureau chief in Tokyo, tells a story about walking home from the office one Sunday afternoon years ago. As he passed the U.S. embassy, he came to a side street that was deserted. After carefully looking both ways, he crossed against the light. A Japanese policeman came charging out at him and shouted in English, "You insolent foreigners. You have no respect for the laws of my country."

It hasn't changed very much over the years. Younger Japanese today, perhaps those with exposure to the outside world, may step off the curb just when the light is about to change, but they don't dare anything more aggressive than that. Older Japanese still scold younger ones for crossing prematurely. Taxi drivers, in their white gloves and neckties, also honk angrily at anyone crossing at the wrong time. In some crucial respects, this battle for control is the group against the violators, not any kind of supreme authority.

The forces of control and conformity are even evident at baseball games. I happened to go to the Tokyo Dome to see the Nippon Ham Fighters play the Orix Braves. Nippon Ham is a meat-packing company; Orix is a leasing outfit. Most major league baseball teams in Japan are company-sponsored.

On the surface, the game was the spitting image of American baseball, but, as Robert Whiting has chronicled so well, there are subtle twists that make Japanese baseball different.[4] In some respects, it boils down to the fight between individualism and the group.

Consider just one play from the Nippon Ham–Orix game. Nippon Ham had a man on first when the player at bat hit a ball off the left-field wall. The lead runner was coming into third and the hitter was heading toward second before the Orix left-fielder's throw began coming in. For the hitter, this was a moment of glory, of individual decision. Do I stop with a stand-up double or go for third? The arm of the Nippon Ham third-base coach was whirling around like a windmill. Go for home, he was signaling. But it was a signal intended for the lead runner, not for the guy rounding second. That seemed clear to me. Sitting behind first base, I saw the ball come in from left field at roughly the same angle as the hitter headed for second. It was clear the lead runner could score, and that it would be suicide for the hitter to try for third.

I was stunned that he kept running. Naturally, the throw was cut off and he was pinned about halfway between second and third. Realizing his fate, he went bravely to his death at third. A good samurai.

"Why did he keep running?" I asked my two Japanese friends. "He was obviously going to be out."

"Didn't you see the third-base coach's arm? He was signaling to keep running."

"But," I protested, "that was wrong. The hitter should have made his own judgment."

"No, *you're* wrong," I was told. "If he had defied the coach, whether he was right or wrong, he would have been punished, probably fined. He would not have been showing respect." In Japanese baseball, the force of control was more important, right or wrong.

There's a similar feeling in the subways, on airport limousines, on the bullet trains, and in department stores. Loudspeakers with recorded messages from polite young women tell you where to stand. Go left here. Watch your fingers. On escalators, stand inside the yellow lines, keep your hands on the red rail. Hold the hands of children. Japanese who have lived overseas find the controlled environment difficult to accept. "This is a police state," one told me. But it's not really the state that imposes conformity and order as much as it is the group. There is a blurring of where the state stops and the group begins.

The irony is that at another level—often invisible to a visiting *gaijin*—anything goes. The same salaryman who scolds someone for jaywalking may be found in the Roppongi district late at night, drunk out of his mind and acting like a high school kid at homecoming. One Wednesday evening at midnight, I was walking back to my hotel from having dinner with a colleague. As I passed through one particularly lively entertainment district, I was surprised to see an executive in coat and tie sprawled on the back of a parked car. When he saw a foreigner, he got up and staggered away. Older men with lithe young creatures on their arms were emerging from bars and dashing for taxis. None of this is considered socially unacceptable behavior. Public drinking and womanizing, if done in the proper way at the proper place, are widely accepted.

These are not just random events. This is a pattern. There is an underside to Japanese society that most foreigners never see. Most foreigners get the traditional "guest room" treatment when they go to Japan. They never see the dirty kitchen. The modern variation is the Hotel Okura treatment. The foreigner stays in a lovely hotel across the street from the U.S. embassy, is surrounded by English-speaking Japanese, travels in a very small area of downtown Tokyo, and then heads for the airport. He or she has not glimpsed the *yakuza* with permed hair hanging out on streetcorners or the sex districts of Shinjuku.

There is no reason to be prudish about it, or judgmental. Everyone knows what happens in crack houses or girlie bars in major American cities. There are adventure seekers in all societies. The point is that so many Westerners perceive the Japanese as a great homogeneous, well-organized mass where everyone works all the time and adheres to a puritanical regimen. But the system allows them socially acceptable safety valves, and there is widespread acceptance of this other dimension to the difficult culture.

One excellent example was a popular 1987 movie called *A Taxing Woman*, by Juzo Itami, one of Japan's hottest directors. The antihero is a gangster named Hideki Gondo who uses every trick in the book. He employs loan sharks to entrap tenants of buildings he wants to tear down, or else uses thugs to intimidate them. In either case, his goal is to quickly resell the property at a huge profit. This strikes a deep chord among Tokyoites in particular. Our antihero also engages in massive violations of company law, cheats the tax authorities, and pays off his Dietman with briefcases full of cash. He uses the name of a dying man to set up a dummy company. He also has a mistress whom he dumps in a most ruthless fashion, after first reclaiming the bank passbooks where he has concealed much of his wealth in her name.

The tax inspector is played by Itami's wife, Nobuko Miyamoto. Diminutive and freckled, she dogs Gondo mercilessly. On the way, she investigates shopkeepers who are cheating on their taxes, *pachinko* parlor operators who are concealing their income, and "love hotel" operators who try to dodge paying taxes completely. It is a devastating portrait of widespread, institutionalized cheating. But the Japanese, as well as some U.S. critics, consider the movie a comedy!

Japanese friends patiently tried to explain it to me. "What you find so shocking is what all of us take for granted," said one. "That's the real Japan. Nothing is as straight as you Americans like to think."

The most intriguing answer came one evening over beer and sake. These evening conversations are the best opportunity to find out what Japanese really think. Americans who live in Tokyo jokingly refer to alcohol as a "truth serum" that enables the Japanese to speak their hearts. When the subject of *A Taxing Woman* came up, I explained my confusion. Why was it funny? My host's reply: "You Americans assume that your fellowman is well intentioned and honest. You assume that human nature is fundamentally good. We don't."

This egged me on, in an admittedly naive quest for the moral heart of this culture. Most Americans with any exposure to Japan know that the Japanese move smoothly from *tatemae* to *honne.* The former is the diplomatic, or official, line that you give to someone you don't really trust; the latter is the level you reserve for someone you have met many times and know well. For Americans, there may be little difference between the two levels, or else it is possible to move from one to the other in the space of a few minutes. It takes much longer and is more complex in Japan. Thus many Americans get the impression that some Japanese are "lying" or "two-faced."

Slightly more complex is the notion of *tsukaiwake*, or situational ethics. If a certain kind of behavior is appropriate in one setting, then it's entirely natural to the Japanese that another kind of behavior is appropriate for another setting. They find it quite easy to switch hats. Specialists have understood these concepts for decades. But where was the moral core? What truths did they hold to be self-evident?

One Sunday I had lunch on the Ginza with an old friend, Paul Fukuda. The father of six and one of a small number of Japanese Christians, Paul considers himself a "very Japanese-y Japanese, with value added." The added value is his religion. He has always struck me as a wise man.

At the Tokyo Union Church that morning, Paul had seen a twenty-two-year-old Japanese man baptized. He was deeply touched and explained it this way, using what he acknowledged was an idealized but still valuable analogy:

"In a village, there are two times of year when a farmer desperately needs help: when rice seedlings are transplanted to the fields in late spring, and again in the fall for the harvest. He absolutely depends on the cooperation of his village and his neighbors. Failing that cooperation, he is ruined. So he must strive to maintain positive relations with everyone around him—that is, his peer group. To this day, the Japanese have two gift-giving seasons. One is in midsummer and one is in December. They stem from the practice of offering gifts to fellow villagers who have helped with the rice crop, to thank them for their help—and to ensure that they will help again.

"This pressure of the group is far more important to the Japanese than any dictums from a supreme being. Christians look up to a supreme being for moral instructions on how to deal with their fellow-man. Even if they are not actual practitioners, they have been stamped with the notion that there are certain ideals of right and wrong that they should observe in dealing with their fellowman. Sure, sometimes they break the rules, but they feel guilt. Many times, if the group is doing something wrong, they stand up and criticize it.

"In Japan, it doesn't work that way. The most important thing is to maintain the relationships with the group. There are very few moral guidelines that have been handed down from on high to regulate these relationships. If the group does something wrong, it's crazy to raise your hand and say, 'This is not right.' That means you will be the nail that gets pounded down. In short, there is no conflict between espousing one thing [to someone outside the group] and doing another, or in having multiple levels of truth. One does what one has to do to maintain power relationships in the group."

Although the Japanese use Shintoism for their weddings and Buddhism for their funerals, and Confucianism has clearly imparted a sense of hierarchy and order, they have not created a true religion with what Westerners would understand as a core of beliefs. Paul concluded: "What the young man at church had done, in agreeing to be baptized, was to cut himself adrift from the Japanese mainstream. He had opted to follow a moral code that would put him at odds with many fellow Japanese. He was no longer part of the group."

It is wrong to say the Japanese lack values altogether. They do have a code of behavior that relates to the group. One has lifelong responsibilities and duties that are often strong and binding to help maintain one's power relationships, but not to help outsiders.

The point is that Japan is not a society driven by a Western moral impulse. Americans like to perceive themselves as involved in moral struggle, in trying to spread democracy around the world or in struggling over issues of conscience at home. Americans rally to what they perceive as a "just cause." Power has a slightly negative connotation. Power, whether it is economic wealth or political influence, is suspect. To be powerful often is to be immoral because one is presumably working against the interests of the average Joe. A nation accustomed to abundance can afford that perception.

But Japan is a society where the struggle for economic power is paramount. The underlying assumption is not abundance but rather scarcity. The group, and by extension Japan, must win at any cost. Any tactic is acceptable. It's revealing that there is no precise equivalent in Japanese for the Western concept of "fair." There are conflicting interpretations. One is that if I have power over you, you submit on the surface while struggling to overturn me by stealth. If you have power over me, I do the same. When Japanese talk about one another, they don't usually say "I don't like him" or "He is not nice." A more frequent insult is to say "He has no power" or "He has no influence."

Conversely, if you perceive someone as having power, you seek a relationship with that person in order to obtain benefits. There is a saying in Japanese that explains this: "If something is long, be rolled by it." In other words, if there is something or somebody with power, don't resist. Attach yourself to the power. Roll with it. On the cultural level, this is how the power game is played.

Japan's value system is not worse or better, just different. It is an ancient, complex, introspective culture that imposes an internal hierarchy and control while resisting destabilizing change from without. At the same time, it can be supremely adaptive and flexible when necessary, hence deceptive to Western eyes. One difference with the Western world is the relations between men and women.

❖ 3 ❖

Women in a Man's World

The headlines of 1989 were hard to miss: "Japan's Rising Women"[1] and "Quiet Revolution: Japanese Women Rise in Their Workplaces, Challenging Tradition."[2] Japanese women were voting for women candidates, part of what was nicknamed the Madonna Fad. Triumphant pictures of Takako Doi, the Socialist leader, were all over the newspapers and on the covers of magazines. In July 1989, a record number of women won seats in the Upper House of the Diet.

The world was intrigued. A U.S.-style women's movement seemed to be breaking out. After enduring the industrialized world's most pervasive pattern of sexism, Japanese women were rising up. That meant that consumer interests would make major gains, because most Japanese consumers are women. As political leaders, women would also shift Japan's priorities. Greater numbers of women in the workplace would soften the workaholic ways of Japanese men, and increasingly assertive wives at home would demand that their men come home and be with their families. All this seemed to imply that Japan would become a kinder, gentler nation whose economic drive was moderated.

The underlying reality, however, was not nearly as heady. There was no question that Japanese women have made and will continue to make strides. But their gains are from a much more modest starting point than that which Western women enjoy. Sumiko Iwao, a social psychologist at Keio University and a former lecturer at Harvard, offers an illuminating set of statistics: Forty years ago, Japanese women finished

31

their schooling at 16; now the average age is 19.2. Back then, women married at 21 and had five children. Today in the Tokyo area, the average age has crept up to about 26 and the number of childbirths per woman is down to 1.8. Longevity today has also risen from a mere 50 years of age to 81.

So, women have made progress on basic issues of education, life-style, and health, but that does not mean they have charged into the male domains of politics, government, or business in a significant way. Japanese women perceive their struggle somewhat differently from American women. The concept of "women's liberation," which is seen as overtly aggressive and demanding, is not popular in Japan. Very few Japanese women perceive their advancement as compromising the economic efficiency of their society, by requiring companies to extend such benefits as flex-time or maternity leave, or by setting a quota for the number of women that should be hired and then advanced rapidly up the corporate ladder.

Nor do Japanese women openly challenge their men. Although some women are beginning to break new ground in politics and business, most are doing it according to the men's rules. The majority of Japanese women are still quite conservative. Over the course of decades, the rise of Japanese women may have an impact on men's life-styles, politics, and the workplace, but there's little evidence that it will blunt Japan's economic advancement. As women fill gaps in the labor force, they may actually enhance Japan's competitive clout.

The response of Japanese men is also different from the American male response. Japan is a man's world, and men intend to keep it that way. Where power is really at stake, in the business or political worlds, there is scant evidence that Japanese men are willing to involve women. The door to this male decision-making process remains firmly closed, more so than in the United States. The cultural and linguistic hierarchy in which men are superior to women is still in place. For many older Japanese men, business is still more important than wife and family. Men's pursuit of sexual pleasure outside the home is also not under assault, as evidenced by the healthy state of Japan's sex industry. To say that Japan has a sexual double standard is an understatement. In short, the appearance that Japanese women were going to quickly reorder Japan was frightfully overdrawn. It was not women's liberation of the sort that swept America in the 1960s.

One Japanese woman challenging old stereotypes is Masako Egawa. At the age of thirty-two, she is a vice president in the Mergers and Acquisitions Department of Salomon Brothers in Tokyo, equipped

with an MBA from Harvard. The first time I saw her was when she gave a speech to a group organized by the three-hundred-member Japan Association for Female Executives. About fifty women got together on a Saturday afternoon in a small speaking hall in Roppongi to hear what Egawa had to say about the value of getting an MBA abroad. Many Japanese women think about studying or living abroad as a way to escape intense social and familial pressure to marry by the age of twenty-five. A particularly stinging label that is applied to single women over twenty-five is "Christmas Cake," meaning that "After the twenty-fifth, it is no good." In Egawa's case, friends and relatives had told her things like "Women should marry soon" and "When you're young, you should bear children." Most listeners in the audience that day were younger than Egawa and were wrestling with the same decisions she had had to make years earlier.

Egawa had wanted to live her own life and resisted the pressure to marry. She was a graduate of the University of Tokyo, like her father and grandfather, but she was the first woman in her family to go there. She does not, however, aspire to the tough, aggressive image that some American women have adopted. Egawa says the goal is to be *ii onna*, which translates as a "nice, attractive lady." "Feminists in America think that to be equal to men they must be as aggressive as men," Egawa says. But her goal is to "seek a life in a feminine way." This is a criticism that other Japanese women leaders make about U.S.-style feminism: It is "too vindictive" or "too confrontational."

Egawa spent five years studying and working in the United States, including a stint at Citibank and training at Salomon in New York. She returned to Japan in 1988 but found it tough to build credibility with the Japanese clients with whom Salomon expected her to deal. "A couple of clients would talk about their daughters when they saw me," she says. "I wasn't really taken seriously. I was disappointed by the reactions."

One of Egawa's limitations is that she can go to dinner with clients, but it is awkward for her to go to late-night clubs and cabarets. She is also excluded from the all-important golfing encounters with clients. These are men-only events, and they are more than just social. Clubs or golf courses are often places where men retreat to nurture their relations and to build consensus, a process called *nemawashi*. It is a critical ingredient of the overall decision-making process.

One of the things that is most striking about Egawa is her ability to shift cultural gears. When she spoke in Japanese to the Japanese women, she bowed often and uttered all the right honorifics. But the moment she encounters an American, her posture and tone change.

Making these cultural adjustments, it turns out, is one of her central challenges. Like many people who are bilingual and bicultural, she is caught in the middle.

When she takes her American boss to visit Japanese clients, for example, getting in and out of elevators is a problem. If she and her American boss are in an elevator with Japanese clients, the American understanding is "ladies first." The Japanese, however, expect the highest-ranking guest to leave the elevator first. Egawa tries to encourage her boss to leave first because that preserves his image in the eyes of the clients. "It's better for him to go out first in front of Japanese clients," she says. "When we go to see a client, I try to operate under Japanese rules." Other women placed in the same situation at dinners or lunches find themselves under pressure to pour beer or tea, even though they are professionals.

Egawa also has to shift gears in conversations in the office. "If I talk to an English-speaking colleague in a very direct way, and [then] turn to a Japanese superior and continue in that tone, he stiffens." She is expected to show greater deference to a Japanese superior and to speak more indirectly. All this is part of the difficulty of developing a new style. "There's no model," she says. "There's no one in front of me. I have to invent my own protocol."

She also pays a price for her career choice, partly because she spent five years in the United States and partly because she is more successful than her friends who work for Japanese companies. She has drifted away from many of her old girlfriends with whom she went to high school, which is somewhat unusual in a society that values long-term relationships. "I find fewer topics of common interest with those people," she says wistfully. "Some classmates today are still working, but because of the limitations of Japanese companies, they're not quite as successful. I can still talk to some of my old friends. We have good memories. But if you shift the conversation to what you're doing today, it's not so good."

She is also perhaps too old, too smart, and too threatening to marry a mainstream Japanese man. "People who have been exposed only to Japanese society have trouble understanding me, not only males, but also females," she acknowledges. Nor is it likely that Egawa will ever be able to work for a traditional Japanese company. So, although she has made a breakthrough as a woman, there are limits on just how far she can take it, and how far she chooses to take it. She has had to make some tough trade-offs. There is little sense of great liberation.

Other women have started companies or joined existing Japanese companies in retailing, cosmetics, marketing, headhunting, or catering.

They also appear to be doing well in medicine and academia. Another growing field for women is translation and serving as a cultural bridge between the Japanese and other nationalities.

Overall, the statistics show that women have been entering the work force rapidly and now represent about 40 percent of all workers, as compared to 57.8 percent in the United States.[3] But a third of these women hold only part-time jobs so that they can still manage their families and households. There is also a higher turnover among the female sector of the work force as younger women leave to marry and have families.

What the statistics and the headlines do not reveal is that the vast majority of women in the Japanese workplace can be seen bowing at elevators, opening doors, and serving tea. At some companies they wear uniforms with name badges while the men wear business suits. At a bank or a brokerage house, women are underutilized. Many sit at desks, shuffling papers and attempting to appear busy. Although some women are breaking into engineering jobs and some have risen to the level of section chief at banks, the number who have broken through to the inner sanctum of decision making at a top-class Japanese company is infinitesimal.

Kyoko Shimada, forty-four, has invested half of her life at Nissan. She spent her first seven years there designing auto interiors. Next, she was in marketing and product planning for seven years, then in corporate identity for two years. After sixteen years, she reached the executive level as a manager and worked in public relations for four and a half years. For the past year and a half, she has been in a staff job planning Nissan's nationwide distribution system.

Shimada is often cited as an example of a Japanese woman who has made remarkable progress in a mainline Japanese company. The less-often-noticed drawbacks are that she has paid a personal price by working long days (about fifty-five hours a week on average) and not being able to or not choosing to have a marriage. Some American women do not consider this a negative, but in Japan, marriage is still the overwhelming desire of most women.

In terms of her career, Shimada has risen to her present position after twenty-two years. While that is decidedly modest progress by American standards, it's about the same speed that some Japanese men face, so there's no evidence that she has been held back simply because she is a woman. But her advance was certainly not made more rapid than that of her male colleagues so as to correct a sexual imbalance, as some American women expect. However slow American companies have been to advance women up the corporate ladder, Japan's seniority system is even more rigid.

The male domain of a major auto, steel, or computer company is a tough setting for a soft-spoken woman like Shimada, who has faced and continues to face awkward or frustrating challenges because of her sex. One of the first obstacles she had to overcome was managing the men who worked for her on specific projects. "I think people whom I managed were confused in the beginning," she says. But those awkward moments eased after she was able to build a track record and after it became clear that she was managing them on a project-by-project basis, not as a career-track manager. Once she establishes her relationships, "then the men listen to me."

She has also broken new ground by including both men and women in meetings where decisions are made. "Most Japanese companies, when they have meetings or conferences, don't allow women to be present even if they're talking about women's products," she says. "I always bring men and women to a meeting."

Prevailing in those meetings is even more delicate for Shimada because most Japanese men think their opinions are more valid than a woman's. "I don't speak loudly or emotionally," she says. "When I say something, it has to be logical and organized, and I have to be persistent."

Like Masako Egawa, Shimada faces limits in her ability to socialize with her male colleagues in the evenings, which is important to the conduct of business. "I'm not good at the *karaoke* bar, but I have started playing golf now. I'm also trying to have working lunches with co-workers, customers, and clients." She still does not socialize with male co-workers after 5:00 P.M., but Shimada does feel she is "building a new style" of consensus-forming.

Although she has persevered, Shimada is not on the same kind of career path as most Nissan men, who know what positions they are competing for. The result is a measure of confusion. "It's very frustrating because I don't know what I'll be [next].... I think compared with American career women, I'm far behind. In the Japanese company system, age counts. Even if you're talented and have many good ideas, you have to wait until the proper age. If I were an American woman, I could be telling my boss 'I'm good at this or that.' But you can't do that here."

It is significant that she does not think younger women just beginning at Nissan will have the same tenacity she has displayed. "Most women cannot wait that long. They will probably quit and move to another company."

The sociologist Sumiko Iwao says this reflects a broader pattern: A relatively small number of Japanese women will pay the price and take the time Shimada has to climb the corporate ladder at mainline Japanese companies. If that's true, rather than spearheading a vast phalanx of women, Shimada will remain one of a hardy band of pioneers.

For every Japanese woman who tries to break new ground, there are many more who represent a fundamental force of conservatism. They do not want to work full time because they fear it would hurt their children's educations, because they have to care for aging in-laws or parents, and because they need to support their husbands' careers. If the number of Masako Egawas and Kyoko Shimadas can be measured in the hundreds, then the number of Sadako Fukudas can be measured in the millions.

Mrs. Fukuda, forty-three, lives about an hour from central Tokyo with her husband, a midlevel executive, and her seventeen-year-old son, plus her husband's mother and father. Their home seems tiny by American standards though it is actually quite spacious by Japanese norms. They own a three-story house roughly twenty-five feet by twenty-five feet, which means each level is more than six hundred square feet. There is no lawn. Instead, the Fukudas have bonsai and other ornamental vegetation outside their home, which is separated from the next house by a wall. The in-laws live in a room off the kitchen on the bottom level, which has a formal dining room and a spare room. Mrs. Fukuda, her husband, and their son live on the second level. On the third level are two apartments that have been rented to single occupants.

Mrs. Fukuda considers herself lucky. For the first ten years of her marriage, she couldn't get along with her in-laws. The usual pattern is that the daughter-in-law and mother-in-law are in conflict. But in Mrs. Fukuda's case, it was her father-in-law whom she could not satisfy. In Japan, fathers-in-law are considered heads of the household. Mrs. Fukuda just didn't live up to his expectations, and he hit her from time to time. One summer she wasn't able to wear a sleeveless dress because of a big bruise on her upper arm where he had struck her. Mrs. Fukuda thought about returning to her own parents during those tough years, but eventually she learned how to cope. The key became using the mother-in-law as a buffer. Altogether, she has been married for twenty-one years and her relations with her father-in-law have been fine for the past eleven. "He doesn't hate me," she says. "Now he needs my help. But it took ten years to reach this understanding."

Her in-laws are both seventy-eight and still healthy, which is a tremendous advantage. Many of her friends have to care for in-laws who are incapacitated for one reason or another, usually failing health.

Some have mental health difficulties, others have serious drinking problems.

Mrs. Fukuda is also pleased that her husband comes home most evenings by 10:00 P.M. Other women have husbands who stay out late every evening; they simply don't want to come home. In some cases, in fact, the wives don't even want them to come home. But Mr. Fukuda works only a few minutes away. "There is nothing bad between my husband and me," Mrs. Fukuda says. She recognizes that he has to be out most evenings for business reasons. And she understands that when he does come home too early, it is awkward. There is no place for him to sit comfortably. If he wants to watch television, it disturbs their son's studying. If Mr. Fukuda is at home on Saturdays, she has to chase him around as she does her household chores. "Having time off is a burden for him," she says.

Another joy for her is that her son is a good student. Many of her friends have children who don't want to study. They would rather spend time in the *pachinko* parlors or watching television. In some cases, when an "education mother" drives her teenage children too hard, they rebel and have been known to physically attack the mother. Some of the women who seek temporary refuge and counseling at the HELP Asian Women's Shelter are Japanese housewives who have been beaten by their teenage sons. But this has not been a problem for Mrs. Fukuda. The way she motivated her son is distinctively Japanese. "Once, a long time ago, when he scored a hundred on a test, I took a piece of paper and wrote some calligraphy on it, praising him. Then I put him up on a table and bowed to him."

She supports her husband and family in other small but important ways. One is taking care of the two gift-giving seasons each year. She must buy a total of fourteen gifts—for her husband's boss, her son's teachers, and her relatives. As the most important person is her husband's boss, she buys him golf balls valued at 7,000 yen ($50). The relatives get new futons and boxes of beer. On average, however, she spends 3,000 yen (roughly $20) per present. In short, Mrs. Fukuda is a driving force in making her men successful.

A final bit of luck is that her in-laws own the house, so the Fukudas have been spared the doubling and tripling of rents that have made life so difficult for many Tokyoites. Mrs. Fukuda knows many housewives who have complete responsibility for managing the household finances. Most Japanese salarymen turn their paychecks over to their wives, so if the money runs short, the pressure is on the housewife. This is a worry that Mrs. Fukuda has been spared.

Because of her many blessings, Mrs. Fukuda is able to do volunteer work and teach a bonsai class to foreigners. She has also made two vacation trips to the United States, a sign of genuine affluence in Japanese eyes. "I'm very happy," she says. "If my mother-in-law becomes sick, I will have to stop all my jobs. But I don't mind because I have had all these years of happiness."

All this is a dramatic improvement from the life she knew as a girl in southern Japan. "Then a man was a man and a woman was very low," she recalls. "There was no cushion for me, even on a cold floor. My brothers got the warm rice. I got cold rice." Mrs. Fukuda had to learn to cook at age eight and wash clothes by hand at age ten. She is scornful of younger Japanese women who don't even know how to peel an apple. She is also shocked by the twenty-six-year-old nurse who lives upstairs and hangs her underwear outside to dry. "I wonder how her mother educated her," Mrs. Fukuda says.

Indeed, Mrs. Fukuda is positively old-fashioned. She doesn't support Socialist leader Doi because Doi was never a wife or a mother. "She doesn't know what she's talking about," Mrs. Fukuda says. Ironically, this is the same criticism many of the men in the LDP make about Doi.

Nor does Mrs. Fukuda support Japanese women who try to change the established order. She tells the story, for example, of a company where some women were unhappy about having to serve the men tea. The suggestion was made that perhaps the men should drink their tea out of paper cups, but one twenty-four-year-old woman objected. "It is in poor taste," the young woman said. The idea was dropped. "I am like that twenty-four-year-old," Mrs. Fukuda says proudly.

As a descendant of samurai, she does not believe in complaining. During the early period of conflict with her in-laws, the key to her perseverance was *gaman*. "I had to do my *gaman*," she says. "Instead of complaining, I would wake up earlier and help them."

Gaman is sometimes translated as perseverance, but it can also mean patience or discipline. It is a broad concept, for which there is no exact English equivalent. "If you go to a hot springs and the water is so hot you can't stand to touch it, but you dip yourself in anyway, this is *gaman*," Mrs. Fukuda explains. "If you have an itch but don't scratch it, this is *gaman*. If you want a car and have the money, you may decide not to buy it now just in case something happens and you need the money for another purpose. This is also *gaman*. Or when I have to spend too much money on something I need, then I do my *gaman* by saving money on another thing."

But the comment that best summarized how she and millions of other Japanese housewives perceive their situations was this one: "We are Japanese. This is our life-style. It's up to the wives to find ways to enjoy themselves."

* * *

However they define their personal missions, Japanese women face the recognition that Japan is still a man's world. At the most elemental level, Japan shares distinctly Asian notions about the worth of a woman. In China, a bucket of water is often kept beside a peasant woman giving birth. If the child is a girl, she is drowned because she would be a financial drain on the family. In India, the families of grooms, in rural areas in particular, burn brides if they do not come with sufficient dowries. Japan is more subtle, and more modern. Doctors who test pregnant women will tell the woman and her husband whether their child is healthy or not, but many will not tell the parents what sex it is. One reason, Japanese parents say, is the doctor's fear that too many parents would choose to abort female fetuses.

Japan also is a virtual Valhalla, where a man can have a wife at the same time that he enjoys mistresses or girlfriends, live sex shows, or simple prostitution, depending on his level of affluence. For a man who is merely lonely, there are hostess clubs where attractive women will pour his drinks, talk and laugh with him, perhaps sing some *karaoke*, and dance. Often that is as far as it goes.

If a man wants to take his mistress to an elegant out-of-the-way night spot, there are clubs that specialize in this, complete with soft lights, American jazz musicians, and showcases filled with jewelry in case he wants to buy her a bauble. If he wants to have sex with her in an exciting setting, there are "love hotels"—with names like Hotel Utopia—only too willing to accommodate his needs. If he is particularly powerful and has a high-class mistress, the teahouses in the Akasaka or Ginza districts of Tokyo are where he will be found. All things in their proper place.

"Soapland" is the current euphemism for prostitution houses. They used to be called Turkish baths, but the Turks living in Japan complained. So the operators changed the name. Going out with one's fellow salarymen to a soapland is part of the male-bonding process. There is nothing secretive about it. Sporty newspapers come out every afternoon at about 3:00 P.M. with advertisements for different soaplands, massage parlors, pubs, "pink salons," "snack bars," and similar establishments. The women are pictured, clad only in bikini bottoms. They are ranked in terms of their abilities and specializations. One, for example, was known for "using her young hands and mouth." The rates for each are quoted and are based on the girls' level of accomplishment. Day rates are much cheaper than those for the evening rush hour. Some of these newspapers offer the opinions of critics who rate the women and their establishments.

There are many other forms of sexual entertainment. In the Shibuya section of Tokyo, it's not hard to find establishments where women strip in front of fifty or seventy-five men and then lie down, rubbing themselves into what appears to be a state of high sexual excitement. With legs spread wide, they rotate on a circular platform so that all the men in the room can have an unimpeded view. One particular club offers a discount for students. Most of the patrons are salarymen or solid mainstream men, not the dregs of society that one would expect in Times Square.

At some clubs, the men even bring flashlights so they can examine the women's genitals. At others, salarymen, late at night after a few drinks, play the child's game of paper, stone, scissors to see which one of them gets to have sex with a particularly desirable woman onstage. In some cases fistfights erupt. "It's amazing," says one American who has spent time in these establishments, "that this society has little old women down in Yokohama scratching out the pubic hairs in *Penthouse* magazines, yet at the same time condones live sex onstage."

One of the less savory aspects of Japan's sex industry is that it relies on the illegal presence of about 100,000 Asian women—from Thailand and the Philippines in particular, but also from Taiwan and Korea. Naive young Asian women are lured to Japan with promises of big money-making jobs, but then are forced into various forms of prostitution once they arrive. The *yakuza* are not the only ones engaged in this form of human smuggling. "Not many women realize what is going to happen to them in Japan," says Mizuho Matsuda.

An English-speaking Protestant lay missionary who has worked in Pakistan and Singapore for eleven years, Matsuda is the director of the HELP Asian Women's Shelter, which is supported in part by the Japan Woman's Christian Temperance Union. The HELP center is located a few minutes from Tokyo's Kabukicho district, where, Matsuda estimates, there are 3,200 sex establishments. Overall, she cites Japanese government figures showing that more than $70 billion a year is spent on various forms of sexual entertainment throughout Japan.

After the newly arrived Asian women present themselves at the bar or club where they expect to make great sums of money waitressing, singing, or dancing, they discover that they owe their bosses the cost of their recruitment. In effect, they have been bought and sold.[4] When the Japanese police cracked down on Thai women one summer, Matsuda said their "price" doubled to 3.5 million yen, or about $25,000.

To pay this back, many of them are forced into "going out" with customers. When they are not on the job, these Asian women tend to be confined and closely supervised. It is difficult for them to escape because most are from small villages in rural areas; they are completely lost in a Japanese city. Unlike the Koreans or Taiwanese who come to Japan, the Philippine and Thai women cannot read Japanese characters, much less speak Japanese. The women are given a minimal amount of money, which they spend on cosmetics and food, so they do not have enough for train fare or airfare. The bosses also typically hold their passports for "safekeeping." The women often try to run away from the nightclubs or snack bars, but they are tracked down and, sometimes, forcibly brought back. Some are subjected to beatings, cigarette burns, or rape. The lucky ones—those who get away—usually have to depend on good citizens to direct them to a place like the HELP center. In three years the shelter has helped 455 Asian women return to their native countries.

It is against this backdrop that fractional changes in attitudes toward marriage and family must be seen. In the traditional urban, upper-class model, a college graduate joins a company at age twenty-one or twenty-two. He is expected to undergo a bonding process with his contemporaries; in fact, most larger companies provide dormitories for these young men. Contact with the fairer sex is not lacking either. It is routine for them to visit the soaplands in small groups. When the salarymen are about twenty-four or twenty-five, the company begins to pressure them to get married. One frequent technique that is a clear signal is to kick a young executive out of the dormitory and to tell him to get an apartment. Another key incentive is that one qualification for a prestigious foreign posting is a wife and, preferably, a family.

Where does he look for a wife? Rather than forcing a man to marry a particular woman, the way a family might, companies simply expose their marriage-age employees to preapproved pools of marriage partners—the company secretaries and office ladies. In this way, the salaryman can be assured that the woman has the proper background. Marrying one of them would probably advance his career because these women are prepared to accept the life of a salaryman's wife. For a salaryman who doesn't like the women he meets within his company, his superiors are only too happy to pay for a marriage service. Again, there is no danger that he will be introduced to a woman of an inferior social background.

If the two young people decide to marry, the two families exchange documents, again to make sure that they are of comparable social background and to screen out any unwanted influences. In some cases, the families hire private detectives to make sure that they are not marrying into a Korean or low-caste family. Should they marry someone beneath their station, they face severe pressure from their families. In one case, a man married a woman of whom his mother did not approve. She refused to see her daughter-in-law and a grandchild for three years.

Assuming that all is approved, a newly married couple will go on a package honeymoon and then set up a household. The period of bliss may last forever. In some cases, the couple enjoys a lifelong and faithful relationship. But in many cases, and there are no statistics that measure this, the pressures at work become too great and the peer group takes over again. The salaryman has to work late many evenings—with his old buddies or with potential new ones. They must go out and build consensus. A key form of male bonding remains the pursuit of women, and in Japan, this rarely results in divorce. In fact, Japan's divorce rate has actually declined despite the supposed new assertiveness of women. Traditional Japanese women understand the institution of marriage differently from the way their American counterparts do: It is their job to run the household and rear the children and it is the man's job to make money. Whether happily or not, many accept their husbands' pursuit of female companionship elsewhere.

This traditional model is undergoing some experimentation at the margins. There appears to have been an increase in the number of love marriages as opposed to arranged marriages. One estimate puts the percentage of love marriages in the mid-1980s at about half.[5] More young couples are postponing having children, so it is not unusual to encounter young couples of, say, thirty years of age who have in effect prolonged their nuptial bliss. There has even been an increase in the number of men who seek other patterns of *nemawashi* with fellow executives. One told me he prefers playing tennis in the evenings to going to the clubs. Many younger couples place greater emphasis on spending leisure time together than their elders would have ever dreamed possible. Western-style romance and courtship are more evident with these younger couples than with their elders. As one Japanese man with a wife and two children put it, these young couples develop split personalities: full attention to their jobs until 6:00 P.M., when they turn to their personal lives.

But as these couples face the challenge of either buying a home or having children, the experimentation stage is put under stress. It becomes more difficult for both to work. If there is a child, the pressure is overwhelming for the woman to stay home. It is not nearly as acceptable for a Japanese woman to turn her child over to a baby-sitter as it is for an American woman. The husband/father also soon confronts the need to work longer hours if he is going to survive increasingly stiff competitive pressure at the office.

The ideal of a happily married couple with two careers and children is not easy to achieve under the best of circumstances in the United States. It remains a hugely controversial question among American women whether they are making satisfactory progress in balancing their needs as career women with the needs of their families and husbands. Some seemed prepared to accept the "Mommy track" in which they accept fewer responsibilities and promotions on the job in exchange for more time with their families.[6] Others argue that women can still have it all.[7] While this debate rages, however, it is clear that American women have far greater flexibility in addressing these challenges than their Japanese counterparts and far greater support from society as a whole. If their husbands work at a mainline Japanese company, the pressures of educating the children, managing the household, and building a career are too great for the vast majority of Japanese women. The experimentation with a measure of equality in the relationship prior to children and prior to the husband's career push often gives way to the old status quo. As younger couples mature, many are "tamed."

Japanese women are thus not challenging the basic functioning of the household or the company, and men have no intention of allowing them to. Many American men believe that a measure of progress for women is a just cause; Japanese men in general do not. There is no question but that they will seek to maintain the male-dominated hierarchy of power.

It is not surprising, then, that Japanese women are nowhere near the levers of political power in Japan. Their numbers in the Diet are much smaller than all the hullabaloo surrounding their gains in the Upper House in July 1989 would suggest. Further, they are concentrated in the largely toothless Upper House and in parties that have little or no chance of actually taking power. In addition, the women are fractured among different parties with varying policy platforms, and they scarcely cooperate with each other.

After the July 1989 Upper House elections, this was how women stood in the Diet:[8]

Party	Lower House	Upper House
LDP	0	6
Socialists	2	15
Communists	5	6
Komeito	0	3
Others	0	3
Total	7 out of 512 (1.4%)	33 out of 252 (13%)

In short, the ruling party had no women in the Lower House, where power in the legislative process, such as it is, is concentrated. Women in the Diet are at the very beginning of a decades-long struggle to assert genuine power. Even Doi was only a figurehead leader of the Socialist Party, with no real power base of union support or factional control. Significantly, the gains that Doi and other women scored in July 1989 were not repeated in the Lower House elections in February 1990. The LDP gave two women bureaucrats positions in the cabinet, which represented progress of a sort, but neither of them was in the power loop. One was publicly humiliated when she was denied permission to hand out the prize at a sumo wrestling competition—still an all-male preserve.

Japanese male politicians are as deeply committed to their men-only pattern of decision preparation in the teahouses as ever. Says Socialist Upper House member Keiko Chiba: "For women to penetrate the male decision-making system, it's not a question of us going to the teahouses. It's a question of whether men will come out and open up the process."

Chiba recognizes that genuine political power still lies in the future. "I hope that in ten years, women will have more power. Toward the year 2000, both men and women will have equal opportunities in politics. To make that happen, we will have to make great efforts. Female politicians are just at the starting point. I'm not saying female politicians have a lack of talents. But they are not trained as well as men and don't have the same experience."

Women will continue making modest gains on the job simply because Japan has a labor shortage. But contrary to Western expectations, there is no evidence that they will crack the male work ethic, which is the lesson Kyoko Shimada has learned at Nissan. At mainline Japanese companies, women either play by men's rules or they leave. Women who start their own companies—in translation, design, headhunting, and similar fields—are in effect filling gaps that Japanese men themselves often ignore or for which they lack the necessary talent. Large numbers of Japanese women are hard-working, driven, committed professionals who have no desire to force the Japanese system to "go soft." Japanese women are, in many respects, just as hardheaded about the need for economic advancement as are Japanese men. Many, if not most, are contributing to Japan's economic advancement, not undermining it.

Because Japanese companies are firing on all cylinders, with high profits and prospects for continued, rapid growth, they need more talented workers. So the women who are hired to fill engineering or technical or marketing positions serve useful functions. Their talents and skills will be absorbed, but there are limits on how deeply they will penetrate the men's decision-making preserves. They will have to work even harder, and be smarter, than the men to prove themselves. Rather than suddenly causing Japanese men to rethink their work ethic, a far more likely result is just the opposite: a fresh supply of dedicated, pliant, and hard-working talent.

Although Japanese women are making some gains, they are starting in a different place, have a different sense of mission, and face a tougher climate of male opinion than American women in the 1960s. It would be more accurate to describe it as a period of experimentation rather than a clear social break. The male domain will not easily yield.

❖ 4 ❖

Hitting the Wall

Tokuo Li's mother and father came to Japan from Korea when they were teenagers in the late 1930s. Under the Japanese occupation of their homeland, millions of Koreans were forcibly relocated to Japan, China, and other parts of Japan's empire to work in mines and factories in support of Japan's military expansion. But in the case of Tokuo Li's parents, they made the decision to go to Japan by themselves. The reason was simple: They faced the prospect of starvation if they remained in Korea.

Today, Mr. Li, forty-six, his wife, and two nearly grown sons live in a modest home on the east side of Tokyo's Sumida River, which is the equivalent of living in Tokyo's Newark. Although it is attractive and scrupulously clean, their house is in a most undesirable location. When a visitor looks out the south window on a balmy summer day, there is a huge cement factory across the street. Immediately to the west is a major expressway. On other sides are warehouses and grimy subcontractor shops. Korean families such as the Lis are not allowed to live in good Japanese-only neighborhoods.

The 700,000 Koreans in Japan also face a consistent pattern of discrimination in schools, recreation and leisure clubs, occupations, and marriage even though they speak native Japanese. The Lis had just been forced out of a golf club and filed suit. As a result, they are now receiving anonymous telephone calls telling them to leave Japan.

One way Japan's difficult culture resists change is by subjecting its

47

minorities and immigrants to a rigorous pattern of exclusion. The Koreans are not the only ones who find it nearly impossible to penetrate the Japanese mainstream (*shuryu,* literally "main flow"). The Ainu, the ancestral inhabitants of the Japanese islands who are now concentrated in northern Hokkaido, and the darker-skinned residents of southern Okinawa island are both held outside the mainstream. So, too, are an estimated 200,000 Chinese, Filipinos, Thais, and other Asians who come to Japan, whether legally or illegally, in search of jobs in the construction, service, or entertainment industries. This is in addition to the estimated 100,000 Asian women employed in the sex industry. The 3,000 Vietnamese and Chinese boat people who arrived in Japan in 1989 received even less enthusiastic welcomes: Japanese authorities imposed a rigorous screening process to distinguish "economic refugees" from "political refugees." Those who fled Vietnam or southern China merely to seek better economic futures were sent back.

Even some full-blooded Japanese hit an impenetrable wall when they try to gain entree to Japanese companies, neighborhoods, and clubs. The *burakumin,* the lower, "untouchable" caste that was only fit to butcher animals and serve as executioners during the feudal era, is still very much resented by mainstream Japanese. During the feudal era, which officially ended with the Meiji Restoration in 1868, there were several different classes of Japanese, including the royalty, the samurai, merchants and craftsmen, and farmers. Below them were the untouchables, who had failed or made mistakes of one sort or another over the course of many centuries. They were outcasts. Over the course of the late nineteenth and twentieth centuries, successive governments have enacted laws and adopted various policies to ease their isolation.[1] Some have managed to infiltrate mainstream Japan, but the class, as a whole, still faces a systematic pattern of exclusion. The government says 2 million Japanese are *burakumin,* whereas the Buraku Liberation League says there are 3 million. Nobody really knows because members of this invisible class look and speak just like mainstream Japanese. It's only their ancestry that is in doubt, and the *burakumin* go to great lengths to conceal that.

In addition to repelling peoples of different race, ethnicity, or caste, mainstream Japanese also spurn their own members who become infected with foreignness. This is most striking in the case of the Japanese who go abroad to help Japan administer its global interests. On a rotating basis, an estimated 2 million Japanese are living outside Japan. Some returnees are able to use their foreign experience to advance in their organizations, but many more find it difficult to reintegrate. As a result, the fathers find themselves off the normal career paths, the mothers have trouble blending back into their communities, and the children often must go to separate schools, segregated from other, "normal," Japanese children. Each member of the family is subjected to a withering crossfire of scrutiny for being "deviant" because of having accepted a measure of Western-style individualism that makes each unwilling to subjugate him- or herself to the group as thoroughly as expected. "While they are Japan's most valuable people in the competitive international economy," writes Merry White in one of the best studies of the returnee phenomenon, "they also face great problems as stigmatized, devalued individuals who are seen as culturally contaminated by their acquaintance with foreign ways."[2]

Likewise, Japanese Christians, a tiny minority, are seen as being outside the fold because of their beliefs. Japanese who marry foreigners or work for foreign companies are also lost to the tribe in most cases. And the offspring of marriages between Japanese and Americans face intense social ostracism as well, particularly as they reach their teens. Even if a Japanese has never come into contact with foreigners but is too unusual, he or she is tagged *henna* (weird, strange) and isolated. A small number of Westerners have tried to penetrate the Japanese mainstream and win acceptance, but they encounter the same resistance.

This attempt to maintain purity is centuries old even though the Japanese themselves are not racially homogeneous. The literature shows, and many sophisticated Japanese will acknowledge, that waves of Koreans, Southeast Asians, and perhaps others arrived in Japan many centuries ago. To this day, some Japanese have the high cheekbone that is characteristic of Mongolians, meaning that somewhere in their family histories are ancestors who must have come from the Asian mainland via Korea. Others have rounder, darker faces reminiscent of Southeast Asia. But because the Japanese maintained their isolation for hundreds of years prior to the visits by Commodore Matthew Perry and other foreigners in the 1850s, their culture is more homogeneous than the people themselves are racially. Many Japanese attribute their homogeneity in part to the fact that they live on islands. But it goes beyond mere geography: The Japanese are obsessed with defining how they are different, and remaining that way.

Thus, Japan's mosaic in some respects is just as complex as America's. In the United States, however, ethnic and racial conflicts among whites, blacks, Asians, and Hispanics are obvious because of their different physical appearances. "Americans are no strangers to racism, but theirs is a straightforward prejudice against people who are physically or culturally different," writes Jared Taylor.[3] The goal of maintaining

Japanese "purity" is accomplished in an almost tribal fashion, through a series of social and cultural checkpoints that screen out undesirables.

Mr. Li, for example, is no slouch. He runs a painting company that has annual revenues of about $4 million. His men, who are mostly Korean, paint highway signs and do other heavy-duty painting. The fumes in his paintshop are thick; Mr. Li's is the sort of work most Japanese do not want. Nor would most Japanese want to live next door to a cement factory. Mr. Li's family is one of three hundred Korean families who purchased land in this area of Tokyo. They bought it from the *burakumin*, who sold out and moved to the other side of the expressway.

The reason Koreans must live in places like this is that mainstream Japanese will almost never rent to them or sell them land. Even though he cannot detect any racial difference in a Japanese-speaking Korean, a Japanese landlord may ask about a potential tenant's current living situation, where he went to school, and what he does for a living. If any of the answers trigger his suspicion, he asks for the would-be tenant's family papers. Koreans need not apply.

Koreans become aware of the problems they face at an early age. Korean children, like all foreigners living in Japan, must be finger-printed so that the government can keep track of them. Then, when they go to Japanese schools, they find that having a Korean name makes them the object of suspicion among Japanese children. Mr. Li once used the Japanese name Kunimoto when he went to school. "I always felt like I was hiding," he recalls now, sitting on a leather couch in his living room. "My character was not open." Eventually he was forced to acknowledge that he was Korean and changed his name. This was a traumatic experience. He feels strongly about being Korean, even though he does not speak the language and does not feel comfortable in Korea, either north or south.

One day Mr. Li's oldest son came home from school and asked to have a Japanese name; he said the other children were teasing him because his name was different. Mr. and Mrs. Li, however, felt it would be best if he and his brother recognized from an early age that they were different. It would be wrong to allow the boys to think they were Japanese when one day it was inevitable that they would be rejected because of their Korean ancestry.

Their oldest son did manage to obtain admission to a night-school program at a mediocre university. The mainstream's checkpoint against outsiders is not entry to a college so much as it is the social pressure once the outsider gets in. University students do not study very hard;

they spend a great deal of time in clubs, playing bridge or sailing, for example. The relationships formed in these clubs are the key to future career networking possibilities. Students who are different tend not to be admitted. But the clincher is that even if the outsider perseveres and gets a degree, mainline Japanese companies will not hire him. These companies routinely hire private detectives to study the backgrounds of job applicants. In the case of the younger Mr. Li, he dropped out of university when it became clear that he would be rejected by Japanese companies when they saw his Korean name on a job application. So he went to work for his father.

The Lis would have lived their lives quietly if it had not been for the golf club incident. Both Mr. and Mrs. Li are avid golfers. "I had a Japanese friend who bought a club membership and said to me, 'Why don't you join? Then we can play together.' Then I told him I was Korean and I didn't think the club would accept me." The friend didn't seem to mind that the Lis were Korean and suggested that he register under a Japanese name. Again, Mr. Li was being put in the position of pretending to be Japanese to gain acceptance. He put up $180,000 to join the club. That may seem like a lot to Americans, but it is cheap by Japanese standards; top clubs in Japan often require entry fees from $2 million to $3 million.

But it didn't work. After they had played only a few times, the politics of the club shifted against them. Mrs. Li said she suspected the reason was that the club wanted to raise its dues and become more exclusive, and that meant it had to become purely Japanese. "Suddenly I was asked to start paying a visitor's fee even though I was already a member," Mr. Li said. The harassment, which included a rumor campaign, became so great that the Lis were forced to withdraw. All their money was refunded, but they filed suit, claiming discrimination. They recognize that they have little chance of winning the suit, but they wanted to publicize the pattern of discrimination that Koreans face. It was soon after their case surfaced that the phone calls started. "We've gotten three calls so far from people speaking Japanese who refuse to identify themselves," Mr. Li said. "They tell me, 'If you are not happy here, go back to your country. You Koreans make big problems out of such small things.' "

The Lis appear to be among the more prosperous Koreans in Japan. In Osaka, I toured a Korean area clustered around the Suruhashi train station on the loop line that runs around central Osaka. In narrow alleyways under and around the station, the Koreans sell their distinctive foods: kimche, a hot spicy cabbage in big buckets, piles of ginseng root, crabs in hot pepper sauce, and pigs' feet. There are also tiny clothing stores and hole-in-the-wall restaurants.

The Koreatown is colorful but poor, and it has been that way for generations. When you ask people why they live here, the answer is: "We can't live anywhere else." Many young Korean women work in Osaka's sex and entertainment districts, as they do in Tokyo, because they cannot get jobs with Japanese companies. Another economic opportunity for the Koreans is owning the parlors where Japanese come to play pinball. Some Korean men, deprived of mainstream opportunities, find a niche in *yakuza* activity.[4]

Of course, any immigrant community in a new country has a tendency to stick together at first, before some are absorbed by the host society. But in Japan, the hardworking Koreans meet active resistance when they try to expand their footholds. They might make faster progress if they were willing to renounce their Korean ethnicity and become naturalized Japanese—that would spare them the hated fingerprinting—but not many Koreans feel they should be obliged to give up their identities. They are not starving and they are not homeless, but clearly the Japanese have little desire to allow them to participate as Koreans in Japan's new prosperity. They remain a trapped people.

Because Japan's economy has been booming for so many years and its own work force is aging, many companies need entry-level employees. Construction companies need laborers, restaurants need waitresses, and subcontractor shops need workers. That's why the presence of hundreds of thousands of immigrant workers from other Asian countries is such an enormously sensitive issue for the Japanese government. While the Asians are needed economically, their presence is, at the same time, feared because of the impact it could have on Japan's perceived homogeneity and social order.

The government is deeply divided. The Ministry of Foreign Affairs would like to admit more of the Asians to improve Japan's international image, but the Justice and Labor ministries are against any broad opening. Even without a formal government decision, the hard-liners may win because more Asians are being rounded up and shipped out of Japan than there are Asians being officially allowed in. "The Japanese government is trying to kick out foreign workers," says Keiko Chiba, the Socialist Diet member. Chiba believes the ministries that are worried about Japan's homogeneity will prevail in the end because "the Japanese don't want foreign workers to make a mess and threaten their jobs. They're worried about crime and social disorder." A poll by the Tokyo Metropolitan Government shows that the Japanese also worry about the impact of Asians on their schools, housing, and social welfare

programs.[5] Right-wing groups complain that the arrival of Asian workers means "our country will be going nowhere with no identity that
people can adhere to."

In the best of all circumstances, some of the more skilled Asians will
be allowed to stay, but only for specified periods. Then they, too, will
have to leave. There is no chance that the Japanese will draw them into
Japanese society any time soon.

Some of the unskilled immigrants who do manage to slip through the
cracks find jobs and send money to their families in dramatically less
affluent countries such as Pakistan, Bangladesh, Thailand, or the Philippines. But many find themselves getting cheated out of their wages or
else are working for a fraction of what Japanese workers get. These
illegals live like fugitives in tiny apartments, worried that their employers will report them to the authorities. Because they tend to work at
dirty and dangerous jobs, some are injured. Lacking insurance, they
face difficulties getting proper medical care. All in all, they threaten to
become an underclass.[6]

Essentially, they have met head-on the unpleasant fact that rights
accorded to Japanese are not willingly extended to newcomers. One of
the few Japanese activists trying to change this situation is Nobuki
Omori, thirty-eight, head of the Cooperation of Asian Laborers for
Liberation. Omori has been trying to organize a European-style trade
union of Asian laborers from different occupations. "Foreigners have
many problems, like housing and medical conditions," says Omori.
"They have problems with other tenants and with landlords and they
have problems with university medical offices."

"How does Japan's commitment to assimilate these people compare
with the American ethic?" I asked.

"Japan doesn't have that ethic at all," Omori said.

The Japanese seem to reserve their worst treatment for the Pakistanis,
who are darker-skinned than East Asians. The National Police Agency,
for example, distributed a 179-page report to regional authorities warning them that it was "absolutely necessary" to wash their hands after
questioning suspected illegal Pakistani workers, and that detention and
interrogation rooms will stink because of their "unique body odor."[7]

While I met many Asian workers, I had a particularly touching
encounter in the Tokyo subway late one evening. As I sat reading,
someone suddenly asked me, in English, what country I was from. I
looked around into the dark, handsome face of a Pakistani.

"Salaam aleikum," I said. This is a greeting widely used in the
Islamic world and means "God's blessing." He smiled ear to ear and

responded in kind. When he offered his hand, it was rough from years of physical labor. Originally from Lahore, he had been working in Japan at an auto parts subcontractor shop and had learned at least some Japanese. The work was physically easy, but getting along with his employers and living in Japan were fraught with difficulties. The fact that he struck up a conversation with a total stranger on a subway seemed indicative of the deep isolation he must have felt. "The British and American people are 90 percent good," he said, "but these people only 5 percent." It was a decidedly unscientific statement, but it reflected his deep frustration.

"So we are both *gaijin*," I quipped. "We're both dangerous."

"Yes," he said. *"Abunai."* It was the Japanese word for dangerous. "They need me, but they can't stand having me here. It's funny, isn't it?"

Unlike the Koreans or other Asians, who cling to a separate identity, the *burakumin* maintain that they are 100 percent Japanese. There is no apparent racial or cultural difference between them and the mainstream. Naturally, it is difficult to locate and identify them because they almost never openly acknowledge their background. Only someone such as Toshihiko Nakashima, an executive of the Buraku Liberation League, would openly identify himself as a *burakumin.*

Nakashima is a man in his fifties with tinted glasses and gray hair combed straight back. A former schoolteacher in the Hiroshima area, he quit teaching after twenty-one years to become involved in local politics. He later joined the liberation league in Tokyo. His most vivid personal experience of discrimination was when he was a young man trying to find a wife. "The first time, I loved a woman who was not a *burakumin* and I was refused," he recalls. He was introduced through a matchmaker to a second Japanese woman of a higher caste, and was refused again. One of the ways the families of his would-be brides identified him was by the neighborhood he came from. Although discrimination against the *burakumin* is officially prohibited, many still live in the same districts as they did in the feudal era. Mainstream Japanese living nearby have simply never forgotten who is who. "If you're from a particular place, the families know," Nakashima said. "Even if you move and someone finds the roots of where you are from, they recognize your status. The worst case is if a woman's family goes to a man's neighborhood and asks the neighbors lots of questions."

It is difficult to prove outright discrimination because many proposed marriages are handled through intermediaries. When confronted directly, families never reveal the real reason for nixing a marriage. "Of course, they never make it clear," says Nakashima. "They say things like 'Your income is not great enough.' " Men or women who marry against their respective families' wishes are routinely ostracized. Nakashima eventually married a *buraku* woman.

The untouchables are concentrated in various cities throughout southern and western Japan, including Kyoto, an ancient capital. Although Kyoto is surrounded by lovely Buddhist and Shinto temples and shrines, its *burakumin* districts are obvious because the residents engage in recycling and selling junk and used tires, which are the kinds of occupations to which they have been traditionally limited. Their dilapidated two-story houses that line twisting narrow streets have been bypassed by Japan's explosion of wealth.

One of the techniques Japanese companies use to screen out *burakumin* is the use of secret book-length lists of *buraku* names and specific *buraku* districts. The existence of these lists was first revealed during the 1970s. The companies, and the detectives they hire, are relentless in exploring city hall records, lists of scholarships, and any other clues to prevent *burakumin* from penetrating their ranks.

Unlike the Koreans or other Asians, some *burakumin* have become successful in Japanese business, entertainment, and academia, but again no one knows precisely how many. These people have had to sever their links to other *burakumin* and to their home districts. "If they say they are *burakumin*, they will lose status," Nakashima explains. "They tell their families not to tell anybody. They conceal their home districts. Successful [*buraku*] people never go home to pray for the spirits of their ancestors."

Returnees from abroad do not have any differences of ethnicity or caste. For them, it is simply a question of mind-set. One returnee who hit the wall is thirty-two-year-old Miyako Mead, who earned a master's in international studies at a Michigan university over the course of three years. Miyako's father is a professor and her mother is from an old family, so she had mainstream credentials. But during her stay in the United States, she clearly had become infected with an unacceptable degree of individualism. "The things I learned and saw, both good and bad, helped me be myself more than before," she said in perfect English. "The sense of being myself, revealing myself, was important. In Japan, we don't know we are concealing ourselves behind a curtain. People think that is usual."

When she returned to Japan four years ago, Miyako joined a Japanese import-export company. After a couple of weeks on the job, her boss took her and several other young women out for lunch. He asked them what they thought. The others, being well-trained Japanese women, swallowed their words and mumbled, or else they simply said, *"Hai, hai"* (Yes, yes, I hear you), and kept smiling. But Miyako, a slender, intense woman, offered her opinions on such issues as U.S.-Japanese trade.

She had failed the test. From that moment, her boss froze her out. She was never again asked to lunch or drinks. In retrospect, she realized she had been expected to be vague, to give indirect answers until it became clear what her superiors wanted to hear. She was supposed to read the signals, *ishin denshin.* "I demonstrated too much of myself," she said. "I was supposed to wait to see what he wanted me to say. I wasn't supposed to have my own opinions. I wasn't modest enough." After a few more months, her isolation made it impossible for her to stay.

No company, Japanese or foreign, likes newcomers who shoot their mouths off, but my impression over the course of several encounters with Miyako was that she was no radical or professional troublemaker. With her degree and experience in the United States, she felt she had a knowledge base that would have helped her company.

She had readjustment problems off the job as well. With her old friends, in the subways, and in other day-to-day contacts, she felt out of place because of her sense of individualism. "In Japan, you have to worry about what others think. The atmosphere makes you hold yourself behind the curtain and try to read the minds of others so that you can fit their expectations. Maybe you can find a way to do something for yourself; maybe not. People say the younger generation is changing, but at the bottom of their hearts, not really. It's only on the surface. They want to look very nice and very fashionable, but they have no social responsibility or independence. Those people don't know how to face problems and solve them. They just turn away and avoid responsibility. To me, they are already being absorbed into this society."

Miyako later met her American husband-to-be, and eventually left Japan for the United States. Like so many other young Japanese who have spent time abroad, she is lost to the tribe forever.

The worst returnee problems, however, are suffered by children, particularly those exposed to the American life-style. Their families have more space and bigger kitchens than they did back home. The fathers tend to come home earlier than they did in Tokyo and spend more time with their kids on the weekends. There is less pressure of space and time at home. The children attend schools that are excellent by U.S. standards but much more relaxed by Japanese norms. Although most go to Japanese schools on Saturday in an attempt to keep pace with their counterparts in Japan, it is an uphill battle. The pressure to perform and conform is much reduced. Moreover, the Japanese children see the American kids around them having fun while they learn, and it can be contagious.

The shock comes as they prepare to go back. Special Japanese schools in the United States try to recondition the children. When an American teacher asks a student a question, the student's response is to simply raise his or her hand. If you know the answer, raise your hand. It's simple. But a Japanese teacher preparing children to go back to Japan scolds children who raise their hands individually without first looking around to make sure that other members of his or her peer group also know the answer. Children who go back to Japanese schools without relearning the concept of group are subjected to bullying and harassment by fellow students, often with the encouragement of the teachers. "You have to conform or you get hit," says Tadashi Yamamoto, of the Japan Center for International Exchange.

The severity of the reentry process depends on a great deal on the age of the child and how long he or she has been in the United States. Within the same family, one child can have severe problems while another can make the adjustment smoothly. Consider the family of Yoshiyuki Izawa, a senior corporate strategist in the Corporate Planning Division of Mitsui & Company in Tokyo. He spent seven years in Los Angeles and one year in Boston. He took along his two sons who were born in Japan, and he and his wife had a daughter while living in the United States.

Their elder son handled the reentry to Japan well, but the younger son had problems. He was in the United States from the age of two until the age of ten. "He was American," says Izawa. "He was so shocked by the culture" when he returned to Japan.

His parents found a special school for returnees, a public school that accepted foreign-experienced people. But one day the boy woke up and said he couldn't move. He was paralyzed. They rushed him to a hospital. Tests didn't show anything. There didn't seem to be anything physically wrong with him. Then all of a sudden he stood up. "It was mental," says his father. Shortly thereafter the boy developed a hearing problem. But gradually he regained his confidence and that problem disappeared, too. It took a full year for him to readjust even to the special school. There is little chance that he will ever be on the same rigorous education track that mainstream Japanese children are on. "To the school they can adjust, but it takes even longer to adjust to the culture," his father says.

As for his daughter, who was much younger during the American sojourn, Izawa is not worried. "She's Japanese," he says proudly.

* * *

Each group that hits the wall has a different history and a different set of problems, yet there is a common lesson: People who are deviant and who attempt to penetrate the difficult Japanese society, much less change it, are almost always stopped cold. Japan is by no means the only country that discriminates—discrimination exists in every country, including the United States. Moreover, people outside the fold in Japan may still live good, prosperous lives. There are no bombs from white supremacists killing federal judges, as in the United States. There are no bulldozers knocking down their homes, as in South Africa or on the West Bank. There are no riots. In that sense, Japan's method of discrimination is eminently civilized. It is not a rigid, institutional wall. Rather, it is subtle, a system of socially and culturally enforced checkpoints. This maintains a sense of boundary.

As Japan's power looms larger in the world and more outsiders scrutinize the nature of Japanese society itself, there is a greater recognition of just how different it is from the stereotypes that have long prevailed. Some experts have understood this for years. "People are discovering there is something unusual here," says Australian Gregory Clark, a professor of Japanese studies at Sophia University in Tokyo. He has lived in Japan for twenty years and ten years ago wrote a Japanese-language book entitled *The Japanese Tribe*.[8] But few outside Japan-watchers were willing to listen. Now that they are finally listening, he feels they are overreacting. "They are giving it a nasty edge," he says in a dry Australian accent. "That's unfortunate. Of course, some of it is nasty, but some of it is very interesting and attractive. It's a package. It's a tribe that has become a nation."

There are more outside-the-fold people living in Japan today than ever before in its modern history, both as a percentage of total population and in absolute numbers. They tend to be visible, and they talk about their problems. This creates confusion for Americans and other foreigners, who see so many signs of "change." For that reason, the foreigners serve as a useful buffer. They create the appearance of change when the underlying system remains silent and strong, as isolated as ever from the threat of contamination.

Perhaps over the course of several decades, the outsiders will be able to alter the mainstream's sense of boundary. But for the moment at least, the mainstream is getting stronger, not weaker. Internationalists and other Japanese in contact with foreigners are under pressure to prove their "Japaneseness" or be labeled outcasts. A member of the Diet who likes to watch CNN tapes says he dares not tell his fellow lawmakers, because they will suspect that he has been infected with "foreignness." The desire to push out Asian workers, to rewrite the history books, to Japanize rather than internationalize—all of these reflect the mainstream's power. "They want to maintain the so-called Japanese race. It's a total illusion. But it has created an appearance of wealth and that's why people want to keep it. The mainstream is becoming more solid and more chauvinistic," says HELP director Matsuda, who is decidedly outside the fold.

There is a fundamental force of conservatism at the heart of this difficult culture that shows little inclination to break with the past. This is what the experts mean when they say Japan is in the world but not of it. Can Japan integrate itself into the world community, or will it forever remain apart, different, and pure?

❖ 5 ❖

The Japanese Prism

McDonald's has done a fine job establishing itself in Japan. Its method of preparing fast food is one of those systems that the Japanese have understood, adapted, and perhaps even improved upon. When one goes into a McDonald's and orders a *biggu makku*, the flurry of activity on the other side of the counter makes most McDonald's in the United States look positively sleepy. The employees take their jobs very seriously. The timing is split-second. The McDonald's outlets are also fully bicultural. The name, which is so difficult for the Japanese tongue, appears as *Makudonarudo* in the *katakana* script.

There is a story about a Japanese family on their first visit to America. They spotted the Golden Arches as they were walking down the street.

"Look, Father," the little girl was overheard as saying. "They have *Makudonarudo* here, too!"

The story may be apocryphal, but the underlying point is still valid. When the Japanese copy a system, a style, or an idiom from the West, it is drawn in and molded in the Japanese way. If it is successful, it *becomes* Japanese. The origin is forgotten.

At the same time, other foreign systems are copied but held in isolation and examined more as objects of curiosity. At the Cavern Club in the Roppongi section of Tokyo, for example, four Japanese men have become the Beatles. The one who portrays Paul McCartney wears his hair in the boyish mod look that the real McCartney sported in his early days and has trained his voice to have many of the same qualities as the Liverpool flash. The musician who portrays John Lennon sports rimless bifocals and wears his hair shoulder length, parted down the middle, imitating Lennon in his hippie days. There are obvious discrepancies in physical appearance but none in the music. From the early ballads to rock and roll to the psychedelic, the band has mastered the sound and the rhythm, down to the last "oooh" and "yeah." If you close your eyes and listen, you would swear it's the real thing.

After hearing a performance, one American went up to the band to tell them what an incredible job they had done and to ask how they managed to pull it off.

"Eh?" one band member responded. It quickly became clear that none of them spoke English. The entire performance had been memorized by rote. There was little chance that anything the Beatles stood for, whether good or bad, would seep into the Japanese psyche.

The Japanese have a prism that allows them and adapt from the outside world on a wholesale basis. The *katakana* script allows the Japanese to smoothly absorb European and American concepts. Like the rays of light that pass through a prism and are refracted, these outside notions are carefully sorted. Japan's history has been characterized by periods of extensive borrowing, from either China or the West. In the modern era, the Japanese have emulated Western models in building a navy and an army, an educational system, a communications system, the police, the banking and legal systems, political parties, newspapers, stock exchanges, and many other attributes of a modern society.[1] This technique of borrowing has a precedent from Japan's own feudal era. If one lord found his enemy too strong to defeat, he would *toriiru* and *toriireru*, which translates to "take in and get in." In short, the lord would study his opponent's system, infiltrate it, and then absorb what would strengthen his own forces.

None of the borrowing from abroad challenges the Japanese view of themselves as a unique society that is different, that is apart, that lies behind the prism. The Japanese have a saying that explains this feeling: Water can absorb salt and water can absorb sugar, but it is still water. In other words, Japan can learn from China and Japan can learn from the West, but it is still Japan. Not surprisingly, the slogan *Ware ware wa nihonjin*, "We are Japanese," takes on an almost religious significance. The implication is that "we are different and must remain that way." This is the ultimate shield from outside scrutiny. We are different; you cannot understand us.

Hundreds of books have been written in Japanese to explain just how the Japanese are different. This is called the *Nihonjin-ron*, or Japanese uniqueness theory. The general thrust also comes across in off-the-cuff remarks. Some Japanese have argued that because Japanese intestines are longer, they cannot digest beef well. One Japanese physician argues that Japanese brains are different. Japan's snow is different, so the Japanese cannot buy Western skis. They cannot buy American shoes because Japanese feet are thicker and wider. American-made aluminum bats do not make the right kind of ping when they hit the ball, so the Japanese do not want to buy them. If a rocket launch goes awry, it must be the fault of an American-made semiconductor. When a JAL Boeing 747 crashed into a Japanese mountainside in 1985, it was universally assumed that the fault was with U.S. manufacturing techniques, not with Japanese inspection or maintenance. Cockroaches in Okinawa must be from America because they are bigger than Japanese cockroaches.

Michio Watanabe, a top member of the LDP and a perennial candidate for prime minister, had a rather earthy explanation for why Japanese would never buy too many American cherries. At a campaign stop in his home district of Tochigi Prefecture, he tried to reassure farmers that Japan's agricultural liberalization would not hurt them because Japanese consumers would simply never buy American cherries, no matter what import restrictions were dropped. The reason? "We Japanese like Japanese cherries," Watanabe said. "They are pink and fresh, just like a virgin's nipples."

Of course, not all Japanese believe in Japan's uniqueness or superiority. But even Reischauer, who has patiently defended the Japanese for decades, shows signs of irritation with them for their obsession with being different. In one of his most recent works he complained that there was a "dichotomy between the actual Japanese position of being among the world leaders and their perception of themselves as being so distinct from the rest of humanity as to be unique. They are both self-satisfied almost to the point of arrogance and at the same time somewhat ill at ease with others."[2]

The point is that despite the prism's ability to absorb so much information from the outside world, it only transmits part of the values that enter, creating a perception gap. Relatively little world opinion about Japan's trading or investing practices, or about the values that prevail in the Western system, penetrates to the Japanese mainstream in a way that it is digested and embraced. And as evidence of Japan's economic achievements mounts, the prism admits less. Indeed, it seems to be turning more opaque.

One important element of the prism is Japan's "victim's consciousness." Memories of World War II, for example, are still quite vivid even though most Americans have forgotten these events, or else glossed over them. Most people know about Pearl Harbor and the Bataan death march and the bridge over the River Kwai, and most people remember the old John Wayne movies. But the sense that memories have faded comes through in the backwaters of America, where Japanese plants are now springing up. Dozens of men from the small central Kentucky town of Harrodsburg, for example, died in the Bataan march; the local chapter of the Veterans of Foreign Wars is called the Bataan chapter. When I visited in 1986, Hitachi was building an auto electronics plant on the northern outskirts of town not far from where the VFW had erected a tank memorial honoring their war dead. Kenneth Hourigan, then seventy-four, was one of the last survivors of the march, but he was willing to forgive and forget. "If the old crowd were around, they wouldn't like it," said Hourigan, wearing his farmer's bib overalls. "But the young people, they need jobs."

In Bloomington, Illinois, where Mitsubishi Motors was building an auto plant with Chrysler as a quiet partner, I sat down with Jennifer Raper, forty, the mother of four and a foreman in the paint shop. Her father had been a marine who landed at Pearl Harbor a few days after it was bombed and fought throughout the Pacific. He criticized Jennifer for working for Mitsubishi and for accepting a training mission to Japan. But she was firm in her insistence that her "children will not grow up hating the Japanese." What's done is done.

It's different when a war is fought on home ground. "I survived World War II," thundered Masaharu Gotoda, one of the grand old men of the LDP, at a campaign rally in Tokyo. "I was here when Tokyo was only burning fields." The speech by the seventy-four-year-old Gotoda was riveting political theater. The phrase "burning fields" is one that pops up often in Japanese politics. It's remarkable that reminding the Japanese that they are victims still sells, but it does, particularly among older Japanese. When one travels outside of Tokyo, many Japanese will tell a visitor about the American bombers flying overhead during World War II. Or one will find in the family living room, near the shrine to the ancestors, photographs of relatives who served as pilots and perished. For residents of Hiroshima and Nagasaki, the memories of being atomic bomb victims are still very much alive. Films constantly examine the physical and psychological suffering they endured, drowning out movies depicting Japanese military brutality in China or elsewhere. That was outside, beyond the prism.

The psychology of being a small victimized nation has not caught up with Japan's status as an economic superpower. To this day, the Japanese seem to have little understanding of the external impact of their actions. For instance, when it became clear that the machine tool subsidiary of Toshiba had supplied the Soviets with equipment that helped make quieter propellers for Soviet submarines, and that the U.S. Navy was having trouble detecting them, Congress was naturally outraged. After all, Japan was supposed to be an ally; they were under the U.S. defensive shield. But here they were supplying key technology to the Soviet military machine.

The Japanese media, as a reflection of the society as a whole, did not see this as the real issue. Their focus of attention was on a different angle. Several congressmen staged a cheap publicity stunt and smashed a Toshiba boom box radio on the Capitol lawn. Most American journalists involved in covering the Toshiba affair were unaware of the PR stunt until pictures of it received wide play in Japanese newspapers. Suddenly the Japanese were the victims. They were being persecuted by aggressive Americans with sledgehammers. The very acceptance of Japanese products in America was under attack. The fact that Toshiba had done something that Americans perceived as "wrong" did not seem to penetrate the Japanese consciousness. It was obvious, to the Japanese, that Toshiba should do whatever was in its best interests and, by implication, in Japan's interests. Japan had to defend itself against the irrational Americans.

This pattern has been repeated many times. Of course, some of Japan's external economic impact has been beneficial, but there are sore points. When these sore points need to be addressed, however, there's little in the Japanese character to accommodate it. The Japanese media look for criticism and magnify it. Japan is victim. Even solid, well-reasoned concern or criticism is dismissed, if not discredited. It becomes evidence of "Japan-bashing" or "anti-Japanese" sentiment.

Americans don't like to hear negative news about their international activities either. They have their own prism, to be sure, but the message does get through. American troops did something wrong and brutal at My Lai. U.S. intelligence forces played a role in toppling and perhaps assassinating President Salvador Allende of Chile. And should navy jets have bombed Libya's Muammar Qaddafi and killed his little girl? These questions become issues of conscience.

One reason so little outside light penetrates the prism is that the Japanese are increasingly convinced that their system is winning. It has created tremendous wealth. It has power. Therefore, it is right.

The view of Americans that the prism conveys is one of failure. It is weighted toward drugs, crime, homelessness, racism, and the supposed education breakdown. The Americans can't make things. Financially, they're broke. Washington is a quagmire.

There is some truth to all these things, but it's only part of the picture. There is also an America quietly going about the business of raising families and giving them solid educations. American universities are the best in the world, bar none. American companies have had a phenomenal export boom and many U.S. multinationals are world beaters. The list is long.

But the message of decline and desperation has power in Japan. It shapes the Japanese response, as Ayako Doi, a Japanese freelance writer based in Washington, D.C., found to her dismay. She approached the editor of a Japanese monthly magazine, for whom she had written previously, suggesting an article on the U.S. decision to declare Japan an unfair trading nation under the Super 301 provision of the 1988 Trade Act. He responded:

> I don't want a straight report on what the Americans are saying. I see no need to listen to rubbish uttered by low-quality American lawmakers. We would do better to ignore those who are busy criticizing Japan while closing their mouths about their own faults.
>
> Japan must argue against American geocentricism in order to protect the free world, although Japan, too, is not without fault. Instead of bowing our heads to listen to the theories of our American "lord and master" . . . we must try to make the sick man realize that he is sick.

The editor concluded by asking for an article that would "reveal America's sickness" and "help us think of ways to deal with this sick nation." Doi declined to provide such an article and instead described the incident for the *Washington Post*.[3]

The Japanese have increasingly less patience for Americans who urge the Japanese to change, to become more like Americans. What the Americans usually have in mind is: relax; open up; spend more and save less; treat women, minorities, and immigrants better; advance the interest of the consumer at the expense of the producer. But most mainstream Japanese see these values as the root cause of American decline. So why should they embrace them?

On the basis of hundreds of conversations with Japanese diplomats, politicians, bureaucrats, professors, journalists, and others over the past few years, I sense this feeling is building in Japan. I first encountered it in 1987 when a thirty-two-year-old Japanese entrepreneur, a rare breed, called on me in New York to promote his company. After a general conversation, I asked him to tell me—off the record—what he really thought about Americans. I was surprised that he did: "The older generation felt the brunt of American power and they still have respect," he said. "But younger Japanese, all they see is Americans working for Japanese companies and Americans taking Japanese money."

By 1989, people like the right-wing Shintaro Ishihara were saying much the same thing but in harsher terms. The new tone was also reflected in the comments of Japanese internationalists. Ambassador Hideotoshi Ukawa talks about Japan as having a "national system that is right." LDP Dietman Koji Kakizawa believes that Japan has "the most advanced human system." Former top bureaucrat Naohiro Amaya, the white-haired sage who is frequently on Western television shows about Japan, believes that Japan's "human software" is better than America's when it comes to making things.

The Japanese have long held a peculiar inferiority-superiority complex when it comes to the Americans.[4] But now it is shifting toward the superiority side of the equation as the results of Japan's economic drive become more apparent. "There's a half-conscious inclination among Japanese these days to say that Japan is superior," says one prominent intellectual.[5]

This is the logic of power, not the logic of persuasion. Many Japanese are uncomfortable debating with Westerners because they don't understand the Western style of reasoning. The Japanese are not schooled that way. Instead, they are trained to recognize power and to roll with it. The *gaijin* have abstract principles and try to argue logically on what is right and wrong, fair or unfair. The Japanese don't have universal, absolute principles of the same sort. They are more flexible and more pragmatic: whatever works for the group. And they prefer what they call "belly-to-belly," or more intuitive, communications that aren't strictly rational in the Western sense. This is one reason some Japanese have said they find Americans to be "cold" and "dry": Americans, like many Westerners, stress the role of abstract principles in their relations with others. Japanese executives spend a year at Harvard or other top American universities in part to learn what they call the "Why? Because. Because why?" style of argumentation. Now some language institutes have popped up in Tokyo to teach English at the same time they teach "why-because" techniques. It is no sudden discovery that the Japanese in general aren't logical by Western standards. Experts have long understood that they have a "cultural tolerance for logical contradiction and ambiguity."[6] Indeed, many Japanese positively enjoy what a Western mind sees as contradiction.

The point is that differences of culture make it difficult to break through the prism with logical argumentation. Once again, the Japanese language provides some of the best illustrations of this perception gap. For example, the Western understanding of the word *fair* is an action carried out on the basis of certain rules or principles, which are defined by religion, morality, or ethics. The Japanese word for fair, *kohei,* has a different connotation. It can suggest an action carried out on the basis of the balance of power. Imagine, for a moment, a rich man meeting a poor man. The Judeo-Christian concept of fairness would have the rich man giving the poor man a chance. He may share only a tiny portion of his wealth, and not all rich Westerners would do that, but it is the ideal by which they are judged. In Japan, if a rich man met a poor man, he would have far less moral pressure to give the other guy a break. The poor man's absence of wealth would be taken as a sign that he had failed as a person. He is therefore to be despised. If the rich man chooses to either spurn or exploit the poor man, it would be considered fair because the poor man had no power, no standing.

This cross-cultural communication gap is pervasive. If an American says he wants better "understanding" with a Japanese, the Japanese might heartily agree. In his context, it might mean you accept his power or agree with his position. The phrase "better relations," which a Westerner would take to mean a change in Japanese actions or behavior, means precisely the opposite to most Japanese: the elimination of carping against Japanese interests.

And what is internationalization? The Western assumption is that internationalizing Japan will result in a change in values and attitudes. But the Japanese word for internationalization is *kokusaika,* which translates into "country-borders-meet." The meaning can be understood as Japan expanding its borders and its relations with the outside world on Japanese terms. An "internationalist" in Japan, then, is not necessarily someone who has thoroughly studied and absorbed Western values and attitudes, but is perhaps someone who is sophisticated enough to manage foreigners. Many Japanese who enjoy exotic cuisines or travel extensively may seem internationalized, but in reality, they regard this foreign exposure as a mere life-style enhancement that has little impact on their commitment to think and act in Japanese ways.

The political events that made headlines in 1989 took place on the other side of this Japanese prism. They had their own internal logic, their own special meaning. Westerners who applied their set of values in interpreting and understanding the Japanese power game were destined to be proven wrong once again.

Part Two

SCANDAL

❖ 6 ❖

The Kingdom

Most outsiders have never heard of one of Japan's most powerful political leaders. That is because he prefers to operate in the shadows. But at seventy-five, Shin Kanemaru controls major flows of political funds from the construction and telecommunications industries. To amass this political power base, he gradually undercut and betrayed Kakuei Tanaka, the former prime minister. His final consolidation of power came after the ambitions of Shinto and Nakasone were crushed.

A master of duplicity, Kanemaru is a man to be reckoned with. Whenever his name or picture surface in public, a major decision is often about to be made, or blocked. He is both kingmaker and troublemaker. "Kanemaru is the grand don," one source told me.

Kanemaru's "front man" is generally reckoned to be former Prime Minister Noboru Takeshita, who, like Kanemaru, was first elected to the Diet in 1958. Takeshita has his own impressive power base, to be sure, both within the party and within his own faction. But Kanemaru plays a broader role of shaping the political environment and troubleshooting. Kanemaru sets the strategy. Takeshita administers on a day-to-day basis and pays heed to the details.

Kanemaru was at the heart of the scandal involving Recruit. Although the Recruit affair touched the Labor, Education, and Agricultural ministries, the key battleground was the telecommunications kingdom. The manner in which Kanemaru dominated the politics of telecommunications is reminiscent of how Mayor Richard Daley ran

71

Chicago. Telecommunications was, and is, a lucrative, fast-growing industry and an object of national pride. The Japanese are trying to ensure their future by transforming themselves into even more of an "information society." Telephones themselves are just one piece of telecommunications. To make a telephone system work efficiently requires advanced satellites, computers, fiber optics, semiconductors, and other critical technologies.

Not coincidentally, telecommunications also generates a large flow of political funds, though nobody knows exactly how much. One official of the Keidanren, the powerful association of Japanese industries, estimates that telecommunications ranks third in the flow of political funds, after the agriculture and tax reform lobbies. Masao Kanazashi, a top political editor at the *Nihon Keizai Shimbun,* Japan's equivalent of the *Wall Street Journal,* puts telecommunications at fourth, but all political analysts agree that it is one of the richest lobbies in Japan. It is the kingdom that Hisashi Shinto wanted to reform drastically. It was the lucrative source of funds that Yasuhiro Nakasone desired in his attempt to expand his own political base. It was an area of business that Hiromasa Ezoe needed to crack.

The Japanese sometimes explain how these kingdoms work by speaking of the "Iron Triangle" (see Figure 1). While it is a dated concept and of limited value in explaining the nation's overall decision-making process, it is helpful in describing the various Japan Inc.'s that dominate the nation's economic and political landscape.

The elites in this triangle may compete with each other for influence and power, and there are, of course, many cliques, factions, subgroups, and other smaller players contained in each. But broadly speaking, they work to protect the system against outsiders, whether other Japanese or foreigners, and they work to expand their triangle's wealth. The

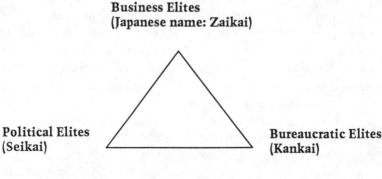

**Business Elites
(Japanese name: Zaikai)**

**Political Elites
(Seikai)**

**Bureaucratic Elites
(Kankai)**

Figure 1

triangle as a concept has greatest application to domestic Japanese industries where government, or "pork barrel," spending plays a key role.

In different industries, real decision making may tilt more in the direction of the bureaucrats, or more in the direction of the private sector. Some ministries are more powerful than others in relation to the industries they regulate. It is different in each case. Although some power shifted to the political elites in the 1970s, politicians are the weakest corner of the triangle in nearly all cases. In fact, it was the bureaucratic elites who created the parliamentary system around the turn of the century. Politicians have rarely been serious rivals for the exercise of real power. They are vastly outgunned by the resources, expertise, and connections of the bureaucrats.

Former Prime Minister Tanaka was a master of this brand of machine politics. A farmer's son with only a sixth-grade education, Tanaka was the first Japanese prime minister who was neither a university graduate nor a general. He served with the Japanese army in China, after which he started his own construction company, quickly striking it rich in the postwar reconstruction effort. In 1947, he won election to the Diet.

Although construction was his original power base, Tanaka became minister of post and telecommunications at the tender age of thirty-nine. Despite his lack of a formal education, he sensed the importance of telecommunications and helped build an Iron Triangle in the quickly developing field (Figure 2).

It was a closed, inbred world. Nippon Telegraph and Telephone Public Corporation (NTTPC), the Japanese version of American Telegraph & Telephone (AT&T), was and remains at the heart of it. A

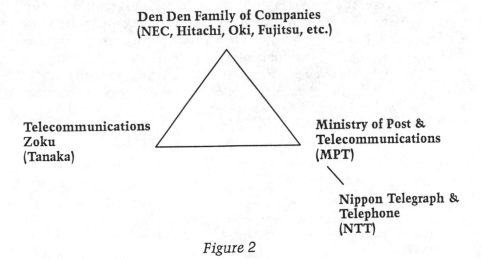

Figure 2

monopoly, it was managed by the Ministry of Post and Telecommunications (MPT). Bureaucrats at the ministry were able to guide NTTPC's procurement and research decisions to their favorite companies, the three hundred members of the so-called Den Den family.*

The largest members of the preferred family of suppliers were NEC, Hitachi, Oki Electric, and Fujitsu, and they dominated the procurement process. Altogether, nearly half of NTT's procurement decisions of $2.5 billion to $3 billion by 1980 went to these companies. NEC, a member of the Sumitomo group, was the single largest supplier, and it won $505 million in orders alone in the fiscal year ending March 1981. These figures cover NTT's purchase of the equipment it needed to operate a telephone system. In terms of total sales, NTT had become a $20 billion giant by the early 1980s. It dwarfed nearly all individual private sector companies and at its height had a staggering 330,000 employees.

Foreign companies were not welcomed into this kingdom. In fact, then NTT president Tokuji Akikusa outraged U.S. trade negotiators in the late 1970s by saying: "The only thing we could consider buying overseas would be [telephone] poles and mops."[1] Even Japanese companies that were not part of the Den Den family were excluded, including Toshiba.

The privilege of belonging to the Den Den family did not come cheap. There were several major sources of political funds generated from within the telecommunications kingdom, and these funds went to the telecommunications *zoku,* or policy tribe, controlled by Tanaka. Factions *(habatsu)* are one level of organization in the LDP. Their existence has little to do with policy differences; they simply include the followers of the various influential politicians who are jockeying for power. Many Western political parties have a conservative wing and a liberal wing. In the case of the LDP, the difference between factions hinges on personality and fund-raising capabilities.

Today, there are five major factions. They can be seen as the base of a pyramid. On top of them are imposed the various *zoku* made up of members of different factions, whose leaders have negotiated with each other to place their loyalists in the best positions. These *zoku* members also happen to be the same Diet members who serve on official committees overseeing a particular industry. The net effect is that the Diet

---

*In Japanese, NTTPC's name prior to privatization in 1985 was Nippon Denshin Denwa Kosha, hence the nickname Den Den. It became NTT after privatization. For purposes of simplicity, it will hereafter be referred to as NTT in all cases.

members in charge of regulating a specific area are heavily dependent on that industry for funding through the *zoku* mechanism. In recent years, as the fund-raising ability of the five factions themselves has declined in relative terms, the flow of funds through the *zoku* has become far more significant.

How important are the *zoku*? In an election year, a moderately successful Diet member needs 250 million yen (roughly $1.8 million) to run his offices and to fund his campaign, a Dietman told me. His salary is 19 million yen, and he receives 5 million yen from the LDP plus another 5 million from his faction. That adds up to 29 million yen, or roughly $200,000.

But that leaves a shortfall of $1.6 million, which he must find elsewhere. Since there is little tradition of individuals giving political gifts, a Diet member is left with devices such as selling tickets to fund-raising events or obtaining funds directly from a company. Although local elites in his district make contributions in return for specific favors, the larger flow of funds appears to be predominantly *zoku*-related. There are laws that supposedly regulate political contributions, but they are widely ignored or circumvented. The *zoku* themselves do not collect funds and redistribute them, as a faction or a party would. The companies contribute directly to politicians who are members of the *zoku*. So there are no records of how much each *zoku* collects.

The assumption among Japanese journalists familiar with the telecommunications sphere is that each Den Den family company sets aside a 2 percent commission on a sale to NTT, and these funds find their way to the members of the telecommunications *zoku*. The 2 percent figure is standard because that is how much trading companies often charge on the transactions they handle. So, when NTT's procurements hit $4 billion in the early 1980s, and the four Den Den family companies accounted for half of that, they would be paying 2 percent commissions on roughly $2 billion in sales, generating $40 million in political funds.

This was not the only source of funds. Another hint of the scale of the political funds available came in a comment that Shinto later made to the *Asahi Shimbun* newspaper. Yasusada Kitahara, Shinto's archrival inside NTT, offered Tanaka a million yen from each of the three thousand NTT subsidiary companies if Tanaka would make Kitahara rather than Shinto president of a privatized NTT.[2] At the exchange rate of the time, this would have been nearly $12 million. There were other channels as well. It is safe to say that in the early 1980s, there would have been between $60 and $100 million a year flowing into political coffers from the telecommunications sphere.

Some commentators have compared the *zoku* to congressional committees whose members receive campaign contributions from the industries they monitor. The key difference is one of degree. The practice of a lawmaker accepting money from an industry he supposedly oversees and granting it special treatment certainly exists in the United States, but it is the aberration, not the standard. Congressional careers have been ruined when such occurrences come to light. In Japan, however, the practice is deeply institutionalized.

Another difference is the degree of dependency on contributions from a specific industry. A Congressman receives money from many different companies in various industries and is much less dependent on a single industry. In the *zoku* system, the Dietman has a far deeper obligation to the industry he represents. To continue the analogy, AT&T contributes to different congressmen, but it has not been able to fully co-opt members of key telecommunications subcommittees that act on matters of interest. Lawmakers on these subcommittees often create trouble for Ma Bell. "We certainly don't own them," said one AT&T executive at the Basking Ridge, New Jersey, headquarters, with an air of exasperation.

Members of these *zoku*, or *zoku-giin*, have a different notion of their jobs. As Professor Tomoaki Iwai of Tokikawa University explains it: "The reality is that the *zoku-giin* act as agents of the connected ministries and they are, in effect, lobbyists for the ministries. These politicians do not set policy, rather they put pressure on the government to adopt the policies and plans of the ministries." In short, there are checks and balances in the U.S. system that are largely absent from Japan's telecommunications kingdom. In the U.S. model, the participants usually regard themselves as adversaries, rather than partners. To a far greater extent, the players in Japan are mutually co-optative.

Japan's bureaucrats play the role of guiding the triangular system and feeding it critical information. Although the word *bureaucrat* has distasteful connotations to American ears, some of the best brains in Japan are in the bureaucracy. The top graduates of the top schools take rigorous examinations to enter the ministries and then dedicate most of their adult lives to public service. They consider themselves patriots, and indeed they have done a remarkable job in guiding Japan's postwar economic recovery and in preventing external trade pressures from threatening Japan's emergence.

In many cases, they have done this through the use of "administrative guidance" rather than by enacting new laws. When a powerful bureaucrat suggests that a company undertake a certain course of action, even if there is no clear legal precedent, that company is well advised to consider it very carefully. The danger of alienating a powerful ministry is simply too great to disregard a bureaucrat entirely, as an American company might attempt to do.

The bureaucrats must contend with strict rules about not accepting money from industry. But, of course, there are abuses. Some of them have accepted half-price membership in golf clubs. In the case of NTT, which was government-owned at the time, a scandal broke out in the late 1970s over how NTT executives padded their expense accounts to the tune of $100 million. This became a scandal in its own right and the then-president of NTT was forced to resign.

Aside from the power and prestige of their positions, the major incentive for the bureaucrats is *amakudari,* which means, literally, "descend from heaven." Top bureaucrats in Japan retire as early as age fifty-two but no later than age fifty-eight, and take positions in companies they have regulated. There are rules, however, about how fast the descent from heaven can be. Sometimes a bureaucrat has to find a temporary resting station for a year or two to avoid the appearance of descending too hastily; for example, he may spend the interim in an "advisory" post.

There are legitimate reasons why private sector companies would want to hire one of the bureaucrats who have lost out in the race to become vice minister or have completed their term as vice minister. They are skilled, motivated, and well connected. But the result of this practice is that the bureaucrats, while in office, have every reason to fight to prevent the system from being opened up. If one of the companies under the purview of MPT bureaucrats were to be seriously hurt by external competition, their own futures might be at stake. "They're scared, and you can't blame them," one U.S. competitor observed. "Where would they go after retirement if there's no business with NEC?"[3]

One mistake Americans often make in trying to understand Japanese bureaucracies is in assuming that the prime minister necessarily has the power to tell a ministry what to do. The LDP appoints the top minister as well as a vice minister for parliamentary affairs. This latter position serves as a liaison between politicians and bureaucrats. But the man, and it is always a man, who really runs the ministry is the vice minister for administrative affairs. He is the top career bureaucrat. Americans place their system in the hands of newly elected politicians and their appointees. The Japanese system does this to a much lesser extent. A prime minister can rarely push around a career vice minister. In the case of telecommunications, Nakasone came from a different faction than

Tanaka and Kanemaru, and they often influenced the appointment of senior MPT bureaucrats, which would mean that Nakasone had less influence. Telecommunications was not his rightful domain.

If you were part of this system, it was a win-win game. Critics argue that the biggest losers were Japanese consumers. Although a local public pay phone call is still only 10 yen (less than a dime), the bills at home are perhaps twice those in the United States. Long-distance calls inside Japan and from Japan to the outside world are more expensive. Installation service is worse than it should be, and it can cost hundreds of dollars to have a telephone line put into a private home. If you buy an answering machine in Japan, it costs more to have it installed by NTT technicians than it does to buy the device in the first place. So even though the Japanese make most of the world's answering machines, they cannot afford to use them extensively at home. There's little question but that the average Japanese has had to pay a price, however invisible, for the abuses inside NTT.

From a U.S. point of view, the kingdom has helped prevent American companies from making major inroads into Japan's telecommunications field. They have been held to a largely token percentage of the overall market. And it gives Japanese companies that are members of the Den Den family a secure, profitable fiefdom that allows them to subsidize their drives into foreign markets, in fields ranging from computers to semiconductors to telecommunications gear. This broad pattern is certainly not limited to telecommunications. "There are NTTs everywhere in the system," Socialist leader Takako Doi told me. "Politicians are used to taking the money."

Very little is known about Shin Kanemaru. He does not grant interviews to foreign journalists or authors and has not shown himself to be interested in Japan's relations with the outside world. On one of the rare occasions when he met a group of American congressmen visiting Japan, it took two translators to interpret his words, and even then it was not clear what he was saying. Not even native Japanese speakers in the room could follow him because Kanemaru is a master of ambiguity. In another incident, a top LDP aide who secured a meeting with Kanemaru admitted: "I couldn't understand him. I had to go talk with his staff."

Although he is said to be charming, Kanemaru is better known for this ability to deceive, for saying one thing and meaning another. "Kanemaru has two faces" is often heard. Clearly, he is a master of subtlety, a master of moving the gears of Japan's decision-making system. One of the keys to his operating ability is his extensive web of informal relations with members of the opposition and the media. He is known, for example, for his "media army," the group of journalists who go to his home each evening to drink and talk. There are three levels of access and intimacy in the Kanemaru home, like three concentric rings. The outer waiting room, which has chairs and other Western-style furniture, is reserved for political leaders, journalists, or business' associates who are only recent members of the Kanemaru sphere of influence. Moving to the next room, also furnished in Western style, more trusted and respected visitors can wait and talk. The inner sanctum, however, is furnished in typical Japanese style, and Kanemaru receives visitors here sitting cross-legged on the tatami mat. The effect is to precisely gauge who is in favor and who is not. Those reporters who become favorites go on vacations with Kanemaru to Hawaii. They are his confidants and they protect his image.

Kanemaru's silence to outsiders is regarded by many Japanese as a sign of great strength. He has wielded great influence at times without actually holding a formal position in the government or party. Today, he is said to suffer from diabetes and from leg problems that make it difficult for him to walk up and down steps. But he is a connoisseur of wine and good food, and a Shinto deputy once brought to Kanemaru's home three chefs from the ancient imperial capital of Kyoto to prepare a classic feast.

Since he began consolidating power, Kanemaru is often the one who puts in the fix for a given political battle, and that often involves an exchange of money. Referring to the scale of the Recruit scandal, one LDP insider said, "What they have done is nothing compared to what Shin Kanemaru gets up to."[4]

Why has Kanemaru never made a genuine attempt to be prime minister? One reason is that it's not a very powerful position. In many ways it would be a step down for him. "For a long time, Mr. Kanemaru tried very hard to make me prime minister of this country," Noboru Takeshita told me. "He himself didn't have the ambition."

Takeshita was surprisingly eager to talk about his relationship with Kanemaru. In person, Takeshita is much more impressive than most Western descriptions, which range from "timid" to "boring" to "nondescript." But up close, it is clear that he is a brilliant technician with genuine cunning. When asked a tough question, he feigns a look of rabbitlike hurt and then proceeds to obfuscate in a most charming way.

Takeshita rejected the notion of Kanemaru, who is ten years his elder, as a mentor or teacher. He prefers to describe them both as "disciples" who received their lessons from the same teacher, former

Prime Minister Eisaku Sato. Tanaka himself, in some respects, was a Sato disciple. By interpreting history in this way, Takeshita evidently hopes he will be seen on a par with Tanaka and Kanemaru.

Both Takeshita and Kanemaru are from sake-brewing families in rural areas. The marriage of Kanemaru's eldest son to Takeshita's eldest daughter in the late 1960s helped knit their fortunes together, and today they share two grandchildren.

While the two men are close, they are also rivals. The relationship between them is one of the central riddles of the LDP leadership. "We are two very different people," mused Takeshita, a diminutive man whose gray-black hair is combed straight back. "I'm very interested in details like exchange rates, whereas Mr. Kanemaru looks at the large framework. Some people say we are like loose balloons going different ways to see where the consensus is. We never intentionally did that. But in retrospect, it probably happened that way."

Their relationship can perhaps be best described as that of two moons circling each other. At any time on one issue, the size of one may seem greater than the other. Only they themselves fully understand the tensions and joys they share. Even other inside players in Tokyo's political district of Nagata-cho do not fully comprehend it. But Takeshita acknowledges that Kanemaru is the one who sets the stage. "Mr. Kanemaru comes out with policies and it was my job to come out with provisions and make it law," Takeshita said. When something goes wrong, Takeshita said, he trusts Kanemaru to be a "good arbitrator" and to be someone who can "settle things."

As these two men rose through the ranks, Kanemaru clearly prepared the way for Takeshita to become prime minister. When Tanaka was implicated for accepting Lockheed bribes in 1972 in exchange for the purchase of Lockheed aircraft, Kanemaru, like Takeshita a deputy in the Tanaka faction, was untouched. Tanaka left the government in 1974 on charges of corruption in property deals but continued to wield enormous influence even after his arrest on Lockheed-related charges. During the 1970s, Kanemaru went on to gradually consolidate his power with stints as minister responsible for the National Land Agency and the Self-Defense Agency. He had set his sights on Takeshita taking over leadership of the Tanaka faction and becoming prime minister. At one point, much later, Prime Minister Takeshita made Kanemaru a deputy prime minister, but it was clear who held the wider-ranging power.

For Kanemaru himself to seek the prime minister's job would subject him to public scrutiny, and that would be dangerous. "In Japan, powerful, influential people naturally have some shady or dirty parts," said

Michio Watanabe, one of the more candid of Japan's top leaders. "That's the way it is. *Shikata ga nai.* The powerful man has to collect political funds not only for himself, but also for tens of other people. It's not against the law, but we have to raise money any way we can. Clean people are not powerful."

Thus it makes far more sense for Kanemaru to remain a behind-the-scenes powerhouse who operates, at least in part, through Takeshita. This is standard in Japan. Truly powerful men place others on the firing line. But to establish firm control of his power base, Kanemaru and other players in the telecommunications kingdom had to contend with some pesky challengers.

❖ 7 ❖

The Challengers

There's rarely a firm and lasting alliance in Japanese politics. "Today my friend, tomorrow my enemy" is a saying that best explains it. Shinto, Nakasone, and Ezoe were very different kinds of men from disparate backgrounds. They were not college classmates or childhood friends. In fact, when Nakasone first became prime minister in November 1982, he sparred with Shinto, who had been in power for nearly two years. "We had to protect Shinto from Nakasone," one top-level participant told me. Aside from any policy difference, they both were, and remain, proud men. Each wants to believe that he is the driving force, and neither is the type that compromises easily.

Although they started out as enemies, they eventually became allies. They never, however, became close personally. Ezoe, the upstart entrepreneur from Osaka, is younger than either Shinto or Nakasone, and he appeared to regard both as mentors. They regarded him as a useful, moneyed disciple.

There is no evidence that Shinto, Nakasone, and Ezoe ever sat down and planned a strategy to attack the telecommunications kingdom. Nakasone, whose power bases included the education and internal security fields, knew Ezoe from contacts primarily in education. Shinto at one point claimed he had met Ezoe only once, but evidence later emerged that they had met several times. Certainly the two could have been in constant back-channel communication through any number of aides or hidden men. Ezoe was not even the most important of the younger executives that Shinto knew and used. Thus, Shinto, Naka-sone, and Ezoe did not have identical concerns. They may simply have recognized their common areas of interest and common goals (Figure 3).

Certainly the most potent player in the assault on the telecommunications kingdom was Hisashi Shinto. An outsider, Shinto was born on July 2, 1910, in the southern prefecture of Kyushu—"among the farmers," as he once put it. He went on to shipbuilding school at Kyushu Imperial University, where he was graduated in 1934. He joined Harima Shipbuilding & Engineering Company and worked in the Imperial ship repair yard in Kure in southern Japan during World War II. After Japan's defeat, billionaire Daniel Ludwig, the reclusive American-born but Brazilian-based owner of National Bulk Carriers Corporation, a shipbuilding company, decided to establish a shipbuilding capacity in the former Imperial ship repair yard. There, a Ludwig lieutenant discovered the young and precocious Shinto, who by all accounts was a brilliant naval architect and he already spoke passable English.

This was the beginning of Shinto's American connection. For the remainder of his career, he was adept at establishing links with the Americans, and this made him suspect in the eyes of many Japanese. Because of his linguistic abilities, Shinto was able to play golf with IBM

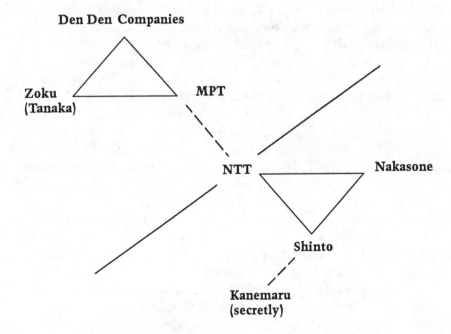

Figure 3

chairman John Akers, hobnob with Hong Kong shipping magnates like Y. K. Pao, have face-to-face meetings with Aristotle Onassis, and eventually meet with President Ronald Reagan. When I hosted Shinto's visit to *Business Week* in 1987, before the Recruit scandal broke, for example, he came by himself and handled the meeting in English. All the aides and public relations executives who had so carefully prepared the meeting were frozen out. In my experience, the gruff, white-haired Shinto was Japan's only top corporate leader who was capable, or desirous, of making such a solo appearance.

By 1972, Shinto had left National Bulk Carriers and become president of what was then called Ishikawajima-Harima Heavy Industries Company (IHI). Toshio Doko, the previous president of IHI who went on to Toshiba, had recognized Shinto's abilities and advanced him rapidly up the ranks. Shinto was to be eternally grateful. IHI had strong connections with the powerful Mitsui group and Toshiba was considered a sister company in the group. Toshiba often built the electrical equipment, such as generators, that Shinto's company used on its ships and Shinto was fiercely loyal to Toshiba. When Shinto was asked about the Toshiba Machine scandal, in which the subsidiary supplied propeller-making technology to the Soviets, Shinto paused for a moment and said, "Japanese technology must be used to develop the Japanese economy." The implication was that Japan should sell its technological products wherever it could to advance Japan's interests. Nothing else was relevant. There was no hint of apology.

By all accounts, Shinto was a modern, tough-minded manager. Some even said he could be brutal. He rationalized the creaky shipbuilding operations by aggressively cutting costs and personnel. When he recognized a talented engineer or executive, Shinto believed in leapfrogging that person over the heads of other, less capable executives, just as he had been. His was a way of thinking directly opposite to the one that prevailed inside the telecommunications kingdom.

Shinto did not go looking for the NTT fight. He had retired from IHI in 1979. Doko, who had become chairman of the Keidanren, the powerful business confederation, had summoned him out of retirement just eighteen months later at age seventy. The expense-account scandal, in which NTT executives had exaggerated their expense accounts to the tune of $100 million, had created the need for a new NTT president. Tanaka's strength in controlling the appointment was weakened by the fact that his leadership had failed to prevent telecommunications from becoming a major irritant in relations with Washington.

Reflecting the logic of factional infighting, Prime Minister Zenko Suzuki, the leader of a rival faction, certainly wanted to cooperate in attacking Tanaka's power base. He therefore had common cause with Doko. These two men were among the players at a closed-door meeting on December 23, 1980, where the decision was made to bring in Shinto.[1] Doko's goal in engineering Shinto's appointment was to open up the Den Den family to Toshiba and the overall Mitsui group. Hundreds of millions of dollars were at stake. In an April 1981 interview, Shinto said Doko "ordered" him to take the job; he had "no choice." Doko was "my senior boss" and "teacher and instructor," Shinto said. "He was my mentor." In the Japanese value system, this implies a powerful, lifelong commitment.[2]

Shinto was in contact with Kanemaru shortly after his appointment. Kanemaru saw Shinto's arrival as a way of achieving his own goal, which was to expand his influence in the telecommunications *zoku*. Kanemaru, astutely, recognized that Tanaka was beginning to lose his grip. He wanted to form his own faction, with Takeshita in charge.

Shinto's key ally was Minoru Isutani, an Osaka businessman in his late forties who had made a fortune in the refrigeration equipment business. He was Shinto's fixer, and he took care of many back-channel communications. (It was Isutani who brought the three chefs from Kyoto to Kanemaru's house.) Sometimes for his own purposes, but sometimes for Shinto's, Isutani entertained influential people, often with geisha. His philosophy of entertainment was "If you play, spend a huge amount of money."[3]

No outside analysts understand the full nature of the Shinto-Kanemaru connection, which was to undergo major strains later and finally rupture, but the best guess is that these early contacts led to a broader discussion. Nothing concrete would have happened in a single meeting. It was subtle and it unfolded over the course of a few years.

But beneath all the maneuvering lay a relatively simple proposition: If Shinto and his allies supplied large-scale political funds to Kanemaru, then Kanemaru would not interfere with Shinto's plans to stage what evolved into an incredibly bold assault on NTT and the Den Den family companies. The money was not destined to flow directly from Shinto's hands into Kanemaru's coffers. Nothing is ever that simple. Powerful people in Japan have aides and secretaries who manage their checkbooks and control the use of their personal seals, which is like having a rubber stamp with someone's signature on it. Shinto's allies and aides would funnel the money to Kanemaru's followers in the telecommunications *zoku*. All this was to pave the way for Shinto to establish his leadership and prepare for the privatization of NTT.

Shinto genuinely believed in this mission. To be sure, he had several different agendas, including helping Toshiba, but he was a man who acted out of conviction. He genuinely believed that a much more competitive environment in Japan's telecommunications industry was good for the country. It is also possible that his decade of working for an American company had imbued him with certain antiestablishment ideals. "NTT is for the society, not the other way around," he repeatedly told his employees after taking over. This was heresy. Shinto was to throw himself so thoroughly into the struggle that he made countless enemies. In the blur of battle, he was to step across the fine line between business and personal life. For Shinto, the struggle was all-consuming.

Shinto's most immediate rival in achieving his objectives was Tanaka's man inside NTT, Yasusada Kitahara. He was the number two man at NTT and he thought he should have been named president. A career bureaucrat, Kitahara controlled important sources of internally generated political funds, represented the interests of NTT's swollen personnel ranks, and protected the interests of the Den Den family. In one remarkable sign of resistance, Kitahara publicly stated that he was opposed to Shinto's restructuring plans and thus, by implication, opposed to Shinto.[4] By all accounts, Shinto hated Kitahara. He represented the enemy.

Virtually no one who knew Shinto believes he ever acted out of a desire to enrich himself personally. He clearly lived better than the average salaryman, but his standard of living was not out of line with his position. "He was never given to a luxurious life-style," says Francis J. Joyce, a New York–based executive vice president of National Bulk Carriers, who has known Shinto since 1951. "He drove a modest automobile. His summer home in the mountains was also modest." Shinto's worst vice appears to have been that he was a compulsive golfer who often made his secretary write down every stroke and every club he used so that he would have a complete record of his game.

Although a man of personal integrity, Shinto had a burning need for money to fight the old telecommunications kingdom, and Ezoe was a key provider. After first making contact with Shinto in September 1983, Ezoe formed a "study group" of up-and-coming business leaders to help Shinto.[5] The Japanese often use study groups as a means of conspiring to achieve greater political power or for fund-raising efforts. Very little actual studying takes place.

The reason Shinto needed funds was that he was badly isolated inside NTT. One view of the balance of power saw executives who were nonengineers as the only clear pro-Shinto force. Backing Shinto's rival Kitahara were the ministry, Den Den family companies, and NTT engineer/executives. The overall telecommunications *zoku* was pro-

Kitahara. It was the flow of funds provided by people like Ezoe that gave Shinto the ability to maneuver.

Most Japanese prime ministers, to play upon an old saying, are complete mysteries to the outside world. Yasuhiro Nakasone was merely an enigma.

Born on May 27, 1918, in Takasaki City, Gunma Prefecture, he was destined to be different merely because of his height. At five feet nine or so, he is taller than most Japanese his age. Thus he could "stand tall" with President Reagan at the 1983 Williamsburg, Virginia, summit meeting. Unlike previous Japanese prime ministers, who shunted themselves off to the side in the group photographs, Nakasone positioned himself directly next to Reagan. It was an important signal and all Japan took note.

Nakasone was a graduate of the University of Tokyo, which should have marked him as an insider. He also had a background in internal security and from 1941 to 1945 had been a lieutenant commander in the Imperial Navy. Nakasone actually witnessed the bombing of Hiroshima from the island of Shikoku, across the Inland Sea.[6] His younger brother, Ryosuke, had already died in a kamikaze suicide mission. Nakasone later wrote that he felt humiliated by Japan's surrender and argued that Japan's national honor should be restored. Up until the early 1980s, many Japanese considered him a rabid nationalist. Yet many Americans, including Ronald Reagan, thought highly of Nakasone for his drive to build up Japanese defense spending, presumably against the Soviet Union. Nakasone's mother had been a Christian, and he occasionally made mention of God in his remarks to foreigners, creating the impression that he was not only staunchly anti-Communist but also pro-Christian. Most Americans did not seem to understand the significance of Nakasone's controversial visit to the Yasukuni Shrine in Tokyo, the state Shinto facility that honors Japan's Class-A war criminals, or the fact that he presided over a gradual watering down of textbooks on Japanese history. Harboring the memories that he must have harbored, what were his real views?

Nakasone could not have been any more different from his immediate predecessors. At a press conference given at the Tokyo summit in 1979, the much smaller, round-shouldered Prime Minister Masayoshi Ohira shuffled into the room and took his position on stage behind a table and microphone. The Japanese press began firing questions at him. He responded in cavemanlike utterances, one or two words that he quickly swallowed. The Japanese reporters privately called him the "bulldog" because he growled a great deal. He had not answered a single question. Ohira's successor, Zenko Suzuki, was cut from much the same cloth.

Nakasone, however, actually believed he deserved to be a full-fledged national leader. This was audacious because he said things that had not been approved by the bureaucrats. His 1983 comment that Japan would be an "unsinkable aircraft carrier" for the United States set off howls of protest at home.

When I first laid eyes on Nakasone it was October 1985 and he was holding a press conference at the Waldorf-Astoria in New York. Security was tight. As he approached the room, his security men, walkie-talkies in hand, began scurrying. Nakasone strode into the room and took his position at the podium. As usual, he said something the bureaucrats had not approved: His foreign minister would travel to Moscow. The next day the papers were filled with bureaucrats in Tokyo denying that anything like that would happen.

By his very nature, Nakasone was at war with the bureaucracy. "There are two types of bureaucrats," Nakasone told me in a 1989 interview, one of the first he granted to a foreign journalist after the Recruit scandal. "One kind of bureaucrat is happy to see the liberalization [of Japan's economy] because they have a broader perspective. But others put the interest of their ministries and of their vested interests above the national interest." To the outside world, here was a man who spoke and acted forcefully, and it was refreshing. Yet in many key respects, he was singularly ineffective in delivering on his promises.

Because of his forceful personality and his direct approach, many Japanese did not appreciate Nakasone as he worked his way up the political ranks. He was given the nickname "Mr. Weathervane" because of how he changed his stance on several issues. But Japanese politicians are always changing position, their votes going to the factional leader who promises the most money. Changing positions, however, isn't what earned Nakasone the nickname; it was the fact that he attempted to take a position in the first place that did it.

Many Japanese also considered him a "Tanaka dummy." Tanaka had given Nakasone the prestigious post of minister of international trade and industry, which he held from 1972 to 1974, and he had to leave the cabinet when Tanaka did. Although Nakasone had his own faction, most Japanese believed that Tanaka, as a "shadow shogun," was responsible for giving Nakasone the prime minister's job in 1982. The evidence that supports this view is Tanaka's ability to place five members of his faction in the cabinet. But dozens, perhaps hundreds, of politicians and bureaucrats were Tanaka dummies. The reason Nakasone

A Chronology of the NTT-Recruit Fight

Shinto named president of NTT, to help break up old Iron Triangle	January 1981
Nakasone becomes prime minister	November 1982
NTT begins privatization in stages; Shinto named head of new entity	March–April 1985
Recruit launches new telecom businesses; Recruit's influence-buying moves into high gear	July–September 1985
Shinto accelerates assault on telecom kingdom	Late 1985–86
Nakasone wins landslide election, refuses to make way for Takeshita	July 1986
Kanemaru realizes he is under attack on different fronts	Late 1986
Nakasone steps down after five years but remains a powerful figure; Takeshita becomes prime minister	October 1987
Recruit scandal breaks	June 18, 1988
Ezoe resigns from Recruit	July 6, 1988
Prosecutor, opposition, media campaign to "get" Nakasone builds	November–December, 1988
Shinto resigns	December 14, 1988
Ezoe is arrested	February 14, 1988
Shinto is arrested	March 7, 1989
Takeshita says he will resign as prime minister	April 25, 1989
Fujinami, Nakasone's right-hand man, charged with bribery	May 23, 1989
Nakasone technically resigns from LDP and his faction; prosecutors conclude investigation	May 29, 1989
LDP loses control of Upper House	July 23, 1989
Kanemaru forces reconsolidate control of telecommunications sphere	Mid-1989

was stuck with the nickname was that he had pride. He dared to believe that he could lead.

When Nakasone first became prime minister, his faction was the smallest of the five major factions. He had emerged by default and therefore was on the fringe of power. He needed more political funds to build his faction and his authority as prime minister.

Nakasone had a vision for accomplishing all this, a key element of which was to use public opinion as pressure against the bureaucracy, a novel tactic in a country where public opinion rarely mattered. Nakasone appointed citizens' councils and other advisory bodies to several different ministries; these were designed to hector the bureaucrats and to give Nakasone a needed wedge. He also authorized former central bank governor Haruo Maekawa to develop a now-famous report that bears his name. This was aimed at opening Japan's markets and rationalizing its systems in such a way that the outside world's frustrations with Japan would be eased. Certain Japanese domestic constituencies clearly would have benefited if the bureaucracy could have been forced to wholeheartedly enact the Maekawa report. In addition, in accomplishing these objectives, Nakasone would be delivering crippling blows to the bureaucrats and his political rivals. So, while Nakasone spoke of "administrative reform," "privatization," and "liberalization," he was at the same time fighting for power. It was a bold, complex agenda.

One young business leader appointed to this advisory council by Nakasone's camp was Ezoe. To attack telecommunications, construction, transport, and other powerful triangles, Nakasone needed money just as Shinto did, but his links with major companies were weak. Like Shinto, he turned to the "new money" crowd. "To break up the old Iron Triangle, money was desperately needed," says Seizaburo Sato, an eminent University of Tokyo professor and key Nakasone confidant. "But the Keidanren would not supply the money. So Shinto [and Nakasone] had to look to businessmen outside the established system."

An important but risky ingredient of Nakasone's strategy was *gaiatsu*, or foreign pressure. Nakasone, who first met Reagan in 1983 in Washington, was to go to extraordinary lengths to cultivate the American president over the next five years that both men were in office. Whether it was Nakasone himself or one of his aides who suggested that Reagan call him "Yasu," it was a brilliant stroke. In Japanese culture, the only people who would have used that nickname would have been the prime minister's parents or other elders. It certainly wasn't the kind of nickname that would have been used between equals. But creating the "Ron-Yasu" relationship helped build a genuine personal relationship between the two men. Nakasone also hosted President and Mrs. Reagan at his private residence in Tokyo, which, again, was without precedent.

When Reagan came to Tokyo in the fall of 1989, he was still talking about his old friend Yasu. He told one gathering at the U.S. Embassy that when Nakasone visited Washington "he told us a very moving and important account of his own daughter's experience with an American host family while she was an exchange student." Reagan did not provide any more details, but it was clear that Nakasone had reached down to an extraordinarily personal level to charm Reagan.

Usually, when a Japanese resorts to the *gaiatsu* strategy, it means he is facing very powerful opposition at home and wants ammunition for the internal fight. Some Japanese who are losing battles at home even suggest to the Americans that they bring back "the black ships," a reference to Commodore Perry's fleet that had arrived in Japan in the mid-1850s. For Nakasone, solidifying the relationship with Reagan was important for a whole host of reasons, but one of the most important was to use Reagan as a lever at home. Shinto, independently, had also cultivated Reagan. When Nakasone and Shinto eventually found a basis for cooperating, the Reagan factor became a powerful weapon in their arsenal.

Hiromasa Ezoe was a pawn—albeit an important one—in a game he did not fully understand. He was fifty-two when his gambit came unstuck in 1988.

It is almost certain that he was a *burakumin*, one of the untouchables. This was widely rumored in Japan, but the Buraku Liberation League declined to confirm or deny it. Ezoe himself has been inaccessible to the press, but even if he were prepared to talk, he certainly would not be willing to shed any light on his class background. The strongest clue appeared in a Japanese book published in late 1989.[7] Author Shinichi Sano goes as far as he can to suggest Ezoe's origins without actually saying what they are. One simply cannot write or state that someone is from the *buraku* caste. This is a strong taboo in Japan.

Instead, Sano describes how Ezoe was born the first son of Yoshiyuki Ezoe and a woman named Masuko on June 12, 1936. He was the product of a turbulent childhood because his tall, good-looking father, a math teacher, lived with a series of three women, only one of whom he married. But the giveaway to a Japanese reader comes when Sano identifies where Ezoe lived: 8-chome, Kamito-cho; then 3-3-9 Suehiro-cho, Toyonakashi, Osaka. His schools are identified and the student mix suggests the presence of *burakumin*. The specificity is all that a Japanese reader would need in order to understand what Sano is saying. Yet no Japanese would ever say it out loud, and certainly not to a foreigner.

The only way to know for sure whether someone is a *burakumin* is to go to the family temple and look at the family's hereditary papers. But this is not easy to do. Sano, however, tells where Ezoe's documents are kept, for anyone powerful enough to secure a peak.

There are other tantalizing clues about Ezoe's class background. He was able to attend the University of Tokyo. At first glance this would suggest that he had passed a screening process, that he was pure. Over the course of his stay there, he became a thriving entrepreneur, selling ads for the student newspaper while his colleagues were attacking the evils of capitalism.

The question then arises: Why didn't he take a job with a major Japanese company upon graduation? The vast majority of the university's graduates have that opportunity. The real screening process against undesirables, whether *burakumin* or Korean, takes place not as students enter college (admission is based almost exclusively on exams) but as they form clubs in college and as they prepare to take jobs. Ezoe was clearly a loner, someone who did not fit in—and rather than taking a job with a big company, Ezoe either chose or was forced to start his own company soon after graduating in 1960. This is rarely done in Japan. One has to be desperate to start a company from scratch just out of college.

Ezoe began in a prefabricated rooftop office. "Our first office was almost as small as a cupboard, only about eight square meters [about eighty square feet], and in the summer it would get as hot as forty degrees Centigrade [104 degrees Fahrenheit] inside," Ezoe said. "My colleagues and I used to say that we wanted to create a company with a good atmosphere even if it was small." The point was that they created a good atmosphere by suffering equally together, not by having a cool office.[8]

His business was a small job-placement magazine, a field ignored by established publishers. It was a logical outgrowth from what he had done at the university and suggests that Ezoe had to find a niche that mainstream Japan did not want to touch.

Whatever his background, Ezoe's business took off. By 1987, he was selling several hundred thousand copies of his recruitment magazine. He had branched out into related fields and had nine magazines with a total circulation of 6.58 million. Costs were modest. The flagship magazine carried mostly advertisements and required modest editorial investment. Japanese companies had always relied on traditional methods of finding young graduates, but as competition became more intense over the years, the graduates flocked to publications that would help them find jobs. Ezoe was sitting on a money machine. Some of his activities posed a direct challenge to major Japanese media companies, such as the *Asahi Shimbun*, which was later to lead the media charge against Ezoe. As early as 1980, the Asahi group was waging anti-Recruit campaigns through *Asahi Shimbun* because of Recruit's increasing competitive challenge to its own magazine business.

Over the years, Ezoe worked hard to expand his business beyond the magazines. Altogether he had four divisions before the roof fell in. One was Recruit Cosmos, a real estate subsidiary, whose collateral allowed him to borrow more than $10 billion from banks. Ezoe had invested aggressively in prime Tokyo real estate prior to and during the post-1985 boom. He was leveraged to the hilt.

None of this need have been well planned. Ezoe was impetuous; he was prone to "thinking after he runs."⁹ He operated his businesses in a most unusual style. One account said it was a "carnival-style" management with decorations hanging from ceilings and workers shouting jokes across the office. Announcements were made over an office communication system whenever salespeople reached a certain target.

Aside from recruiting temporary staff and managers for hotels, ski resorts, and other companies, the last piece of his business was telecommunications, which Ezoe entered in 1985. The reason telecommunications was so important to him was that, as his business grew, he needed more computing capacity and the ability to transmit his information over telephone lines. He told several interviewers that he feared he would soon have to begin transmitting his data electronically rather than distributing it in printed form.

The key to achieving this was a relationship with NTT. Ezoe's drive to crack the telecommunications business was a major force behind his decision to distribute unlisted shares of Recruit Cosmos stock to dozens of political leaders, bureaucrats, business leaders, and others. "At the core of the scandal is the company's aggressive advance into the information and telecommunications area," one analyst observed.¹⁰ By late 1984, the process of buying in was starting.

Why did he have to do it? In many respects, he had no choice. To run most large-scale businesses in Japan requires dealing with the bureaucracy. He needed continued cooperation from the Labor and Education ministries simply to run his core business. Education Ministry officials were needed to persuade schools to keep advertising in a Recruit student guidebook despite its high rates. The Labor Ministry was considering revising the Employment Security Law, which would have tightened control over job-placement magazines. Recruit also wanted to develop a resort in the Appi Highlands, and that required "understanding" from the Ministry of Agriculture.

Whatever specific problems Ezoe had, he knew he was vulnerable because he lacked extensive connections inside the inner circles of power. Even if he had not been of questionable class background, the sheer speed with which he had burst into the big leagues marked him as a newcomer. Unlike Americans, who lionize successful entrepreneurs, the Japanese have intense suspicions of them. As he tried to penetrate important business associations such as the Keidanren, mainline executives were quoted as saying, "These days there are many artificial companies which are successful money-wise, but I don't want their presidents to say they are businessmen."[11]

As a newcomer, another stinging phrase that was applied to Ezoe was *narikin,* and this group of people have been despised in Japan for decades, if not centuries. As Ruth Benedict explained in *The Chrysanthemum and the Sword:*

> *Narikin* is often translated "nouveau riche." . . . In the United States, nouveaux riches are strictly "newcomers"; they are laughable because they are gauche and have not had time to acquire the proper polish. This liability, however, is balanced by the heartwarming asset that they have come up from the log cabin, they have risen from driving a mule to controlling oil millions. But in Japan, a *narikin* is a term taken from Japanese chess and means a pawn promoted to queen. It is a pawn rampaging across the board as a "big shot." It has no hierarchal right to do any such thing. The *narikin* is believed to have obtained his wealth by defrauding or exploiting others and the bitterness directed toward him is as far as possible from the attitude in the United States toward the "home boy who makes good."[12]

Was his assault on power all Ezoe's idea? It seems incredible that an upstart entrepreneur would dare attack one of the bastions of state-dominated industry without some prior indication that he might be successful. The Japanese media have speculated that a Shinto intermediary, Ei Shikiba, helped persuade Ezoe that his future lay in telecommunications. Naturally, something would be expected in return— namely, political contributions.

Ezoe's connection with Nakasone was formed as a result of their contacts in the educational field. In 1985, Nakasone's government named Ezoe to an ad hoc committee on taxation, and to the Curriculum Council under the education minister. The two men played golf together on at least one occasion. In 1987, Ezoe was appointed to a post as counselor for the government's committee to consider land issues. Nakasone was using him to build pressure on the bureaucracies; Ezoe was using his connections at the top. The money was flowing.

But there was nothing shocking about all of this. There were no heroes and no villains. There were no burning moral issues. All the parties involved in fighting for control of the telecommunications kingdom had their own agendas. Drawing Recruit into the web was simply the way the Japanese power game worked. As Michio Watanabe was to say later, "What's wrong? It's just another business deal."

❖ 8 ❖

The Attack

When Westerners play a game like chess or checkers, there is usually a clear battle line. One player controls a certain space on the board; his line of attack may be subtle, but it is clear to an experienced eye. The fight over the telecommunications kingdom was more like the game of *go,* which is distinctly Asian in its complexity. It is a game of gradual encirclement with no single brilliant move, no sudden crashing breakthroughs.

Kanemaru seems to have been uncharacteristically slow in recognizing the nature of the game being played against him. He supported Shinto and Nakasone's plans to privatize NTT in 1985 and to appoint Shinto as president of the new entity. In fact, Kanemaru played a leading role in making the privatization happen at all.

Unbeknownst to Kanemaru, however, privatizing NTT was at the heart of the challengers' assault on the telecommunications kingdom and, by implication, on his influence. The privatization scheme helped draw Shinto and Nakasone together. They suddenly had a common objective. Privatizing NTT meant reducing the ministry's control of its procurement decisions, and it also held out the prospect of diminishing the flow of political funds into the old kingdom while greatly enhancing the flow from new telecommunications businesses into the challengers' coffers.

Although Nakasone and Shinto couched their plans in language that was suitably lofty, their intention was to do nothing less than crack the

Iron Triangle. Kanemaru did not realize the scale of the challengers' ambitions. Perhaps the old-fashioned Kanemaru could not imagine the daring and audacity that Shinto, Nakasone, and Ezoe were to demonstrate.

It's also likely that Kanemaru was blinded by his own ambitions. Tanaka's health was failing in 1985, when maneuvering over naming a president for the new NTT reached its height. Tanaka had viewed Shinto as a transitional character and wanted to put in his own man, Kitahara. The behind-the-scenes struggle was intense and lasted for months. It was at this time, according to Shinto, that Kitahara offered Tanaka one million yen from each of the three thousand companies under NTT's control if he, Kitahara, was named president. Despite the fact that Tanaka held no official position, he had retained major power in the ministry and NTT, in part by remembering the birthdays of even midlevel bureaucrats and executives and influencing their appointments or promotions.

Kanemaru had been nurturing his secret relationship with Shinto now for four years. Shinto had been able to make some progress in implementing his program, but not nearly as much as he wanted. He had no allies inside the monster. His room to maneuver was still quite limited. But Shinto's unofficial lieutenant, Minoru Isutani, had moved millions of yen to Kanemaru.[1] With Tanaka weakened and a major decision at hand, this was the moment for which both Kanemaru and Shinto had been waiting—but for different reasons.

On March 4, 1985, Tanaka was hospitalized. His enemies moved quickly. Shinto's appointment as head of the new NTT was announced only a week later, on March 11. Tanaka's power over the telecommunications kingdom was crushed. Kanemaru quickly staged one of the events for which he is famous. Allowing Shinto to be named was part of his strategy to choke off the flow of telecommunications funds to Tanaka. He was attempting to strangle his mentor. But in public, Kanemaru complained bitterly about how Shinto had been appointed. "This is not the right way," he said. "This is ridiculous."[2] Kanemaru wanted to pose as a Tanaka loyalist to maintain his position in the *zoku* and faction, while at the same time actively seeking to break Tanaka's leadership. It was a brilliant performance. The power configuration had shifted (Figure 4).

The privatization unfolded. As agreed, millions of shares of NTT were sold to the public in two major offerings. The share price made NTT the most valuable company in the world in terms of its market capitalization. Financial control, however, had little to do with actual management control. The ministry still exercised significant influences

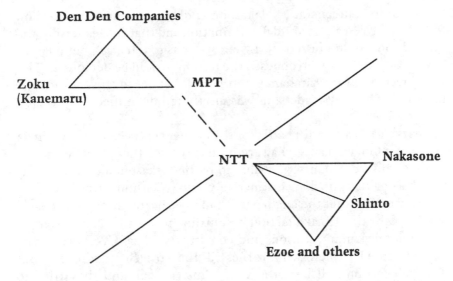

Figure 4

over the privatized NTT. There had not been as clean a break as the term *privatization* would imply.

In the months ahead, the scale of the challengers' assault on the telecom kingdom became apparent. There were at least three levels to the struggle: the fight for bureaucratic and political control; encouraging domestic competition to NTT; and the use of *gaiatsu,* or foreign pressure.

Fight for Control

In the fight for control, a newly empowered Shinto was able to put talented loyalists in several key positions inside NTT for the first time, and this helped expand his power base. Nakasone was also able to put more of his loyalists in the Ministry of Post and Telecommunications at the same time he attempted to neutralize members of the Tanaka-cum-Kanemaru telecom *zoku*. "There were two elements we had to deal with," Nakasone later said. "First, within the LDP, there were the *zoku-giin* [members of the telecom *zoku*], who were in collusion with the bureaucrats." This is a reference to Tanaka loyalists in the party and in the bureaucracy. "The basic strategy was how to persuade them to go along with reform," Nakasone continued. "We used all sorts of methods to persuade them. We offered help in their districts with campaigning. We offered them better positions in the party." All of which required money. Lots of it.

"As for the bureaucrats," Nakasone said, "it was important to show that the LDP had a very solid determination and that the leadership was unified and would not retreat. I went so far as to tell a cabinet meeting that any bureaucrat who opposed the reforms would be demoted." This was directed toward Kitahara and other old-school loyalists inside the kingdom. The LDP leadership was anything but unified. It was split wide open.

It was clearly an uphill battle for the challengers because of the sheer depth of influence Tanaka had accumulated. Even though he was in the hospital, his lieutenants were able to battle Nakasone because all the members of the kingdom instinctively knew, without ever having to have a meeting, that the challengers had to be beaten back. "Nakasone tried to fight the Tanaka faction by putting his men in as ministers of post and telecommunications and construction," said Watanabe, one of the top LDP men who witnessed the struggle firsthand. "But Tanaka's faction still held the vice minister level, and they tried to increase their power within the LDP. The Tanaka faction strategy was to control the construction and telecommunications ministries through the bureaucracy. It was a no-win game for Nakasone. The Tanaka faction had more depth. Nakasone only had the top positions."

To the outside world, therefore, it may have appeared that institutions, as Westerners understand them, were making decisions. There was a ministry, a huge telephone company, a political party, a cabinet. But all these institutions had fault lines running through them, pitting those who wanted to cling to old ways against those who wanted to change. Essentially two tribes were fighting for the spoils. The challengers had allies in politics, government, and business, as did the kingdom's defenders. The challengers wanted to open and revitalize the system; the defenders believed Japan's interests were best served by the existing system. Any public policy debate was largely camouflage for the real power struggle, where the tool of combat was money.

Even though Kitahara was vice chairman of the new NTT and Shinto was chairman, they were on opposite sides of the fault line. Kitahara still influenced the flow of political money from NTT subsidiary companies and played a role in directing the funds from NEC and other Den Den family companies. Shinto had to resort to other devices. One was an organization called the All-Nation Electronics Telecommunications Association, which had been established in the NTT building in Uchisaiwai-cho, in the General Management Department, in 1983. It had about 45,000 professional employees and 15,000 retirees who paid nominal dues. On the surface, the organization was aimed at promoting telecommunications use, but in reality it was a Shinto political group.

In the three-year period beginning in 1986, Shinto collected 800 million yen through this organization. At an exchange rate of roughly 150 yen to the dollar, this would be more than $5 million. He spent 300 million yen to buy party tickets and to contribute to Diet members, probably those in the telecommunications *zoku*.[3]

Shinto used other organizations and "study groups" inside NTT to collect money, and he put his own lecture fees into an entertainment account for politicians and journalists. As he later openly admitted to Japanese reporters, his personal finances became blurred with the company's. On some occasions he even spent money from his personal bank accounts on political causes—and this was his critical error.

But all these were relatively minor sources of money. Isutani and other young business leaders whom Shinto had nurtured contributed more, although no one knows exactly how much. The most flamboyant of these allies was Ezoe. In December 1984, Recruit had directly distributed some unlisted shares of Recruit Cosmos, the real estate subsidiary. But the process picked up steam in 1985, when Recruit began using dummy subsidiaries with names like Do Best, Big Way, and Eternal Fortune to transmit the shares. In some cases, the shares were simply given away. In others, a different subsidiary of the Recruit group, First Finance Company, approached influential people and offered to finance their purchase of the shares. It was virtually the same as giving the shares away, but it was a shade more subtle.

Prosecutors are aware of Recruit giving millions of shares to political leaders, bureaucrats, and business leaders, but no one has been able to estimate their value with any degree of accuracy. What did it cost Ezoe? The face value of the shares would not have been an accurate reflection, because Ezoe was so heavily leveraged. If he could borrow $1 billion to buy a piece of property whose value soon rose to $2 billion, as was common in the 1985–87 period, he could use that position to issue shares worth tens of millions of dollars that did not necessarily "cost" him anything more than the expenses involved in setting up his distribution channels.

His primary method of gift-giving was offering unlisted shares of Recruit Cosmos at bargain-basement prices. Then, when the company went public, the beneficiaries of his largesse could sell their shares in the open market or, in some cases, back to Ezoe's group. At this time, the Tokyo stock market was in the process of doubling and tripling in value. Ezoe was riding the crest of the new money wave. To be sure, Recruit was using other channels, such as making direct contributions, and this was "real money." But the unlisted shares were not. We can only stab at the order of magnitude. It is likely that the cost to Recruit was in the neighborhood of tens of millions of dollars, but the value to recipients would have been a multiple of that because of the explosive rise in the stock market.

The shares went to at least 160 different people, including bureaucrats, lawmakers, company executives, bankers, and publishers—all of whose names have been listed publicly. Nakasone lieutenants figured prominently. Recruit gave shares to Hideko Ota, Yoshihiko Kamiwada, and Yasuo Tsuihiji—all of whom were in Nakasone's camp. As many as 29,000 shares went to the Nakasone camp, for an estimated profit of $1 million. The shares likewise flowed into Shinto's camp, as well as to Kanemaru and Takeshita. Takeshita eventually was to admit that he received 151 million yen in donations or contributions from Recruit over three years, which would have been about $1 million at prevailing exchange rates.

But just knowing who got the shares is not enough. When Recruit Cosmos went public and recipients began cashing in their shares, the money kept moving. There are no records, and there are only fragments of evidence, but the forces of Nakasone and Shinto used much of the profits to curry influence with political leaders. In the case of Nakasone, prosecutors were never able to lay a finger on him because none of the profits went into his personal bank accounts. Everything had been handled through aides and assistants. Shinto's error came when an aide realized a profit of 22 million yen from selling shares. The aide used 13 million for political contributions, and placed 9 million ($75,000 at prevailing rates) in Shinto's personal bank account to make up for Shinto's own money that had been used for his cause. It's unlikely that Shinto put the money into the account himself because he didn't manage his bank accounts; his aides did. So even if some funds were skimmed off the top, the bulk of the profits from Recruit's shares seems to have been used in the fight for control of the telecommunications *zoku*.

On the whole, there was relatively little that was illegal about what Ezoe was doing. It has been standard for companies to convey untaxable, undeclared income to politicians. One favorite technique has been "political stocks." A company executive may know of a certain development that will drive his stock price higher, or he is about to issue a new stock. He tips off the politician, who obtains the stock from a brokerage house. Sometimes the brokerage house itself runs a stock up for the purpose of assisting the politician. The point at which political funds-giving becomes illegal is if the recipient of the political funds does a favor for the person who gave him the money. Thanks to the different techniques developed by the political elites, including dummy companies and bank accounts in other peoples' names, it is extremely difficult to prove a clear quid pro quo. The code of ethics that the Diet had adopted in 1985, on the heels of the Lockheed scandal, never took hold.

The real mistake that Ezoe made was in being too obvious about what he was doing, and doing it too quickly. But he had encouragement from the men leading the charge. Ezoe's new money was helping Shinto and Nakasone stage their assault.

Domestic Competition

Ever since Shinto came to NTT in 1981, he had wanted to radically restructure it, to break it up into independent organizations. Lacking the power to achieve that vision all in one fell swoop, he resorted to the next best thing: doing it piece by piece. After NTT was privatized, he established at least two hundred new subsidiaries. Their role was to compete for business, in many cases against established units of the old NTT. It was creative destruction at its best.

Shinto also used outsiders. His friend Isutani, for example, was able to establish the Japan Card System Company in March 1986, using NTT's technology. Prepaid telephone cards are quite the rage in Japan. Rather than carrying a lot of coins, the Japanese like to buy thousand-yen cards in vending machines that allow them to pay for calls from pay telephones. When a card is used up, it is discarded. So Shinto helped Isutani get started with this hot new company. Some sixteen banks supported the upstart. Shinto didn't see this as depriving NTT of an opportunity; he saw it as innovation, as competition.

It was much the same pattern with Ezoe. Shinto's lieutenants in NTT allowed Recruit to lease some high-speed, large-capacity digital circuits at a very low cost. Recruit, in turn, leased these circuits to other users at 40 percent of the price that NTT itself was charging. Ezoe called this his Information Network Systems (INS). Not surprisingly, Recruit obtained 60 percent of the domestic Japanese market for this kind of circuit.[4] Shinto's forces even allowed these circuits to be specially coded so they could be identified and repaired quickly when there were breakdowns. This helped Recruit offer excellent service to its customers. NTT executives loyal to the kingdom openly fought this arrangement. They would later charge that Shinto and Ezoe had set it up in direct negotiations. "This clearly shows the close ties between the two," one was quoted as saying.[5] There was never any confirmation that the two men met face-to-face to discuss this subject, but certainly they collaborated to make it happen.

In September, two months after launching his high-speed circuit business, Ezoe's Recruit began offering the Remote Computing Service (RCS), which involved the online use of two Cray supercomputers that NTT had acquired. This was later to emerge as a central thread of the prosecutors' inquiries. These two supercomputers were placed in the Yokohama Nishi Building of the NTT Data Communications Company and in the Dojima Building in Osaka, also owned by the NTT Data Communications Company. But they were either leased or resold to Recruit. A fog has enveloped the precise arrangements, but NTT, in buying the two computers from Cray, did disclose that the end-user would be Recruit; however, it was not obliged to spell out the precise nature of any NTT-Recruit understanding. Clearly, again, NTT was incurring major costs to help Recruit. NTT's expertise and facilities were being used to help Ezoe launch a new business. By himself, Ezoe almost certainly could not have obtained clearance from the Japanese government to buy the supercomputers directly, and he lacked the expertise to service them.

Dozens of other companies—many of them more reputable than Isutani's and Ezoe's—were also entering the competitive fray against NTT. Toshiba was one of them, and it was suddenly winning projects. Mitsubishi Electric was another. The titans of Japan's electronics and telecommunications industries were squared off against each other. Shinto had made it clear very early in his tenure that creating this kind of truly competitive environment was a key goal. "Besides NTT family members, we now have many stronger competitors among the Japanese manufacturers, such as Mitsubishi, Toshiba, Matsushita, Sony, that used to be 'outsiders,' " Shinto said in 1981. "Now those companies have to be considered evenly."[6] Shinto's vision was finally beginning to come true.

Shinto was trying to crush the old kingdom, shifting business and profits to outsiders and younger, more aggressive companies, and in general trying to expand the role of competition in bidding for NTT work. Traditional suppliers were suffering because they no longer had guaranteed access to the NTT honeypot. The fact that, in some cases, the newer companies were funneling money to Shinto's camp was just one piece of the strategy. Shinto never really saw this as bribery, and it was certainly not intended to enrich him personally. He had a much larger ambition.

Use of Gaiatsu

The challengers repeatedly used foreign pressure, particularly the prestige of Ronald Reagan, as a means of prying open the telecommunications kingdom. The sword, however, cut both ways. On the one hand, it clearly benefited the Americans. U.S. and European equipment sales to NTT rose from a tiny $17 million in 1980, before Shinto took over, to $366 million in 1988, according to official NTT figures. Some 90 percent of those purchases in later years were from American companies. This is not quite as dramatic as it looks because the value of the yen doubled, but there's no question that outsiders made gains.

NTT executives never fully disclose, however, what percentage foreign companies have of that procurement pie. It is an extraordinarily complex game that they play by making distinctions between total purchases and purchases of technology goods, by distinguishing between budgeted expenditures and actual expenditures, and by using the rise in the value of the yen to show greater progress than actually achieved. By 1989, NTT's total purchases had reached $8.6 billion. But this would include uniforms and other items of little technological content. The best estimate is that about $4 billion was being spent on equipment. Thus foreigners still had less than 10 percent of the real action, a token amount in view of the rapid gains Japanese companies were making in U.S. technology markets.

By far, the major beneficiaries were Japanese companies, like Toshiba, that had previously been excluded. The traditional Den Den family companies suffered a decline in absolute sales, but it was not a sharp decline. "The impact on the traditional companies was small," said an NTT procurement executive. "But even if a small amount of business is lost, it's a big worry to them." Of even greater concern was that the Den Den family companies did not share in the dramatic growth of expenditures as fully as they would have liked. This went to the newcomers, overwhelmingly Japanese, not foreign.

Shinto's use of IBM was particularly interesting. In September 1985, NTT and IBM announced a joint venture that was publicly described only in the vaguest terms. It seemed to represent an effort to make IBM computers compatible with Japanese-made computers.[7]

Den Den family members and ministry bureaucrats were alarmed by this development and asked Shinto, in effect, to put any genuine cooperation on hold. Shinto ignored that advice and continued negotiating with IBM. The following year, in December 1986, another IBM deal was announced, apparently reflecting a deepening of the existing cooperation. Under this accord, IBM would work with Mitsubishi Electric on a project aimed at creating a new computing environment inside NTT. This joint venture, called the Japan Information and Communication Company, would use hardware products made by IBM-Japan to sell value-added data network services to Japanese companies. If taken to its logical conclusion, it would undercut traditional Den Den companies. The traditional Japanese companies were "terrified" by the IBM joint venture and called Shinto a *kokuzoku,* or nation-betrayer.[8] The man making this accusation, NTT sources later confirmed, was none other than NEC chairman Koji Kobayashi, one of the giants of Japanese industry.

NTT's purchase of four Cray supercomputers, however, was the centerpiece of the *gaiatsu* campaign. Shinto spent hundreds of thousands of dollars on several different Washington lobbying organizations to open a channel to Reagan. He did this in defiance of legions of Ministry of Foreign Affairs officials and other bureaucrats. Finally, on June 6, 1983, Shinto met Reagan at 3:45 P.M. for fifteen minutes to talk about NTT purchases of U.S. equipment. Shinto started off the conversation by saying, "Yasu kicked my ass."[9]

The impression Shinto was trying to create was that he was under tremendous pressure from Nakasone. Later that day or the next (the precise timing is unclear), Shinto went to see his old friend Francis Joyce at National Bulk Carriers in New York and told him, "I had a difficult meeting with President Reagan. He wants us to buy more equipment. He leaned very hard on me." Then on June 7, 1983, Shinto reported to Nakasone at the prime minister's private residence. Shinto seemed to be consciously cultivating the pressure. Few heads of Japanese companies would go to such extraordinary lengths to meet an American president and a Japanese prime minister for the sheer privilege of being abused.

Shinto was developing a mandate to act, and this suited Nakasone perfectly. This is where the interest of all three challengers intersected. Shinto wanted Cray supercomputers to help create a non–Den Den computing environment. Buying Cray supercomputers was a direct slap in the face to NEC, Hitachi, and Fujitsu. The big Japanese companies were being thrown onto the defensive.

Ezoe and Nakasone also had keen interest. Ezoe wanted to use the machines. Nakasone wanted access to a supercomputer for the Institute for Global Peace that he was creating. And diplomatically, Nakasone clearly wanted to make himself look good by smoothly handling the American pressure. What better way than highly visible purchases of symbolic American supercomputers? Shinto wanted to co-opt Nakasone and did so by giving him a tool for dealing with the Americans. "As a result [of these purchases], Nakasone owed Shinto a lot. This helped Shinto survive the battle against Kitahara" and the telecommunications kingdom.[10]

The supercomputer purchases started in 1984. Four had been purchased as of 1988. The purchases were usually timed around Nakasone meetings with Reagan, or at times of keen U.S. trade pressure. Out of the four Crays that NTT bought, two were put to use for Recruit. The sheer power that the Nakasone-Shinto-Ezoe axis had amassed began to become evident.

As a result of this multilevel assault, the telecommunications king-dom was in clear retreat by mid-1986. Procurement was shifting away. New competitors were rising up. The Americans were getting slightly more of the market, and Shinto and Nakasone were directing what appeared to be a massive flow of political funds.

It's not clear at what point all this began to alarm Kanemaru. With someone like NEC's Kobayashi on the warpath, the political heat must have been building on Kanemaru to take action. As in a game of *go*, he gradually found himself maneuvered into a difficult position. He had to find a way to stop the rot.

The final break came when Nakasone, after four years in office, refused to leave office gracefully and allow Kanemaru to install Take-shita. Instead, Nakasone's smashing victory in the July 1986 elections, in which the LDP took 308 out of 512 seats in the Diet's Lower House, up from 258, consolidated his power just when Kanemaru was confi-dent he could get rid of him. Nakasone's faction reached 62 members in the more powerful Lower House, surpassing the Miyazawa and Abe factions. The Kanemaru-Takeshita faction had 71 members. Nakasone was closing in. To make matters worse, Nakasone won an unusual one-year extension for himself as prime minister. He was headed for real political power. He had to be stopped.

❖ 9 ❖

Tripping on a Small Stone

When Shinto was arrested in early March 1989, he said, "I tripped on a small stone."[1] The larger objective of completing the reshaping of Japan's telecommunications industry and smashing the old kingdom had eluded him because a relatively small piece of the drama had blown up in his face.

I asked Nakasone whether he also felt that the two of them had tripped on a small stone. Reading Nakasone is an art in itself. Sometimes he answers in an abstract way, other times he looks you in the eye. Sometimes he speaks with fatigue, other times with emphasis. When I asked him this question, he looked me dead in the eye and said emphatically, *"So."* His answer should be translated as "Absolutely."

Was anyone in Kanemaru's camp or the broader telecommunications kingdom responsible for his troubles? "I have no way to know," Nakasone answered. "If there was such a thing, it was invisible. They could not do anything obvious."

Indeed it wasn't obvious. What Shinto, Nakasone, and Ezoe did is well understood and well documented. The real mystery begins in the role the kingdom played in stopping them and why the scandal suddenly dried up when it did. No coherent explanation has been presented, even to the Japanese, so we are left with only tidbits of information to assemble a plausible scenario. As usual, there is much information available about the losers, but very little about the winners and the real decision makers.

The scandal surrounding Recruit began in June 1988, when *Asahi Shimbun* printed an article about the vice mayor of the city of Kawasaki accepting unlisted shares from Recruit, apparently in exchange for permission to erect an office building. It was a minor, obscure flap, the sort that ordinarily would be forgotten after the official made a public apology or resigned. Japan's entire postwar history is marked by periodic political scandals that flare up and then subside with no lasting impact on the underlying structure of power or on the ever-growing link between money and politics. It wasn't until July that the Recruit flap even began receiving serious attention in Tokyo. That's when *Asahi* identified Nakasone and Takeshita as recipients of Recruit shares. They had not necessarily done anything in exchange for the gifts, so there was no evidence of wrongdoing.

There is no hint that forces within the telecommunications kingdom planted the *Asahi* story. Asahi, as a communications company, had its own competitive reasons for making trouble for Recruit. Its reporters knew that Recruit was an acceptable target. They were simply doing their jobs.

For months, the scandal focused on Recruit itself. The links to big-name politicians seemed to have been forgotten. Although it was clear that Ezoe was in trouble, no truly powerful people seemed threatened. It was not the kind of affair that was destined to bring down a government. It was punishing the usurper, the *narikin*.

Then, in November and December 1988, it took a more serious turn when the media as a whole, the prosecutors, and the opposition in the Diet all moved into higher gear. The information war being played out in the media began striking closer to men of real power. Each story that was leaked produced just one more piece of information or made one more vital connection. Part of the explanation for this sudden, serious turn is the presence of Yusuke Yoshinaga, the same prosecutor who broke the Lockheed case. NTT officials opposed to Shinto also began leaking information about his involvement with Recruit. By December, Finance Minister Kiichi Miyazawa was forced to resign. Then Shinto was forced to quit. All the earlier assumptions about Recruit being a scandal headed nowhere were out of date. It had taken on Lockheed-like proportions.

There were several underlying reasons why things seemed suddenly out of control. The emperor was clearly dying, and that created a sense of flux. The issue of imposing the new consumption tax was growing larger. At the same time that the "new money" usurpers were driving fancy cars, buying new homes, and playing on the stage of national power, the average Japanese were being asked to pay a new tax. This created a very real, but in the final analysis temporary, flare-up of public opinion against the LDP.

It was just the kind of fluidity on which Kanemaru, the master of silent fear, thrives. Although there is no smoking gun, Kanemaru had at least two major levers to use to advance his interests: his ties to opposition parties, and his ties to the media. He had the motive and the weapons to fan the flames of the Recruit scandal. It strains credulity to believe that he would have remained completely passive after having been handed an opportunity to create trouble for pesky challengers who were mounting an increasingly powerful assault on his power base and to enhance his leverage over Takeshita and other top LDP leaders.

One of the keys to Kanemaru's power has been his ability to funnel money to the Socialists. The other two major opposition parties, the Democratic Socialist Party and Komeito, are also thought to receive funds from Kanemaru. It is taboo to discuss this. Only the Communists, who are outside this cozy arrangement, complain about it. "It happens very often and everyone knows about it, but no one dares talk about it," says Communist Diet member Haruko Yoshikawa. It is likely that the LDP makes some payments without Kanemaru's instructions, but he appears to be a leading practitioner of this pattern of activity. Outsiders will never understand the details, only that it happens.

In exchange for the money that he sends to the opposition parties through a variety of channels, Kanemaru is able to broker deals in the Diet, to defuse difficult situations. At least in part, this is what Takeshita means when he says that Kanemaru is "a good arbitrator when something goes wrong. He settles things."

Kanemaru's links with the Socialists go so deep that the former secretary-general of the Socialist Party used to visit Kanemaru's home on New Year's Day. Japanese journalists who cover Kanemaru were surprised to find the Socialist leader sitting on a tatami mat in the inner sanctum of Kanemaru's home one New Year's Day while Kanemaru's wife poured sake. Paying a visit to someone's home on New Year's Day in this way is tantamount to expressing loyalty. It is the day that power relationships are maintained and developed.

The veil on Kanemaru's channels to the Socialists was lifted slightly in April 1989, when Construction Minister Hikosaburo Okonogi made an unusual, public complaint. In his previous position as chairman of LDP's Diet Affairs Committee, Okonogi had funneled 2 million yen to the Socialist Party by buying tickets to a fund-raising party in that amount. Somehow the Socialists failed to send the actual party tickets or even a thank-you note. This angered Okonogi, who was quoted as saying he was "furious that they don't know how to behave." He was not angry over the fact that the LDP was paying money to the Socialists, only that the Socialists were not observing the normal courtesies.[2]

One opposition Diet member involved in the Recruit investigation disclosed to me that Kanemaru was enraged by this disclosure; he felt it threatened to reveal the mechanism by which he was funneling money to the Socialists so that they could fund their investigation into Recruit. Obtaining information costs money. People with valuable information do not give it away for free.

The disclosure came less than a month after Shinto had been arrested and just as pressure against Takeshita and Nakasone was rising to a crescendo. After only two days of coverage in *Asahi* and *Mainichi*, the payola incident died a quiet death. It was never described in the English-language newspapers that both *Asahi* and *Mainichi* publish. Okonogi declined to comment, and the account is unconfirmable, but it does offer another fragment of evidence. Kanemaru had long cultivated the Socialists and often paid them money to help cut legislative deals. Why not help fund their Recruit investigation as well?

The Socialists certainly had their own reasons for going after Nakasone. He had privatized Japan National Railways (JNR) and had played a role in attacking NTT. "When I got into the Recruit thing, the Socialists attacked me viciously," Nakasone told me. "It was retaliation. I had fired the president of Japan National Railways, who opposed privatization. That privatization of JNR devastated a base of Socialist support. They were broken into six divisions. That led to the collapse of unions in JNR, which was a mainstay of Sohyo, the General Council of Trade Unions of Japan [a Socialist base of support]. They had very good reason to retaliate. The Socialists were vehemently opposed to the privatization of NTT."

When I asked the Socialist Party's Takako Doi whether that was true, she laughed broadly, as if gaining time to compose an answer. Then, suddenly serious, she said, "There is no cause-and-effect relation." But of course there was a relation, and it would have been handy to have additional funding to help square accounts.

Kanemaru's second major tool was the press corps that covers him. Japanese journalism, so much like the Western model on the surface, is fundamentally different in a subtle kind of way. Japanese journalists who are assigned to cover a certain industry, a ministry, or a major political leader usually spend many more years in that position than their American counterparts. In some cases, a Japanese journalist spends his entire career covering the same companies, ministries, or political leaders. They enter into a far deeper relationship with their subjects than most American journalists. For example, in covering a ministry, a Japanese journalist becomes part of a club—also called a lobby because the members sit in the lobby so much. The journalists obtain a great deal of information that they never disclose. It is not their job to provoke or attack or criticize. This would lock them out of the club and threaten their careers. There are exceptions, but this is the general pattern. In effect, these journalists become advocates for the interests they cover.

This is particularly acute in politics. Once assigned to cover a particular faction leader, journalists only rarely cover another one. A journalist who arrived from the Nakasone faction, for example, to cover the Komoto faction would be suspect. His loyalty would be in question.

Kanemaru has spent years and millions of yen developing his personal relations with the journalists who make up his media army. "We can call them Kanemaru's SS," says the political expert Takao To-shikawa. "With some of them he goes out drinking and socializing, sometimes with their families as well." These journalists, from major media organizations, actively promote him. When Kanemaru makes a pronouncement, it is headline news, even though he holds no formal position in the LDP or the government. The stories usually identify him simply as a former deputy prime minister and as one of the "most influential" leaders of the party. They never explain why he is powerful or how he wields that power.

Many of these journalists were assigned by their publications and their television stations to cover Recruit. Several journalists outside the Kanemaru camp confirmed this but declined to name names. Could Kanemaru have subtly shaped their inquiries or provided bits of information? It's possible, but it would not have been necessary. From long years of covering Kanemaru, these journalists understood Nakasone's challenge to Kanemaru; they were the old man's confidants and part of his camp. Not only did they understand Nakasone's challenge to their patron, but also the threat it represented to their own careers.

The point is that Kanemaru had tremendous and largely hidden strength to create a climate for the Recruit investigation and to fuel it. In short, he could make sure that the small stone proved large enough to trip. Could it have been a complete coincidence that the ultimate goal of both the opposition parties and the media was to "get Nakasone" and not push into the roots of structural corruption inside the telecommunications kingdom?

One difficulty with this line of analysis is that there were many other victims of the Recruit scandal, not just Shinto, Nakasone, and Ezoe. Takeshita, Abe, and Miyazawa all were tainted, and these were the men whom Kanemaru wanted to rotate through the prime minister's job.

Kanemaru himself was a recipient of Recruit shares. Why would he allow pressure to build on a number of LDP men, presumably including himself? And what about all the bureaucrats at the Labor and Education ministries who were hurt?

The explanation, according to one source in Nagata-cho, is that Kanemaru thrives on crisis. If there is a problem, he is the fixer. If the LDP men were under assault, they might turn to him to extinguish the flames. He could be both persecutor and savior, and few people, even in Japan, would understand what he was doing. Although Takeshita was forced to resign, his underlying power base as a factional leader was not challenged. He remained powerful. In Japan, resigning does not necessarily mean giving up power. It may only mean finding a front man. As for Kanemaru himself, he was never in danger because he held no formal position other than his seat in the Diet. In a sense, he is beyond the full scrutiny of the law. The officials at other ministries were a sideshow, caught up in a larger drama.

Whatever the precise nature of his involvement, the end result was a clear victory for Kanemaru. "He eliminated Shinto and Nakasone," said a source in the Democratic Socialist Party. Kanemaru was able to emerge as an even more powerful kingmaker in coming months, in the maneuvering that followed the July 23 Upper House election. All the evidence suggests that he was also able to consolidate his grip on the flow of political funds from telecommunications. "Historically, the profit of Den Den Kosha [NTT's political funds] had been fought over between the Tanaka faction and Nakasone," Watanabe explains. "Now the Kanemaru group is winning. This is the story of the fight."

To understand why the scandal was stopped in its tracks, there is another strand of the tale that must be explored, which has little to do with Kanemaru. As suddenly as the Recruit crisis had begun toppling major leaders in December 1988, it was abruptly halted by the end of May 1989 when the special prosecutor agreed to conclude his investigation. The media and the opposition also went largely mute. It was as if someone had thrown a switch. The scandal that supposedly threatened to bring down the entire established order was over. To be sure, the parties geared up for the July 23 Upper House elections to deal with the political aftermath and test each others' strength, but no sensational new revelations were forthcoming. Many influential Japanese understood this. In fact, as early as March, some of Japan's internationalists began telling their foreign contacts that the scandal would end in May. But it was difficult to believe them. The scandal seemed in full fury.

At the eye of the storm was prosecutor Yusuke Yoshinaga, fifty-seven, who was chief of the Tokyo district Special Prosecutor's Office. He is known as the "giant of special investigators" because of his role in prosecuting Tanaka for accepting money from Lockheed to secure the sale of U.S. jets in Japan. Special prosecutors have a reputation for wide-ranging independence, but they operate within the overall purview of the Justice Ministry, which is outside Kanemaru's sphere of influence. Kanemaru may have been able to create an environment of politics and opinion that allowed the prosecutor to mount his investigation, but he had no direct pipeline. The prosecutors are not immune, however, from political considerations. The ultimate weapon that hangs over them is that if they push too far, their independence could be sharply limited.

Yoshinaga's office had a special score to settle with Nakasone, who had been a minister in Tanaka's government when it fell. The prosecutors had tried to nail Nakasone back then; he wriggled away, and there was still some bad blood.

Yoshinaga has not granted an interview to a Western journalist in years. One Japanese journalist working for an American publication did manage to secure an interview several years ago but sat for hours with Yoshinaga unable to elicit a single fact from him. The prosecutor operates only through his own "lobby" of Japanese journalists whom he knows and trusts. Through them, he took part in the campaign of leak and counterleak. "They are utilizing the press very skillfully," Takashi Kakuma, a journalist and author of several books about corruption, said. "Without these press leaks, I'm sure their investigation would have been stopped by now. The pressure is very intense."[3]

By April 1989, following the arrests of Shinto and Ezoe, Nakasone was on the ropes. The combined effect of media, opposition, and prosecutor was overwhelming. If the investigation were to be taken through to the logical conclusion, Nakasone was in trouble. The entire process was aiming at him because the new money usurpers had exploded onto the national stage during the time he was prime minister. He was being blamed. He helped create the environment and the mechanisms for Recruit's money to flow, even if he was careful enough to never personally accept any funds or to personally extend any favors. To completely ruin Nakasone, the prosecutor could merely have arrested him and subjected him to weeks of cross-examination without recourse to a lawyer. Legally, the prosecutor had that power. If that wasn't enough to extract damaging information, he could have subjected Nakasone to grueling years of trial. To fatally injure Nakasone, the prosecutor didn't necessarily have to achieve a conviction.

Why didn't Yoshinaga deliver the knockout blow? One explanation is that Nakasone was simply too smart and never crossed the line from the gray zone to outright illegality. Another explanation is that the prosecutor was worried that it would threaten the LDP's grip on power. It was a moment of real drama. The Diet was tied up in knots over a new budget because of an opposition boycott, and public opinion polls showed astonishingly low ratings for the LDP.

But a more plausible analysis is that pushing further would have threatened the prosecutor's own relative independence. In other words, he had reached a political limit. Although the prosecutor's office enjoys a genuine measure of autonomy from the Justice Ministry, it is not completely independent. Time and time again during Japan's history of postwar scandals, prosecutors have been leaned on to stop investigations of prime ministers or former prime ministers.

Rather than continuing his investigation, Yoshinaga accepted the end of May as the date for completing it. This was to allow the LDP time to prepare for the July 23 elections. Yoshinaga had interviewed hundreds of people over 260 days and indicted twelve on charges of bribery, plus an additional four for violating political fund-raising laws. But he only questioned two politicians. If he had been fully independent and fully determined to dig to the bottom, he would not have stopped when he did.

Nakasone testified in the Diet, technically resigned from the LDP and his faction, and sacrificed his aide Takao Fujinami, all in the space of a few days at the end of May. It had all the hallmarks of a brokered deal, a precisely calibrated settlement. Japanese newspapers were virtually unanimous in complaining that the investigation had been aborted, but none of them felt obliged to offer a theory of how this had happened.

Judging by his own remarks, Masaharu Gotoda played a role in that. Gotoda was another top Tanaka deputy and was so influential that he was nicknamed "Tanaka's brain." He even lists himself as a member of the "ex-Tanaka faction." He does not belong to any of the five major factions, so his power cannot be explained on the basis of being able to deliver votes. As a former head of the National Police Agency, however, he has access to information. He knows how to identify the bureaucrats involved in a given decision, and where any dirty secrets may lie hidden. Another of his nicknames was "Tanaka's enforcer." Even if he no longer held a formal position in the security apparatus, he would understand where the pressure points were at the Justice Ministry. In addition, by virtue of his age (seventy-four) and the fact that he survived the "burning fields," he also commands genuine respect as an elder. He is in the same league as Kanemaru, another of the powers behind the curtain.

Gotoda had known Nakasone for years. They had both served in the security apparatus and Nakasone, like Tanaka before him, had used Gotoda as a right-hand man in dealing with recalcitrant bureaucrats.[4] Even though Gotoda was older than Nakasone, he had served in the younger man's government in the powerful position of chief cabinet secretary. Moreover, Gotoda was on the board of Nakasone's new International Institute for Global Peace. If Nakasone had a guardian angel, this was him.

Gotoda granted me a rare interview and I asked him to tell me who specifically Nakasone was threatening in his overall assault on NTT. He looked me straight in the eye and replied, "I have never thought about it." It was clearly stonewalling, a man at the heart of power who had never thought about it.

In response to a different question, Gotoda charged into a defense of the way the Recruit case had been resolved. A lean, craggy man with thick glasses, Gotoda responded emotionally. There was electricity in the air. He was dressing me down, as he might an errant schoolboy:

"When a scandal like Recruit happens, we can respond any number of ways. We can have a trial and involve the police. Or it can be a question of ethics and having the politicians involved take responsibility, to make sure it never happens again." The phrase "taking responsibility" means that someone apologizes or resigns.

"Japan is a modern civilized country," Gotoda continued. "Penalties are strictly provided by law. If there is no evidence, you cannot prosecute. On the contrary, the mass media will dig up the facts but this cannot happen [implication: we cannot allow this to happen] because it will interfere with human rights. The Japanese government will be blamed because it pressures prosecutors. This is what the mass media is blaming the government for. The result is not as big as the media expected, so the media says the government intervened to protect the criminals." He concluded by adding that preventing politicians from allowing such scandals to happen again was better than "having them hanging by their thumbs."

Interpretation is left to the hearer, but it is clear that Gotoda opposed hanging Nakasone by his thumbs and felt that the drumbeat against him was interfering with Nakasone's human rights. Nakasone "took responsibility" by resigning from the party and from his faction. In the absence of any proof that Nakasone personally accepted money or administered favors, Gotoda clearly stood opposed to prosecution. It is obvious that he used whatever clout he had to protect Nakasone.

This is by no means a complete explanation, merely a tantalizing clue. There were almost certainly other power brokers involved. Moreover, there would have been no need for a formal decision to stop the investigation. No one had to "put in the fix." Prosecutor Yoshinaga may simply have understood the balance of power and realized there was a limit to just how far he could push.

If the prosecutor ran into political resistance, why did the media and opposition prove suddenly quiescent? The answer, as it relates to the media, is that Japanese journalists wear their own distinctive set of blinders. When I asked Hiroshi Yamamoto, the *Asahi Shimbun* reporter who coordinated his newspaper's investigative team, why he did not press ahead to reveal the structural corruption inside NTT, he replied, "The Japanese people already knew about the close connections between politicians and companies. The Japanese are used to people bribing each other."

But that means the system won, right?

"Yes, unfortunately."

But how can you explain that people got upset about the small thing and not the large one?

"It's just like the Americans, before Gorbachev, getting excited about Nicaragua but not the Soviet Union," said Yamamoto. In other words, the challengers to the telecommunications kingdom were interesting, but the kingdom itself was not. Once it became clear that Nakasone was off-limits, the game was over.

As for the opposition, there were some lawmakers who wanted to continue the inquisition against Nakasone, but the ground had been cut out from under them. The climate had changed. I asked one top Socialist who helped whip up the campaign, Masao Nakamura, why he did not go after the institutionalized abuses inside NTT. "That's the way it is," he said. "*Shikata ga nai.* There is a triangle. These bonds have existed for many years. You cannot change it."

This has been the pattern of Japan's postwar political scandals since 1948, when executives of a big fertilizer producer were accused of bribing senior government officials for low-interest loans. Some forty-three public and private sector officials were indicted, including a former prime minister. In the 1950s, shipping companies were at the center of scandal, bribing officials for contracts and subsidies. A central figure was Eisaku Sato, a future prime minister, who was indicted, but the charges were later dropped. During the mid-sixties, there were the so-called black mist scandals, which involved links between organized crime and key politicians. The black mist was so thick that no one could see what was happening. Then came Lockheed, the granddaddy of them all prior to Recruit.[5]

As old as the pattern is, it also seems preordained that someone must die. There must be a letting of blood. About two dozen political aides or secretaries have committed suicide as a result of these postwar scandals. Tanaka's secretary-driver asphyxiated himself in his car in August 1976 when it appeared authorities were preparing to grill him. As the Recruit crisis heated up, longtime observers of Japanese politics expected that, again, there would be a loss of life. It was just a question of who.

It turned out to be Ihei Aoki, Takeshita's secretary and confidant for thirty years. As a fund-raiser, he had accepted $400,000 in loans from Recruit. Although the loans were repaid and were not illegal, Takeshita had failed to disclose them. This is the technicality that tripped him. It did not ruin Takeshita; it merely forced him to resign as prime minister and retreat to the time-honored position of kingmaker. Aoki, however, had failed and his failure had cost Takeshita an honored position.

Aoki's body was discovered after he had slashed his wrists and legs, and then hanged himself with his necktie from a curtain rail at his home. His wife found him. He left four suicide notes, none of which were ever publicly revealed. But to his high school alumni newspaper, he had earlier written a chilling passage: "Behind the scenes of this peaceful democracy are the same bloody power struggles to the death that were waged time after time by medieval warlords."[6]

The losers in this particular struggle were the challengers, the people who used new money, who tried, however modestly, to open the system to the outside world, the people with questionable backgrounds. They were the heads of nails that were hammered down. As one wag put it, this was "maintenance of the status quo with a vengeance."

That Ezoe was arrested and most likely ruined was foreseeable. He was destined to become fodder for the cannons from the moment he tried to penetrate the establishment. He had no right to do that. His class background was questionable and his business was "artificial." He was not legitimate.

There is also a logic to how Nakasone was handled. Aside from losing a top aide, he was forced to resign from the LDP and from his faction and therefore "take responsibility." He soon lost control of his faction to Michio Watanabe. Although spared the ultimate humiliation of imprisonment, Nakasone paid a terrible personal price. In the space of four years, he aged ten. The forceful head of government who strode into the Waldorf-Astoria had become gaunt and gray. Although still a proud man, he evoked the air of a warrior who had fought his last battle.

The price that he paid is striking when compared with the appearance of Takeshita or Miyazawa or Watanabe. All these men were tainted as well, but they are still very much alive politically. They were forced to give up very little, and this is reflected in their faces and demeanors. Only politicians who dare to be leaders run into major trouble. "The politicians who demonstrate leadership, like Tanaka and Nakasone, achieve temporary success, but ultimately they build up resentment and they stumble," says Professor Iwai.

It is hardest to explain why Shinto, at age seventy-eight, was humiliated by being taken to the Tokyo Detention Center, a prison that dates from before World War II. There he was held in a small solitary cell and subjected to twenty-three days of questioning without being charged. Now he faces the possibility of years of trial. Aside from Aoki's death, his is the most shocking human casualty of the Recruit affair.

His sin was that he was drawn into the struggle too deeply. His aide bought ten thousand shares of Recruit real estate and realized $170,000 in profits. Less than half of that ended up in Shinto's bank account. "I had to pay the money for dealing with politicians who were personal friends of mine," Shinto said. "I used the profits from the Recruit stock deal to make up the deficits in my bank account."[7]

If he used any money for his personal needs, it was minor in comparison with the vast amounts changing hands throughout the telecommunications kingdom. In many ways, he was the ultimate samurai. He responded to a call from his mentor, and he did his job unflinchingly. Nor did he complain when he was cut down. "Shinto doesn't feel he did anything wrong at all," says Watanabe, an ardent Shinto supporter from the start. "He did it for NTT as a company. He should be praised for taking care of the company. He was brave to take all the responsibility for what was wrong. Perhaps they should build a statue for Shinto."

Aside from the technical miscue of allowing his own bank account to be used, Shinto's greatest mistake was that he allowed himself to become resented as arrogant and too individualistic. An outsider from Kyushu, he was not a team player, not part of the group. He was also perceived as being too close to foreigners. Lastly, Toshio Doko, his mentor, had died and Shinto lacked a powerful protector in the inner councils of power. He was isolated, and he had made powerful enemies. Aside from Kanemaru, archrival Kitahara, Tanaka's choice to head up NTT, cooperated with prosecutors and built a damning case.[8]

Kitahara has often been portrayed as having lost the power struggle with Shinto. But in late 1989, he was still on salary at NTT as a consultant-adviser and still had an office. He rejected several requests for interviews, but it is obvious he is still employed, while Shinto is on trial. The kingdom protected its own.

Was there outrage among the Japanese people? Yes, and it was directed against the usurpers, the fast-money people, the outsiders. Not against the face of power itself. In his book *The Enigma of Japanese Power*, Dutch journalist Karel van Wolferen argued that the Japanese system lacked the ability to reform itself in a way the outside world found meaningful, and that its various crises did not alter any underlying reality. "From time to time, the Japanese nation throws itself on a particular subject with a real vengeance as the media hit it day after day," he wrote. "A subject that attracts such intense negative attention is known as a *mondai*, which in various contexts means 'problem,' 'issue,' or 'question.' . . . Most press-generated *mondai* are on the front pages for a couple of months at the most."[9]

These *mondai* are almost like a form of entertainment, an outlet for frustration, and indeed Recruit proved to be a momentary upheaval of precisely the sort about which van Wolferen wrote. Almost totally absent was the sense of moral outrage that most Westerners read into the scandal. Few people in Japan were shocked that their leaders were bribing each other behind closed doors. That's simply the way Japan works. *Shikata ga nai.*

❖ 10 ❖

The Uno Affairs

In the early evening in the Akasaka district of Tokyo, men in elegant suits saunter down the neon-lit streets past restaurants and drinking establishments to enter old, traditional-style buildings that look like homes from a different era. The markings on the outside of these wooden teahouses are subtle, just a few characters written in classical style. No bright lights, no neon. One needs a proper introduction to enter.

These are the teahouses of Akasaka near the Diet Building and political offices of Nagata-cho where many of Japan's LDP politicians go in the evenings to meet each other and to meet business supporters over elegant multicourse meals. Also to meet geisha and former geisha. Hundreds of years old, this is the "flower and willow world."

There are many different kinds of teahouses and different kinds of women. The government officially estimated that there were thirteen thousand geisha in 1985, but the number has shrunk. Today, there are only a thousand or fewer true geisha, women with a full training in the arts. But there are many more hostesses and others at bars, cabarets, and clubs who are eager to establish relationships with well-to-do patrons. After dinner and drinks, some of the men move to nearby hotels or apartments for an hour or two of intimacy with their chosen women. Others limit their evenings to drinking games, playing mah-jongg, or simple conversation in the presence of these women. Intentionally losing at mah-jongg, a Chinese domino-style game, is one way of transferring funds to political leaders with total discretion. Proper geisha never reveal anything they have heard, seen, or done.

Just as important as the women is the sense of trust and friendship that develops with the other men. This is a time for bonding and deepening trust relationships, as part of the *nemawashi* process, usually translated as consensus-building, but literally meaning "binding the roots." The men are exchanging money and strategies in an environment of trust, deepening their ties with each other. "Japanese policy is not decided in geisha houses, but the preparation, the *nemawashi*, is done there," complains Upper House Dietmember Haruko Yoshikawa, who, as a woman and a Communist, will never penetrate the flower and willow world.

By 11:30 P.M. or midnight, long lines of taxis form in Akasaka to take the men home. Others have black limousines with drivers and perhaps their aides waiting for them. "There's probably more political power concentrated in the teahouses of Akasaka on a given evening than anywhere else in Tokyo," quipped one longtime Tokyo resident, a Japanese-speaking American.

Many of Japan's top political leaders have mistresses or maintain illicit relationships. It is institutionalized, it is pervasive, and it is accepted. To establish themselves in the pecking order, politicians demonstrate to each other that their women are the most attractive or the most desirable. They demonstrate to each other how well they manage these relationships. This builds a man's prestige. The Japanese, among themselves, make no secret about it. "Everybody knows politicians are deeply connected with women," says Michio Watanabe. "The Speaker of the House has been living with his mistress. Everyone knows it. The education minister has been living with his mistress for so many years that no one can distinguish who is his real wife. All this is well known, so it's not a scandal. Some leading political figures have had mistresses for thirty years, with grown children. It used to be that these kinds of stories were never carried in the newspapers. Wives usually do not make this subject a big deal."

The reason it became a big deal for Prime Minister Sosuke Uno was not that he engaged in a series of extramarital affairs for as long as fifteen years, but that he chose the wrong kind of women. Uno picked women who were not first-class; women who were part-time or faded geisha, who were former legal secretaries or over the hill. He didn't pay them well, and he broke off his affairs with appallingly bad manners. In one case, he failed to offer a girlfriend a sufficient amount of hush money. In another, he failed to give a lady friend a ten-year anniversary memento. The scandal had little to do with the concept of marital fidelity. In fact, Uno's wife, incredible as it may seem, later made a public apology for the controversy surrounding her husband.

The bespectacled Uno, then sixty-six and serving as foreign minister, was not a powerful man. In fact, the ultimate statement about his relative lack of power was that Ezoe did not even bother to try to give him Recruit shares. The result, however, was that he was relatively clean. Thus he was installed as prime minister only after one of the most agonizing searches in modern Japanese history. The top LDP leadership had been discredited, at least temporarily. Everyone knew that the party was headed for losses in the July 1989 Upper House elections. No one wanted the job, certainly not on the terms it was being offered. Whoever took it was a sacrificial lamb. But Uno either did not care or did not know. Glory was knocking on his door. The only thing Japan-watchers disagreed about was whether he was a Takeshita puppet or a Nakasone puppet. Perhaps he was both.

Whatever pretensions he had toward exercising power quickly unraveled. It wasn't surprising; he was merely holding down the fort while the real power brokers maneuvered. But Uno fell apart faster than anyone had anticipated because of his poor management of his women. In early July, less than a week after he had taken office, the first quasi-geisha publicly accused Uno of being vain and pompous. She claimed he had paid her only $2,300 a month for four or five months—the accounts vary. He immediately became a laughingstock among Japanese men. He may have aroused some ire among Westernized Japanese women, but that was beside the point. To have one's mistress go public represented the ultimate failure for a Japanese man.

I'll never forget a conversation I heard between a senior LDP man and one of his top campaign contributors. I was accompanying the LDP politician on a campaign swing through his district on the southwest outskirts of Tokyo and he stopped in to see a Toyota dealer, who was obviously quite successful and a major donor. My assistant and I were allowed to sit in, like flies on a wall, only if I agreed not to identify either party. The exchange went like this.

Car dealer: "What do we need with this fool Uno? He can't even manage his women." This was in reference to Kagurazaka Geisha. Her real name was Mitsuko Nakanishi and she was forty years old when she disclosed her story.

LDP man: "Yes, I know. What happened was that the woman called him on the night he was named prime minister. His secretary took the call and didn't put it through. So the woman was angry. Then, when Uno offered her the hush money, he didn't offer enough."

Dealer: "Ten million yen would have been enough."

LDP man: "Even five million yen would have been enough. But he only offered three [$21,500]."

Dealer: "So he was stingy. He didn't know what he was doing."

LDP man: "Right."

Soon after, it was revealed that Uno had also had a ten-year liaison with a woman identified only as Hatsuko, who had been a geisha in Akasaka for twenty years. Having been born in the fifteenth year of the Taisho emperor (1926), she would have been nearly fifty when she began her tryst with Uno. In 1985, on their ten-year "anniversary," she asked him, "Aren't you going to give me just a little anniversary memento?"

"Oh? Ten years? So we've been f——ing for ten years, eh?"[1]

Uno left her house and never came back. That was that. He didn't even offer any consolation money. The former geisha nursed her wounds in silence for four years.

But after Scandal No. 1 broke, Hatsuko told her story in excruciating detail. Uno, who served in a series of cabinet positions during the relationship, came to her house once a week, either a Tuesday or a Wednesday night. He liked to wait until it was dark so that he would not be recognized, but if it were still light he wore sunglasses. His male secretary would come with a car in the morning to pick him up.

For his evening's amusement, Uno used to demand that she go and rent pornographic movies for them to watch while they had sex. Sometimes they would take a room at the New Otani Hotel.

Hatsuko had to prod him to give her a monthly stipend, and when he started doing so in 1975, it was only 100,000 yen a month (roughly $400) rather than the going rate of 200,000 yen. And in the ten years he saw her he never gave her a raise, nor did he remember her birthdays. One reason this geisha came forward was that she read that the later girlfriend had received $21,500 as hush money. Clearly Uno's financial resources had improved over the years, but the discrepancy in how much the younger woman was paid outraged Hatsuko. Uno never denied any of the details that were disclosed, nor was he available for confirmation.

Did the Uno affair reflect a sudden American-style abhorrence of adultery? I paid a call on Shuntaro Torigoe, the man who decided to break the story of Uno's most recent affair, that with Mitsuko Nakanishi. He was editor-in-chief of the *Sunday Mainichi*. Torigoe, in his late forties, had an unusual appearance for a Japanese because of his longish hair that hung well below his ears and kept swinging into his face. But he was no softie. He had spent a year and a half in Tehran enduring

Iraqi bombardments. Having been in neighboring Afghanistan during the Soviet invasion, I compared notes with him. We had a common basis for understanding.

The quasi-geisha Nakanishi had gone to both *Mainichi* and *Asahi* to promote her story, trying to play the two newspapers off against each other. She was very aggressive, calling Torigoe every day. She had been working in a law office and didn't earn much money. It was clear to Torigoe that Uno's political rivals in the LDP were encouraging her. It was unlikely that any Japanese woman would have the courage to publicly attack a prime minister without some sense that she had powerful support. Torigoe explained that the prevailing view at the time was: "There's no personality beneath the navel. You must not touch those things." It was taboo.

The *Sunday Mainichi* editors discussed whether they should publish the story. They were divided fifty-fifty. They were aware of recent U.S. coverage of the sexual improprieties committed by Gary Hart and John Tower. *Mainichi* had been under financial pressure and needed to generate a larger readership, but Torigoe denied this was the reason they printed the sensational story. "We concluded there is personality under the navel," he said. "It is a reflection of personality. Sex is very important."

Was Torigoe outraged that Uno had cheated on his wife? "No, it has nothing to do with the wife. It has to do with Uno's personality and character [toward the mistress]. His manner was so bad."

As a veteran of international journalism, Torigoe promoted the story with the American media. He knew that if his story was not noticed outside of Japan, it would fall flat. At first it appeared that it would be ignored. But then the *Washington Post* ran a modest account in a back section of the newspaper, based on the *Mainichi* report, and that did it. Japan had been embarrassed internationally. If the affair had been kept on one side of the prism, it would have been quickly forgotten. But now the Americans, in Washington no less, knew about it. The scandal took off. Uno was destroyed by rivals within his own party who found his weak point and encouraged the women to come forward. He had no power to stop them from talking. He could not be respected.

How did the idea spread that Uno was humiliated simply because he cheated on his wife, that he was some sort of anomaly? Again, the outside world interpreted the event through its own lens, not through Japan's. To be sure, there were voices from within Japan who suggested that there was a major shift in attitudes. One female Diet member charged that the prime minister had "treated women as pieces of merchandise." The Japan Housewives Association went on the attack against Uno. Kuniko Inoguchi, associate professor of political science at Sophia University, and a well-respected commentator, said Uno's problem "represents a fundamental and important transition."[2]

There's not the slightest hint that Japanese who proclaimed fundamental change were attempting to lie or deceive. There are several possible explanations. One is that the Japanese, like the Chinese, have a different concept of truth. If they want something to happen, they proclaim that it is, in fact, happening. Another factor is that the Japanese think in ten- to fifteen-year terms. When they see something on the horizon that might have a major impact over that time frame, they get excited. It's big. By Western standards, it is still a dim and distant prospect. Last, most of the people who proclaimed a watershed in Japanese attitudes toward women were outside the mainstream. They were vocal but on the fringe. They said things the outside world wanted to hear.

The result was headlines like "Sex Scandal Rocking Japan's Premier Shows Traditional Attitudes Changing."[3] Some pundits went so far as to argue that Japan was no longer male-dominated, which was a wild leap of imagination.

But the fact of the matter is that, despite the flare-up, the *mondai*, underlying attitudes barely budged. In the silent mainstream, some Japanese women did not criticize Uno as much as they did the forty-year-old quasi-geisha. She had violated all the unwritten rules. "That woman is nothing but a prostitute," raged one former geisha. Of the four events of 1989, the so-called four-piece set, which included Recruit, Uno's affairs, the consumption tax, and agricultural liberalization, Uno's peccadilloes were the least significant, the least challenging to the established order.

One of the events that largely escaped outside attention came a few days before the July 23 Upper House election. Uno's wife, Chiyo, went to an auditorium in Yokohama and, before a predominantly female audience of six thousand, offered her "heartfelt apologies over the controversy surrounding my husband." She did not say she was sorry for what he had done, or that she was angry with him, only that she regretted the controversy. No matter what had happened, she was a good Japanese wife. An election was about to be held. Power was at stake, as were all the benefits that might flow to her as the wife of a top politician.[4]

After the LDP took a beating in the Upper House, Uno was forced to resign. By the fall, both he and the scandal were forgotten, an almost comical interlude. And the lines of taxis waiting for lawmakers to come out of the teahouses of Akasaka were as long as ever.

❖ 11 ❖

Socialists: A Flash in the Pan

The rise and decline of Japan's Socialist Party in the space of a half dozen months in 1989 was a remarkable political riddle. To put these events in perspective, it is important to understand three essential truths about the Socialist Party. The first is that it's not really a party, and it's not really Socialist, in the fullest sense of either term. It is a grab-bag collection of unions from government sectors such as teachers, railways, the post office, and local government workers. Other sectors that are represented include farmers, shopkeepers, and a sprinkling of white-collar salarymen and blue-collar workers. In view of this breadth of membership, it is of little surprise that the party has been racked by a particularly bitter, long-term wrangle over who it is and what it stands for. Beneath a thin veneer of rhetoric, it has no real policy because of a schism between more left-wing ideological elements and more pragmatic party leaders who were prepared and eager to play the traditional power game. The left wing consisted of old-school ideologues who were prominent in the years following World War II. Their major preoccupation was opposition to rearmament and to the U.S.-Japan Security Treaty. Over time, as these issues became less critical, the appeal of this brand of socialism faded. As a result, the party had been locked in a long, seemingly permanent decline. The distinctions between right wing and left wing blurred.

In an excellent treatment of the Socialist Party, Gerald L. Curtis, an expert on Japanese politics, suggests that the Socialists were in "perpetual opposition."[1] The party might better be called the Loose Coalition for the Protection of the Status Quo Ante. But under no circumstances could this motley collection be seen as advocating a comprehensive socialist vision of redistribution of income, nationalizing big business, turning away from capitalism, or any of the views that many Westerners attribute to socialism.

In fact, after traveling to Niigata Prefecture and spending the day with Kinuko Ofuchi, a so-called Madonna candidate who had won a seat for the Socialists in an Upper House special election on June 25, it was clear that two major driving forces behind the Socialist Party's increase in popularity in May and June 1989 were from an overwhelmingly conservative direction. Rice farmers in Niigata, Kakuei Tanaka's old stronghold, were defecting in droves from the LDP because rice prices had gone into decline. They were defending an ancient way of life from the "lords" in Tokyo. Theirs was a populist revolt, one which demanded that the quaint but hugely inefficient Japanese agricultural sector be protected. As Socialist candidates walked the streets of small provincial towns, it was also obvious that shopkeepers, upset about the 3 percent consumption tax, were another source of strength. Thus the Socialists went into the July 23 elections attacking the LDP not from the left, but from the right. "The Socialists are Japan's most conservative party," says Professor Iwai.

The second essential truth is that the Socialist Party was not big enough to govern by itself. Even if it won in the largely honorific Upper House and forced an election in the more powerful Lower House, it could not mathematically field enough candidates to win a majority in the Lower House. In this sense, it was fundamentally different from a European Socialist party or a party in opposition, such as the American Democrats, who are always ready to move smoothly into power.

So, a victory in the Upper House would be only marginally important; when it came to the most powerful body, it was certain that the Socialists, even in the best-case scenario, would have to form a coalition with other opposition parties in order to rule. They had been trying to do that for decades with no success. The Democratic Socialist Party and the Komeito want to have little to do with the Socialists. They have traditionally been more inclined to flirt with the LDP. So it would have taken several years of spectacular upsets and precedent-setting agreements with other opposition parties before the Socialists could genuinely exercise power and even try to implement their own program, whatever it was.

A third essential truth is that the Socialists were nowhere close to the real levers of power in Japan. The trading companies, banks, and manufacturing companies have levels of organization, resources, expertise, and savvy that are simply unsurpassed. Next in the power ranking are the bureaucrats, who are worldly, highly educated, and have access to large quantities of high-quality information. Their decisions affect the flow of billions of dollars around the world. At a third level would be the LDP politicians who have big black cars with chauffeurs, cellular telephones, a fancy headquarters building, and spacious private offices in office buildings near the Diet. Not to mention their mistresses.

A sorry fourth are the Socialists. They know very little of what transpires in the inner councils of government. Party leader Takako Doi acknowledged that she did not really know Japan's defense policy toward the United States, for example, because "all the information that the Japanese bureaucrats have has not been made public. We don't have the information." In other words, the Socialists were not in the loop. In terms of resources, the Socialists' offices, even Ms. Doi's, were tiny and cramped. When they went campaigning in the prefectures, they had little more than megaphones.

For them to develop the resources, connections, and expertise that the LDP possessed, and which the LDP used to help the bureaucracy shape public policy, the Socialists would have had to tap into major flows of political funds. Their promise to sever the link between money and politics was wildly naive—and misleading.

They were already participating in money politics, just on a smaller scale. As evidenced by the funneling of money from Kanemaru and the LDP as a whole, the Socialists were dependent on the ruling party and thoroughly compromised. "To a considerable extent, the Socialists must depend on the goodwill of the LDP to make their lobbying efforts pay off [on behalf of their constituencies]," Curtis concluded. "To be in such a position of dependence on the ruling party, while maintaining a stance of adamant and uncompromising opposition to it, is fundamentally and unavoidably corrupting."[2]

Very much aware of this backdrop, most veteran Japan-watchers in Tokyo took the July 23 elections with a grain of skepticism. There was no mass outcry, no sign of excitement in the streets. On election Sunday, shoppers were strolling on the Ginza as usual. The kids were doing their thing in Harajuku. The Socialists had gained ground in the Upper House, but they did not have a majority. It represented forward movement for the Socialists, but only incrementally. It seemed to be a protest vote, a wake-up-the-LDP vote. After the election, the distribution of seats in the Upper House was as follows:[3]

LDP	109
Socialists	66

Komeito	20
JCP	14
DSP	8
Others	35
Total	252

To be sure, it was a fascinating moment. The polls showed Doi as Japan's most popular politician. At an unusually tall five feet six, the sixty-year-old former professor of constitutional law was a natural politician for the electronic age. With a deep voice, she seemed assertive and in control and, at the same time, quite feminine. She was an attractive personality and she knew how to campaign. Like most women in the Diet, she was single.

As one might expect, she encouraged the belief that she was on the verge of seizing real power. When I interviewed her on August 1, 1989, and asked how long it would be before she could exercise power, she said, "It's right in front of us. It's in front of our eyes." This is the Japanese style of trying to make something come true by insisting that it *is* true.

Japanese newspapers and electronic media gave the election massive coverage. Political specialists talked about an "enormous amount of fluidity" in Japanese politics. In normal conversations, the Japanese themselves told foreigners how thrilled they were that they had dealt a blow to the LDP. "This is real democracy," went the refrain. But very few Japanese actually believed in anything the Socialists stood for, assuming they could identify what the party did stand for. But even an incremental change that might take many years to play out is of keen interest to the Japanese. It is magnified, held up, and examined in detail.

Most of the Western press corps reported on the confusion and predicted a long period of uncertainty. Doi was a figurehead of a crazy nonparty that was nowhere close to taking real power, and the bureaucracy and LDP had many tools for dealing with the challenge. It could be merely a summer thunderstorm, but it was prudent to at least acknowledge the possibility that she might, over a long period of time, make further gains. Headline writers in London and New York were a tad too enthusiastic: "Japan's Next Revolution," proclaimed *The Economist*.[4] "Woman of the Hour," trumpeted *Time*.[5] But the overall treatment by Tokyo-based reporters and analysts was about right.

It was the pie-in-the-sky analysis from U.S.-based columnists and pundits, however, that seemed to carry the day in terms of the American perception of the event. Max Lerner, whose column is distributed by the *Los Angeles Times,* wrote from New York: "Historians will see the July 1989 election as a well-mannered revolt—yet a revolt nonethe-less—that revealed the fissure in the layers of [Japan's] stability." Japan's very stability was suddenly at stake. Lerner also argued that "the sensitivity about public ethics, the new independence of women against macho arrogance, the consumer's anti-tax revolt" were all im-ports from America, which they most decidedly were not. Lerner seemed pleased that Japan could no longer escape "the invasion of pressure groups and the discontents that come with the territory of postmodern man" and that Japan, like America, "will have to battle its internal demons of democracy."[6]

Flora Lewis, the respected columnist for the *New York Times*, wrote in an article appearing on July 26 that there could be "profound changes in the Japanese approach to politics, a broadening of concerns beyond the business interest of Japan Inc. to civic issues, consumer problems, everyday questions. In a way, it could make Japan easier for its foreign partners to deal with, more open, readier to accept a role in the international issues of human rights, environment, poverty and development."[7]

Others argued that Japan's political fund-raising system would be reformed. The link between money and politics would be severed. The old machine politics would be overturned. The presence of Doi's So-cialists would suddenly create a more truly democratic and pluralistic system that was more responsive to external demands. "Paradoxically, a bit of socialism in Japan may further capitalism in the United States!" proclaimed Charles R. Wolf from Santa Monica, California, where he is director of research in international economics for the Rand Corpora-tion.[8] It was one of the wildest statements ever made about Japan.

This line of analysis was terribly seductive and gratifying. Japan was cracking. The Japanese were human after all. The desperate desire in the outside world to see all this happen, however, obscured the fact that it had not occurred. Many Americans simply chose to believe that it had.

Even at the height of uncertainty in Tokyo, the bureaucrats and business leaders were never genuinely rattled. There could have been total political chaos in Nagata-cho, but what did it mean to the coun-try? Very little. The stock market took it all in stride. Business went on its way. The streets were calm. The troops were in their barracks. This was no coup.

Politicians have never been the driving force in Japanese government. They do come in handy for absorbing foreign brickbats over trade, and sometimes they are useful for coordinating or troubleshooting within the bureaucracy.

The bureaucrats, however, are really the ones running the government. They were quietly preparing to expand their influence if the Socialist gains continued. If the Socialists managed to seize top political positions, they would not have been able to impose their vision on the bureaucracy. It would have been the other way around. The bureaucrats would have managed the Socialists. Several told me how they hoped to use a "period of confusion" to advance their ministry's mandate. "Confusion might be helpful," said my old sparring partner, Ambassador Hidetoshi Ukawa. "The political parties get wedded to industries. That may be a block to rational policy action." One senior bureaucrat in a different ministry asked, "Who cares if Doi wins the Upper House? Who cares if she wins the Lower House? If she becomes prime minister, we will send her to America and you Americans will be charmed. But nothing in the relationship will change."

The LDP was also considering laying a trap for the Socialists. The only other time in Japan's history that the Socialists have run the government, for a short period in the 1950s, they were chewed up and discredited. One of the worst-case scenarios being debated by LDP strategists was to let the Socialists have another shot at it. That would have allowed the LDP to retreat and revitalize. At the same time, the LDP and the bureaucracy would cooperate in making the Socialists look like fools. The Socialists lacked a realistic program for managing Japan and its international relations, and everyone knew it. As *Fortune* correctly put it, "think of [the Socialist win] as something like a college all-star baseball team scoring three runs off the San Francisco Giants in the top of the first inning. There are 8½ innings to go—and the major-league team has patience, experience, and better batters."[9]

Indeed, by the second and third innings, the college all-star team was on the defensive. Within two months after her July triumph, Doi was facing bitter fights within her party over the number of women who would be allowed to run in the Lower House election and over the policy of the party itself.

Particularly disappointing was that the men who really controlled the party were not willing to allow a repeat of the Madonna strategy in the vastly more important Lower House. Doi's goal was to field at least 50 more Socialist candidates to add to the already decided list of 130, among whom only two were women, including Doi. Even a full list of 180 would not have been enough for a majority in the 512-seat Lower House, but it could conceivably allow the Socialists to emerge in a position to lead a coalition.

Doi naturally hoped that a large percentage of the new Socialist candidates would be women. But because of Japan's system of multiple-seat constituencies, that meant some of these Socialist women would run against old-guard Socialist men. These incumbent male Socialists were not about to allow themselves to be overturned. "Given these facts, it is almost a wonder that the JSP remains popular with many women and feminists, who believe the party will increase the role of women in politics," wrote one Japanese journalist.[10] This was only one sign that the Japanese media as a whole were turning against Doi. They had built her up, and now, with equal speed, they began tearing her down. In the end, Doi was able to field only eight female candidates in the February 1990 Lower House elections, a far cry from the high expectations that prevailed only a few months earlier.

Doi also ran into trouble with former party chairman Masashi Ishibashi, who had allowed Doi to become party chairman but who attempted to continue exercising real control. In September he said he would give up his seat in Parliament to protest Doi's "fascist" leadership style. She was trying to exercise real power, but she was running into brick walls.[11]

To compound her troubles, the LDP whipped up a minor but nasty scandal about the Socialist Party accepting contributions from the *pachinko* industry. Many of the *pachinko* parlor operators are Korean and some of them are sympathetic to Communist North Korea. Suddenly there were allegations that North Korean money had flowed into the Socialist Party's coffers. Ideological conflicts among the various wings of the party erupted at about the same time. "Three months after its historic victory in the Diet's Upper House, the Japan Socialist party's honeymoon is over," Konosuke Kuwabara wrote in the *Japan Economic Journal.*[12]

At the same time, the LDP was moving smoothly to co-opt Doi's issues. Indeed, the ruling party is famous for this, as Princeton University's Japan specialist, Kent Calder, has observed. When the LDP faces a crisis, it compensates by absorbing, co-opting, or preempting the source of the challenge.[13] On agriculture, the LDP switched gears and announced that it was going to increase the amount of food Japan produces domestically to reduce dependence on imported food. This would slow the liberalization of Japan's agricultural imports. The LDP also said it would spend more on housing and seek tax breaks for housewives who worked part-time. The Japanese began getting used to the 3 percent consumption tax and the popular Ryutaro Hashimoto, as finance minister, began using his own photograph in advertisements to persuade the Japanese to accept the tax. Some minor changes were contemplated, but essentially the Japanese were being asked to buy something they had rejected only a few months earlier.

To compete with Doi's telegenic ways, a new generation of LDP men was pushed into the limelight. The new prime minister was Toshiki Kaifu, fifty-nine, who had been plucked from the obscurity of the smallest faction. He had even less power than his predecessor, Uno, but he made a big public relations hit by going to America and, with his wife standing by his side, throwing out the first ball at an American baseball game. This was an entirely new brand of slick LDP packaging. The voters loved it.

By October 1989, the atmosphere was entirely different. The LDP was consolidating, as evidenced in a by-election win and by the polls. The LDP's support level, once as low as 20 percent, had now returned to 42 percent. The leadership set the Lower House elections for February 18, 1990, when memories of the events of 1989 had faded further. Recruit was over. Uno was over. The consumption tax problem was easing. The agricultural issue had been defanged.

Doi recognized, well before the February balloting, that her forward momentum had been checked. In December, when young supporters held up a poster declaring, "Doi for Prime Minister," she said: "It sounds a bit premature."[14] Power was no longer right in front of her eyes.

The final results showed that the Socialists did make gains in the Lower House, but they came almost entirely at the expense of other opposition parties. The LDP's majority was barely dented, and nearly all the senior LDP men tainted by Recruit, including Nakasone, were re-elected.

The LDP used all the resources and all the levers at its disposal to turn the Socialists into a flash in the pan, but there was also a shift in thinking among Japanese voters. As former Prime Minister Takeshita put it: "They used the iron fist against the LDP, but they realized it was too strong."

Party	(Lower House) Seat Distribution Following the February Elections	Previous Distribution
LDP	286*	295
Socialists	139	83
Komeito	46	55
Communists	16	27
Democratic Socialists	14	26
Others	11	26
	512	512

*Including 11 independents who chose to align with the LDP.

Ultimately, the Japanese have a conservative streak that makes them unwilling to accept untried alternatives. Voting for Doi and the Socialists in the July Upper House elections had been cost-free. They did not have to bear the risk that she would exercise power. "There may be growing discontent, but people are not that unhappy," said Tadashi Yamamoto of the Japan Center for International Exchange. "They're not willing to go to the other alternatives. Although we got mad at the LDP, it became clear that the Socialists were not a better alternative."

This was the pattern veteran Japan-watchers had seen time and again in Japan's postwar political history. There were moments of fluidity, but the supremely adaptive system had never cracked. Top Japanologist Chalmers Johnson put it best: "All of us who work in the field of modern Japan have files of articles from the past forty years claiming that 'Japan is at the crossroads' when all that Japan actually did was look at the crossroads but not choose a new direction."[15]

If the LDP was reconsolidating its grip, so, too, were Kanemaru and the forces of the telecommunications kingdom. With Shinto and Ezoe on trial and Nakasone subdued, the decade-long fight for control appeared to be moving toward a denouement. One key tool was the Ministry of Posts and Telecommunications (MPT) and its renewed attempt to break up Nippon Telegraph and Telephone (NTT). Although Shinto had also tried to spin off pieces of NTT, this time it was the bureaucrats who were proposing it. And it seemed clear they were proposing to do it with a twist: Breaking up NTT would smash Shinto's old power base and greatly expand the ministry's grip. The phrase "organizational reform" was particularly threatening.

This fight had been building throughout the Recruit crisis, but in Shinto's absence and after the LDP's convincing comeback, it appeared to escalate. The new NTT president was Haruo Yamaguchi, who had been the number three man under Shinto and Kitahara. By all accounts, he had survived by remaining neutral throughout the civil war.

There were economic arguments flying back and forth between the two camps about tariffs, management efficiency, and the need for effective competition. But the real struggle was, at least to some extent, along the old fault lines. Yamaguchi, incredibly, issued a public statement alleging that the MPT was trying to "tighten political control" over NTT. Other players—such as the Ministry of International Trade and Industry (MITI); the Ministry of Finance, which still held 70 percent of NTT's shares; and the Keidanren—were again engaged in a fluid, multisided struggle.

At a small luncheon meeting with foreign correspondents in the Palace Hotel, overlooking the Imperial Palace, Yamaguchi, a former bureaucrat himself, was asked who was trying to tighten political control. "It is not that I know clearly and specifically who are the ones who are trying to tighten control," said Yamaguchi with a stone face. It seemed hard to believe that he simply did not know, though the fight was taking place through a bewildering series of panels, advisory groups, and the like. Perhaps individual bureaucrats and politicians were shielding their personal stands. All Yamaguchi would offer by way of explanation was that "Japanese bureaucrats want to have stronger control over our approvals and various rules."[16]

Although it seemed clear that Yamaguchi was involved in another political struggle, his only comment was: "Apart from what Dr. Shinto was doing, our policy is to try to talk to people in politics who have an interest in telecommunications to seek their understanding." This appeared to be a reference to the LDP men in the telecommunications *zoku*, whose understanding is gained in only one way. The fact that Yamaguchi was willing to be even this candid with foreigners, combined with Shinto's absence, suggested that he was on the defensive in the battle to establish a new telecommunications order.

It was going to take months, if not years, to establish the new order. The betting was that even if the MPT did not succeed in actually breaking up NTT, it would gradually win its struggle to expand influence. Seizaburo Sato, the Nakasone confidant, believed the ministry would not only have broad sway over the old Den Den family companies but also over the telecommunications companies that had previously resisted its influence under NTT domination. It would not be the same kind of control the MPT exercised in the old days, controlling every procurement decision. It would be a step more subtle. "Even if their power is limited, their territory expands," Sato said. As in feudal days, it was better to have limited power over a broader territory than absolute power over a tiny area.

NEC, Fujitsu, Hitachi, Oki, and others would not enjoy the same degree of preferential treatment they had traditionally enjoyed, but then they did not need it. "It's not fatal for them," Sato explained. "They are the biggest companies in the field. They can compete without government protection."

As for the politicians, they would also gain because as the telecommunications field grew, there would be more opportunities for funding. Politicians in the telecommunications *zoku* did not particularly care where the money came from, as long as it kept coming in increasing quantities. The historical pattern would suggest that a period of *wa*, or harmony, was in the making.

So a new kind of harmonious triangle appeared to be developing. The old Iron Triangle was no longer needed. A greater measure of competition had been introduced. The ministry's control had been diluted by one step. But it seemed that much the same reality was being reestablished—only in a different, more subtle form.

In the political sphere, Kanemaru was triumphant. Doi's gains in July actually helped him wield influence over a somewhat chastened LDP leadership. In August and September, he was at the high point of his career. He was kingmaker. The unavoidable implication was that he had bound Takeshita into a tighter orbit. Kanemaru's cograndparent had been disciplined—not too much, but enough. Power was coursing through Kanemaru's veins.

The *Financial Times* of London wrote:

> It is Mr. Kanemaru who has been pulling the strings as the LDP lurched its way toward selecting a new leader, even though he holds no party or government post. Mooted as a candidate himself, he craftily withdrew last week and then insisted that no one else within his [also Takeshita's] faction—the LDP's largest—run either. That put him in a position of being able to deliver the votes that any other candidate would need to win. And sure enough, he was the one who, through backroom negotiations with other factions, orchestrated the emergence of Mr. Toshiki Kaifu.[17]

The pictures of Kanemaru on the front pages and the images of him on television showed that he had aged dramatically. His hair was much thinner. The lines and pockets of his face had deepened considerably. But not only was he a driving political force, he was winning major pork-barrel projects. He was able, for example, to secure a magnetically levitating train project, the dream train of the twenty-first century, for his home constituency of Yamanashi Prefecture in the best of the old Tanaka fashion. The research and development (R&D) stage alone would cost $2.3 billion, and his prefecture would get much of that. Miraculously, Kanemaru had invested in a lavish country club right next to a proposed interchange on the dream train and stood to make millions.[18] He may have been aging, but his instincts were still razor sharp.

All this is not to say that the events that culminated in late 1989 were not significant. They were. But the events on the surface were a by-product of deeper phenomena. One was the sudden and sensational explosion of wealth in Japan, another was the implicit but clear recognition that Japan had emerged as a player on the world stage. It had power. It no longer needed to give in to the Americans on agricultural or distribution reform. Pressure to open up the telecommunications sphere was suddenly not as important as it had been. This all contributed to a heady feeling. The system needed to strike a new balance and a new tone. Some steam needed to be let off. If one subscribes to the theory of tribe in explaining Japan, it was a tribal cleansing ritual, a purification. But there was no cracking of the postwar order, no sudden deviation from Japan's chosen course.

Part Three

INTO THE FUTURE

❖ 12 ❖

The Political System Rolls On

After a year of scandal and embarrassment, some Japanese leaders argue that Japan's politics is headed for major reform. A new generation of LDP men will adopt a new code of ethics and a new style, and the system, as a whole, will evolve from essentially a one-party system toward a more thoroughly Western multiparty style. This line of reasoning pleases the outside world because Japanese politics is widely seen as holding the key to improved U.S.-Japanese relations. Much foreign commentary concentrates on how it is just a matter of time before Japan's political system makes "concessions" to ease economic friction with the Americans. As younger, more cosmopolitan LDP leaders move up the ladder, they will presumably act more on the basis of Western values.

But rather than fading, the money-politics link shows signs of actually deepening as more money than ever before pours into politics. The flow just shifted channels; it did not dry up. The flow of money will continue in probably ever-growing amounts, certainly in election years. In some respects, this implies less transparency in fund-raising, not more. The new generation of LDP men in their fifties who are moving into power are certainly more articulate and "internationalized" than their elders, but they clearly have a stake in maintaining the flow of funds and the LDP's dominance in Japanese political life. Rather than being fresh blood, many represent the consolidation of power in the hands of Japan's traditional political families.

As we'll explore further in Chapter 13, powerful, conservative forces are on the move throughout the Japanese governing structure. The traditional political system is consolidating in some respects, adapting in others, but it is clearly rolling on with no real challenge. Arguably, it is becoming more Japanese-like, not more American-like. In view of Japan's success and vast power, it is only natural that the Japanese would move toward a decision-making system more in consonance with their traditional values and attitudes. As a result, the weight of real decision making is shifting to more distinctively Japanese ways that lie beneath the trappings of a democratic edifice partly imposed by the United States.

There did appear to be minor disruptions in political fund-raising in the May–July period of 1989 as companies turned down some politicians' requests to buy fund-raising tickets, but later in the year and early in 1990, as preparations moved into high gear for the Lower House elections in February, the use of political stocks, whose value is manipulated to benefit politicians holding those shares, resurfaced. The LDP itself was engaged in a virtual feeding frenzy of fund-raising from Japanese business. The party, its factions, and its candidates were widely reported to have raised and spent nearly $1 billion in the months leading up to the February election. Fund-raising and spending were running at higher rates than ever before.[1]

In view of the sensitivity about money-politics displayed only a few months earlier, the brazen manner in which political figures sought to literally buy votes was surprising. In one incident, envelopes containing a 5,000-yen note (about $35) and a letter from an LDP candidate seeking support were delivered to dozens of homes in the Kobe area. In other constituencies, politicians handed out riceballs and confectionery containing 10,000-yen notes.[2]

Keeping track of the channels through which this money flowed was becoming increasingly difficult. It was widely agreed that the flow of funds to Diet members who belonged to individual *zoku* remained strong. The flow of funds from individual factions to their members was clearly in trouble, but the LDP leadership itself, above the factional level, charged back into the fund-raising fray and was attempting to raise an estimated $200 million from the banking, construction, electric machinery, securities, and auto industries.[3] Another increasingly important source of campaign funds was businesses and local elites in Diet members' districts who had traditionally not been big contributors.

The fact that Japanese politics is fueled by money was also reflected more and more in the choice of candidates, resulting in greater concentration of power in the hands of political families. The United States has had its LaGuardias, Daleys, and Longs, but their grip on political power has gradually eased, if not faded altogether, over the years. In Japan, however, the number of second-generation lawmakers is increasing rapidly. In the Lower House, which was standing for reelection, 84.2 percent of the Dietmen under the age of forty had inherited their seats; of those aged forty and above, 50.3 percent inherited. For those over fifty years of age, 44.2 percent of the seats have been passed down, and for those over the age of sixty, a mere 25.6 percent have been passed down. Thus the younger the politician in Japan, the greater the chances that he represents inherited family-based power.[4] They are not rebels.

Nearly half the 275 LDP representatives elected in February had inherited their seats. Why is so much political power inherited in Japan? The answer stems from the way the Japanese view their politicians, what specialists call the "values context." The Japanese do not expect political or moral leadership from the politicians they elect, the way many Americans do. What they expect is that their elected officials will be able to bring them tangible, physical benefits. This, in itself, is not terribly different from the way many Americans—who want better bridges, dams, and highways—view their congressmen. It's part of the political game in virtually any country. But the Japanese concentrate on the material benefits far more than any abstract moral or political principles. There is little principle other than money itself.

In Japanese politics, the pundits speak of *"jiban, kaban,* and *kanban."* *Jiban* means a regional organization of supporters. *Kaban* refers to the amount of money a candidate has. *Kanban* means fame, or the degree to which someone is known. One needs all of these qualities to be in a position to provide the material benefits that one's constituents expect. The Japanese, for example, expect their politicians to give them money when they get married or when they bury loved ones. Accounts vary, but it is not unusual to hear that a Diet member has to attend six or seven weddings and as many as twenty-five funerals in a given month. He needs to bring about $75 to a funeral, and double that to each wedding.

One Dietman told me that a Little League system in his district even demanded that he send a trophy to the team that won the championship. If his constituents are having a banquet, the Dietman is expected to send bottles of whiskey. Although Japanese politicians do not engage in massive television campaigning, Dietmen do face enormous pressures to keep the benefits flowing to their constituents.

This helps explain why Japanese voters want to elect the sons or sons-in-law of well-established politicians to replace them: They are more likely to be able to keep the gravy train rolling. "From the party's point of view, there is safety in nominating family members and relatives of well-known politicians, because it is easier to get the recognition and support from voters throughout the campaign," says Professor Iwai. In short, there is a bias against outsiders breaking into the political system. The fact that several members of the LDP must compete against each other for a given seat also means that the competition to dispense money at weddings and funerals will continue, if not accelerate. There is no sign that the government will scrap this system in favor of single-seat constituencies any time soon.

Thus, despite talk about a more Western-style democracy that increasingly operated on the basis of international standards, the greater force was toward more diverse and in some cases subterranean forms of political fund-raising. "The hugeness of the money required is beyond anyone's honest toiling work," complained former Finance Minister Kiichi Miyazawa, one of the five LDP faction leaders. Can the link between money and politics be severed? "It's almost impossible," he replied.

In the final analysis, the LDP's ability to beat back the Recruit investigation and smoothly reconsolidate power meant that fundamental political reform was not necessary. The LDP was going to remain in power on its own terms. If it had been forced into the opposition, it might have had greater incentive to push for genuine change. Although Prime Minister Kaifu was pressing for electoral reform, Japan's top poltical fund-raisers were remarkably candid (in private) in telling foreigners that this was designed merely for public consumption. "At the *honne* level, we will resist," said one.

This has been part of the pattern of Japan's postwar political scandals. When the LDP is on the defensive, as it was in early and mid-1989, major changes are suddenly brought up to help regain public trust. These included eliminating the multiseat constituencies, requiring all legislators to disclose their personal assets, imposing tougher restrictions on corporate ticket purchases for fund-raising parties, and even disbanding the party factions. There is an outcry after every scandal. A new measure may be rushed into place but little changes. There was just as much chance that lawmakers would suddenly transform their fund-raising habits as there was a chance that they would respect the code of ethics that was rushed into place after the Lockheed scandal— and that was precious little. Diet member Yohei Kono, who once left the LDP to set up a short-lived reform party called the New Liberal Club, put it in a particularly stinging way: "The LDP is not capable of true reform."[5] Professor Takeshi Sasaki, professor of political science at Tokyo University, added, "When it comes to reform, the Liberal Democratic party will only do what's good for the party."[6]

Predicting the future of politics is risky. The Japanese have a saying that reflects confusion in their own minds about how their political system works: "In Japanese politics, darkness lies only one step ahead." Although it is impossible to foresee the precise configuration of political power, it is relatively easy to pinpoint the leaders who will be increasingly important.

Kanemaru appears to have begun the process of grooming Ichiro Ozawa as his heir apparent. Ozawa, only forty-seven, is also said to enjoy good relations with Takeshita. In fact, this is one of the keys to Ozawa's power base: He can maneuver smoothly between Kanemaru and Takeshita. He is one of the boys. Ozawa, who is now secretary-general of the LDP and who has been instrumental in the party's fund-raising, would exercise power in much the same way his mentors have and would presumably represent the construction industry in particular. He is emerging as a heavyweight in the inner circles and easily dominates the distinctly unpowerful Prime Minister Kaifu in party affairs. His detractors have nicknamed him a "mini-Tanaka" because of his fondness for the direct exercise of raw power. One problem Ozawa might face, however, is that if both his mentors were to leave the scene, his base of support might not be as broad as he thinks.

Two other members of this new generation of prime-ministerial candidates are Finance Minister Ryutaro Hashimoto, and former Self-Defense Agency chief Koichi Kato. There are others, but these two represent the spread of attitudes and styles.

Hashimoto, fifty-two, possesses a combination of traits that make him a major force in Japanese politics and suggest he will play an even more powerful role, which is the reason he poses a threat to such party elders as Kanemaru. Hashimoto is a second-generation political leader. His father was health and welfare minister twice, once during the Occupation and again later. He obtained control of the health and welfare *zoku* and later it was handed down to his son, who also served a stint as minister. There's no firm evidence of just how much money this *zoku* generates; probably not as much as telecommunications or construction, but it is considerable nonetheless. To top it off, the younger Hashimoto is married to a relation of the Imperial family. So he is a personal example of how the system is consolidating. He sits astride several key channels of power from the LDP, the bureaucracy, the world of electoral finance, and the Imperial family.

With his long sideburns and slicked-back, Elvis-style hair, he is personally charismatic. It is clear from the way he greets voters that he is accustomed to power. With foreign journalists, he knows when to smile, when to flatter, and when to turn to steel. To put it in Buddhist terms, he is a man in control of his vehicle. As finance minister, he is already one of the most powerful men in the government, and he almost certainly will be prime minister one day. He is not a man enamored of the United States. "I experienced Japan losing the war when I was in second grade," he said in an interview. "Japan regained independence when I was in junior high school. I am positioned in the midpoint of the generations who lived prior to and after the war." He believes that Japanese who are older than he, and who remember the magnanimous manner in which the Americans administered and fed a hungry Japan, have a certain sympathy for the United States.

But Hashimoto clearly defines his life, at least in part, as one of struggle against the U.S. "I graduated university in 1960 and joined the private sector," he recalled. "It was a textile company and I was a salaryman. The first thing I encountered was U.S. restrictions against cotton exports. It had been the textile special relationship. Then it became the textile war." This was the beginning of postwar U.S.-Japanese trade friction. Although a minor footnote in the minds of most U.S. analysts of trade relations, it obviously left a deep impact on Hashimoto. It was soon thereafter that his father died and his father's supporters lured the younger Hashimoto into running for the Diet and assuming control of the health and welfare *zoku.*

"Our generation," Hashimoto continued, "has keenly felt the recognition that the U.S. is doing away with the stance of helping from above and has now come to see us as an equal competitor. The present [Japanese] leaders are not able to ease their perception that the U.S. will always understand and always make concessions."

The point he was building to came quickly thereafter: "In the past, Japan was asked to give way and make concessions to an extreme level. But now there will be fewer cases. That trend will be in decline. Japan will make compromises where reasonable and appropriate. So what happens in the years ahead is that Japan will be speaking more clearly and expressing itself more accurately. We're just in the process of making that transition. Due to lack of mutual understanding, the relationship could be hurt in a very destructive manner." This is as tough a line as any mainstream Japanese politician can take publicly.

Hashimoto faces some resistance within the LDP because he's too assertive and too popular. He is not self-effacing enough. Even though he is a member of the Takeshita faction, he is a bitter enemy of old man Kanemaru. Soon after the Kaifu government was formed, the old guard maneuvered Hashimoto into the usually prestigious job of finance minister. The intent was to saddle Hashimoto with what appeared to be a thankless, and politically damaging, task: managing the consumption tax issue. But Hashimoto cashed in on his popularity and launched the apparently successful advertising campaign to sell the tax to the voters. He will be a hard man to keep down.

Fellow prime-ministerial contender Kato, fifty, is roundish in physique with thick black-rimmed glasses, but his modest appearance conceals a phenomenal intellect. With credentials from both Tokyo University and Harvard, Kato is fluent in English and his Chinese is impressive. His linguistic ability, and his command of Japan's foreign policy issues, make him a hit with Americans even while he clearly defends Japanese interests. He is a second-generation politician and former bureaucrat who has a strong position in the Miyazawa faction and sits astride flows of funds from the defense and agriculture *zoku*. At the same time that Kato is accessible and appealing, he is an increasingly influential power player. It is a fine line that he walks.

Kato is considered somewhat dovish in comparison with Hashimoto. His colleagues in the LDP see him as too soft, too intellectual. He visits the United States occasionally and nurtures relations with prominent Americans, which would be crucial to managing U.S.-Japanese relations but at the same time raises questions at home about his Japanese credentials. He believes that the Japanese "cannot survive without strong international relations." That does not mean he wants Japan to cave in to anyone, but rather that Japan should manage its relations with other countries to its own best advantage. He may sound more dovish than Hashimoto, but in many respects he is simply more sophisticated.

Part of the difference in view between Hashimoto and Kato can be attributed to the ways they responded to the American Occupation. "Along with neighboring children and friends, I rushed to see the American jeep," Kato said over an evening drink in Tokyo. "We were so glad to be given chocolate. My father was mayor and made a courtesy call to the officer in charge. The officer offered him a bottle of Coca-Cola. My father said, 'Do I have to return the bottle?' The Occupation officer laughed and said, 'No, you can keep it.'

"But glass was very precious. I took it to my home, and dropped it. The bottle didn't break. I was amazed at its quality. This was the United States. This kind of perception of the U.S. existed for a long time in my mind. You gave us food. You gave us time to protect our infant industries. If you had not allowed us to make the barriers, Japanese industry could not have existed. We know the past. We are very efficient. You are not competitive at the moment. But we have to think about the future."

Although Kato today thinks the Americans are "not competitive," which is quite a stark judgment, he does recognize that the Americans have potentially broad economic power. His basic advice to Americans is: "Recover your confidence in your basic capacity. You accomplish things when you are determined. Against the Soviets in space, you won."

The irony is that at the same time he is able to appear almost sympathetic to Americans, he also says things that would sound ominous coming from a tough guy like Hashimoto. At the Asia Society in New York, for example, Kato was asked whether Japan would follow the U.S. lead in managing relations with China following the Tiananmen massacre. He replied that "we are going to be a little bit independent on this one." That is tremendously controversial because it harks back to the period when Japan occupied large parts of China, but no one in the room batted an eyelash. And Kato does not have any interest in moderating Japan's economic pace: "If you Americans can't compete, we have the right to continue innovating," he says bluntly. If Hashimoto said this, he might trigger an angry American reaction.

Ozawa, Hashimoto, Kato, and other members of the emerging generation of political leaders are called "neo-new leaders" to distinguish them from the "new leaders" (Takeshita, Miyazawa, and Abe) who were in line to succeed Nakasone. Members of this new generation define themselves not in a postwar sense but rather in terms of their response to Occupation. They remember little about how World War II started, only that the Americans ended it and occupied Japan. There would be some differences in tone between a more combative Hashimoto and a more sophisticated, disarming Kato, but none of the neo-new leaders would be a pushover. Americans waiting for a generational change of LDP leadership because it would usher in a period of dramatic Japanese concessions on trade and investment are destined for disappointment. The next generation of LDP leaders are in many respects a more powerful, sophisticated breed than their predecessors.

Entire books have been written comparing the similarities of the official U.S. and Japanese political systems.[7] These similarities definitely exist. But what most traditional analysis fails to consider is just what percentage of the *total* decision-making process in each country can be accounted for by the observable political process. Transparency is the U.S. ideal, as spelled out by the Founding Fathers when they devised a governing system. It is credible to argue that 70 percent of what the U.S. government does is transparent. That means that an outsider can figure out this percentage of the process. But he or she can't see everything; 30 percent is still invisible. One does not fully understand what the lobbyists are up to, or what takes place in subcabinet meetings, or what the president says in a confidential chat with the Speaker of the House.

Transparency is not the ideal in Japan. About 70 percent of the total decision-making process takes place where no outsider can see it, and 30 percent where it can be seen, the opposite ratio of the United States. Japan's underlying decision-making system was never written down and codified. It has developed over many hundreds of years. Today, the deliberations of the Diet represent just a fraction of the real process. "The Diet is becoming rather ceremonial," observed former MITI vice minister Makato Kuroda, who in his three decades inside this ministry earned a reputation as a tough negotiator. "Everything is decided before a bill is tabled [introduced]."[8]

Beneath the Western-style political mechanisms, who drives the decision making? How does it happen? According to Naohiro Amaya, a predecessor of Kuroda's in the job as MITI vice minister and a graduate of the University of Tokyo's Law Department, "We cannot objectively explain our decision-making system to the outside world. Even Japanese don't understand it. It's like the brain of a child that grows up as the child grows."

In the case of Japan's brain, the common link between many of the different nodes is the educational background of the participants. This is why the University of Tokyo's Law Department is so important. Van Wolferen was correct in identifying the Law Department as being at the heart of this underlying decision-making system.[9] It is probably more accurate to think of this level as a neural network of personal relationships that takes an organic form than as a "system," which implies that it has been codified and structured.

Some 90 percent of all top civil servants are graduates of Tokyo University's Law Department, which produces only six hundred to seven hundred graduates each year. "We don't really practice law in law school," explained Kuroda. "It's more general. To become a real lawyer, it's necessary to pass a very difficult examination. It requires two to three years of study [after law school], then two years of training. Then you become a lawyer or a prosecutor or a judge. Only a few become lawyers."

The most important aspect of going to Tokyo University's Law Department is not the academic training, but the kind of *jinmyaku*, or network of acquaintances, it provides. Taizo Watanabe, the official Foreign Ministry spokesman and another Law Department alumnus, for example, occasionally has dinner with a Keidanren official, or meets socially with business or political leaders. This is made possible by clubs for Tokyo University graduates who were born in the same year. Watanabe belongs to the Year of the Dog Club. "It's like a country club," he remarked. "You can talk to anyone." Likewise at MITI, Hirobumi Kodama, a key official involved in U.S.-Japanese relations, proudly tells visitors that he is the coach of the University of Tokyo sailing club, and it's clear that this is an important conduit for identifying and recruiting talented new bureaucrats.

These informal networks throughout "the brain"—some horizontal, others vertical—may be nearly as important as the way bureaucrats and politicians execute their official functions. It is through these channels that information and influence often move, not in a predictable manner but on a constantly shifting course.

In this Japanese decision-making system, there is no center, no president where the buck stops. The trade men know about trade, the scientific men know about science, the finance men know about money. They have different networks or channels, often the result of their educational ties. No one has a complete overview. "We don't have a center the way you have a center," former Finance Minister Miyazawa said. "In our power structure, everybody knows everybody else. It is elitist perhaps. We can tell by rule of thumb what the likely outcome [of any given situation] is going to be, what kind of decision is going to be made. There is no foreign element. It is homogeneous. It is not a system the way you have a system."

Not all of Japan's leaders are from the University of Tokyo. Keio and Waseda universities also produce their own networks of graduates, though there are differences between the quality and sophistication of the networks generated by these schools. Tokyo and Keio graduates tend to dominate the ranks of Japanese serving abroad, whereas Waseda graduates are more prevalent in Japanese domestic politics and the mass media. The University of Kyoto is also important in grooming future elites. Despite any differences among these leaders owing to their university backgrounds, they are stamped with a common culture. "The system is not monolithic," says one top LDP man. "The culture is."

So, on an institutionalized scale, Japan's top leaders can engage in a form of personal networking and clue-reading that America's top leaders certainly cannot. It's almost like *ishin denshin*, the ability to anticipate what the other desires. When it becomes obvious to the most powerful participants that something must be done, that recognition is transmitted to the official, visible decision-making apparatus. The "brain" has functioned smoothly—and invisibly to the outside world.

Although some Japanese point to evidence that their political system is suddenly evolving along Western lines, it is more likely that precisely the opposite is occurring. The underlying level of decision making is less transparent and less Western than ever. This is the level that harbors more important clues to understanding the future shape of Japanese politics. How any new prime minister conducts himself, for example, depends on the attitudes that prevail at this level. Unlike an American president, who sweeps into office and imposes his vision on the government as thoroughly as possible, most Japanese prime ministers are shaped by the group and the nation, the mood of which is becoming more confident, assertive, and, indeed, nationalistic.

❖ 13 ❖

Nationalistic Drift?

Near the entrance to Yasukuni, arguably Japan's most important State Shinto shrine, Japanese veterans of World War II stand with microphones, haranguing passersby about General Douglas MacArthur and asking if the Americans really needed to drop two atomic bombs. The entrance gate itself is marked by chrysanthemum seals. The flower is the official symbol of the Emperor, and inside the compound can be found exhibits of chrysanthemum that have been precisely nurtured, shaped, and clipped.

Inside the temple compound, a handful of children chase white doves, the symbol of purity, while on an outdoor stage older Japanese men sing samurai war songs and women perform the traditional *kenbu* dancing. Perhaps fifty yards away is an exhibit of Japanese World War II military equipment, including battleship turrets, antiaircraft guns, and artillery. Signs praise the Japanese technology displayed in these weapons. Overhead, the Imperial Navy's war flag, the rising sun at dawn, flutters in the October breeze. In a museum can be found an old Zero fighter plane. There are many buildings in the compound, and at some outlying private shrines can be found businessmen in dark suits who ease into the temple grounds in big black Mercedes Benz cars. Elsewhere can be glimpsed Shinto priests in their clog shoes, white robes, and distinctive hats.

The main event of this autumn festival is at the big shrine, where priests usher hundreds of Japanese, overwhelmingly over the age of fifty, into the inner recesses to honor the 2.5 million Japanese who have died in various wars over the course of the past century, including all those killed in World War II. What the Americans call Class A war criminals are among them. All these names are listed and kept on record for posterity. Foreigners have never seen the innermost sanctum of this main temple.

It's difficult for an American to assess Yasukuni dispassionately. It's wrong to suggest that the Japanese do not have the right to honor their war dead. This is a subject that leads very quickly to highly emotional responses. "You Americans assume that American war dead are more valuable than Japanese war dead," snapped Seizaburo Sato, the University of Tokyo professor and Nakasone confidant. "Americans should go to Arlington, but Japanese shouldn't go to Yasukuni. It's not fair. It's only common compassion for people who died on the battlefield."

It is indeed natural to remember those fallen in battle. But to some extent, the State Shinto religion and the symbols of Japanese culture are being used in a political context. The original Shinto religion does not embrace the Emperor, military strength, or technology. State Shinto is a creation of the late nineteenth century, and it was designed as a rationale for glorifying the Emperor and consolidating political control. It was also used to lead the nation into war. Thus, Yasukuni brings together the Emperor, religion, the military, technology, traditional Japanese culture, rice, and other symbols. This is not just a place where the dead are honored. It is also a place where there is an attempt under way to give new birth to old ideas.

Yasukuni has made a gradual comeback over the years. Americans who lived in Tokyo in the 1960s recall the shrine as abandoned and dilapidated. Twenty-five years later, it is obviously well endowed and is being renovated. It claims 8 million annual visitors. And many ministers of the Japanese government visit it in their official capacities each August 15, the anniversary of the end of World War II.

Ivan Hall, an American professor of Japanese history at Keio University, believes the Germans did a more thorough job in turning the corner on their prewar ideology than have some of Japan's conservative elites. "The conservative forces here have not cleansed themselves," says Hall. Helmut Kohl, the West German chancellor, may have visited Bitburg, where some SS troops are buried, but he also laid a wreath at the Auschwitz death camp in Poland. "They have never gone through the process of reflection that the Germans went through after World War II. A few have done it, but not many. Under the cover of an American alliance, they have a sort of gridlock on the Japanese political system. The people who are leaders of the establishment of the postwar period do not really represent a change of heart or a real break in motivation and outlook, whereas in Germany they did." It is a well-documented point. Many of the men judged war criminals in Japan were allowed to leave jail in the early 1950s and help Japan's government organize the postwar economic recovery.

Although this attempt to revitalize State Shinto is being supported by business and political elites, as well as the criminal underground, a clear majority of Japanese do not support it. Nor do they openly support attempts to revive the Imperial tradition, an acceleration of Japan's rearming, or the rewriting of Japanese history textbooks. Most Japanese under the age of forty or forty-five scoff at the rightists and at those attempting to resurrect the past. Right-wing sound trucks have coursed through the streets for decades, blasting their messages out over loudspeakers, but they are almost universally ignored. The polls indicate a clear rejection of their message.

The danger is not an overt embrace of the right-wing message as much as it is that the attitudes will seep into a broader body politic that is peculiarly vacant. If love of country is called patriotism, the word *nationalism* implies a desire and willingness to see one's country prevail over others. There is a fine line between revived self-confidence and pride in Japan, which could be considered mere patriotism, and more alarming nationalism. At least some experts believe they detect an implicit and unknowing drift toward nationalism that is more important than any conscious embrace of Emperor-worship. "Our educational system, for all its rigor, does not produce truly cultured people. In terms of nonmaterial values, Japan is a wasteland," laments Mikio Sumiya, a professor emeritus at the University of Tokyo. "Promoters of a prewar style of nationalism have rushed to fill the vacuum. The public, immature and aimless, is easy prey for these opportunistic charlatans."[1]

The notion that healthy patriotism in Japan too often veers into nationalism, in a way that does not happen as readily in Germany, is becoming more widely accepted by American historians and intellectuals. Historian Arthur Schlesinger went so far as to say that Japan "is even more mystical, portentous and humorless in its hypernationalist traditions than Germany and far more scornful of other countries."[2]

Movies are part of the effort to spread old ideas. At night on the Ginza, the bright neon lights of NEC and other Japanese companies glitter atop the many-storied buildings. In a cinema in the Yurakucho Marion building one evening, two American movies were showing: *Working Girl* and *Indiana Jones and the Last Crusade.* Also showing was a Japanese-made movie called simply *2-26*.

February 26 was the date in 1936 when a group of young military officers staged a coup against Japan's civilian government. Believing, apparently falsely, that they were acting on behalf of the Emperor, they charged into the homes of government ministers in the middle of the night and assassinated them. The young officers thought the ministers were resisting the Emperor's will. Although their coup attempt was put down by more senior Army officers, it represented one step in the military's consolidation of power and the launching of World War II.

The new movie, which will never appear in English and certainly never be distributed commercially outside Japan, depicts the instigators as young heroes. When they gun down a cabinet minister in front of his wife and family, they stand at attention and salute, their white gloves rising in unison. One decapitates a minister with his sword. The director often flashes back to the young officers at home with their charming wives and bubbling children. They are just a bit misguided, but their fundamental mission is correct. They're nice guys, but they are betrayed by their generals. In the end, they must commit suicide. They are martyrs.

A handful of older Japanese in the audience walk out. They recognize that the film is militaristic propaganda. They lived through the insanity that this kind of thinking produced. But the vast majority of the Japanese in the theater, almost all of them under forty-five, see the movie through to its bitter and totally predictable end, munching popcorn all the while. The younger Japanese may overtly reject anything that smacks of old-school right-wing nationalism, but they are fascinated nonetheless.

Conversations at the *honne* level are also a good way to sense the drift. During an evening at the Hitotsubashi Club, where alumni of Hitotsubashi University meet, the conversation one evening veered into the sensitive territory of U.S.-Japanese relations. My host, a Mitsui salaryman, had agreed to gather a handful of friends to talk about the lives of salarymen. Mr. Mitsui was quiet as the discussion unfolded, and kept pouring more Suntory Royals for everyone. Finally he exploded.

"American troops must leave Japan," Mr. Mitsui insisted. "Having the Americans here is bad for our children. It is bad for our nation-building. It makes for bad feelings. You're not protecting Japan, you're protecting your own interests. This is our land. This is a very serious issue. It's a very basic issue for the nation-people."

His colleagues were embarrassed. Mr. Mitsubishi, wide-eyed, vainly tried to change the subject.

"Our country is better than the United Kingdom, France, or Canada, sometimes even the United States. Why don't we defend ourselves?" Mr. Mitsui continued, his hand chopping the air. "To build our own nation, we must have nation-management. It is a matter of identity."

"Why are American troops bad for your children?" I asked.

"Because every day when I go to the office, my children ask me, Father, but you work for Mitsui . . ." The implication is that if you work for Mitsui, why are you not running the country? Why are there American troops here?

"My father's generation failed forty-five years ago," he continued. "My generation's mission is how to rebuild our totality. We are a failed country from World War II. This is a reality." His father had been wounded in the Truk Islands. My father had been on a naval supply vessel near Okinawa.

It was stunning that Mr. Mitsui expressed regret not that the war broke out but that his father played a role in losing it. It was one thing for the last Class A war criminal to issue a final statement before he died apologizing for losing the war rather than for having started it. But it was another to see the same view propagated by a contemporary. Of course, not all the salarymen agreed with Mr. Mitsui, and many Japanese use their evening drinking sessions just to let off steam. Nonetheless, it is significant if only a fraction of Japanese in this age group harbor similar feelings. Overall, 52 percent of the Japanese believe they should be less dependent on the United States for defense.[3]

It was approaching 10:30 P.M. and Mr. Mitsui had to catch the train for the ninety-five-minute ride to his home in the suburbs. As we parted and bowed, he said, "Thank you very much. We need your understanding."

These anecdotes are part of a larger drama: History is up for grabs in Japan. Being essentially ahistorical, many Americans scarcely comprehend the significance of this struggle over Japanese history, which has been unfolding for at least twenty years.

The standard American view is that the Emperor and his army charged into a reckless course of foreign military expansion in the 1920s and 1930s, which included atrocities against the Chinese and Korean peoples in particular. This policy of military expansion culminated in the Japanese attack at Pearl Harbor. The Americans were forced to respond. It was a terrible war for everyone. Finally, atomic bombs were dropped. It was over. The Americans helped rebuild Japan and shielded it. They were remarkably generous in providing technology and allowing access to their market. The Japanese "owe" them something.

But there is an alternative interpretation that a Japanese patriot might espouse: Japan has been emerging ever since Commodore Perry's black ships arrived in an attempt to colonize Japan. The Japanese were forced to defeat the Russians in 1905. Then, as Japan emerged, the Americans and British tried to contain Japan, which forced a military response. The Emperor really did not have anything to do with it. It was just a handful of military leaders who got a little bit out of control. President Roosevelt lured them into attacking Pearl Harbor so that he could drag the United States into a war against Japan. Then the Americans dropped atomic bombs on the Japanese, not the Germans, because they are racist. Now that Japan has become an economic superpower, it does not need the Americans. The Japanese system is superior.

These views are extreme simplifications, but they suggest the range and scale of the debate about history in Japan. To an extent far larger than with the European theater, historians and authors and journalists are still arguing over the Emperor's role, Pearl Harbor, the decision to bomb, and the success or failure of the U.S. Occupation. Very little has been resolved. They are still open wounds.[4]

To the extent that Japanese students learn about the war, the educational curriculum has traditionally been tilted toward the conventional American view. Now the pendulum is swinging toward the alternative Japanese interpretation. The Education Ministry, backed by the LDP, is leading this fight and it is winning against professors and teachers who are worried about revived nationalism. In early 1989, the ministry succeeded in pushing through regulations that will oblige elementary and junior high schools to fly the Japanese flag at important events. At some of them, students will also be called upon to sing the "Kimigayo," an unofficial national anthem that praises the Emperor. While Americans debated the merits of burning their flag, the Japanese institutionalized respect for theirs.

It's entirely understandable that the Japanese would want to instill a greater measure of patriotism in their children. Certainly, one cannot expect that decades after the events of the 1930s and 1940s, the Japanese would want textbooks that rub their children's noses in misdeeds and defeat. "The old textbooks were anti-Japanese," complained Professor Sato.

But the Education Ministry is going beyond merely restoring a healthier balance to the books. Education Minister Kazuya Ishibashi has been quoted as saying it is important to develop students' awareness of themselves as "Japanese nationals." He added that "we will be jeered by the peoples of other countries unless we resolutely seek a national identity as Japanese."[5]

In October 1989, the Education Ministry also won a long fight against Saburo Ienaga to significantly alter Japanese history textbooks. Ienaga, seventy-six, a well-known former professor at the old Tokyo University of Education and an author of history textbooks, has pursued three lawsuits since the 1960s against the Education Ministry's insistence that it be allowed to screen, and mandate changes in, history textbooks. This is a higher-stakes struggle than it would be in the United States because Japan's curriculum is controlled at the national rather than the state or local level. To a large extent, what the Education Ministry approves is what Japanese students study.

Ienaga has tried to convey what he considers a balanced view of Japanese history, which includes the good and the bad. But the Tokyo District Court ruled that the Education Ministry's screening of textbooks is not unconstitutional. This forced Ienaga to rewrite portions of his textbook. One of the sore points in the struggle about Japanese history has been the seizure of the important Chinese city of Nanking (now called Nanjing) and the wholesale slaughter of at least 100,000 Chinese that followed at the hands of Japanese soldiers. This is not hearsay. Documentary films and pictures exist. Americans know this 1937 incident as the Rape of Nanking.

Ienaga had written that many Chinese were killed by the Imperial Japanese Army. But the ministry wanted the passage to read: "Many Chinese soldiers and civilians were murdered in the chaos." This makes it unclear who actually did the killing. Several other passages about military actions, including sexual assaults by Japanese troops and biological experimentation on thousands of Chinese in Harbin, were either excised or revised beyond recognition. This was in line with the ministry's overall campaign to turn "invasions" into "advances" and, in general, to rewrite history as most of the outside world understands it.

Ienaga, tired and sick after his long struggle, has clearly lost the fight. "There is Japanese nationalism and it's dangerous," he wrote in response to questions submitted to him. "It is important to admit Japanese sins and faults from the past so that they do not happen again. Regarding the Nanjing Massacre that the Japanese inflicted on the Chinese, every Chinese knows about the cruel behavior, but the Japanese don't know. If a Japanese goes to China and doesn't know about it, it's a shame. It's important for Japanese to admit that beautiful things are beautiful. But if they're not, it's also important to admit that they are not."

The efforts by the Education Ministry and its backers in the LDP have not escaped the attention of Japanese teachers, who have been longtime, bitter enemies of the direction the government has taken in educational matters. The Japan Teachers' Union, known as Nikkyoso, is widely reviled in conservative circles as a militant, leftist organization. This is a war in its own right. There have been so many right-wing threats and intimidation attempts that the union's headquarters in Tokyo has two video cameras mounted outside in the elevator lobby to deter harassment. The door is locked and a visitor can enter only after being thoroughly screened. Any major event that the union tries to hold is also subject to right-wing disruption. In February 1988, for example, 250 right-wing organizations mobilized 2,000 rightists and 500 cars to stage a counterdemonstration against the union's annual convention in Fukushima.[6]

Behind the locked door and two video cameras sits the union's manager of education and cultural activities, Tadashi Yaguchi. Born in 1931, he retired four years ago after a thirty-year teaching career. He acknowledges that his personal politics would be characterized as socialist, although he is not a member of the party. As someone who experienced old-school nationalism as a child, he is concerned by what he sees today. "The policy of the LDP and the ministry is nationalism, rather than internationalism," he said. "They want to create people who are useful for Japan. This contradicts the principles of the postwar educational system, to create people who seek truth and peace. They want to create elites, people who are merely talented and efficient and who are loyal to big Japanese corporations. They are teaching how Japan can have more power than other peoples. This is wrong. This allows them to believe Japan is number one. Japan is the best. I am afraid of this. This will allow Japan to do wrong against other people. They cannot force this system on the adults, so they are trying to impose it on the children."

Yaguchi's views seem to have been shaped more by his own personal experiences in the school system during the late 1930s and the war than by any infusion of Marxist cant. "When I was in primary school, the teachers didn't teach me facts about history or social sciences, only the Emperor," he recalls. "The Emperor's ancestors don't really exist, but as children we had to believe in this [Emperor is divine] system. We were taught that the Emperor system was the traditional system. We couldn't resist it.

"Back then, we didn't learn about science, for example. We learned about the kamikaze, the divine wind. If some struggle happened, the Emperor, the living god, blew a good wind so that he could win. But what was a typhoon? Was that also a kamikaze? So the teachers had to connect a typhoon with the god-wind. It wasn't just a weather system."

Like Ienaga, teachers are clearly on the defensive in the face of sustained, institutional power—and they are vastly outgunned. "The

ministry is on the offensive," Yaguchi said with an air of resignation. "We are losing."

Who is this mysterious right? In *Yakuza: The Explosive Account of Japan's Criminal Underworld*,[7] David Kaplan and Alec Dubro use the word *nexus* to describe how some elements of the LDP, bureaucracy, business elite, military, and *yakuza* underworld cooperate to create a powerful right-wing force. Ever since the 1984 death of Yoshio Kodama, a former Class A war criminal and right-wing mastermind, the far-right fringe has been without a real leader. It is a loose confederation now, a web of cooperation. The fact that leaders of the criminal underworld enjoy links with prominent politicians is not as shocking as it would be in the United States. The LDP and government used the *yakuza* to crush the left wing during the 1950s and 1960s. Some of Japan's most powerful men owe their grip on power to the underworld.

According to one of the leading authorities on the right wing, Masayuki Takagi of the *Asahi Shumbun*, the number of right-wing groups has grown during the 1980s to more than 1,000, with a total of more than 200,000 members.[8] One problem in analyzing this right wing is that the distinction between clearly criminal elements and purely political groups blurs. Among the right-wing groups, there are prewar right wings and postwar right wings. There are some right-wing groups that limit themselves to policy debates, whereas others believe in acting violently to achieve their goals. Overall, more than 80 percent of all right-wing groups have *yakuza* connections, Takagi wrote. These *yakuza* right-wingers brag of connections with top LDP men, including Tanaka and Nakasone, and they are believed to be a major source of funding for some political leaders.

What binds all these shadowy groups and factions together is their commitment to the Imperial system, called *tenno sei*. Unlike Britain, where the issue of the royal family's status is firmly resolved, the questions of the Emperor's divinity and his supposedly direct descent from the Sun Goddess more than two thousand years ago are very much alive in Japan. At Emperor Hirohito's funeral, for example, there was only a thin curtain separating State Shinto rites from the official state ceremony attended by world leaders. The devotees of Emperor-worship are also gearing up for the coronation of Prince Akihito in late 1990 at the grand shrine in Ise, central Japan, where the Sun Goddess supposedly resides. Japanese who publicly question this attempt to revive the Imperial tradition are often intimidated by right-wing thugs. When Hitoshi Motoshima, the mayor of Nagasaki, made a controversial comment in December 1988 on Hirohito's responsibility for starting World

War II, he soon found himself the subject of harassment from rightist groups. In January 1990, he was shot and badly wounded in broad daylight by an ultranationalist who was offended by his remarks about the Emperor. The attempted assassination occurred just a few days after the end of the one-year mourning period for the late Emperor.

It is not the ugly, brutal face of Japanese right-wing nationalism that sells among the Japanese themselves, but the modern face, as personified in LDP Dietman Shintaro Ishihara. He speaks very little about the Emperor. He is telegenic, well-groomed, and charming. But he has become the most visible political personality representing the right, broadly defined. A former prize-winning novelist, Ishihara, fifty-seven, is often dismissed as "fringe" and a "maverick." But younger Japanese consider him the equivalent of John F. Kennedy. They pay little attention to the content of his speeches and articles. Few of them know, or care, that one of his heroes is Minoru Genda, who planned the attack on Pearl Harbor.

A member of the Diet for twenty-one years, Ishihara first expressed his views prominently in July 1989 in *Chuo Koron,* an opinion magazine, in which he openly discussed the need for Japan to undertake major shifts in its relations with the Americans. What had angered Ishihara was the flap over whether the Americans would transfer technology to the Japanese as part of the FSX jet fighter codevelopment plan. "The time has come for us to give up the postwar consciousness and postwar systems," he wrote. "The suitable way is to proceed with domestic development of FSX, think about the constitution, and think about Japanese self-defense. We cannot fail to do this for the sake of Japan."[9] The implication is that Japan should go its own way and revise the U.S.-imposed constitution to allow for an accelerated Japanese military buildup.

Because of the linguistic barrier, the *Chuo Koron* article did not attract much attention in the United States. But Ishihara's book with Akio Morita, chairman and founder of Sony Corporation, caught on like wildfire. *The Japan That Can Say No* was the result of conversations that were recorded and transcribed. The book appeared only in Japanese in the spring of 1989 and both authors apparently assumed it would remain on that side of the prism. But bootleg translations began popping up in Washington and New York in August and September 1989, and spread rapidly through the U.S. political, journalistic, governmental, and corporate worlds. The book received wide publicity in major U.S. publications. Morita made a grievous error in publicly associating himself with Ishihara, particularly at the same time that he

was buying Columbia Pictures, but his actual comments are much milder.

In the book and in subsequent interviews, Ishihara makes blunt, and often erroneous, claims of Japan's technological dominance in semiconductors and other fields. He says Japan should "stand up" and break free from its "postwar stepchild mentality." Perhaps his single best-known statement was that if Japan sold its semiconductor chips to the Soviets and stopped selling them to the United States, this would upset the entire superpower military balance.

One of Ishihara's most revealing, and shocking, themes is his preoccupation with race. He argues that America's racial prejudice is at the heart of U.S.-Japanese frictions. "It may be true that the modern era is a creation of the white race, but you have become somewhat presumptuous about it," he writes. The Soviet Union and Americans, because they are predominantly white, may one day "gang up" against Japan. Ishihara therefore argues that Asia is Japan's franchise. This is reminiscent of Japan's creation of its Greater East Asia Co-Prosperity Sphere earlier this century, when Japanese troops occupied much of East Asia.

Although they are attention-grabbing, Ishihara's views are not particularly well thought out. The Soviets do not have enough money to pay for Japan's output of semiconductors, and the Japanese fear the Soviet Union far more than they resent the United States. For Japan to tilt the world balance of military power to the Soviet Union would be to cut its own throat.

Ishihara may look upon Asia as Japan's franchise, but the Asians are hardly unanimous in sharing that view. If the Japanese were to abrogate their treaty with the United States, it would call the nature of their military buildup into greater question and undercut their image throughout Asia.

Despite his popularity, it is unlikely that Ishihara will become prime minister. He lacks a strong factional position and more middle-of-the-road LDP men say they are determined to block him. But Ishihara has helped create a new climate in two ways. First, he has redefined the spectrum of acceptable political opinion. Only a few months earlier Hashimoto would have been perceived as hawkish, but after Ishihara, he appears more moderate. "Doves" such as Kato, although better able to communicate with the outside world and to shape a less confrontational policy course, seem positively meek in comparison. They are now under pressure to get tougher toward the Americans.

Second, Ishihara's statements have resonance among many average Japanese. Even if they do not explicitly embrace what he says, his views pop up in day-to-day conversations. The wildly irresponsible theory that the United States and the Soviet Union are about to gang up on Japan, for example, is already being recycled on the cocktail party circuit. Japanese may not remember where they first heard it, but I was asked about this prospect on more than one occasion in Tokyo. "Ideas like this and the emotions that have been articulated by Ishihara will be picked up by ordinary people who are on the fence or don't think about it very much," says historian Hall, at Keio University. Indeed, a *Business Week*/Harris poll showed that 55 percent of Japanese believed America's growing dependence on Japanese technology gave Japan more clout in its dealings with America; 18 percent said it did not. Whether Japanese recognize it or not, this echoes Ishihara's position.

As we look into the future course of Japan's foreign policies, it is clear they will be shaped by a growing sense of nationalism. The risk is not that the prewar Emperor-worshiping nationalism will be revived, at least not overnight. There is resistance to this. But there is far less resistance to a more implicit, modern, slicker version.

In fact, there is no significant, internally generated vision that is competing with it. Aside from a few holdouts in the media, the teachers' union, and the Socialist and Communist parties, the left in Japan has been decimated. In view of China's massacre in Tiananmen Square and troubles in the Soviet bloc, communism and Marxism of all varieties have even less appeal than ever. The left scarcely exists in comparison with the political and economic power possessed by the other end of the spectrum.

Indeed, some elements of what is generally described as the left share in the newly assertive stance toward the United States. The Socialists' resistance to U.S. pressure on the agricultural and distribution sectors, combined with the left's clamor against the U.S. military presence, are in many respects part of the same general trend. There are traces of patriotism-cum-nationalism across the political spectrum.

If this momentum builds, fewer and fewer Japanese will tolerate American criticism about their trading or investment practices. They will turn a deaf ear. "Japan is moving to the right, but it is different than the move to the right before World War II," says the Socialist Keiko Chiba. "Then the Emperor was the center of the movement. Japanese people would kill themselves for him. He was a god. Now it's more individualistic. If I have a good life, I'm okay. I don't want to help other people. I don't want to take a risk to change." The implication is that Japan will be more resistant than ever to the kind of change demanded by the outside world.

* * *

One factor that will shape this nationalism is the speed and success of Japan's economic emergence. If the United States is perceived as powerful, its views carry a certain weight in Japan. If America's economic strength and determination are seen as cracking, then the U.S. loses credibility. This is the way the power game is played. The weak and the failed do not receive sympathy in Japan, but rather contempt. Consequently, the future of Japanese attitudes and policies is linked with its economic strength. If we have the power, we are right.

❖ 14 ❖

Economic Lift-off

When Commodore Matthew Perry's "black ships" reached the entrance to Edo Bay in July 1853, the Japanese were shocked by the technology that he possessed in the form of giant cannons. The power that Perry was able to display was simply on a different level than anything the Japanese could hope to achieve by themselves.

It may be on a different order of magnitude, but many Americans are headed for a similar shock in the early 1990s. Japanese companies are not passing their huge profits through to their shareholders, or giving their employees big bonuses as an American company might. They are reinvesting their profits in a new drive to commercialize new technologies, develop new products, improve their efficiency, expand their investments in the United States and around the world, and in general to move into the next phase of economic lift-off. Whereas an American or European might be tempted to relax or coast under these circumstances, the Japanese are accelerating.

Simply put, the United States is in only the early stages of understanding the enormity of Japan's challenge. Japan is just beginning to hit its stride after a century of striving and experimentation. It is not a sun about to set. In finance and autos, in aerospace and computers, and even in Hollywood movies, the Japanese are marshaling their strengths in what promises to be an effective, long-term method.

The equilibrium that some Americans felt they had reached with Japan after the 1985–88 yen-shock period has ended. In 1989, the U.S.

trade deficit with Japan, in terms of percentage of the total U.S. trade deficit, was actually growing again. Japan accounted for nearly half of the total U.S. trade deficit. The devaluation of the dollar was working with Europe, along the lines of classical economic theory; the United States had gone into trade surplus with Europe and was making progress in narrowing the gap with Canada. But it wasn't working with Japan. The trade deficit had been stuck in the $50 billion range for five consecutive years. Trade is just one piece of the picture. On the invest- ment, finance, and commercial technology fronts, the Americans faced growing, not receding, challenges from Japan.

It is easy to identify the U.S. industries and companies that are on the firing line: Detroit is in trouble—Japan already has the power to deliver crippling new blows not only to U.S. automakers, but to the Europeans as well. Anyone in computer-related hardware industries, aside from well-ensconced giants, is in for a withering assault—and that includes Cray Research, which is up against NEC, Fujitsu, and Hitachi in supercomputers. The last full-fledged manufacturer of consumer electronics, Zenith, has been forced to sell off its profitable computer division and now faces a do-or-die effort in consumer electronics. In machine tools, where the Americans account for only about 40 percent of their own production, companies like Cincinnati Milacron, one of the giants of the industry, may be forced to retreat further as Japanese machine-tool companies expand in the United States. Goodyear faces renewed competition now that Japan's Bridgestone and European com- petitors have been able to establish positions in the United States by buying Goodyear's competitors.

American banks and securities houses are waking up with a bad hangover. First it was Bank of America that needed help from Japan. Now Manufacturers Hanover is the most recent major bank to turn to the Japanese for a capital infusion, with the long-term risk that it could slide deeper into the embrace of the giant Dai-Ichi Kangyo. In retailing, Japanese acquisitions span the gamut from the 7-Eleven convenience stores to Saks Fifth Avenue. Although it is the American management of Saks that is theoretically in control of a proposed leveraged buyout, a Japanese retailer is bankrolling it and is therefore in control. These everyday names have thus gone the same way as Firestone, CBS Rec- ords, Columbia Pictures, and Rockefeller Center.

Even aerospace, pharmaceuticals, satellites, and other areas Ameri- cans thought "safe" have been targeted. Even at the same time that it promotes certain kinds of imports, the Ministry of International Trade and Industry (MITI) is subsidizing an effort to build up a Japanese aerospace industry, for example, to compete with Boeing, a centerpiece of America's manufactured exports. Komatsu is readying a new drive at Caterpillar. The Japanese once spoke of the notion of "horizontal division of labor" in which the Americans could excel in some areas and the Japanese would excel in others, but that has been forgotten. The Japanese are pushing for supremacy in virtually every field. There does not appear to be any middle ground, any stasis point. Kenneth S. Courtis, one of the better-known Western economists in Tokyo and senior economist at DeutscheBank Capital Markets (Asia), argues that Japan is headed for a new "economic miracle" in the 1990s.[1] Respected Japanese analysts such as Yoichi Funabashi of *Asahi Shimbun* predict that Japan is entering the third phase of economic emergence. The first was based on its mass manufacturing abilities, the second on its financial clout, and the third will be based on its superiority in critical technologies.

Japanese companies won't necessarily make it across the board. There are many fine American companies that will beat them in certain sectors. Some of these U.S. companies, ranging from smaller specialty niche players to large multinationals, will continue making inroads in Japan. But the overall competitive pressure from Japan, first felt in the form of cheap imports in the 1970s, has moved to an entirely different plateau. The ante has risen so high that at least some U.S. players cannot stay in the game.

In effect, Japan has changed the rules for the entire industrial world, particularly the United States, which has been far more willing to face the full brunt of Japanese competition than Western Europe. The new rules are these: Match our work ethic, our productivity, and our long-term drive, or we win. If you blink, you lose. It is the external face of the power game. It is fair. In many cases, the Americans will find themselves outclassed as the cost of innovation, distribution, and marketing on a global basis increase. "Japanese money and advanced technology are coming to dominate the world," proclaimed Yoichi Masuzoe, a commentator who was an assistant professor at Tokyo University.[2] Most Japanese who follow industry trends would agree with him.

How can this be? Isn't Japan supposed to be cracking? What's all this about Socialists and women and consumers? About the work ethic collapsing? The young rebelling? What about the stock market? Bad aging problem? Labor shortage? And what about the political crisis?

The answer is that Japan does face some long-term problems, but it has recognized them and is dealing with them, long before they reach the proportions of, say, the drug crisis in the United States. When

Japanese newspapers are filled with headlines about a particular issue, it may be a problem that they fear will develop over ten or fifteen years. By identifying a potential disruption far in advance, the Japanese are able to develop solutions. The relatively rapid increase in the proportion of Japan's population over the age of sixty-five and its labor shortage are genuine problems. But Japan's new 3 percent consumption tax is designed to help pay for taking care of the aged, which will not become a real problem until after the turn of the century. Japan also has means for dealing with the labor shortage, including allowing some foreign laborers into Japan for a specified period, raising the retirement age, hiring more women, moving more production offshore, and relying on more automation. As we've seen, the Socialists, women, and consumers may eke out fractional gains, but these are not likely to come at the expense of Japan's productive capabilities. The young may not be quite the workaholics their parents were, but many are still more effective than their counterparts elsewhere, and as they are drawn deeper into their companies they will have to work harder and smarter.

As for Japan's stock market, its 25 percent correction in the first quarter of 1990 had scant impact on the underlying strength of the Japanese economy. It did not, for example, put a dent in the capital spending plans of most major Japanese companies, or curtail their international expansion plans. In some respects, the decline in the Nikkei index served the useful purpose of taking speculative steam out of Japan's financial and real estate markets, punishing some of the more aggressive speculators and disciplining the most conspicuous consumers. It was the new money crowd, more than the underlying power structure, who were feeling the pain. There was little of the sense of Armageddon that prevailed in the United States following the Wall Street crash in October 1987, in part because the Tokyo market, which had reached a high of about 38,900 yen in late 1989, recovered to the 32,000 mark by May. The stage appeared set for for further gains. It was a sign of Japan's remarkable strength and confidence that such a financial shock could be absorbed so smoothly. To suggest that Japan was suddenly cracking was just as fanciful as hoping the Recruit crisis was going to result in a transformed political world. If anything, the corrective action was likely to make Japan's long-term economic emergence more sustainable, not less.

The argument that Japan's star is fading is put forth most comprehensively by Bill Emmott, who was the Tokyo correspondent for *The Economist* of London for three years. In his book *The Sun Also Sets* he argues that Japan's huge trade, current account, and capital surpluses are destined to disappear within a decade as more Japanese become consumers, pleasure seekers, pensioners, investors, and other forms of presumably less-productive individuals. The savings rate will decline precipitously and Japan's declining merchandise exports will be more than offset by its consumption of foreign services, including tourism.[3]

Emmott's is a theoretical proposition, put forward on the basis of an understanding of how Western economies might function, but certainly not of how Japan's economy works. It is based on the assumption that the Japanese will cooperate in blunting their own emergence, and fall into the same traps that Britain did. Emmott's argument is also off-target because it concentrates on macroeconomic surpluses without considering Japan's technological and manufacturing prowess. In addition, several current trends are headed in directions completely opposite to what he supposes may happen sometime in the 1990s. For example, the Japanese government is projecting that Japan's 1990 total trade surplus with the world will dip from $81 billion to $78 billion thanks to an import-promotion scheme. Otherwise, the surplus would have grown. As Japanese companies prepare a new wave of products for export markets, it will be a battle to prevent the surplus from growing again. Another basic mistake Emmott makes is suggesting that Japan's overseas investments will reduce exports sharply. So far at least, those investments have helped expand Japan's exports. As for the Japanese savings rate, it is increasing, not decreasing.

From the Japanese point of view, the Ministry of Finance projects that Japan will generate at least $100 billion in savings a year, including export earnings, in excess of what the Japanese system itself can absorb. Morgan Guaranty estimates that Japan's long-term capital outflows in 1989 totaled $170 billion, and this is growing at a rate of roughly 9 percent a year.[4] Accordingly, the Japanese will have at least $100 billion a year more than they know how to use in Japan. The money, therefore, will continue to be invested outside Japan for several years at least. It will be managed and invested largely by Japanese institutions, which is an essential difference from the petrodollars that the Arabs earned but could not adequately manage. Nor do Japanese government officials see any significant decline in Japan's trade surplus with the United States for at least three years. Something may happen in the dim and distant future that no one can predict, but to the extent that anyone can foresee, this is what Japan's top bureaucrats say.

The other factor that is supposed to sink Japan is the nation's political upheaval. But that upheaval is largely over. Moreover, Japan's econ-

omy is becoming increasingly decoupled from politics. Japanese companies have sufficient financial and technological strengths that they do
not need the cozy triangle for political protection. This was put to me
most forcefully by Mitsui's Jitsuro Terashima in New York. "Frankly,"
he said, "we are quite comfortable with second-class politicians."

The link between politics and economics is also being reduced in
North America and Western Europe. National political leaders have
much less influence over the movement of capital, technology, and
people across their borders than they would care to admit. But it is in
Japan where this is being felt most recently. Companies that were once
struggling exporters, dependent on the support and protection of politicians and bureaucrats, are emerging as multinationals able to win in the
big leagues of global competition.

One top Ministry of Finance bureaucrat, Eisuke Sakakibara, likens
Japan's large corporations to "autonomous kingdoms" that operate independently of the government. It is ironic that at the very moment
that there was ferment on the surface in Japan, creating the impression
of a break in the postwar order, these autonomous kingdoms were
completing their recovery from the yen-shock period and were emerging as stronger competitors than ever.

For the foreseeable future, the Japanese economy will be firing on all
pistons. Household income is up, savings are up, and consumption is
up. To be in Japan today is to feel a little bit like being in the United
States during the late 1950s or early 1960s. Japan's economy is growing
three times as fast as its U.S. equivalent, about 4.5 percent versus 1.5
percent. The result is that enormous opportunities are unfolding. Infrastructure is being built for the future. Careers are being made, not
destroyed. New technologies are being mastered. The impossible seems
possible.

Just as the Japanese once moved upscale from textiles and toys, so,
too, are they preparing new waves of products that could include high
definition television in the consumer electronics field, specialty materials for steel producers, and biotechnology-based drugs in pharmaceuticals. Voice-activated cameras and cordless telephones with built-in
answering machines are on sale in Japan in preparation for introduction
in the United States. New products will be based on superconductivity,
robotics, liquid crystals, and other sophisticated technologies. In virtually every industry, the Japanese have the money and the ambition to
maintain their economic momentum. *Forbes* best summarized this
dawning recognition about Japan's economy with the headline "How
Do You Shut the Darn Thing Off?"[5]

Consider these very simple profiles of several industries.

The Automobile Industry

It is difficult to express sympathy for Detroit. With the possible exception of Ford, the Big Three have done their very best to lose against Japan. One major strategic error was failing to penetrate the Japanese market when they could afford to and when the Japanese automakers might not have been strong enough to resist them. That time is long past. The result is that the Japanese have a virtual monopoly in one of the world's largest and fastest-growing auto markets, namely their own, giving them a source of profits to subsidize their competition against the Americans and Europeans around the world.

More recently, however, Detroit was handed a once-in-a-lifetime opportunity to regain lost market share in the United States when, beginning in 1985, the high yen slowed the Japanese automakers. But instead, they raised prices, gave top executives big bonuses, and failed to forge an improved relationship with labor. Rather than using their strategic alliances (General Motors with Toyota, Isuzu, and Subaru; Ford with Mazda and Nissan; and Chrysler with Mitsubishi Motors) as tools for cracking the Japanese market, they have relied much more on these partners for engines and made-in-Japan "captive imports." This is a defensive, losing strategy.

Overall, the American companies have made progress with their products in terms of quality and technology. In any other environment, they would be applauded. But with notable exceptions, their products have not kept up with the blistering pace set by the Japanese. They are being measured by someone else's yardstick.

The Japanese transplant factories will be a primary tool for the further humbling of the Big Three. For the most part, these are brand-spanking-new facilities with the latest equipment. Their work forces are typically white, rural, hard-working, healthy, overwhelmingly male, and mostly nonunion. The Japanese manufacturers have received hundreds of millions of dollars' worth of incentives from American states, which helps their competitive position. They also import components heavily from Japan and have brought in their own supplier networks. While General Motors and Chrysler in particular are slashing costs by shutting down plants and laying off white-collar workers, the Japanese are building their dealer networks and doubling their U.S. capacity. They are gearing up to produce as many as 2.3 million vehicles in North America annually.

They are only halfway toward that goal, and the Americans are already closing plants. When governors lured these factories to their states, the assumption was that every car produced by a transplant would replace one imported from Japan. But it is not working out that way. The generally accepted estimate is that every three autos made by the transplants will displace one import—but two from Detroit. By 1994, the Japanese and American automakers together may be making 3 million more cars in the United States than Americans can buy, creating a huge glut.[6]

The Japanese industry's other primary tool is a wave of new products, including new luxury cars and sports cars, built in factories in Japan. Remember when it was universally assumed that the Japanese would only be able to make cheap, fuel-efficient subcompacts that rattled on the freeway? Now the Japanese have shocked the European luxury makers in particular. Jaguar, Saab, Volvo, and Audi all are reeling in the U.S. market, at least in part because of new Japanese models. Even mighty BMW and Mercedes are under big competitive pressure in the United States. The Japanese are also pushing for the heart of the market dominated by the likes of Cadillac, which is a major reason so many auto analysts are pessimistic about GM.

Aside from styling, the Japanese have pushed to develop new technologies. Some of them, like the "fragrance-control system" that pumps fragrances through a car's air-conditioning system, are almost laughable. But others, such as hydraulic active suspension systems, multivalve engines, two-stroke engines, and traction-control systems, could outclass U.S. autos if they are introduced successfully. One reason the Japanese are able to introduce new technologies and styling changes faster is that they are shortening the model cycle. It generally takes eight years for Detroit to design a completely new car, whereas Honda and others are coming in at four years and pushing for even faster cycles.

So, at the same time Japanese industry has spent billions in the United States, it has also put on a blitz of new investment at home in new technologies, new efficiencies, and new capacity. This will keep exports from Japan to the United States at high levels.

There will be some losers on the Japanese side, which is already a subject of speculation in Japan. The consensus seems to be that Fuji's Subaru, Suzuki, and Isuzu will be forced to seek new alliances or equity infusions to survive. Daihatsu, another member of this second tier of Japanese automakers, also faces tough times. But clearly the greatest pain will be felt by Detroit. In the coming competitive fray, rebates and financing terms could become even more important. A company like Toyota, with $11.8 billion in cash reserves, would be able to virtually give cars away at cost for a period of time, all for the purpose of gaining market share. It is easy to see how General Motors could shrink from its current 35 percent of the market to 25 percent sometime in the early 1990s, and how Chrysler could be faced with another battle for survival. Only Ford has a clear chance to go toe-to-toe with the Japanese and win. The auto parts industry, which actually employs more people than the Big Three, is in even worse shape as Japanese auto manufacturers bring in their networks of suppliers.

It is widely assumed that Japan's share of the market will increase from about 25 percent today, double what it was a decade ago, to 40 percent by 1992. No one knows if there is an upper limit. The manner in which both Toyota and Nissan rolled out their luxury models with advertising blitzes that cost hundreds of millions of dollars provides some idea of the resources that they command and the sheer power it gives them to develop new markets for their products. "Not content with strong sales and rising market share, Japanese carmakers want more—they want to prove they are No. 1 in the world," wrote Sally Solo of *Fortune*.[7] For the U.S. auto industry, that will produce the worst competitive shakeout of the postwar period.

High Technology

Like autos, America's information technology industries are often likened to a "food chain." At the bottom of this food chain are the companies that produce raw silicon wafers, or that make the equipment which "prints" tiny circuits on this material, or that design and assemble the semiconductor chips themselves. At the top of the chain are the finished computer products such as laptops, personal computers, minicomputers, mainframes, and supercomputers. This broad industry is one of the mainstays of the American economy and, like autos, it has clearly been targeted.

Once a Japanese company has established a presence in one of these food chains, they use that position to establish themselves at other levels. The eventual goal is to have a strong position at each level of the chain, just as they attempt to do at home. That is the way the Japanese compete with each other—strategically rather than financially. Companies like NEC, Hitachi, Fujitsu, Mitsubishi Electric, and others tend to be vertically integrated, which means they try to make everything themselves or obtain their needs from other members of their group. Only IBM in the United States can claim to possess a similar range of capabilities, from semiconductors to mainframes. (IBM lacks the raw materials and semiconductor equipment–making capability at one end of the chain. At the other end, it does not yet make supercomputers. Thus, although IBM frequently stirs complaints inside the United States that it is too powerful, it is not as fully integrated as its Japanese competitors.)

The Japanese quite rightly perceive semiconductors as the "rice" of the Information Age. Because their companies have other successful product lines, the Japanese were able to absorb huge losses to penetrate the U.S. semiconductor market. In the face of $2 billion in losses in the mid-1980s, American companies walked away from the lower end of the market, which is memory chips. The Japanese swallowed an estimated $4 billion in losses and kept going. They now enjoy a virtual monopoly over these memory chips, while the Americans have retreated to more sophisticated chips. Overall, Japanese semiconductor makers control half of the world market.[8]

The Japanese are not likely to knock off Motorola, Texas Instruments, or Intel, but companies like Advanced Micro Devices and National Semiconductor face long-term trouble.[9] They may lack the manufacturing muscle and the capital to stay in the game as new generations of chips enter the marketplace, each requiring greater technology and capital.

From a position of strength in semiconductors, the Japanese have moved into the equipment and materials used to make the chips. This is called integrating backward. In the space of two months in 1989, Sony acquired Materials Research Corporation, and Kyocera Corporation swapped shares with AVX, a maker of ceramics for semiconductors, to obtain control. The last major U.S. company in this field, Perkin-Elmer Corporation, of Norwalk, Connecticut, is hemorrhaging and barely avoided having to sell itself to the Japanese.

As the Japanese position has strengthened, there has been an equal increase in the accusations from American semiconductor makers that the Japanese are holding back supplies of the latest sophisticated equipment. The Americans claim that other Japanese chipmakers get first crack, giving them a head start. In this brutally competitive field, even a six-month delay can be crippling.[10]

Having secured the low end of the food chain in semiconductors and related fields, and in certain computer components—such as printers and disk drives—the Japanese are now preparing to drive at the heart of the American computer industry itself. In 1988, they reaped just $2 billion of some $49 billion in U.S. hardware sales. "But quietly, Japan has readied an offensive that will test America's computer might," one expert wrote.[11] Thanks in part to a growing number of plants in the United States, the Japanese are taking market share in personal computers and laptops, and beginning to make headway in mainframes. "Piece by piece they have staked out the inside and the outside of what's a computer," says Andrew S. Grove, president of Intel Corporation. "The trend is unmistakable."

At the pinnacle of the food chain are supercomputers. After Control Data's retreat from this field, only Cray Research is left as a U.S. manufacturer, and it faces relentless pressure from NEC, Hitachi, and Fujitsu. "The Japanese have three companies that are committed to taking over," says one supercomputer expert. "Cray will probably be able to hang on for five years or so, but the writing is on the wall."[12] These three companies, not coincidentally, were all beneficiaries of special treatment at home as part of the Den Den family of companies.

Thanks in part to the Japanese government's active support, the Japanese companies already have faster processors in their supercomputers, but that's only part of the battle. Cray maintains that its machines are still quicker if one considers the amount of time required to enter the data. Scrappy Cray executives hope to stay in the fight on the basis of sheer entrepreneurial innovation, but the company has split into two because of a dispute over direction. Cray Research may lack the resources to continue the never-ending technological battle; it also depends on Fujitsu to supply semiconductor chips, which is a dangerous vulnerability in view of Fujitsu's goal of beating Cray in supercomputers.

The United States retains more distinct advantages in computers than in cars. The Americans are generally better at software, networking, and systems integration, and they are quicker to invent new technologies, such as parallel processing, which in the final analysis may prove more cost-effective than supercomputers. But the Japanese have huge capital, which means they can take bigger long-term risks. They place greater focus on commercializing new start-up technologies. And they enjoy more government cooperation, encouragement, and support. It is overwhelmingly clear that the Japanese will expand their presence in this food chain. As a result, some American companies will lose, and jobs will be lost.

Aerospace

The Japanese want to design and build their own civilian airliners. This has been a national priority for decades, and the crash of a Boeing 747 in Japan renewed their determination. Four "heavies" are leading the charge: Mitsubishi Heavy, Kawasaki Heavy, Fuji Heavy, and Ishikawajima-Harima Heavy. MITI has guided this effort and has pumped hundreds of millions of dollars into different projects to help these companies develop the necessary technologies. Thus, at the same time MITI professes a desire to redress imbalances in U.S.-Japanese relations, it is building a new competitor.[13] An equally important part of the strategy has been to form "partnerships" with U.S. and European manufacturers to obtain their technologies and skills. Mitsubishi's new partnership with Germany's Daimler-Benz is particularly significant for its potential to equip the Japanese with German aerospace know-how.

Boeing, one of America's largest exporters of manufactured goods and the cornerstone of the Pacific Northwest's manufacturing economy, is thus targeted. Boeing is notoriously tight-lipped, and in view of the competition it faces perhaps that's the way it has to be. But we can describe the nature of the finely tuned game it is playing with Japan.

On the one hand, Boeing needs Japanese components, partly to create an environment to sell its jetliners in Japan, its largest foreign market. If it did not have any Japanese components, the Japanese would be unhappy. To keep suppliers happy, it has to draw them deeper into its manufacturing process.

Yet at the same time, Boeing does not want to create new competition. So it draws out and stalls, and starts again, on joint projects. Boeing spent several years during the 1980s on developing an advanced one-hundred-fifty-seat plane with Japanese participation, called the 7J7. The project was not judged commercially viable and was scrapped. It turned out to be a "paper plane."

Now the game is entering a new round, but no one outside Boeing fully understands the Seattle giant's thinking. In October 1989, Boeing began discussions with three of the heavies—Mitsubishi, Kawasaki, and Fuji—on starting a $3 billion project to build a new three-hundred-seat passenger plane initially called the 767-X. Boeing needs a model for this segment of the market and it cannot, and probably would not choose to, turn to other American companies or the U.S. government for help. After several more months of negotiations, the Seattle giant in April 1990 announced the three Japanese companies would not become full-equity partners, but would provide as much as 20 percent of the new plane's body. It was only an incremental step for the Japanese, but a step forward nonetheless.

To the extent Boeing is able to use Japanese skills and capital to develop a new model and at the same time gain greater acceptance for its products in Japan, without giving away crucial secrets, it is a brilliant game. To the extent that Boeing transfers technology or skills, it is taking a risk. The major Japanese problem appears to be systems design and integration, which is the overall process of translating aerodynamic theory into reality and drawing together and managing thousands of different parts and subassemblies.

Thus, how Boeing handles itself will be much more important than the FSX fight. That was a public controversy because it was a government-to-government decision, and therefore open to persistent challenge from Congress. Whether the Japanese can extract any commercially valuable experience from the FSX project is yet to be seen. Clearly it will help them develop skills for military aircraft. "There is no debate over whether the FSX program will give Mitsubishi Heavy and its Japanese subcontractors broad capabilities in the design, development, and integration of current-generation fighter aircraft," acknowledges the Japan Economic Institute, which is sponsored by the Ministry of Foreign Affairs. The question is whether these skills can be applied to commercial aircraft. It is only obvious that the Japanese companies will try.

Although Japan's bid to enter the commercial aircraft industry has not been either easy or smooth, the chances are that sometime in the late 1990s a Japanese company will design and build its own commercial airliner. Soon thereafter, Boeing and McDonnell-Douglas and Europe's Airbus will begin to feel competitive pressure as the Japanese try to sell their jetliners internationally. This is foreordained. The Japanese market is too small to absorb the costs of development. MITI has set a goal of 10 percent of the world passenger jet market by the turn of the century. This is a major challenge for the Japanese heavies, and they may not make it. But they are not likely to ever stop trying, no matter how long it takes or how much money it costs.

Capital Power

In an astonishingly short period of time, the Japanese have swept the world of finance. True, the Japanese securities companies have had difficulty cracking Wall Street, but all ten of the world's largest banks are Japanese. Even mighty Citicorp, once the world's largest bank, has been blown away in terms of size. "Japanese financial institutions are poised to dominate the world financial system during the 1990s while American banks will be constrained," concludes David D. Hale, chief economist at Kemper Financial Services, Inc.[14] This is also the thrust of Daniel Burstein's too-shrill *Yen! Japan's New Financial Empire and Its Threat to America.*[15]

We will examine some of the implications of this later. But aside from creating competition for U.S. financial institutions, Japan's raw financial power translates into productive activity. Unlike American moneymen, the Japanese do not just play games with their money. They invest it to achieve long-term objectives. As we have seen above, financial power is playing a crucial role in autos, high tech, and aerospace.

Smart capital spending prepares a company for a new leap in quality or quantity. This money can either be generated by a company's own earnings, or it can be borrowed from financial institutions. Because of its abundance, money is relatively cheap in Japan. Japanese companies can borrow this money for as little as 4 percent compared with the 8 or 9 percent that a blue-chip American company would be likely to pay.

Partly as a result, Japan's capital spending has for the first time surpassed that of the United States, even though its economy is smaller. "Japan is positioning itself to become the new-product laboratory for the world in the 1990s, like America was in the 1950s and 1960s," says the economist Kenneth Courtis. "That has enormous long-term competitive implications. The frightening thing to me is that people [in the United States and Europe] aren't focusing on this. By the time they do, we'll be in the fourth quarter of the game."[16] In addition to Toyota's $11.8 billion treasure chest, Hanwa steel trading company is sitting on cash and securities worth $17.2 billion and Mitsubishi Corporation, the trading company, has $15.2 billion. There is no sign that the cash buildup is ending.[17]

The money can also be used to expand the competitive position of Japanese companies abroad. Sony was able to raise $5.5 billion to buy CBS Records and Columbia Pictures in the space of two years. There are tens of billions of dollars ready to move down the same pipeline. The only limit is the U.S. political response. Some pundits proclaim that the nineties will be "the takeover decade." That means Japanese companies taking over American ones, not vice versa.[18] Yukuo Suzuki, general manager of Sanwa Bank's merger and acquisition business, said, "The huge volume of Japanese idle funds cannot be kept from flowing overseas in search of higher returns.[19] Overall, the latest estimates put Japan's direct investments in the United States at $75 billion for 1989, up 40 percent since 1988.

In view of the emerging pattern, it's not hard to understand the growing Japanese sense of self-confidence. Despite overwhelming evidence of Japan's economic lift-off, Americans are still debating whether it is for real and whether a response is required. The bureaucrats in Tokyo must be particularly amused by the Japan-will-go-away school of thought. At the same time that some Americans believe Japan is fading, the U.S. business press is filled with warnings of a broad economic offensive. While in some cases these warnings are overdone, they are also broadly accurate. The pattern is clear, but the conclusion isn't necessarily that Japan will win in every area. The important point is that in the new wave of Japanese competition, nothing is sacred.

There is little chance that government-to-government negotiations can stop it. The Japanese do not want to. As Ambassador Hidetoshi Ukawa said, "It is unnatural and irrational for us as a government to intervene to restrain our private sector. Intervention would be artificial."

What does all this mean for Americans? Some economists would say, That's fine. Whatever is good for the consumer.

But it's not that easy. Assessing Japan's impact on the U.S. economy is much more complex. Start with the simple model of imports. In the old days, when a Japanese car got off at the dock, it benefited the distributors, the ad agency, and presumably the customer. The people it hurt were the competing U.S. auto company, its employees, suppliers, shareholders, and dealers—the chain of people who had a stake.

The Japanese challenge of the 1990s will also create winners and losers. Thanks partly to Japan's manufacturing and financial strengths inside the United States, this competitive foray is stronger and poses tougher issues. Now, hundreds of thousands of American workers and many more suppliers and joint venture partners are on Japan's side of the equation. But the stakes for the other side are higher. To even stay in the game, U.S. industries have to come up with capital they may not have or can only borrow at higher rates. In some cases, the competing U.S. industry may not just be hurt, but decimated. All those "stakeholders" will be hurt.

Before trying to draw any broader conclusions, it is important to understand that Japan's lift-off is not just limited to economics. Economics does not exist in a vacuum. It is a bedrock that supports values. As Japan lifts off, it naturally becomes more confident about exporting its own systems and values.

❖ 15 ❖

Going Global: Values

It is often said that Japan lacks a coherent foreign policy, that it does not understand why it is doing what it is doing in the world. "Power without purpose" is how one writer described it.[1] Many others have chastised the Japanese for being too reluctant to assume a larger global leadership role.

But the Japanese mission is clear. The driving force behind Japan's economic expansion around the world is to create and extract enough wealth to satisfy the demands at home for material progress and to create an overall economic position that is unbeatable. It's wrong to say the Japanese lack a goal. They do have one: a better and richer Japan. To do that, they require a world that is economically efficient, where it is possible and safe to make money.

The Japanese are able to articulate a sense of mission about why they do what they do. Rather than focusing on the geopolitical and ideological issues that fascinate Americans and Europeans, the Japanese are more interested in creating climates of economic growth. The Japanese see economic tools as just as important as more conventional tools of diplomacy, like sending off the fleet. Some of the fruits of economic growth may accrue to countries in which Japan invests, trades, and lends money, but more importantly it builds wealth for Japan itself.

The fact that this may destroy or severely damage the industries of other nations is not a matter of great concern. Taizo Watanabe, the Foreign Ministry's official spokesman, argues, for example, that mounting Japanese challenges to American auto, semiconductor, computer, and other industries are not a threat. "Ultimately it is for the benefit of humanity as a whole," he says. "Some nations [i.e., Japan] have innovated and it spills all over the world. That is to be welcomed."

It's true that Japan has innovated and that this is spilling over into the world, but it creates winners and losers. It does not benefit all of humanity. Watanabe's argument, however, is beguiling. It lays the foundation for believing that whatever Japan does in the world should be welcomed. It is all innovation.

The Japanese have also been chastised because they have no broader sense of mission. Repeating an oft-quoted analogy, the British believed they were civilizing the world when they built their empire. The Americans believed they were making the world safe for democracy. But the Japanese have no such notions to export. Being Japanese is nontransferrable.

Watanabe, who has emerged as one of Japan's most articulate spokesmen on these issues, is quick to point out that the British also created losers. Not everyone enjoyed the uplift of civilization. "When the British built their empire and thought they were civilizing the world, millions of people in Africa were being made slaves," Watanabe says. "Millions of people were colonized. That should never be repeated. Japan cannot do that. Japan has been suspected of following this kind of colonization. But we are determined not to follow this path." He argues that Japan will be like a landlord who helps his tenant by sacrificing his own short-term interests.

The Americans also had victims. One man's vision is another's exploitation. The Europeans were worried about American multinationals as expressed in *Le Défi Américain.*[2] Salvador Allende in Chile certainly would not have believed that the Americans were saving the world for democracy. Many people feared and disliked the ugly Americans.[3] The point is that any powerful nation is able to construct a system of beliefs to justify its external behavior. The Japanese now have that system in place and their cause is just. Prime Minister Kaifu and top bureaucrats have begun calling for a "new world order" in which Japan's brand of economic diplomacy would play a truly global role. As one LDP Dietman put it to me late one evening over sushi and sake: "We have the technology. We have the money. We can shape the twenty-first century."

As the Japanese attempt to shape the twenty-first century and as their innovation spills over into the world, they are bringing their own values, perceptions, and systems with them. It is not realistic to expect them to play the power game internally in one fashion and play it in an entirely different way as they emerge onto the world stage.

Japan's tools are investment, aid, bank and government lending, trade, and technology. This impressive economic complex is managed by bureaucrats, bankers, executives, and intellectuals who are skilled, highly educated, and worldly. In the field are an estimated 2 million Japanese who live overseas. This infrastructure is backed by a world-class information flow—the news provided by an internationally deployed Japanese media as well as the intelligence that flows through the worldwide data linkups of the major trading companies, banks, and manufacturers. Other major information flows take place through the Ministry of Foreign Affairs and MITI, which operates around the world through the Japan External Trade Relations Organization (JETRO). The net effect is something akin to an early warning system, a DEW line. Threats can be identified well in advance.

Some pundits say Japan can never be a world leader without being a military superpower, but they are missing an essential point: War is largely obsolete, at least among industrialized nations. Strategic arsenals are becoming ever less influential. In some cases, the Japanese use economic levers to persuade governments to take appropriate policy actions. They are attempting to do this, for example, with governments in Burma and Cambodia. It also happens with American states: California was pressured to drop its unitary tax law largely by the threat that Japanese investment would shift to other states.

In other cases, as with the U.S. government, the Japanese use their economic levers to prevent decisions from being made that would adversely affect Japan's interests. In these situations, Japan does not want to "lead" as much as it wants to block. In a world that is placing far greater emphasis on economic growth than military or ideological confrontation, Japan's tools could prove even more effective in the coming years. We will explore this subject in more depth in Chapter 17.

One cannot complain about it, though. That's the way power among nations works. The nation that has power tries to shape the world in its image. The Americans wanted to impose democracy and respect for human rights, to beat back communism, to raise up the poorest of the poor, and to build market economies. These goals were sometimes mutually contradictory, but all of them were, and remain, part of the American gestalt.

The Japanese vision has considerable overlap with U.S. interests. Both countries want to maintain political stability around the world, free from Soviet or communist domination, and both are committed to preserving some form of international trading and financial systems.

But Japan's vision places a greater emphasis on economics. The Americans may try to help a people throw off a dictator or they may try to avert famine. But in Thailand or Britain or Mexico or the United States, the overriding Japanese goal is to create an environment where Japanese companies can get their work done more efficiently and wealth can be created. Many critics say the Japanese have no values, but they do. They are just shaded in different tones. One's attitudes toward the creation of wealth and the need for hard work, for example, are important values.

The fact that Japan is spreading its values is overwhelmingly positive on some counts. Japanese managers have often been welcomed by hourly, or blue-collar, workers in different countries because they treat laborers with more respect than other managers. Time and time again, particularly in the United States, the Japanese have acquired companies where management-labor disputes were so bitter that those companies had failed. In other words, executives and workers feared or hated each other so much that they decided, explicitly or implicitly, to simply close a factory or sell the company rather than resolve their differences.

The Japanese are able to transform that kind of confrontational atmosphere. The best-known example is the old General Motors plant in Fremont, California, which had been the scene of radical labor activity. When Toyota took over management as part of a joint venture with GM, it used many of the same UAW employees, but productivity and quality soared. Toyota's managers worked with, not against, their employees.

It was a similar story at an old Firestone tire tread plant in Danville, Kentucky, that had been purchased by ATR, a consortium consisting of C. Itoh, Mitsubishi, and Tokyo Rope. The plant had been the scene of nasty management-labor disputes when Firestone owned it. The equipment had been allowed to run down. The workers had been subject to frequent layoffs. The plant had failed.

But now the Japanese were working extremely hard with the blue-collar workers, most of them from farm backgrounds, to instill a new sense of commitment and cooperation. This kind of manufacturing is particularly numbing mentally because it consists of taking in steel at one end of the factory and turning it into the thin cords of metal that go into tires. It consists of the bending and manipulating of steel rather than creating a finished product.

One morning after an all-night shift, a thirty-four-year-old shift foreman who had worked for Firestone told me over coffee how pleased he was to be working for the Japanese instead. He had been to Japan for a few weeks of training and came back to Danville determined to make the factory a success. "Pride is back," he said. Others told me how thankful they were that ATR, when demand had been slack a few months earlier, redeployed the workers to other tasks in the plant rather than laying them off.

The Japanese have made a real contribution to manager-worker relations. For years, American managements had said American labor was to blame for U.S. competitive problems. But it turns out that if executives give up the special parking places and corporate dining rooms, and if workers are given a measure of power about when to stop the line and how to improve the design of their workstations, it is possible to unlock new levels of productivity and performance, not to mention commitment to quality. Of course, American workers have not embraced the singing of Japanese company anthems and they have resisted doing calisthenics before starting work. But overall, the exposure to Japanese management has been positive.

Part and parcel of this Japanese value system is a whole-hearted commitment to see that their company survives. Americans are never going to adopt mystical attitudes toward their companies, but Sony's Akio Morita is right when he says that Americans have a shocking tendency to strip the assets of their own companies, carve them up, and sell off the pieces to the highest bidder. The Japanese have also proven that the notion of a postindustrial economy is a myth. Americans must make things if they want to generate wealth. Manufacturing is no longer a dirty word. Honda executives, for example, speak of "the joy of manufacturing."[4]

What is less understood are other subtle but no-less-influential Japanese values that they seek to implant or American values that they fail to respect. This is particularly evident when it comes to women and minorities. American women and minorities have not advanced as far or as fast as they would like in American companies, but they have advanced at a far greater tempo than their counterparts in Japan. To a certain extent, Japanese companies apply their homegrown values toward those who are different when operating in the United States.

Sumitomo and Honda, for example, have both had suits filed against them by women employees. Although there has been a rash of such discrimination suits against all companies, the Japanese have found the issue particularly difficult to deal with. "In effect, the Japanese have imported into this country the notion that women are office flowers," says Lewis Steel, a New York attorney who has represented American women in these lawsuits. "These women claim, in effect, broadstroke, that they are held down in inferior positions. Even when they do get a title, it's a show title rather than a real title."

Whereas women are often limited to being office ladies or secretaries in Japan, one trap American women face is the PR ghetto. Unable to absorb women in mainline executive positions, Japanese companies tend to hire women as their public relations or marketing liaisons. But they are still little more than tokens. American women working for Japanese companies have the same problem that Japanese women have: Men make the decisions. Women are not absorbed into decision making. Unless Japanese companies can cross that threshold with Japanese women, it's unlikely they will be able to develop management styles that can accommodate American women as full-fledged managers and decision makers.

It's not exactly utopia for women in American companies either, but some women do rise to senior positions in major companies and exercise real responsibility. Some, certainly by no means all, have been able to balance maternity leaves and family obligations with their careers, although this is difficult. Many companies accept a slight diminishment of commitment to work in the short term because they believe that it is the proper, ethical course of action and because they believe it will engender long-term loyalty. Japanese companies are far less inclined to do so.

As for race, Japanese attitudes toward American minorities are well known. Nakasone, in a September 1986 comment he came to regret, said the presence of so many blacks, Puerto Ricans, and Mexicans had helped lower American "levels."[5] This was not an isolated incident. Toyota Chairman Eiji Toyoda shocked Massachusetts Institute of Technology president Paul E. Gray in a meeting in Japan by remarking: "The reason Americans can't make good cars is that they are a mongrel race."[6] Japanese friends have taken me aside and tried to explain that where America went wrong was in the 1960s when it started trying to raise the status of American blacks. In the *Business Week* poll conducted by Louis Harris in Japan (see Appendix A), Japanese respondents were asked to identify reasons for America's economic problems. A decisive 42 percent said "too many different minorities." Other factors were a lazy work force (35 percent), insensitivity to foreign markets (29 percent), and too interested in short-term returns (25 percent).

Melding disparate peoples together is simply not an article of faith for the Japanese, at home or anywhere else. One can argue whether the Americans have done it fast enough or well enough, but the fact of the matter remains that, by international standards, America is a truly multiracial society that is open to economic, political, and social progress for minorities.

The key question is how Japanese attitudes are translated into action, or the lack thereof. One well-known case was Honda, which, ironically, is often perceived as the most Americanized of all Japanese manufacturing companies in the United States, with the possible exception of Sony. In March 1988, Honda of America Manufacturing, Inc., agreed to give 370 blacks and women a total of $6 million in back pay, resolving a federal discrimination complaint. They were not given jobs; they were given, instead, compensation for the wages they would have received if they had been working.

The strongest piece of research on this subject suggests that the Japanese auto manufacturers and parts suppliers have attempted to avoid American minorities by simply locating many of their manufacturing facilities away from black population centers. This study was done by two professors at the University of Michigan, Robert E. Cole and Donald R. Deskins, Jr.[7]

Cole and Deskins note that the Big Three employ a disproportionate number of blacks. Blacks represent almost 11 percent of the overall U.S. civilian work force, but 17.2 percent at General Motors, Ford, and Chrysler. The Japanese, however, have been careful to ask for profiles of communities, including census data, before making decisions on where to build new factories. The result is that Japanese auto companies have situated their factories in places like Bloomington, Illinois; Lafayette, Indiana; Marysville, Ohio; Georgetown, Kentucky; and Smyrna, Tennessee. These are all overwhelmingly white and rural. Mazda did locate in Flat Rock, Michigan, south of Detroit, obviously near a major black population, but the location decision was largely ascribed to Ford's influence, which insisted that its displaced workers be given special preference. The broader pattern remains. "By siting their plants in areas with very low black populations, they, in effect, exclude blacks from potential employment," Cole and Deskins write.

At the same time, the U.S. auto plants that have borne the brunt of the competition from Japan and been closed are those with disproportionate concentrations of blacks. "There is an extraordinary mismatch between the heavy toll on black unemployment taking place among U.S. manufacturers and the small number of opportunities for blacks being made available at the new Japanese plants," Cole and Deskins argue.

A flap involving Recruit's two U.S. subsidiaries suggests that the attempt to avoid women and minorities is part of a broader pattern that is not limited to the auto industry. In the summer of 1989, when the Recruit scandal was on a low boil back in Japan, the *San Francisco Chronicle* broke the story of how Recruit USA and Interplace/Transworld Recruit used an elaborate system of racial and sexual discrimination in picking the employees it placed with many different Japanese companies. The San Francisco office of the U.S. Equal Employment Opportunity Commission began an investigation and took Recruit to court.[8]

The way Recruit identified the ethnicity and sex of job applicants, in alleged violation of U.S. law, was to use code phrases such as "see Adam" on job documents when a Japanese company wanted to hire a Caucasian male employee or "see Eve" when a Caucasian female was desired. "Talk to Haruo" was used when a Japanese male employee was sought, "Maria" to indicate a female Hispanic, "Maryanne" to indicate a black female, and so forth. The company denies any wrongdoing, and the case is still pending in court.

Some American companies, of course, discriminate, and indeed companies around the world discriminate. What's striking about the Japanese practice in America is that U.S. laws and U.S. values are relatively well defined, but the Japanese, reflecting their own attitudes and values, have not fully accepted them as a price of doing business in the United States. Just as the Japanese reserve their worst treatment at home for darker-skinned Pakistani workers, so, too, is it clear that American blacks are the least desired employees in the United States. Cole and Deskins cite one study showing that most Japanese businessmen view blacks as "streetwise, rioting, stealing or drugged."

From time to time, American blacks get angry about remarks made by Japanese politicians, or about their fascination with Little Black Sambo clothing and toys. The NAACP sends a delegation to Japan, and the Japanese offer to advertise in more black publications or to give money to the United Negro College Fund or certain black universities. Perhaps a Japanese real estate developer talks about a new construction project in Harlem. But there is little sign of change in underlying attitudes or behavior. The values that the Japanese demonstrate at home toward their own minorities and immigrants are applied internationally.

The Japanese also have had difficulty with male executives. This is more than a mere management problem. It reflects different notions about how and where decisions should be made, about the role of the individual versus the group, and about the need for hierarchy versus egalitarianism. It is a vast subject in its own right, but we can draw the broad outlines.

Most major Japanese companies depend on a higher degree of personal connection-building among their executives than do Western companies. The standard Japanese pattern, and there are, of course, exceptions, is that a group of students is hired from a university and advances through the company at about the same pace until a winnowing-out process starts during the group members' forties. By their fifties, the numbers have been narrowed down but the cultural and social cohesion among them is still intact. The homogeneity is essential to the Japanese style of decision making, which places a greater emphasis on being able to read signals and on implicit understanding than on formal decision-making systems and procedures. The *nemawashi* process of building consensus is part of this pattern.

To interrupt this system, by introducing outsiders of any sort, imposes a genuine strain. "It's very difficult for the Japanese to have people who are older working for younger people," notes management guru Peter Drucker. "And it's difficult for them to work with each other unless they went to school with each other. In practically every Japanese company, it is still true."[9]

The Japanese have taken this basic model and attempted to apply it globally. Harvard management expert Christopher Bartlett has nicknamed this phenomenon "jet age *nemawashi.*" Japanese managers assigned to the United States or other distant postings keep in much closer contact with headquarters than most country managers for a Western multinational would. In the United States, Japanese executives write memos and other correspondence and send them back to Tokyo on the fax machines for overnight answers on how to proceed on a particular problem. Many U.S.-based executives spend hours every evening on the phone with their colleagues back home, where it is morning.

The most grueling aspect of trying to maintain the group management concept over such long distances is flying executives back and forth at a dizzying rate. Some Japanese companies have been known to fly an executive from New York to Tokyo for a single day of meetings and then send him right back. Anyone who has ever flown from New York to Tokyo would understand the physical price one pays for making a round trip in the space of three days. According to Bartlett, NEC in a single year flew executives in or out of Tokyo ten thousand times. That was in 1985, before the company accelerated its international push. Some Japanese jokingly refer to these rapid journeys as "kamikaze trips" because of the physical grind.

Japanese executives have to do this to keep in touch with the group at home, to remain visible. If they stay in the United States too long, they risk being edged out of the group and will not be able to understand the decision-making dynamics at headquarters. This is a risk for an American manager overseas as well, but it is particularly acute for a Japanese. "After a while, they don't smell right," says Drucker. "They're out of the loop." For that reason, some savvy Japanese managers remain based in Tokyo and commute to the United States, even in the case of Honda. The president of Honda's North American operations, for example, lives in Tokyo, but crisscrosses the United States each month.

The point is that there is relatively little room in this modified group-decision-making model for foreign executives who wish to play important roles. The conflict is particularly sharp with American executives, many of whom approach decision making with a different mindset. The Americans often believe that decisions about what a Japanese company does in the United States should be made in the United States whenever that is practical. None are naive enough to believe that a U.S. subsidiary would ever have complete autonomy from Tokyo, but they expect that routine personnel decisions and other matters that are still typically controlled from Tokyo should be devolved to the U.S. These managers also believe that they should be given individual decision-making roles—that is, specific areas of responsibility and the right to make decisions on the basis of certain broad guidelines. Many also feel that the Japanese company's hierarchy is much less important than indigenizing the company's U.S. management. In other words, they should be advanced fairly rapidly up the chain of command because it makes sense for a Japanese company to have Americans managing their U.S. subsidiaries. In a sense, this is the American notion of egalitarianism over the prevailing Japanese commitment to hierarchy.

To be sure, some U.S. executives looking for advancement in Japanese companies are quick-hit artists, but even genuinely good American executives often find themselves in a kind of attitudinal conflict with their Japanese employers. "It's real combat," says Clifford Clark, a California-based management consultant. "The combat line is between individuality and group consciousness."

The Japanese have experimented with a number of solutions. Nissan has an American who manages its Tennessee factory and an American who manages its U.S. marketing, but a Japanese executive oversees them. Matsushita has an American executive as chief operating officer of its North American activities, but a Japanese executive based in Secaucus, New Jersey, is still chief executive officer for the hemisphere. Sony has appointed Michael P. Schulhof as president of Sony USA, which encompasses Sony's entertainment activities, and he has a reporting relationship to Tokyo. He also sits on the Sony board, the only American to hold such a post for a major Japanese manufacturer. Still,

Morita's younger brother Masaaki Morita is chairman and chief executive of Sony of America, which is the Sony subsidiary that oversees actual manufacturing activities. Americans not versed in these matters might obtain the impression that American executives working for Nissan, Matsushita, Sony, Honda, and similar Japanese companies run the American operations, but, in fact, they do not exercise full-fledged responsibility.

It seems easier for the Americans when they clearly report to a Japanese executive than when they have someone on their staff who monitors them. This "shadow" manages relations with Tokyo and with other Japanese managers. "If you were the manager of a department, you would have a shadow," says Robert J. Wilkinson, who resigned as U.S. corporate controller for Kubota Tractor Corporation in Compton, California. "You would have a man who was assigned to learn what you were doing, and assigned to 'help' what you were doing. They were actually grading you—whether you realized it or not."[10]

As a result of all these conflicts, the Japanese have not only experienced some unwanted management instability in the United States, but they have also been hit by a rash of suits by American executives who claim breach of contract or outright discrimination. Although some American executives find the Japanese decision-making model appealing, the majority find it a dead end. "The perceived exclusion from decision making and strategic planning, the absence of training and management development programs, and the apparent lack of career opportunities discouraged even the most loyal and determined individuals from long-term commitment to the [Japanese] company," concludes a study by the University of Michigan and Egon Zehnder International, a Swiss executive recruitment firm. The authors surveyed 133 American executives at 32 Japanese companies in the United States, making it the most extensive study that has been done of the issue.[11]

With the possible exceptions of Sony and Honda, none of the mainline Japanese multinationals have established management models in the United States of the same nature that U.S. or European multinationals often establish in countries where they operate. In Japan itself, U.S. and European multinationals often employ Japanese as presidents or general managers of their Japanese subsidiaries. Although none of them are completely autonomous, they enjoy a measure of latitude that the Japanese have rarely allowed their foreign subsidiaries. Perhaps it is only a question of time before that changes. Some executives believe the Japanese will be forced to absorb more foreign nationals and allow decision-making responsibility to become much more decentralized.

But the stronger evidence, at least for now, is that the Japanese will maintain their own uniquely Japanese model where decision making can remain relatively centralized in Tokyo and Osaka. Mitsui & Company, the trading company, has operated in the United States for a hundred years and during that time has never been able to find an American to become head of its North American activities. Yoshi Tsurumi, a Japanese who is a professor at New York's Baruch College and one of the best analysts of Japanese multinationals, believes that for ten years at least the Japanese will attempt to further centralize, rather than devolve. "The last time I was in Japan, I castigated my audience," Tsurumi says. "This is really occupation-force style. You just send everybody in. It's really bad."

One key to maintaining the centralized model is the so-called hardware solution. Just as the Japanese use a piece of hardware, the fax machine, to maintain their expanded group decision-making model, they hope to use video conferencing and other electronic systems to facilitate communications back and forth. Some Japanese are interested in building a new supersonic aircraft because it would cut the commuting time from Tokyo to the United States to three or four hours. This would help them manage from headquarters.

The struggle over where and how decisions are made inside major Japanese companies is one of the most important but largely underrecognized issues surrounding Japan's global emergence. It is a particularly keen issue between the United States and Japan. Not only does it affect business, but it also reflects a battle of values. It is the front line.

With so many Japanese living in American communities, the temptation is to see them as another wave of immigrants who are buying into the U.S. system and U.S. values. But of course, Japan's managers are in America on rotating assignments, and it is dangerous for them to assimilate into American society because of the price they will have to pay when they return to Japan. Although some visiting Japanese do "go native" for a period of time, the greater trend is for the Japanese to remain in their own circles. Japanese-language newspapers are delivered to their homes, they buy Japanese food products at Meidi-ya and other Japanese food chains, they build and operate their own schools, and they buy and operate their own golf and ski clubs. Mitsui's Izawa, who lived in Los Angeles for seven years and then spent a year at Harvard in an intensive management program with U.S. executives, told me he learned more about America in a single year in Boston than in all seven in Los Angeles because he had remained in the Japanese enclave there.

Japanese tourists also flock to Hawaii, the West Coast, New York, and elsewhere in growing numbers, but few mix intensively with Americans. The majority tend to go to a Japanese travel agency that puts them on a Japanese airline. They are booked into a Japanese-owned or -managed hotel, and they get on Japanese-owned and -operated buses when they go sightseeing or shopping. Part of the reason for this insulation is the fear of crime, with which the Japanese as individuals are simply not prepared to cope. They also face linguistic barriers. Americans have done much the same when they get on an American airline, stay at a Sheraton, and go on tours organized by their travel agencies. For people who choose to travel this way, it is perfectly acceptable by international norms. But one side effect is that the Japanese, like the Americans before them, are protected against becoming exposed to too many alien concepts.

Although some Japanese-Americans have assimilated and have even become U.S. senators, the process required generations of living in the United States. Visiting Japanese, whether rotating managers or tourists, are usually not interested in assimilating. They are unfailingly polite and they pay top dollar, but with few exceptions they are not immigrants. The trend toward exclusivity and separateness is far stronger. It is a kind of cultural chauvinism to believe that just because the Japanese are physically present in the United States, they will begin to think like Americans.

So, as the Japanese go global and export their values and systems, the issues and the challenges they pose are profound. It is not possible, nor desirable, to completely adopt Japanese values or systems. But it is possible, and indeed desirable, to use the shock of exposure to Japan's success to sharpen American values. Americans have allowed management-labor conflicts, a lack of attention to detail and quality, a cavalier attitude toward the survival of their own companies, and an overall short-term mentality to undermine their own system. Americans need a better balance.

But some of the values that Japan exports clearly conflict with American values. Some Americans may wonder, If the Japanese want to run our economy so badly, why not encourage them? The answer is that values come with economics. Ownership of the means of production is not value-free. Economic power supports, nurtures, and expands values. Japan affirms hierarchy, duties, harmony, and exclusivity. It subjugates individuals to group conformity. Americans savor their diversity, and it is hard to develop a harmonious framework, much less consistency. Then there are tensions over Japan's commitment to ethnic and sexual pluralism and its willingness to allow Americans a greater say in managing the Japanese economic presence.

If the Japanese were to remain a minor player in the American economy, their impact on American values and American society might remain so small that it scarcely merits discussion. But they are not a minor player. And if the Japanese expansion continues at the current rate for another ten years, the relative weight of their values and systems will be greatly enhanced.

❖ 16 ❖

Going Global:
Exporting a Keiretsu

Americans distrust great concentrations of economic power. Over the course of the century, there have been periodic waves of antitrust action. AT&T was too big, so it was broken up, not once but twice. Companies like Exxon (itself the result of an antitrust action), Citicorp, and IBM, rightly or wrongly, also face constant low-level skirmishing over whether they are too big, powerful, or arrogant. "Big business" is synonymous with the monopolization and abuse of power. Americans like to think they have an open marketplace where there is full-throated competition and a sense of fair play. A person with a bright idea, an entrepreneur, can make it big. This is an ideal that is, of course, only partly applied in practice. But it is a deep streak in the American psyche.

This is virtually the opposite of the Japanese model, which places a premium on large integrated groups that wield immense economic and political power. Entrepreneurs are not appreciated, much less lionized. The small guys, like subcontractors in the auto industry, are subjected to the most relentless long-term pressure to squeeze out costs. Wide-open competition is often eschewed as promoting a "disorderly" market. It is fine for the Japanese to use whatever systems they wish within Japan. The issue is what impact it has when they replicate those systems in the United States or elsewhere in the world as they go global.

Mitsubishi is Japan's largest industrial and financial group, and it has exported a hybrid version of its vertically integrated auto assembly system to the cornfields of Illinois and surrounding states. The Diamond-Star assembly plant in Bloomington, Illinois, a $650 million joint venture with Chrysler Corporation, sits at the apex of a powerful, integrated system that Mitsubishi group companies have been painstakingly building for decades.[1] This is only one industry where Mitsubishi companies have built Japanese-style industries in America, and Mitsubishi is only one of the groups that has done it. By examining Mitsubishi and its joint venture with Chrysler, however, we begin to understand the scale and the organization of Japan's manufacturing investment in the United States and the model upon which it is based. Aside from the competitive impact this has on American companies, the issue is how it squares with American notions of economic diversity.

In the old days, the Mitsubishi, Mitsui, and Sumitomo groups were called *zaibatsu*. Blaming them for supporting Japan's war effort, the Americans removed the families who owned the groups from active involvement, assuming the groups would then collapse—but they didn't. Because of a network of social and educational links among executives, as well as extensive cross-holdings, interlocking directorships, and long-established business connections, members of these groups have retained a measure of coordination and cooperation.[2]

Today they are called *keiretsu*, meaning groups. In addition to Mitsubishi, Mitsui, and Sumitomo, newer groups include the Fuyo, Sanwa, and Dai-ichi Kangin groups. Each of them have different personalities and business mixes, but taken together they represent the heart of corporate power in Japan. Other companies such as Hitachi, Sony, and Matsushita control *keiretsu*-like structures. None of these groups is completely self-contained. Sometimes they establish consortia or cartels with each other. Sometimes they compete with each other. To a lesser or greater extent, member companies also do business with nongroup customers. The linkages are subtle, not ironclad.

Major Members of Six Largest Groups[3]

Mitsui group (24 companies)
  Toray Industries, Inc.
  Toshiba Corp.
  Toyota Motor Corp.

Mitsubishi group (29 companies)
  Kirin Brewery Co.
  Nikon Corp.
  Mitsubishi Heavy Industries

Sumitomo group (20 companies)
  NEC Corp.
  Sumitomo Chemical Co.
  Sumitomo Metal Industries

Fuyo Group (29 companies)
  Marubeni Corp.
  Nissan Motor Co.
  Canon Inc.

Sanwa Group (44 companies)
  Teijin Ltd.
  Ohbayashi Corp.
  Kobe Steel Ltd.

Dai-Ichi Kangin Group (47 companies)
  Seibu Department Stores Ltd.
  Shimizu Corp.
  Yokohama Rubber Co.

These groups are on the list of items being discussed by U.S. and Japanese negotiators as part of the Structural Impediment Initiative (SII) talks. The American side argues that the bonds which tie these groups should be relaxed because they encourage Japanese companies to buy from each other, rather than from foreigners, and create an overall climate in which it is difficult for American companies to break into Japan. As part of the group structure, for example, some manufacturers have captive distribution chains that make it hard for outsiders to penetrate with their products. Thus Japan's ability to export its *keiretsu* structure to the United States should be of keen interest.

The Americans do not have any corporate structure that comes close to the scale of a *keiretsu,* and as a result, they tend not to understand them. I once received a call from a 3M executive in Minneapolis who was in the business of making upholstery for the interiors of automobiles. It seemed that a Mitsubishi company had just purchased one of his U.S. competitors, but his division at 3M did not know who Mitsubishi was. I explained that he was up against Japan's largest industrial group and therefore had a problem. "I thought maybe we did," said the 3M man. "But I've been having the hardest time convincing anyone around here to take this seriously."

Many major American companies have numerous subsidiaries and affiliates and on the surface may appear similar in organization and management style, but there are crucial differences with Japan's groups. Typically, different subsidiaries of a major U.S. company run their separate businesses and have different customers and different suppliers. They are united in the sense that the parent company consolidates their financial results and imposes budgetary targets, but the subsidiaries often actively resist doing business with each other because of conflicts of style or because of fear of losing autonomy. Although two subsidiaries may have some business with each other, it is extremely rare that numerous subsidiaries of a multidivision corporation or conglomerate would engage in a vertically integrated "food chain."

If Citicorp owned 10 percent of DuPont, Ford, Bechtel, Caterpillar, and several other U.S. giants, and if each of these companies owned 5 percent of other group members, this would be the beginnings of an American-style *keiretsu.* Their top executives would serve on each others' boards and they would have extensive educational and social links. Perhaps 30 percent of a company's shares would be held by friends, so that short-term earnings pressure would be greatly reduced and there would be little risk of hostile takeover. At the same time, the members of the group could link up with each other on an ad hoc basis to bid for specific projects. If Bechtel were competing to build an airport, for example, it could offer the best rates of financing from Citicorp and the best prices on construction plastics from DuPont and airport vehicles from Ford, and other inducements. Caterpillar equipment would be used in the actual construction. This is the kind of scale on which the Mitsubishi group sometimes operates. Other times, members go it alone.

The three flagships of the Mitsubishi group are its trading company, simply called Mitsubishi Corporation, Mitsubishi Heavy Industries, and the Mitsubishi Bank. Aside from imports and exports, the trading company concentrates on creating an environment for Mitsubishi companies to operate in and to act as a kind of coordinator of their activities outside Japan. For the group's investment in Illinois, Tetsuzo Nomura, vice president and general manager of the Mitsubishi Corporation branch in Chicago, was the point man for political and media relations.

Mitsubishi, which means "three diamonds," was established by a samurai family in 1870 and traditions from that era still apply. Mitsubishi companies tend to stick more closely together and have more extensive dealings with each other than, say, the Mitsui group. "If you are united and cooperate, you will not be defeated by your enemies," Nomura said, quoting an old Mitsubishi tradition. "But if you go this way and that way, you will lose."

Altogether there are twenty-nine companies in the core Mitsubishi group, almost all of which carry the Mitsubishi name. They include major players in metals, finance, real estate, chemicals, construction, electronics, heavy manufacturing, petrochemicals and plastics, and aerospace. The CEOs of these core companies have a luncheon meeting on the second Friday of each month in a Mitsubishi-owned building in the Marunouchi district of downtown Tokyo. This Friday Club is not a formal board of directors and does not make formal decisions. Some accounts have described it as largely a venue for building personal friendships. Others have said the executives merely discuss ways of protecting the Mitsubishi name and trademark. But they do establish joint committees on specific group issues and thus are able to provide a form of coordination.

Outside this core group are several concentric rings of other companies that do not necessarily carry the Mitsubishi name, but they are still considered "Mitsubishi companies." The level of ownership and cross-holdings varies. One key distinction is that these companies do not participate in the Friday Club. As of March 1987, the Mitsubishi Public Affairs Joint Committee listed forty-one companies as being in the core and the first inner ring. There are dozens more joint ventures, loosely held affiliates, and other companies that could be considered members of the broadly defined Mitsubishi group. In the outer rings, like small Plutos circling the sun, are countless small suppliers that have traditional, long-term relationships with Mitsubishi group companies.

Mitsubishi executives say their group accounts for 10 percent of Japan's GNP. This is impossible to document because it is hard to know where the Mitsubishi group starts and where it ends. It is also difficult to sort out how much they sell to each other versus how much they sell to the outside world. In 1987, the group's directory of forty-one companies in the core and first tier showed $165 billion in sales. This includes some double-counting of sales among companies within the group, so it is not a fully accurate reflection of the group's sales to outsiders, but it is close. By 1989, those sales had grown to $197 billion. In effect, in two years the Mitsubishi group added sales equivalent to those of AT&T, one of America's largest companies.

In terms of assets, Mitsubishi Bank had $232 billion in 1987 and Mitsubishi Trust and Banking had $151 billion. The explosion of real estate and stock market values, combined with a near doubling of the yen, had swollen assets of these two institutions to more than $380 billion, which is nearly twice the size of Citicorp. By 1989 that figure had risen to $468 billion, or nearly half a trillion dollars. In short, Mitsubishi operates on a scale that is virtually inconceivable to Americans.

Although Chrysler put up half the money for the Diamond-Star plant and its executives are present, Mitsubishi is in the driver's seat. The Chrysler executives are trying to learn how the Japanese do what they do, and to ensure that Chrysler has a supply of automobiles to market. Chrysler has had a relationship with the Mitsubishi group since 1970, when Mitsubishi Motors was broken off from Mitsubishi Heavy and established as a joint venture with Chrysler. Mitsubishi Heavy is the largest shareholder and Chrysler has a minority stake, which started out at 15 percent but has been whittled down as Chrysler has sought to raise cash. The more Chrysler sells out and the more it depends on Mitsubishi for parts and cars, the more obvious it becomes that Chrysler is just along for the ride.

In building and equipping the joint venture, the group used Mitsubishi International, the U.S. subsidiary of Mitsubishi Corporation, as general contractor. Kajima, one of Japan's largest construction companies, did the construction work and Tokio Marine, a Mitsubishi company, underwrote the project. Japanese companies provided most of the capital equipment. Komatsu, which is not part of the Mitsubishi group, sold giant presses for stamping sheets of metal into car bodies, but Mitsubishi Electric provided robots for the assembly line and Mitsubishi Heavy provided a die-sinking machine.

Equally fascinating was the supplier network. When I met top Chrysler and Mitsubishi managers in the plant in 1987, I was given a list of sixty suppliers. A casual examination revealed only a handful of obviously Japanese suppliers, including Nippondenso in Michigan and Toyoda Gosei in Missouri, which are both Toyota affiliates.

On further research, it became clear that suppliers such as Bloomington-Normal Seating, Vuteq Corp., and others were either Mitsubishi-related or related to traditional Japanese suppliers. AP Technologies in Bellefontaine, Ohio, which was to supply glass, turned out to be an Asahi Glass joint venture. Asahi Glass is a Mitsubishi company.

Then there was Eagle Wings Industries in Rantoul, Illinois, a couple of hours east of Bloomington. Although Illinois residents knew that Eagle Wings was Japanese and that it was going to supply Diamond-Star, very few understood what Eagle Wings was or the nature of its relationship with Mitsubishi. The origins date back to 1962 when sixteen small suppliers in Okayama Prefecture formed a cooperative to supply the Mitsubishi Motors factory a few miles away.

This cooperative had now invested $36.5 million to build the Rantoul plant. The plant manager, Isamu Kawasaki, had the air of someone who did not particularly want to be building a factory in the Illinois corn belt. But Mitsubishi had not left him much choice. "We had a direct request from Mitsubishi to have a project here in the United States," he said.

The reason it was so important for him to come to Rantoul was that he and his men were familiar with specifications for parts, Mitsubishi style. They knew how to make brakes, steering assemblies, axles, bumpers, engine mounts, and other important items. They could also act as a staging area for parts made by other suppliers. Eagle Wings would paint things that needed it, inspect the parts, and deliver them at precisely the time Diamond-Star needed them. "This is our method to manufacture our cars in Japan," Kawasaki explained.

The list of suppliers was still in the formative stages because production had not actually started. Other Mitsubishi companies not on the list were positioning themselves to get a piece of the business, either then or at some future point. For example, Mitsubishi International was building a steel processing center in Illinois to handle steel imported from Japan; Mitsubishi Metal was building a plant in Columbus, Indiana, that would make cast parts for auto engines and transmissions; and Mitsubishi Electric had established a subsidiary near Cincinnati, Ohio, to make electronic auto components. All these companies naturally would be seeking business with other Japanese and American companies. None would ever fully depend on Diamond-Star.

Diamond-Star President Yoichi Nakane was very sensitive about his suppliers. He was worried about his American suppliers because they had not yet met desired quality levels, nor had they proven their ability to meet the rigid requirements of just-in-time delivery. Mitsubishi and other traditional Japanese suppliers had been obliged to bid for the work to win it. Many probably did have better quality.

But the result was that the only parts coming from American companies were such things as carpets, trim, bolts, paint, and molding—in other words, all low value-added material. The engines, drive trains, chassis, and other highly engineered parts of the car were arriving from Japan as part of "knock-down kits." These were arriving on U.S. soil with very little duty because Mitsubishi had succeeded in declaring its factory site a foreign trade zone, which entitled it to a reduction of federal duties. Parts that were of moderate importance were being provided by traditional suppliers who had been "transplanted." The American role, aside from labor, was limited. "The things they're buying domestically are bulky or else things with high-energy costs," complained Lee Kadrich, director of governmental affairs at the Automotive Parts and Accessories Association in Washington, D.C. "The so-called local sourcing is none other than migrant suppliers [from Japan]. If they can replicate the structure of the Japanese auto supplier network in the U.S., then it's a detriment to the U.S. industry." This group of about a thousand U.S. auto parts suppliers fought Diamond-Star's effort to win foreign trade zone status, but lost. This is where Mitsubishi's political clout came in handy.

Diamond-Star maintains that its U.S. content is 60 percent, but this could be misleading. The U.S. government, as a whole, has never defined "U.S. content." Instead, the Environmental Protection Agency set a standard for determining the difference between imported and domestic cars for emission control purposes. That definition of U.S. content includes labor, transportation, advertising, and other costs. Kadrich estimates that in terms of actual parts, American content at the Mitsubishi plant may only be 25 percent. In short, Mitsubishi imported the majority of its production system from Japan.

That was great for Illinois, but it also had wider regional and national impact. The Japanese construction industry was given one more platform to compete against U.S. companies while the home Japanese market remains largely closed. Komatsu and other capital equipment suppliers also received a boost, to the detriment of the already decimated U.S. machine tool industry. American auto parts suppliers were hurt, as were General Motors and Ford. Chrysler will market some of the cars produced in Bloomington, as it does other Mitsubishi vehicles.

Illinois subsidized all of this by assembling a package of incentives for Diamond-Star of as much as $177 million, which affected local, state, and federal governments. Such incentives as tax abatements, training, road improvements, water and sewage improvements, and reduction in federal import duties were put in place. Eric G. Pitcher, the state's senior coordinator for foreign direct investment, acknowledged that Mitsubishi Motors had to find a place to build a factory in the United States if it wanted to stay in the American auto market. This was because the yen was in the process of doubling in value, and Toyota, Nissan, Honda, and Mazda had all announced plans to build plants. Moreover, he knew that Mitsubishi was Japan's largest industrial group. The question was: Why use taxpayer dollars to help it? "The only reason a company this size needs incentives is if you're in close competition with another state," Pitcher said. "And we didn't want Indiana to get it."

So what does all this mean? First, what Mitsubishi is doing in autos in the United States must be multiplied many times over. This particular group is also active in high technology, metals, petrochemicals, and other fields, from California to North Carolina. Its most sensational investment was in Rockefeller Center, and at about the same time it announced a joint venture with Westinghouse to, in effect, take over the American company's electrical power generating equipment business. Shortly thereafter, Mitsubishi group companies bid successfully against GE Plastics in a $850 million fight for Aristech Chemical Corporation. Sumitomo, which is similar in scope and affiliated with Mazda, NEC, and other major companies, is also expanding throughout the United States. Mitsui is slightly different in business mix because it has a focus on trading, banking, real estate, venture capital for high technology, and other areas outside of traditional manufacturing.

There are many other major Japanese companies in the United States that have *keiretsu*-like structures. It is simply the way the Japanese do business. Individuals band together as groups. The groups band together as companies. And the companies band together as parts of bigger systems. The pattern of vertically integrated, inward-looking activity that Mitsubishi is creating in autos is being created in many different sectors and many different American states.

The Japanese *keiretsu* system may be more efficient economically. Diamond-Star can produce a car more cheaply than General Motors or Ford in part because of its new low-cost base in Illinois, but also because it has so many members of the Mitsubishi group willing and able to accept such a low rate of return for a sustained period of time. These companies, all dedicated to enhancing Mitsubishi's role in the auto industry over the course of decades, also do not face pressure to enhance shareholder value or to pay big dividends. There is no contest in terms of the scale of the competing organizations. If General Motors or Ford tried to establish the same degree of vertical integration as the Mitsubishi group, there would be howls of indignation. If it is bad for an American company to be vertically integrated inside the United States, why is it good for a Japanese company? In effect, the U.S. government has one set of rules that apply to American companies in America, and another set that applies to Japanese companies in America.

Chalmers Johnson puts it this way:

> The *keiretsu* form of industrial organization is one of Japan's most important contributions to modern capitalism. At the same time it clearly violates Western conceptions of anti-trust and makes a mockery of much of the economic theory that is predicated on the workings of "market forces." Western nations have yet to come up with a competitive match for the Japanese *keiretsu*, and the problem is becoming acute as *keiretsu* relationships are extended to North America and Western Europe through direct investment by Japan.[4]

Whether a Mitsubishi-style pattern of activity actually violates U.S. antitrust law would obviously depend on a court, and that is unlikely in the current enforcement atmosphere. Proving antitrust violations in an American court of law would be problematical because whatever coordination takes place happens in Tokyo, not on U.S. soil. Plus, it is so subtle and informal that obtaining evidence would be difficult. The Mitsubishi companies do not have absolute financial control over each other, and even proving that they were actually members of the same legal entity would be difficult. Mitsubishi executives naturally deny they are engaged in inappropriate or unfair conduct. "We are not colonizing the world," said Nomura.

Whatever the legal issues, it is clear that Mitsubishi is creating a concentration of economic power in the United States that is at odds with long-prevailing American notions about diversity and pluralism. To compete, American companies are obliged to enter into deeper relationships with a smaller number of suppliers and win government permission for a handful of joint research and production arrangements. The point is that the structure of Japanese groups at home affects the nature of their presence in the United States and around the world and challenges the economic pluralism of host countries. The Japanese values and systems that prevail at home are exported. This is critical in understanding the broader issue of Japanese investment in America.

❖ 17 ❖

Is Japanese Investment Created Equal?

The influx of foreign investment in general and Japanese investment in particular into nearly all spheres of the American economy is one of the most profound economic trends of the postwar era. A subject of encyclopedic scope, it is extraordinary how much ink has been spilled on it and yet how little Americans understand it, much less agree about it. What is foreign investment and what is it for?

American companies have invested hundreds of billions of dollars in other countries to guarantee entry to those markets, to secure access to raw materials, to hedge against the vagaries of currency swings, and to protect themselves against protectionism. The Americans began their postwar investment push at a time when Western Europe and East Asia were devastated. Over the years, most countries in Europe and Asia have continued to seek American investment.

The creation of jobs is only one piece of the equation. The Americans have a reputation for stimulating local supplier bases and transferring new technologies, knowingly or unknowingly. In a bustling area like Taiwan's Hsinchu Science Park, the Taiwanese companies getting off the ground in high-tech fields are peppered with Taiwanese executives, scientists, and engineers who once worked for American companies. American investment is usually seen as positive for a nation's trade balance because allowing a U.S. company to make something in one's country usually results in a decrease in that company's imports into the country, and helps that country win access to international markets. A large percentage of Taiwan's exports, for example, are from the plants of U.S. companies. Additionally, American companies usually actively attempt to localize their managements. Today, many top American multinationals rely more heavily on third-country nationals or local residents than on American managers.

American investment is not always so beneficial to a host country, particularly in natural resource industries such as oil, agriculture, and mining. In some cases, American investment has remained in a fairly primitive stage of extraction. These countries have not been notably successful in using the American presence to their own long-term competitive advantage. South Korea and Taiwan used American investment as a launching platform for economic success. Nigeria and Angola have not.

Whether American investment has been a form of exploitation or genuine economic stimulation has depended, to a considerable extent, on the skills and determination of the governments and populations of countries that have been on the receiving end. Those who approached American investment intelligently won. "Europe got 20 times more out of American investment after the war than the [American] multinationals did," Lord Lever, a prominent British businessman, once said.[1] Part of this enlightened response was driven, of course, by fear of U.S. domination.

Over time, as Europeans, Australians, and Canadians have emerged as investors in the United States, they seem to be playing by much the same rules as the Americans. These countries have more formal and informal limits on American investment than the United States imposes on their investments. German companies are difficult to acquire because of the commanding presence of DeutscheBank, which holds shares in many German companies. French bureaucrats have blocked American acquisitions as well. But with all these countries, there is a broad degree of balance and reciprocity. Open investment has worked.

When it comes to Japan, the key question is this: Is all foreign investment created equal? In other words, is Japan's investment push taking place on the basis of the same Western model?

At the popular level, the argument about Japanese direct investment almost always centers on jobs. Of course, it depends on what kind of Japanese investment is at stake. When a Japanese company merely buys an American company, that does not usually create jobs. A few jobs may actually be lost in the short term as Japanese managers or engineers arrive, but the continued existence of other jobs may actually be safeguarded. When a Japanese company invests in real estate or buys a stake in a bank or buys U.S. government bonds, that does not necessarily create jobs either. It is when the Japanese build manufacturing plants that politicians get excited about new jobs. Although only a fraction of Japanese investment is for building new plants, it generates the most political mileage for governors and mayors.

But does that create jobs for the entire United States, or merely redistribute them? Norman J. Glickman and Douglas P. Woodward, in a book entitled *The New Competitors,* have contributed to this debate with an analysis of how Japanese and other foreign "greenfield" investment destroys jobs in the United States at the same time it creates other jobs.[2] It's naive to argue that because a foreign investor creates a thousand jobs in Georgia, the United States as a whole has gained a thousand jobs. Other jobs in Pennsylvania or New Jersey may already have been lost as a result of the foreign investor's competitive challenge, and still others could be destroyed as a result of the foreign investor's strengthened competitive position in Georgia. In the final analysis, Americans do not have the statistical tools for measuring the national impact of this investment.

But to obtain the full benefits of Japanese investment, of all sorts, Americans must look beyond jobs. We have examined the issues of Japan's commitment to indigenizing management, the impact of Japanese investment on U.S. values, and the *keiretsu* structure of some investments. Rounding out the debate are issues of technology transfer, local sourcing and trade impact, and reciprocity. Each of these issues are building blocks for a more complete portrait of Japanese investment practices so that Americans can absorb all possible benefits and promote their own revitalization. That is the enlightened response, consistent with how U.S. investment has been received by successful host countries.

Technology transfer is a crucial but messy concept. The genuine transfer of technology usually happens over a period of time as skills are transferred, person to person, as part of a training process. It is doubly difficult to discuss technology transfers between the United States and Japan because so many different channels are currently in use: from U.S.-Japanese joint ventures among large companies to Japanese acquisition of or investment in smaller U.S. technology companies. The Japanese also maintain a research presence in the United States, and American companies conduct research and development (R&D) in Japan. One can argue whether this multifaceted technology relationship is balanced or fair, but technology is undeniably flowing in both directions.

In general, the Japanese are tougher-minded about technology than Americans. Much of America's nonclassified research is carried out at universities and laboratories, and the results are published openly. Most of Japan's research at home takes place within specific companies and is proprietary. And whereas Americans sometimes want to give away their technology, the Japanese rarely do. I have met American businessmen who went to Japan in the 1960s and licensed their technology to Japanese companies virtually for free because they believed the Japanese, as a nation, needed help. The Japanese, however, rarely give technology away. The Koreans, for example, have obtained entire industries from the United States such as telecommunications switchers, but they complain about receiving little technology from Japan.

While the American food industry may not immediately spring to mind when one discusses Japanese technology transfer to the United States, it is important because a large percentage of U.S. exports to Japan are foodstuffs. In this respect, the Americans resemble a developing country. In such cases, the key question is whether the provider of raw materials is successfully moving downstream into more "value-added functions" and becoming sophisticated enough to extract more profits from the overall process of getting his product to market. To some extent, this involves greater technological sophistication as well as marketing know-how. Call it mental technology.

In the case of fishing, are American companies processing and packaging the fish or simply sending off raw fish? In the Pacific Northwest's lumber industry, are Americans driving down the value-added chain to make finished wood products such as furniture and cabinetry or are they shipping out round logs? In the case of Washington wheat, or Iowa corn, or Illinois soybeans, are Americans making finished consumer products to sell to the Japanese or selling their raw products in bulk?

The Japanese have invested in the value-added end of most of these industries. Although there are some exceptions, one impact has been to hold American providers at the raw material stage. When the Japanese buy grain elevators and barges for shipping the grain, or build a brewery, or construct a tomato processing plant, they are extracting much of the value-added from American natural resources, while the Americans remain mere providers of raw foodstuffs. In the case of beef, for example, the Japanese have stampeded to buy U.S. ranches, feedlots, and packing plants.[3] Of course, in cases where Americans are content with shipping out raw materials and do not demand Japanese technology and know-how, the Japanese cannot be faulted for not providing it.

In manufacturing, a great deal of attention has been focused on

Japan's purchase of major American companies or the building of large new plants. Technologically, however, a more significant trend has been Japan's purchase of hundreds of relatively small American technology companies. To what effect? Lawrence Krause, at the University of California at San Diego, believes that the large-scale Japanese acquisition of these smaller American companies interrupts the process by which technology normally flows to major American companies. Big American companies have normally been able to count on having a small company come to them with a bright idea. For the right price, the big company would make the little guy rich and take the idea into commercial production. "But now the Japanese buy these small firms and the Japanese become a serious competitor for U.S. enterprises," Krause argues.[4] "This has a very bad impact on the competitive balance. The Japanese don't want to develop small companies, but just ship their technology back to Japan." It then arrives back in the United States in the form of products.

Krause is not alone in arguing that the technological impact of Japanese investment is different from that of the Dutch, British, or Canadians. "Nearly once a week, a high-tech U.S. firm is acquired or receives equity from a Japanese firm," says John P. Stern, a vice president of the American Electronics Association's office in Tokyo and a frequent commentator on U.S.-Japanese technological relations.[5] "This constitutes a massive transfer of future potential from the U.S. to Japan. Japanese investment is used as a vacuum cleaner for acquiring technology. In contrast, the investment by most other countries in the American high-tech industry is for the purpose of capital gains, but not for importing technology back to the home country for competitive uses there."[6] Other owners of small- and medium-size technology companies argue that the United States is becoming a "science colony" for others, particularly the Japanese.[7]

The best single example is how Kubota, Japan's largest manufacturer of agricultural machinery, transformed itself from the backwaters of technology into a manufacturer of mini-supercomputers by buying or taking a major equity stake in a series of small American technology companies.[8] By spending less than $75 million, Kubota acquired stakes in Ardent Computer, Exabyte, MIPS Computer Systems, Akashic Memories, and Synthesis Software, all in the Silicon Valley area. It thus won access to the technology of all these companies and launched a new division selling cutting-edge computers in competition with American computer makers. The same pattern is being repeated in biotechnology, solar energy, and other sensitive fields. Smaller U.S. companies clearly get benefits when they win infusions of long-term "patient" capital from Japan, but these seem eclipsed by the broad outflow of technology.

One other area where Japan's investment results in technology outflows is research at American universities. A congressional study has found that, by taking part in industrial liaison programs at American universities, Toshiba is developing a new technology for recording images on disks, Toyota is devising new engineering stress sensors, and Asahi Chemical is computerizing its manufacturing process. In many cases, the research is being underwritten by the federal government.[9] Japanese companies have access to research in some of America's most sensitive technologies. Hitachi Chemical, for example, has provided $12 million for a research facility at the University of California at Irvine, which will give it access to biotechnology research that will be carried out for the next forty years.

MIT has been at the center of this controversy. Of two hundred endowed chairs, twenty-one have been funded by Japanese companies. At the Media Laboratory, Japanese companies have researchers working with Americans to find new applications for video, digital audio, and personal computer technologies. MIT President Paul Gray steadfastly defends his institute's deepening ties with Japan. U.S. federal funding is on the decline and if MIT wants to continue its "chase for knowledge," it must obtain funding somewhere. Further, he argues that American companies could participate more aggressively in these research projects but they choose not to, and therefore are not reaping as many benefits as their Japanese competitors. The Japanese also make scientific contributions to the research. "It's a net gain for us," he says.

Still, the result is that Japanese companies are obtaining commercially valuable technology from federally funded institutions that U.S. companies are not obtaining, at least not as fast or as much. NEC Honorary Chairman Koji Kobayashi, for example, credits access to MIT research for much of his company's success in computers.[10] There is no easy solution. The best research into new scientific vistas is done when scientists openly exchange results. To impose a straitjacket on MIT would be a terrible tragedy. But Japan's presence is giving its companies an edge over their U.S. competitors.

There are clear-cut cases where Japanese investment is resulting in technology transfer into the United States, mostly in heavy, troubled industries. NKK Corporation, which has management control of National Steel, is struggling to modernize the American steel-making facilities, and LTV won technological help from Mitsui and Sumitomo. Bridgestone is making a major commitment to upgrade Firestone's tire-making capability, and involves some new production technologies. Some Japanese auto parts companies also have transferred technology to American joint venture partners. These are genuine efforts to up-grade industries that the Americans let slide, but one does not find this in resource-based industries or in sophisticated fields at the high end of the spectrum. In many cases, it is limited to American companies that are owned or managed by the Japanese. In that way, it is kept within Japanese control, not genuinely transferred.

It is not possible to reach any definitive judgment about whether Japanese investment results in a greater flow of technology out of the United States or into it, but certainly there is a greater outflow than that associated with U.S.- or European-style investment in other host countries. And certainly the blithe assumption that Japanese direct investment always results in technology transfer does not stand the test of scrutiny.

Another key issue in assessing the Japanese investment model is what impact it has on the American trade balance. Although some Japanese companies have begun exporting products and components they make in the United States back to Japan, this is still a tiny current in comparison with the flood of components and capital goods being imported into the U.S.

John Kageyama is a lovely, grandfatherly man. About age sixty, he has worked in fifty countries for Matsushita Electric Industries, the world's largest maker of consumer electronics. Although Matsushita is in general a progressive investor, Kageyama manages a "screwdriver" VCR assembly facility. That means the American value-added is little more than turning a proverbial screwdriver to assemble things that are really manufactured someplace else. This facility is in an old Del Monte warehouse in Vancouver, Washington, just across the Columbia River from Portland, Oregon. Ten Japanese work there and 170 locals.

In this plant, the electronic innards of VCRs manufactured in Japan move down conveyor belts for testing. American-produced plastic is fed into American-made plastic injection molders to create bodies for the VCRs and American-made paint coats them (but this is done by Japanese-made painting robots). The American employees seem happy and Kageyama appears to be a wise and benevolent boss.

In one sense, Matsushita is to be congratulated for moving even the assembly of VCRs to the United States. Other Japanese manufacturers have not even taken that first step. But the U.S. content of Matsushita's VCRs, broadly defined, is only about 15 percent. Why? "We are looking for local suppliers but we find it a little bit difficult," Kageyama explains patiently. Americans don't make VCRs themselves, so there is no American supplier industry.

One hears variations on this theme time and time again. Keiji Endoh, chairman of Ricoh, once explained to me that, for years, about 90 percent of the components he used in his copier assembly facility in Southern California were imported from Japan because he had not been able to find any "blue-eyed"—American—suppliers as opposed to "black-eyed"—that is, transplant Japanese—suppliers. "The suppliers are very weak," he said. Although Ricoh executives say they have made progress in localizing their production, it was accomplished at least in part by shifting some manufacturing functions from Tokyo to California. While that may be better than mere screwdriver assembly, the best result from the American point of view would be for American suppliers to learn how to supply the heart and brain of Japanese products being manufactured or assembled in the United States.

Lost in the arguments back and forth is a generally accepted principle of cross-border investing: It is the responsibility of a foreign investor to identify capital goods suppliers and other equipment and parts suppliers in the host country and use them. If that means transferring some technology or skills to upgrade their quality levels, that is part of the price that must be paid for the right to own a piece of another country. A foreign investor is not obliged to have 100 percent local content—that would be extreme. But investors are expected to make the effort, and to continue making it over a period of years. This is one of the major stimulative effects of foreign investment. Countries that do not insist on this are missing the boat.

There's no question that some Japanese have done it well. Honda's U.S. content, including both Honda's transplant suppliers and genuine U.S. suppliers, is now higher than some of Detroit's U.S.-assembled cars.

But the broader pattern is that the Japanese operate through their *keiretsu* and other traditional relationships for a surprisingly large percentage of their sourcing, whether in the host country or from back home. Mordechai Kreinin, a professor at Michigan State University, spent a year in Australia, a neutral testing site, to study the subsidiaries of twenty Japanese, twenty-two American, and twenty European manufacturing multinationals. He found that the Japanese relied on within-the-family buying decisions there as well. "The purchasing behavior of Japanese-owned subsidiaries is definitely different from that of their American-owned and European-owned counterparts," Kreinin writes. "They are tightly controlled by the respective parent company, procure their equipment mainly in Japan, and own and operate mainly Japanese machinery." Western companies have a far greater tendency to purchase locally. Japan's very industrial structure shapes its buying preferences.[11]

The Europeans are more sophisticated about these matters. Whenever the European Community bureaucrats identify a Japanese screwdriver plant, erected by a company that has been cited for dumping, they demand that the facility be upgraded into genuine manufacturing or else face dumping tariffs. The Americans are simply content with jobs. This is a leap in understanding that the Americans need to make. In Europe, trade policy and investment policy are linked.

Japan's sourcing patterns are one reason Japan's trade surplus with the United States has remained at the $50 billion mark despite a major investment push. As Japan has shifted to assemble and manufacture more finished goods in the United States, the import of Japanese capital goods and components into the U.S. has increased. The mix of Japan's exports has shifted. In other words, rather than shipping a laptop computer from Japan, Toshiba sends the components and perhaps some equipment for assembling them to California. Companies in dozens of industries have done much the same. If they had procured their capital goods and components in the United States, the trade picture would have been dramatically different.

In short, Japan's investment has helped it sustain its export drive, rather than slow it. "Japan's strategy to build factories and assembly plants overseas has permitted total Japanese exports to rise," concludes Ron Napier, the Salomon Brothers economist in Tokyo.[12]

This broad portrait of Japan's manufacturing investment practices, from its management style to its sourcing patterns, suggests that it is, in fact, a different model than U.S. or European equivalents. Some Japanese argue that it only appears this way because they are in the early stages of internationalizing, and that over time the models will converge.

But this does not ring true. The pattern is too consistent. Japan has a smaller propensity to indigenize management. It implants its own systems and values rather than adapting to local standards, and it does not provide technology as readily or use local suppliers as extensively as most U.S. or European multinationals. One result is that the impact of Japanese manufacturing investment on trade patterns is less stimulative than normally expected.

Moreover, Japanese manufacturing investment differs from the waves of European investment in America that helped build the railroads and the canals. That European investment, although feared by many at the time, did not threaten the existing American industrial base, whereas Japan's investment is often concentrated in industries where it attempts to displace American companies. Another frequent argument is that U.S. foreign investment in the postwar era has been positive for host countries and therefore Japan's is positive for America. But to compare Japan's investment today with earlier European or American investment is to miss an essential point: Japanese investment practices are based on a different model.

He was an unlikely figure to put the spotlight on the issue of investment reciprocity and investment balance between the United States and Japan. Texas oilman T. Boone Pickens, Jr., must have been out in the sun too long when he decided to attack the Toyota empire in its own backyard. Pickens acquired 26 percent of Koito Manufacturing Company, a piece of Toyota's vertically integrated production system. Toyota owned 19 percent of the company, had three board seats, and played a role in appointing key managers; it was also Koito's largest customer. This was enough to secure Toyota dominance. Many such suppliers fall under Toyota's sway. It drives them each year to improve quality and reduce their costs, but it protects them from outsiders. This almost feudal network of subcontractors and suppliers is part of the key to Toyota's success.[13]

We may never know for sure why Pickens attacked Koito. It is universally assumed in Japan that a shady Japanese coconspirator put him up to it. And certainly he made no secret of his desire to run for governor of the Lone Star State—a little visibility wouldn't hurt.

But even though he had become the company's largest stockholder, Koito refused to give Pickens a seat on the board or to provide him with basic financial information. Pickens tried to whip up a lynch mob. On his behalf, seventeen U.S. senators complained that Koito is "dominated by a cartel-like group of corporate and financial institutions." Pickens alleged that Japan had a closed monopolistic economy. But at the end of the day, Pickens could not—and cannot—win because he was fighting the very structure of one of Japan's most powerful manufacturing empires.

Specialists have understood the inward-looking group nature of Japan's economy for years. Not only do members not wish to sell out, the Japanese government reserves the right to reject any foreign takeover attempt that is not 100 percent agreed upon.[14] The only surprise about the Pickens raid was how candid Japanese bureaucrats were in acknowledging what it proved. A Ministry of Finance bureaucrat put it to me this way:

> We are not a [U.S.-style] capitalist country. We do use market mechanisms a lot. But that doesn't translate into capitalism. The majority of companies are not owned by capitalists, in your sense of the word. Our

system may be called managerial capitalism. It is not managed for share-holder interests.

We don't like capitalists just coming over and buying companies by sheer force of money. A corporation is a community. I have some pride in the Japanese system in this regard. I don't want LBOs and all that. It's not healthy. We have a different system and we think it's a better system.

Another reason more Americans are not investing in Japan is that it has become prohibitively expensive. While it is not unusual to hear about a Japanese company investing $1 billion or $2 billion in the United States, investments by big American companies in Japan often come in the $50 million to $100 million range, and these are often expansions of existing facilities rather than brand-new plants. Indeed, many major American companies have actually sold out of Japan to help prop up their quarterly earnings or fend off raiders.

Moreover, Japan does not offer incentives for investment. Their prefectures do not maintain offices in New York or San Francisco wooing investors. Every prospective foreign investor has to submit a report, through the Bank of Japan, to the Ministry of Finance and other relevant ministries as part of one of the industrial world's most elaborate approval processes. It is an entirely different mentality. The Japanese do not like foreigners owning any more of Japan than necessary. It's as simple, and as complex, as that.

Although American companies have investment positions in Japan, many dating from the early days after the war, the statistics clearly show an investment imbalance between the two countries. Direct investment includes manufacturing, stakes in banks, real estate, and other tangible assets. This kind of Japanese investment in the United States increased to a total of $53.4 billion, a thirteen-fold increase, from 1980 until the end of 1988, according to official U.S. Commerce Department statistics. The Japanese government measures this direct investment in a slightly different way and on that basis Tokyo analysts expect cumulative Japanese direct investment in the United States to reach a total of $75 billion by the end of 1989, double the level of two years earlier.[15] Clearly, billions of dollars more are in the pipeline. The United States could be in only the early stages of Japan's investment drive.

By contrast, U.S. Commerce Department figures show accumulated U.S. direct investment in Japan of $14.7 billion at the end of 1987, which increased to $16.8 billion by the end of 1988. These statistics are enormously complex, in part because of difficulty in knowing whether to measure a company's original investment or its value in today's market. Nonetheless, the official figures indicate that Japan's direct investment in the United States is triple the same kind of American investment in Japan.

The broadest measurement of investment includes shares in companies when the stake is less than 10 percent, corporate bonds, government debt instruments, and other so-called portfolio investments. By this measurement, Japan's total investment in the United States is nearly twice America's investment in Japan, or $284.8 billion versus $156.3 billion at year-end 1988, according to Commerce Department economists in Washington.

A question that official figures cannot answer is whether Japan is the largest single investor in the United States. The government does not provide a specific accounting for each country in Europe, but it does acknowledge that much of the money that is registered as "British" investment is coming from other nations who use London's money markets as a convenient platform for managing their American investments. "Everybody in the world uses London as their vehicle for investing in the U.S.," says one Commerce economist. "We don't know who the ultimate investors are." This includes money from as far away as the Middle East and Hong Kong. And since London is a major financial center where Japanese companies maintain a presence, an unknown percentage of Japanese purchases of U.S. stocks and bonds are recorded as originating in London. One other channel for Japanese capital is purchases or investments made by the U.S. subsidiaries of Japanese companies. If a U.S. subsidiary of a Japanese company makes or borrows money in the United States and invests it, this is not technically considered foreign investment. Billions of dollars a year in Japanese real estate purchases, for example, are not reflected in Commerce Department figures, and they may be coming through this channel.

It is likely that Japan is already the single largest investor in the United States if one considers that a significant share of what is described as British investment isn't really British. And few would argue with the fact that if current rates of investment continue, Japan will clearly lead all other nations investing in the U.S. by 1991 or 1992.

The obvious imbalance in U.S.-Japanese investments is only one reflection of an overall economic relationship that is dangerously unbalanced. This has led the Japanese to make another kind of investment—attempting to influence the American decision-making process.

❖ 18 ❖

Managing the Americans

There are two jokes in Tokyo, one old and one new, that speak volumes about Japan's perception of its ability to shape the American political system.

The old one is: Washington is just as easy a place to do business as Jakarta. You can get anything done for a price.

The newer joke made the rounds as Ronald Reagan was being paid $2 million to appear in Japan in October 1989. It must have been a source of tremendous satisfaction; bureaucrats still have tapes of old Reagan movies like *Jap Zero* sitting on their cluttered desks. They know exactly what he stood for during World War II, and here he was appearing as a hired hand for the upstart Fuji Sankei media group. Takeshita had raised nearly $8 million in a single evening's fund-raising event and Reagan had come cheap in comparison. He was the second former American president to enjoy a financial relationship with the Japanese. Jimmy Carter's center at Emory University in Atlanta also receives funding from Ryoichi Sasakawa, a famous right-wing philanthropist. As related by a journalist, Japanese politicians were saying to each other: "We have Carter and Reagan. Now who can buy Bush?"

These remarks reflect the surface of a much deeper phenomenon. Most Americans believe their government is still in a position to shape Japan and its policies but that it simply has not found the right formula. What they do not understand is that Japan has been gradually turning the tables. There have been no sudden moves. It has happened painstakingly slowly, step by step. The instruments that the Americans once used to cajole and prod the Japanese have declined in their effectiveness. At the same time, the potency of Japan's levers has gained exponentially.[1]

To manage the Americans, the Japanese have promoted the development of an impressive intellectual and political edifice in the United States. Although other nations have also played the influence game, Japan's is the broadest, most sustained, and most richly endowed effort the Americans have witnessed. It is wider in scale than what either Israel or the Arabs, armed with petrodollars, have tried to achieve. South Africa's Informationgate and South Korea's Tongsun Park scandals were minor in comparison.

Japan has been the largest spender on identifiable lobbying activity in Washington since 1984. "This ain't OPEC all over again," said Richard J. Whalen, chairman of Worldwide Information Resources, a public relations firm that has Japanese clients. "This is different." By 1988, Japanese entities were spending a conservatively estimated $310 million a year, not including advertising, in shaping and guiding the overall American decision-making system. This spending has continued to escalate rapidly.[2]

Japan's infrastructure for monitoring and shaping U.S. decision making is national in scope. The Ministry of Foreign Affairs (MoFA) maintains fifteen consulates throughout the United States, more than any nation, and these consuls general are active in nurturing relationships with local opinion leaders and decision makers. MoFA is also the broad umbrella organization for the Japan Society of New York and the Japan Economic Institute, two respected bodies that have come to play more clearly advocatory roles. MITI's JETRO also maintains a wide geographic reach and over the years has increased its concentration on "soft-side" activities, as opposed to the "hard side" of trade promotion. Also at the grass-roots level are Japan-America societies and Japanese chambers of commerce, which are coordinated and quasi-official. Naturally, Japanese companies, banks, and trading companies with investments in specific communities are part of this network. At the local level, these players often cooperate, but there is also competition. Both MoFA and MITI believe they should be the preeminent ministry managing the American relationship, and they therefore have been known to squabble. "The coordination is not as much as desired," the Foreign Ministry's Taizo Watanabe said, when still based in Washington.

At the national level, aside from lobbying and information-gathering in Washington, the Japanese use a variety of tools to build relationships with major universities and think tanks. Corporate and foundation philanthropy, including the endowing of chairs and sponsoring exchange visits, is a key tool. American companies that have joint ventures with Japanese companies, that allow themselves to become dependent on Japan, or that simply want to protect their positions in Japan are effective levers for helping shape American political decision making on Japan's behalf. From the grass roots to the state level to Washington, the Japanese are active participants in the political process.

Although the leading Japanese executives and officials involved in this effort have periodic meetings in Washington or New York, there is no evidence that one particular agency or committee is in charge of managing it. It is only loosely coordinated, but it is systematic and long-term, like most things the Japanese do. Some wags in Washington say that Japan has done to lobbying what it did to the transistor.

As a result of Japan's bid for influence, lobbyists, former congressmen and government officials, law firms, consultants, public relations firms, and other influence-peddlers are enjoying a bonanza. It is not limited to one party. Frank Fahrenkopf, the chairman of the Republican Party, has worked for Toyota and goes to Japan to look for more work. On the other side of the aisle, former Democratic national chairman Robert S. Strauss has worked for the Japanese. Other household names who, according to official Justice Department records, have worked for Japanese interests include former National Security Adviser Richard Allen, former Deputy Assistant Secretary of State Stanton Anderson, former director of the CIA William Colby, former U.S. Special Trade Representative William Eberle, former Deputy Trade Representative Harold Malmgren, former White House domestic policy chief Stuart E. Eizenstat, and dozens of others. The list is like a who's who of Washington's toughest, savviest political operators.

The U.S. Trade Representative's office, which handles U.S. trade negotiations with Japan, has become a kind of training ground for Japan's lobbyists. "A remarkable percentage of people in the Special Trade Representative's office graduate to Japanese companies or to law firms working for Japanese clients," says Stephen S. Cohen, director of the Business Roundtable on International Economy, at the University of California at Berkeley.[3]

Indeed, it has now become a standard career path in Washington: A talented American works for the U.S. government for several years to obtain needed experience and connections and then goes to work for a Japanese company, either directly or indirectly. Japan's wealth has thus contributed to polarizing the intellectual and policy debate among American elites about how to respond to Japan.

It is not surprising that Japan would seek any available avenue for wielding influence. A powerful nation cannot be blamed for trying. It deserves some form of representation to protect its interests. This is only fair. The greater responsibility is on the side of the one that is influenced. If the Americans were able to manipulate an African dictator or a Latin American despot to their advantage, the Americans would consider that fair in the calculus of international relations. The client-state had a dependency and Washington able to manage their government as a result. It also works in reverse. Some of America's best and brightest have not been forced to work for Japanese interests. They have chosen to do so. "The fault lies not with the Japanese," says TRW vice president Pat Choate, author of *Agents of Influence*, which concentrates on Japan's influence in Washington.[4] "It lies with us. This is an issue of the governing class in government and academia and finance."

The pivotal question is whether, as a result, U.S. political and governmental elites, from time to time, make decisions or fail to make decisions in a way that advances Japan's interests to the detriment of the American commonweal. It is a complex question to answer because different Americans naturally define the national interest in different ways. Moreover, it is difficult to quantify a real impact from many of the bitterly contested turf battles in Washington, which take place behind the beltway prism. But the general pattern is clear.

The classic case was the Toshiba Machine flap in 1987 and 1988. Toshiba beat what appeared to be a clear majority in the U.S. Congress that wanted to impose tough sanctions against it for the shipment of submarine propeller–making equipment to the Soviets. By using a combination of grass-roots politicking and Washington lobbying, Toshiba was able to escape with only minor damage. Whether it was wise to penalize Toshiba or not is beside the point. Toshiba, backed by the rest of Japan's influence network and coached by some of Washington's top political experts, was able to identify companies, plant managers, suppliers, and other Americans who would suffer if Toshiba were penalized.

This was the first time that a Japanese company was able to leverage its U.S. investments and business relationships across the United States in such a way to deploy genuine, high-profile political muscle. Companies such as Apple, which depends extensively on Toshiba parts, went to bat in Washington, as did Honeywell Incorporated, which buys semiconductor chips from Toshiba. Westinghouse, which has a joint venture with Toshiba in Horseheads, New York, also pitched in.

So did political leaders such as Ned McWherter, the governor of Tennessee, who has Toshiba plants in his state and wrote a letter to Tennessee's congressional delegation counseling caution. In Washington, Toshiba used veteran political operators Jimmy Jones and Leonard Garment—one a Democrat, the other a Republican—to get through to the decision makers. "Toshiba was able to purchase access to those who were writing the legislation," complained Congressman John Bryant (D-Tex.). "They won."[5] Altogether, Toshiba spent an estimated $30 million on its campaign.[6] In the end, Toshiba left clearer footprints than Japan has on most other issues.

It is widely assumed that Japanese interests played a key role in watering down the 1988 Trade Law by blocking such items as the Bryant Amendment, which would have required foreign investors to register with the Commerce Department. Congressmen are rather candid in acknowledging the pattern: "If you have three Japanese high-tech firms employing 6,000 people in your district, as is the case in Vancouver [Washington], it lowers your political rhetoric on trade," Congressman Donald L. Bonker of Washington was quoted as saying.[7]

In other cases, Japanese construction industry lobbyists apparently succeeded in persuading the White House to kill the appointment of J. Michael Farren, who had a reputation for being tough-minded, as lead negotiator in talks to open the Kansai Airport project to U.S. builders. This was brought to light by Senator Frank H. Murkowski of Alaska. The White House denied it and Farren later took another key job at Commerce.[8]

These are not the kinds of fights, like abortion or flag burning or congressional pay raises, that excite the American populace. They are complex infights, and Japanese faces are rarely seen buttonholing congressmen. It is largely done through American intermediaries, which makes it doubly difficult to identify and quantify.

Also, the Japanese are not as interested in ramming bills through as they are in blocking something from happening. One key technique is simply stalling a piece of legislation, repeatedly. The Japanese do not have to defeat a piece of legislation such as the Bryant Amendment decisively, they merely have to delay it to maintain the status quo.

They also play agencies against each other. This is one reason that their efforts to "collect information" are so important. Much of JETRO's governmental effort, for example, is dedicated to collecting detailed information. Because of MITI's infighting with the Ministry of Foreign Affairs, JETRO cannot maintain an office in Washington. But it frequently flies its officials down to Washington from New York, and they employ a range of American companies and consultants. By all accounts, JETRO spends far more money on these activities than the embassy, which is part of the Foreign Ministry.

Once information about a certain department or committee has been obtained, it can be passed to another player in the decision-making process who is against a particular course of action. This does not involve direct lobbying, and therefore does not have to be registered with the Justice Department, which is charged with the task of monitoring all foreign lobbying activity. If Commerce is planning something that might affect Japanese interests, information can be relayed to Treasury, which is the department most sensitive to the government's dependence on Japanese capital to fund the budget deficits. Getting information to Treasury about something Commerce is planning can, therefore, intensify interagency bickering. "Then they sit back and let the interagency process eat itself up," says a former Commerce trade negotiator. As described by Michael B. Smith, a veteran U.S. trade negotiator, Japanese diplomats are eager "to find inconsistencies in the positions of different U.S. agencies and drive a wedge in there."[9] This is similar to the techniques Japanese bureaucrats use at home to manipulate politicians in the Diet.

Japan's effort may be concentrated on what some Americans may consider obscure fights, but collectively these battles shape U.S. governmental economic and trade policy toward Japan. The fact that an effective U.S. policy toward Japan has never coalesced cannot be blamed on the Japanese. Overwhelmingly, the responsibility is in American hands. No power on earth could have inflicted this degree of confusion on the American political elites if they were not already confused and prone to corruption in the first place. Japan's effort can only work when the infighting in Washington is severe and the ethics poor.

One of Japan's top lobbyists is James Lake, a principal in the firm of Robinson, Lake, Lerer and Montgomery. A talkative man who exudes excitement about the political game, Lake came from California as part of the Reagan revolution. One of his key relationships in Washington was a friendship with former U.S. Trade Representative Clayton Yeutter. Aside from an enviable set of connections, he became then-candidate George Bush's principal (unpaid) communications adviser and coordinator of press operations at the GOP convention.

The ultimate insider, he is also a registered lobbyist for Suzuki Automotive, the Japan Auto Parts Industries Associations, and Mitsubishi Electric. It is next to impossible to measure the "efficiency" of a lobbyist because of all the loopholes in the laws governing them. But Lake's records filed with the Justice Department show that during a six-month period in 1987, he met or spoke with Yeutter or his deputies twelve times on behalf of Mitsubishi Electric, for which his firm received $129,000.[10] Access does not always produce results. There is not a shred of evidence that it had any impact on a major semiconductor fight that was raging at the time and which was a matter of concern for Mitsubishi Electric. It may have been that Yeutter had already decided to exclude Mitsubishi Electric from a list of Japanese companies that were going to be slapped with $300 million in duties, as a penalty for violating a U.S.-Japanese semiconductor accord. But the fact of the matter is that Mitsubishi Electric did escape, while others did not. Lake is not obliged to reveal anything more than the fact that he made the contacts on behalf of a given client.

The same pattern, however, has unfolded for other Lake clients. In another instance, Colombia's flower sellers needed to beat an anti-dumping complaint filed by U.S. growers. Lake's records show he made calls to Yeutter. The U.S. growers' complaint was rejected. Even if Lake is wasting his clients' money, he certainly has created the appearance that he has been effective.[11]

Lake is a man who knows how to press the flesh, how to engage, how to wield the symbols of access, which is the ultimate elixir in Washington. We had an 8:30 A.M. appointment, but he did not show up at his sleek office a couple of blocks from the White House until 9:00 A.M. "You'll have to excuse me," he apologized, "I ran into some congressmen." At the same time, he is also what insiders refer to as a "spin-control artist." In a town where headline management is a consuming profession, he is a master at articulating the implausible. Certainly Washington is filled with special interests eager to twist the system to their own advantage. Isn't it different when it comes to foreign special interests?

"I think the Japanese as well as some Americans are beginning to realize we have an international economy," Lake said. "Sophisticated people in the U.S. and Japan understand there is an inextricable link between the U.S. and Japan. The pressures on the political side here have forced the Japanese to look and see if they were doing enough politically. Political necessity has forced them to expand the scope, breadth, and intensity of their communications. They are getting more sophisticated and American-like in their approach."

Lake and other lobbyists for Japan acknowledge that Americans cannot engage in similar efforts to shape Japan's decision making because that system is not as open. If it is not reciprocal, and the Japanese are the largest player in town, it seems that creates an imbalance. Is that the way our system was designed?

"The guy with the message and the organization wins," Lake replied.

"I don't think it's a perversion of our system. That *is* our system."

Sometimes when Americans disagree among themselves about relations with Japan, it is helpful to consider the European perspective. Some Europeans worry about the U.S. propensity to become so emotionally charged about Japan, but the European perspective is that the Americans are a bit naive about Japan. "There's no other major country in the world where foreigners can come in and manipulate the system like this, I promise you," says Tomasz Mroczykowski, a professor at American University in Washington and a specialist in U.S.-Japanese relations. "The Europeans simply don't allow it. It's amazing that [in Washington] I can leave government, open up my own company, and make fifteen times as much working directly against the interests of my country."

Having an "international economy" and "inextricable links" are one thing. Germans, French, Dutch, Canadian, and other world leaders all acknowledge these trends. But they never lose sight of their national interests, nor do they countenance their own former officials working against these interests.

Crucial to the success of any major lobbying effort is the ability to shape the marketplace of ideas itself. To support Japan's attempt to shape U.S. government decision making, the Japanese play a surprisingly sophisticated perception game to shape the way Americans think about trade, investment, technology, military relations, and other issues of keen importance to Japan.

The power game is played on several different levels. The most obvious level is one where information and views are disseminated and are readily identifiable as Japanese in origin. The English-language publications of the Japan Economic Institute, JETRO, and sometimes the Japan Society of New York clearly advocate and defend Japanese interests.

Less savory are the propagandistic techniques employed by some Japanese diplomats, industrialists, and U.S. specialists. Akio Morita says Americans can't make things. Shintaro Ishihara says Americans are racists. Diplomats say Americans don't really want to sell their products in Japan; Americans can't understand Japan; and America is a broken society. One of the most recent additions to this list, from JETRO's New York President, Mikio Kojima, is that Americans are too America-centric. In other words, they insist on seeing the world through American eyes. All this is designed to keep Americans preoccupied with internal divisions and to prevent them from focusing on Japan.

Japanese diplomats also have become increasingly candid in threatening Americans with a "divorce" if they attempt to redress their economic imbalances with Japan. A particularly threatening set of remarks came from one of Japan's top New York–based diplomats in an off-the-record lunch with magazine editors. When the subject of managed trade came up, he warned of Japanese retaliation. "The flow of Japanese money [into America] will be smaller," he said in a matter-of-fact tone. "Interest rates will go up. That will result in a recession or a depression. It's almost suicidal, I think." After a pause, he added, "I'm not threatening at all." But of course he was, and it naturally has a chilling effect on any journalist who wants to probe to the heart of U.S.-Japanese relations. There is often a hard edge to efforts that can be readily identified as Japanese attempts to shape American perceptions.

But far more effective is the subtle manner in which Japan magnifies the voices of American elites who benefit from their association with Japan. One strand of this intellectual edifice consists of Peter G. Peterson, Fred Bergsten, and Stephen Bosworth, all former U.S. government officials.

Peterson is chairman of The Blackstone Group, a New York investment banking firm that has played a role in upwards of $8 billion in acquisitions by Sony, Bridgestone, and the Mitsubishi group. A former Commerce secretary in the Nixon administration and a former head of Lehman Brothers, Peterson has made tens of millions of dollars by helping Japanese companies buy American companies. Nikko Securities, one of Japan's four largest securities companies, has invested $100 million in his firm and supplied another $100 million for a leveraged-buyout fund that Blackstone manages.

At the same time, Peterson is chairman of the prestigious Council on Foreign Relations and the Institute for International Economics, which Fred Bergsten manages. Bergsten's institute, one of Washington's more respected think tanks, was originally set up with funding from West Germany and some U.S. companies, but now the Japanese supply funds as well. Bergsten's institute received $280,000 of its $3.6 million annual budget in 1988 from Japanese-supported sources including the U.S.-Japan Foundation.[12]

This is a foundation originally endowed by the right-wing philanthropist Ryoichi Sasakawa, the same man who supports Jimmy Carter's center at Emory. Bosworth, a tall, distinguished-looking former ambassador and top State Department official, runs this foundation. He argues that it has a U.S.-dominated board of directors and is, therefore, an independent entity. But he acknowledges that the organization serves the purpose of shaping American perceptions of Japan; it is also clear from the foundation's pattern of activity that it supports Japan's agenda.

Peterson is quite active with speeches and articles that support his argument that the United States needs massive amounts of foreign capital and should not, therefore, devise new policies for managing or coping with Japanese investment. In making his argument, he often cites work in progress at the Council on Foreign Relations or at Bergsten's institute. Bergsten and Bosworth also give speeches, write articles, and move in top policy circles. There is no hint that Peterson or Bergsten or Bosworth have changed their public policy pronouncements simply because they either profit or obtain funding from Japanese-related sources. "I've been for open trade and open investment since the 1950s, at a time when it hurt my short-term interests," Peterson claims. Bergsten adds that the Japanese have never sought "one iota of influence" at his institute. Bosworth says there is "nothing nefarious" about what his foundation does.

The point, rather, is that Japan has advanced their weight and their prestige in the marketplace of ideas at least in part because they sing the right tune, and this has advanced Japan's agenda as well. Bergsten, in particular, has been valuable for the Japanese. As a devotee of free market international economics, it was his argument that the dollar-yen relationship was the key problem in redressing the trade imbalance that helped prepare the intellectual groundwork for the dramatic strengthening of the yen. His assumption was that Japan would respond to this kind of market force. But it did not, and does not. Without identifying his Japanese funding, he also publishes studies that support the view that foreign investment in general and Japanese investment specifically do not require any new policy responses. That helps create an intellectual climate that supports Peterson's business.

There are many other members of the U.S. intellectual establishment who benefit from their association with Japan and, coincidentally or not, articulate views that are in consonance with Japan's. All this is part of a broad effort to tilt the marketplace of ideas itself. On the one hand, this involves magnifying or amplifying the voices that Japan identifies as sympathetic, while isolating, neutralizing, or discrediting voices that are troublesome. In the former case, Japan supplies funds to professors and think tank experts who are either sympathetic to Japan or are ardently subscribe to the notion that free trade and free investment theories apply to Japan. The Japanese also provide access to their top thinkers, and this advances the careers of American professors. Some, like Stanford University's Michael Boskin, have made it all the way to the White House, as economic adviser to Bush. Boskin and others like him have had unpaid consulting or advisory roles to Japanese government–supported bodies. This has triggered congressional criticism, but there is little prospect for corrective action.[13]

There is no evidence that obtaining funds or access somehow changes the views of any of these experts. Rather, their studies and opinions are broadcast more widely. They use the funding to print their studies on glossy paper and distribute them with a more concerted public relations effort. They advance the prestige of their think tanks and centers at major universities. Their careers are enhanced because, in effect, they have been given megaphones.[14] "In the marketplace of ideas, the Japanese seek people who will amplify their views and then pour in the money," says Pat Choate. "You dominate the adviser corps."

One reason this is particularly important is that journalists who cover U.S.-Japanese issues require sources—government officials, experts, consultants, academics, investment bankers, and others. As a participant in this marketplace of ideas, it is obvious to me that Japan's wealth has had an impact on the range and breadth of views that are expressed, and therefore reported. On the one hand, it is difficult to find credible sources because many professors, experts, investment bankers, consultants, and others have worked, are working, or hope to work for Japanese interests.

On the other hand, longtime sources who are even mildly critical can go mute or silent. For example, I had a source for a *Business Week* cover story on Japan's influence in America who was a Japanese-speaker with years of experience; he was able to offer comments that were balanced and clearly in the midrange of the broader marketplace.

When I called this source back a year later to talk about Sony Corporation's acquisition of Columbia Pictures, he said, "I really can't comment."

"Why not?" I asked.

"I'm doing a couple of deals with Sony myself."

"Well," I pressed, "who would you recommend that might have some balanced views of this acquisition, someone who is not too critical but someone who is not on Japan's payroll?"

"Gee, I'm sorry, I just can't help you."

And that was it. If some Americans self-manage, others self-censor. In fact, a majority of the people who are identifiable as "experts" owe a certain measure of their career progress to their Japanese connections. They protect and support one another. In effect, they represent their own intellectual establishment. "Where is the independent analysis?" asks Peter White, president of Atlanta's Southern Center for International Studies. "The Japanese have been smart. They've learned to buy the talent. But we've been very naive."

Americans who are identified as critical of Japan often find themselves subjected to subtle campaigns of isolation. This is similar to the hammering-the-nail technique that the Japanese use against one another at home. Former trade negotiator Clyde Prestowitz, American journalist James Fallows, and Dutch journalist Karel van Wolferen, all of whom have written books or articles that have received wide attention among American policymakers, were apparently identified as irritants, so Japan's information-control machine went to work on them. They are subjected to massive attention from the Japanese news media and the diplomats and U.S. specialists who monitor American opinion. The key is to identify their weak points and then broadcast and magnify those weaknesses.

One small example: Fallows, who wrote an article entitled "Containing Japan" for *The Atlantic* magazine, has some good instincts, some bad. One of his weakest points is arguing that the United States can and should impose sudden tariffs against Japanese imports. He gave a speech one day in Seattle making this argument. His remarks did not appear in the American national media, but they did receive attention in Japanese newspapers that were distributed across the United States. A Japanese diplomat based in New York with whom I had lunch the next day knew what Fallows had said the previous day in Seattle. No matter what else Fallows had said, his remarks about a tariff were held up to me as an example of why Fallows was dangerous. Fallows had been monitored, his weak point identified, and he was being hammered behind his back, Japanese-style. It was an attempt to discredit him in the eyes of someone who acts as a gatekeeper in U.S.-Japanese news coverage.

Even American businessmen in Tokyo find themselves under pressure if they are too outspoken. As explained by one Japanese-speaking executive who had lived in Tokyo for several years: "If you stand up at a meeting and say, 'Let's wake up,' they go back to headquarters and say your guy out there in Japan is rocking the boat. That is bad for business. Then, bang, you're transferred out." A few weeks later, this executive lost his job in large part because of his outspokenness.

Not only does Japan's power have an impact on governmental decision making, it also shapes the breadth and the nature of the U.S. debate itself.

In addition to conventional lobbying and perception efforts, Japan has become increasingly sophisticated in using its direct investments and American technological and financial dependencies on Japan to shape the U.S. political climate. Sometimes the Japanese use these explicitly. At other times, Americans simply recognize the dependencies, whether they admit it or not, and manage themselves accordingly.

The Toshiba case was just one example of a systematic, nationwide campaign to use political muscle at the grass-roots level against Washington. The three key areas where the Japanese have been able to do this are the West Coast, the Southeast, and the Midwest. The Japanese are certainly cognizant of regional differences in the United States. Even though many Californians are originally from the East, California as a whole resents the East. One way this resentment has been expressed is by keeping New York banks out of California. Instead, California has allowed itself to become a major U.S. platform for Japanese banks. Walking down the streets of San Francisco's financial district feels a bit like being in Tokyo: Sumitomo, Sanwa, Mitsui, Mitsubishi, and others are there in force. No Citibanks or Chases. Although there has been a federal prohibition against interstate banking, Californians have consciously helped to keep the New Yorkers out while letting the Japanese in. When interstate banking goes into effect, the Japanese banks will be able to use their California base for a nationwide expansion.

It is also obvious that Midwesterners suffered enormous economic damage during the 1980s when many East Coast elites were writing off the "Rust Belt." Staring into the economic abyss, they were left to fend for themselves. Governor Richard Celeste of Ohio, for example, still speaks bitterly about how Washington allowed the U.S. machine tool industry, a major employer in Ohio, to be nearly wiped out in the face of Japanese competition. The South, particularly Tennessee, Georgia, Virginia, and North Carolina, hosts major concentrations of Japanese investment and staunchly protects these companies against critics from the North. "If we could get used to the Yankees, we could get used to the Japanese," Jesse Coe, the public-works commissioner of Lebanon, Tennessee, was quoted as saying. "Life here goes on."[15]

The Japanese manage their relations with these different regions through organizations such as the U.S. Midwest/Japan Association and the U.S. Southeast/Japan Association, which are loosely affiliated with the Keidanren, the powerful business federation. Top CEOs, trading company presidents, key diplomats, and other top-echelon Japanese attend annual meetings of these organizations, clearly outgunning local and regional American participants in terms of experience and organization.

The Midwest was the last of the three key regions in which the Japanese established their investment base, but it was important politically. Because the Midwest was so hard hit in the early 1980s, it became a hotbed of political pressure to take tough retaliatory action against

Japanese imports, whether rightly or wrongly. American embassy officials, labor union leaders, and governors themselves told the Japanese
they should invest in the Midwest to create jobs and therefore mitigate
the political pressure. "We've told [the Japanese] that a strategy of
investment in the Midwest could produce less trade pressure in Congress," Michigan's governor, James J. Blanchard, told me at a meeting
of the U.S. Midwest/Japan Association in Columbus, Ohio. "That's
what they've done. They'll deny it has any political connection, but
it's not a mere coincidence."[16]

The $5 billion that six auto manufacturers invested in six states,
making up a new "auto alley," did have a political impact. Although
this impact is difficult to quantify, governors and other state and local
leaders began sending different signals to their representatives in Congress, warning them against jeopardizing the new links with Japan. "In
Washington, we hear noises every day from Congress and the Hill,"
said Yoshiyasu Sato, a top official at the Japanese embassy in Washington. "The feeling here [in Columbus] contrasts. I think it will be quite
influential in Congress." The irony is that now, having established
their auto alley, the Japanese are in a position to deliver more crippling
blows to the U.S. auto industry, forcing even more plant closings.

The lesson is that, in view of a kind of balkanization that the Americans have accepted, the Japanese have learned to play the ends against
the middle. The Japanese have become increasingly vocal in acknowledging and advocating this strategy, particularly as it relates to Congress. The key architect of this grass-roots activity is Sony's Morita. As
early as 1984, Morita was leading a delegation of executives from the
Keidanren who promised California $1.4 billion in investment and
eleven thousand jobs if California dropped its unitary tax. That was an
important lever in persuading California to accede, and in demonstrat-
ing the effectiveness of this carrot-and-stick approach at the state
level.[17]

By 1988, Morita was leading a group called the Council for Better
Investment in the U.S., which included 160 major companies that had
investments in the United States. Also under the aegis of the Keidanren, the group's objective was to beat back adverse political develop-
ments at the state and federal levels. In 1989, this group was renamed
the Council for Better Corporate Citizenship. This provided for the first
time tax-deductible status to Japanese corporate contributions made to
U.S. communities hosting Japanese investments.

Morita has shown himself to be a master at coordinating the use of
investment and corporate contributions to eliminate political problems
in the United States. "In the future, if Japanese business circles are

regarded as a really good American corporate citizen, sometime I hope the Japan-bashing attitude by congressmen will disappear," Morita said in an interview at Sony headquarters in Tokyo. "If congressmen or a politician bashes his friend [Japan], then that politician will lose the election." This is astonishingly ambitious: Morita is trying to neutralize Congress and he is showing his fellow Japanese chief executives how to do it.

Another advocate of using these investment levers is Kenichi Ohmae, of McKinsey and Associates, the prestigious management consulting firm, in Tokyo. The author of such books as *Mind of the Strategist* and *Triad Power*, Ohmae cultivates the image of an enlightened internationalist in the United States while fostering one of a tough guy at home. The linguistic prism allows this. But one of his interviews appeared on the front page of *Nihon Keizai Shimbun* and attracted attention from Japanese-speaking Americans in Tokyo. It read:

> If you really want to exercise political power in the United States, invest strongly in a state that is pro-Japanese, also buy their products, and finally raise up [cultivate] Congressmen from those states who would be supportive of Japan. There were Congressmen who smashed Toshiba products on the U.S. Capitol lawn with a hammer. It would be good to simply halt investment in the states and localities of Congressmen who do such things. The states and localities will want the investment. In this way, I think Japan should use its economic power to put a stop to one-sided Japan-bashing in the U.S.[18]

What allows Morita and Ohmae to speak so openly about shaping the American political process is that the United States has allowed itself to develop dependencies for a variety of economic inputs, ranging from direct investments to spare parts to funding the federal budget deficit. Virtually every nation depends on another nation for something. The key question is how a country manages its dependencies, and whether they are increasing or decreasing. The Americans, long accustomed to being supreme in the world, have paid scant attention to the dependencies they have developed on Japan. Now these have reached the stage that they are politically significant.

As early as 1986, some of Washington's savviest political analysts recognized that Japan's financial clout in particular would translate into political influence. "The Japanese are developing a whole arsenal [of political levers]," Kevin P. Phillips, a well-known Republican strategist, said. "You've got this incredible investment in the U.S., particularly Treasuries. They use that as leverage. Any time they want to steer more of their money into the U.S., they can step up their direct investment. They can say, 'Hell, we're not going to buy Treasuries. We're going to buy Arkansas.' That's not a joke.''[19]

Recognition of Japan's financial power went largely unheeded until the October 1987 stock market crash. Although there were a variety of factors such as program trading and the specialist system on the floor of the New York Stock Exchange, one underlying influence was that the Japanese had bought heavily into the U.S. government bond market and then started selling when inflation worries cropped up. There is not the slightest hint that the Japanese did this with malice. It was merely a by-product of their overall power in the market. Nicholas Brady, co-chairman of Dillon, Read & Co., currently Bush's secretary of the Treasury, conducted a presidential task force study into the October 19 crash. Although his report did not mention the Japanese role, he told a meeting of pension fund managers that this was "the real trigger." The Japanese have come to acknowledge this as well.[20]

As time passed, it became obvious that Japanese interest in buying or not buying U.S. government debt was the single largest driving force in determining U.S. interest rates. Each time the U.S. government goes to the market to sell IOUs, it is obliged to adjust the interest rate it is willing to pay depending on demand. If the Japanese, as the largest single external force in this market, are not particularly active in buying the bonds, the U.S. government has to increase the yield. That means interest rates go up.

The longer Washington allows politics-as-usual to prevail and the budget deficits keep widening, the more the government's dependence on Japanese capital continues to grow. All told, Japan owns about $500 billion of U.S. government debt.[21]

How does this financial power translate into action, or inaction, by the U.S. government? Soon after taking office, President Bush himself offered a revealing insight in a news conference in February 1989. When asked how he would reassure Americans who were afraid that the Japanese were buying and owning too much of the U.S. economy, Bush said:

> I'd tell them that the Japanese have the—are the third largest holder of investment in the United States, behind the U.K. and the Netherlands. I'd tell them that it is important, if we believe in open markets, that people be allowed to invest here, just as I'd like to see more openness for American investors in other countries. I'd tell them that we have to do a better job in knocking down barriers to American products in the various markets.
>
> I'd tell them don't get so concerned over foreign ownership that you undermine the securities markets in this country. We have horrendous

deficits and foreign capital joins domestic capital in financing those deficits.[22]

One can quibble with some of Bush's facts. In terms of direct investment, the Japanese were indeed third at the time, but soon thereafter displaced Holland. Of course, if one includes Japan's financial investments, there was strong evidence suggesting they might already be the largest overall investor.

But the key passage was in the last two sentences, and it is an amazing admission. It would be inappropriate to address the broad subject of Japan's buying and owning too much of the U.S. economy because it might interfere with the flow of Japanese funds into the financial markets. As long as Japanese money continues to allow the U.S. government to avoid facing up to its fiscal responsibilities, there is little prospect that the Bush administration will seriously address the issues posed by foreign investment in general or Japanese investment in particular.

Japan's inherent power has been demonstrated elsewhere, as in the case of financial reciprocity—another obscure spat between the United States and Japan. Congressman Charles E. Schumer of New York engineered a provision in the 1988 Trade Law requiring the Federal Reserve to issue a report on whether U.S. securities houses enjoyed as many opportunities in Japan as Japanese counterparts do in the United States. If the answer was no, the penalty was to deprive four big Japanese securities companies of their right to be primary dealers in Treasury bonds.

When August 1989 rolled around and the Fed report was due, it was clear that although the Americans were making some money in Japan, they did not enjoy anywhere near the same access that the Japanese do in the United States. But most insiders knew it was inconceivable that the Federal Reserve could reach this firm conclusion. It would force action against the four Japanese securities firms who were buying the government's debt. Depriving them of their right to buy U.S. bonds would be suicidal. The U.S. government needed every buyer it could find. It had a dependency. So although the headlines warned of a major Fed report and how it might have dire consequences, it came as no surprise that the report adopted a conciliatory tone. No Japanese lobbyist or agent had to make any threats of retaliation. It was obvious.

In this climate, it has become the rule for Japan to win on the issues it chooses to fight in Washington, rather than the exception. Sometimes it prevents Americans from making bad decisions. Sometimes it prevents them from making prudent ones. Whether Japan's lobbyists and consultants are able to put in a "fix" on a particular issue becomes much less important in view of the overall weight of Japan's investment base and U.S. financial dependencies. Japan now has achieved the necessary power to no longer give in to Washington's demands, and indeed to help keep Washington looking like "a district of confusion" rather than the District of Columbia. As one U.S. diplomat in Tokyo acknowledges: "Every time we sit down with them, we have to be aware of their economic and financial power."

Rather than adapting to any American vision, the Japanese are in the process of declaring policy independence from the United States and indeed, as part of the Structural Impediments Initiative, they have finally found an official platform for lecturing the Americans about their own failings.

None of Japan's tools would be of concern if the Americans had equal clout in Japan. This is the reciprocity test. Is U.S. involvement in Japan's decision making growing? Is the United States developing some powerful new tools that allow it to shape Japanese thinking? Are tough decisions increasingly being made in Tokyo that hurt some Japanese so that the overall relationship can be maintained and enhanced?

The short answer to all of the above is no. Although the American government and American businesses are entitled to engage in Japan as deeply as they choose, the real decision-making system is subterranean. It is tremendously difficult to identify the key, informal decision makers, much less seduce them. To be sure, some sophisticated American companies have learned to exploit differences between two ministries or to align themselves with one business group to attack another, but they have not achieved influence nearly on par with Japan's use of former American ambassadors, heads of CIA, heads of political parties, and other elites.

Compared with the MoFA's geographic spread in the United States, the State Department's embassy in Tokyo and the consulate in Osaka have only a superficial presence. A limited number of diplomats are bilingual, and they tend to move in relatively narrow circles. Many are transferred from other countries and have to spend years learning the ropes in Japan. By the time they do, they are transferred out. The Americans have no equivalent of MITI's JETRO. Although there are talented American diplomats in Japan, particularly Ambassador Michael H. Armacost, the American presence is distinctly modest compared with Japan's diplomatic reach in the United States.

In the Japanese media world, there is also no comparison. Japanese journalists, think tank experts, and professors are almost universally preoccupied with putting forth Japan's point of view, not serving U.S. interests. It is inconceivable that a preeminent Japanese intellectual would accept funding from the American government or business sector to openly advocate that Japan give in, accommodate, or "change." They would risk losing everything. "The Japanese are operating here [in the United States] on a scale that no U.S. company does in Japan," says Peter Grilli, former director of the Japan Project at New York's public television station WNET/Thirteen, who coordinated public TV's fund-raising from Japan. "We're not as adept or as sophisticated."

Then there is the bribery problem. It is against American law for U.S. corporations to give money to foreign agents under most circumstances. Lockheed, for example, ran into this problem in Japan. So even if an American company were to identify a truly critical decision maker who was inclined to shape the decision-making process to advance that company's purposes, it would require a large transfer of resources. American companies are denied that tool.

Overall, the levers the United States has with Japan have declined, not increased, in potency. Washington is an emperor who has no clothes. It has much less negotiating leverage than it pretends to wield. Its two pressure points have traditionally been the U.S. military presence and Japan's need for access to the U.S. market. But Japan is working as hard as it can to achieve self-sufficiency in defense and the Soviet menace has declined. Japan's booming domestic economy also has helped ease Japan's dependence on the U.S. market. At the same time, it has demonstrated the ability to either prevent Washington from imposing barriers or to circumvent them if they are put in place.

Sovereignty is not an absolute, a black/white thing. The Japanese lack complete sovereignty in their defense, and it is a matter of some irritation to them. In an interdependent world, it can be argued that Americans must sacrifice some sovereignty. The United States and Canada have ceded tiny pieces of their sovereignty for the sake of a North American market, and the Europeans seem headed down a similar path for the sake of unifying their markets by 1992.

But to be prudent, it must be reciprocal. The Americans are rapidly accumulating dependencies on a single nation, Japan, which is working diligently to build its own room to maneuver and to strengthen its identity, rather than submerging its interests in a grand international scheme of things. This unfolding pattern has triggered alarm from solid, middle-of-the-road thinkers. Arthur Schlesinger, Jr., argues that the United States must begin the post–cold war era by "recovering its independence."[23] Investment banker Felix Rohatyn has also warned that America's "economic independence" is at risk.[24]

It's too shrill, and indeed unfair, to argue that Japan is conducting a nefarious campaign to take over American decision making. A more balanced assessment would be that Americans are ceding it in some cases, giving it away in others. Piece by piece, they are trading it away. "Japan will [soon] be in a position, if not to dictate to us, at least to constrain the range of options we have for ourselves," says Kent Calder, the Princeton professor who holds the Japan Chair at Washington's Center for Strategic and International Studies.[25]

At the Foreign Correspondents Club in Tokyo, Murray Sayle, an Australian and one of the grand old men of the Tokyo press corps, has a slightly less diplomatic way of explaining it to Americans, who, like his countrymen, were British colonial subjects. Says Sayle: "Once again, you Americans are being told what to do by a small island nation with no apparent right to do so."

Part Four

THE
AMERICAN
RESPONSE

❖ 19 ❖

Rethinking Japan

Americans have long been able to reassure themselves about Japan's rapid inroads into the United States by choosing to believe that, at the right time, and under the right mix of internal and external pressures, Japan would gradually start managing its economic machine in a manner that the United States found more acceptable. It is a simple assumption, yet it has been the cornerstone of the U.S. stance toward Japan for decades. If only Japanese consumers or women understood how exploited they were, Japan would suddenly become a more egalitarian, consumer-oriented society that would be more inclined to buy American goods and moderate its pressure on U.S. industries. If only the value of the yen were higher, U.S. goods would be cheaper and more widely accepted. If only the Japanese stimulated their domestic economy, it would draw in a huge influx of American goods. If only we could find the right prime minister to talk to, we could persuade the bureaucracy to seriously address trade and investment imbalances. If only we waited a little longer, the Japanese would inevitably change and become "more like us." Many experts spoke of "convergence" as the two systems naturally evolved toward each other. The Japan Problem was destined to disappear.

As Americans head into the 1990s, this line of reasoning started to unravel. The prospect of social and political change in Japan—of the sort that would give a quick boost to U.S. interests—faded as quickly as it had arisen. The disruption or unrest that Reischauer and others had foreseen was not happening, nor was it likely to happen. Far from representing a break in the postwar order, or a "revolution" in values as some Japan-watchers had proclaimed, the Recruit and Uno scandals were more significant for what they revealed about the way in which power is exercised in Japan, and from what cultural and ethical plat-form. Rather than being crippled, Japan's power elites were proving surprisingly resilient.

In economic terms, the equilibrium that some Americans felt they had reached with Japan in the 1985–88 yen-shock period came to an abrupt halt at about the same time Japan was supposedly in the throes of a political crisis. The American deficit with Japan actually grew as a percentage of the overall U.S. trade gap and by late 1989 accounted for nearly half of the total. Auto plants were again being closed. Nearly two decades of attempts by waves of U.S. negotiators, officials, and congressmen to reverse the trade gap had been a miserable failure. It had grown from less than $2 billion in the early 1970s, a level President Richard Nixon then declared unacceptable, to the $50 billion level. U.S. exports to Japan were up, but Japan's exports to the United States were much larger and still growing. The flurry of tentative U.S.–Japa-nese accords that were reached in the spring of 1990 were billed by the Bush Administration as a major breakthrough, but they contained much less substance than advertised. There were major questions whether such structural changes in Japan as reforming the law against large retail chains would actually be adopted by the Diet. Further, it was unclear whether American exporters to Japan would benefit even if the law was changed. Agreements were reached on satellites, telecom-munications, and supercomputers, but there was little to suggest that they would fundamentally alter Japan's determination to develop its strengths in these fields.

On the investment front, Japanese kept buying American companies and moving into sectors that had long been immune. Sony's purchase of Columbia Pictures, capping a $5.5 billion spending spree in two years, was one of the signs that there were fewer limits than generally reckoned. Then came Rockefeller Center in New York. Japan was still on the march. It was clear that there was a gap in overall level of economic momentum between the two societies, which had an impact on the realms of values, systems, politics, and perceptions. The United States did not face such an imbalance with any other nation in the world.

In short, Japan was not reacting as it had been expected to. It was accelerating, not cracking up. It became increasingly clear that Japan was a late-twentieth-century Asian power that could not be explained by nineteenth-century Anglo-American concepts about the efficiency of the marketplace and the free flow of trade and investment. As they related to Japan, Smithism and Ricardoism were quaint Anglo-American notions. Grounded in assumptions about human, and therefore corporate, behavior that may have been accurate about Americans and Europeans fifty or a hundred years ago, this school of economics could not explain how the Japanese economy would act as it approaches the twenty-first century. Certain concepts are valuable, but in the final analysis this free market economic framework is based on assumptions about whether societies will advance the interests of their consumers over producers, whether they will allow economic imbalances between nations to reach an equilibrium point, and whether they will respect the precept of reciprocity.

But Japan was not advancing the interests of its consumers in a way that undercut its producers. Nor was Japan showing any haste in reversing what had come to be obvious economic imbalances with the United States. In a smoothly functioning global economy, the United States would have gone into trade surplus with Japan to earn the money to help repay its debt. This is the essence of a global economic system that is reciprocal and in balance. But one Japanese-speaking U.S. executive in Tokyo put it this way: "When you arrive at Narita Airport, you might as well put Adam Smith in a locker. Then come into Tokyo, do your business, and pick Adam Smith up on the way out. He's not relevant here." The Japanese themselves became increasingly candid in acknowledging that they did not believe in the same notions of unfettered competition, the invisible hand, and open investment. Top bureaucrats began to acknowledge that Japan had a different kind of capitalist system than the United States. All this was part of the rethinking of Japan in government, academia, business, labor, and other sectors of the United States.[1]

There were megatrends underlying this rethinking, which we can only briefly sketch here. One was the rapidly declining power of communism in general and the Soviet Union in particular. Ever since World War II, the Americans had organized themselves to confront communism around the world and to focus their energies and resources on that mission. This was ideological and military struggle of the sort the Americans could rally around. The good guys against the Evil Empire. Although the Soviet military apparatus was still very much in place, and tricky issues loomed throughout Eastern Europe, the prospect of a full-fledged European conflict had receded dramatically. The American effort had been spectacularly successful—but at a huge cost.

Partly because of these military costs, but also partly because of a lack of attention to economic fundamentals, it was now time to repair the damage, to rebuild economic security. That meant a modest shift in attention toward revitalizing the U.S. economy and toward America's economic relationships in the world. Inevitably there was renewed attention to Japan, with whom the Americans have a larger trade relationship than they have with any single European country.

Several public opinion polls showed that Americans were concerned about the imbalances with Japan. According to a Harris poll in July 1989 (see Appendix B), 69 percent of Americans said they felt the trade deficit was a "very serious" issue and 23 percent said it was "somewhat serious." It was a slightly misleading comparison, but several polls showed the Americans rated Japan's economic challenge greater than a Soviet military challenge. Moreover, 68 percent cited Japan's economic threat versus 22 percent who cited the Soviet military threat. The reason this comparison did not represent a complete picture was that other polls showed the Americans rating the drug problem or the environment as of greater concern than Japan. But still the evidence was clear that there had been a watershed in American thinking about Japan.

As a result, Ambassador Mike Mansfield's insistence that political, diplomatic, and military relations with Japan take priority over all other aspects of the relationship began to deteriorate during a series of flaps such as Fujitsu's proposed acquisition of semiconductor maker Fairchild, the Toshiba Machine Tool controversy, and finally the FSX debate. Japan's economic power had become so great that it no longer existed in isolation from U.S. strategic and defense-related interests. Its economic power also had become so great that it no longer made sense to continue transferring technology for defense purposes that could come back to haunt U.S. aviation and aerospace companies. "Mike Mansfield was a great man and I admired him," Peter Drucker told the Foreign Correspondents Club of Japan. "But he had one simple line: The political importance of Japan was so great that all economic considerations be subordinated to it. That is no longer operational. The balance of interests are shifting very fast."

Suddenly, the old patronizing notions about Japan were out of date. Japan's economy had surged past the Soviets' and had become 60 percent of the size of the American economy. Growing at a rate of about 4.5 percent, it was clearly going to become even larger proportionately. For decades, the Americans had consciously allowed poor, little Japan to exploit the international trading system, even to help it destroy entire industries in the United States, such as cameras, watches, shipbuilding, and consumer electronics. The United States helped create modern Japan because it wanted an anchor that would be strong enough to help offset Soviet power in the Far East and resist communism but also because it was the "right" thing to do. It was a price Americans were willing to pay, and the strategy worked.

But now the United States felt economic vulnerability, particularly in view of the financial shocks it received and the continued pressure on its auto, computer, machine tool, and other key industries. It was no longer acceptable for Japan to play the same old game. When a country enjoys the degree of success and power that Japan does, it is no longer realistic to view it as a quirky little island nation dominated by mysterious clans. It's not droll anymore. The standards and expectations change. It was Henry Wendt, the chairman of SmithKline Beckman and chairman of the U.S.-Japan Business Council, who put it best when he said: "Now the Japanese have become so large in the international trading system that they have to behave as a full-fledged partner, not just as a marginal player that exploits the system."[2]

Central to the rethinking of Japan was a better understanding of Japanese cultural precepts. The Americans have a much stronger commitment to egalitarianism, compared with Japan's sense of hierarchy. The United States, despite stops and starts, believes in absorbing people from foreign lands, whereas Japan has a much greater tendency to exclude. The Americans celebrate the individual, Japan the group. By accepting so much foreign investment and waves of immigration, the Americans have shown a greater willingness to allow their country to be internationalized, which is in contrast to Japan's continued preoccupation with national purity and national identity.

Americans also find it difficult to understand how they can be allies with another nation at the same time that they are locked in deep, seemingly permanent economic conflict. In the Judeo-Christian ethic, you are either my friend or my enemy. You cannot be both at the same time. But to the Japanese mind, this contradiction is not disturbing. As masters of long-term, low-level conflict, the Japanese find it only natural to embrace at one level and struggle at another. At the official level, the *tatamae*, I can be polite to you. At heart, the *honne* level, we can struggle. In conversations with Japanese, it is not unusual to talk about how two companies or two individuals were shaking hands above the table while fighting beneath the table, or how they may be embracing with one arm while holding knives behind their backs with the other. The Japanese have the phrase *kyoryoku shi nagara kyoso*, meaning "cooperating while competing." Most Americans would call this duplicity. Most Japanese call it natural.

This notion is at the heart of Japan's power game with the United

States. When the experts pose big questions like "The U.S. and Japan: Cooperation or Competition?" most Americans would perceive the answer as being either one or the other. But, in fact, it is both, which the Japanese have understood better than their American counterparts. For the Americans, either the market is open or the market is closed. Either they are free-traders or protectionists. They are either allies or enemies. Ambiguity and contradiction are difficult for a yes/no American mind.

The U.S. approach to Japan has also been remarkably naive because it presupposes that Japan will conduct itself on the basis of Judeo-Christian ideals. To reduce the argument to very simple terms, many Americans feel that Japan owes them a moral debt. After a terrible war, the Americans allowed and encouraged Japan to rebuild from the ashes and extended its defense umbrella to make it possible. Thus Japan should respond to moral arguments to "share" its wealth.

But the Japanese, as a whole, do not accept or understand this appeal. There is very little in their culture that allows them to suppose that the interests of an outsider should prevail over the interests of a member of the group. The notions of charity and generosity do not figure prominently. When the Americans pressure the Japanese to increase their aid to other countries, the American expectation is that the Japanese will literally give money away, as the United States once did. But the Japanese use their aid programs to advance their own economic interests to a greater extent than the Americans did, and the Americans are surprised. When governors and congressmen first cajoled the Japanese to invest in the United States as a way to redress the trade gap, they expected a certain measure of largesse. It was a way of compensating for lost jobs. Instead, the Japanese have used their investments, particularly in areas such as automobiles, to expand the flow of capital goods and components from Japan and at the same time build new pressure on U.S. auto companies. More jobs will be lost. When American negotiators cajole the Japanese into opening their beef and citrus markets, Japanese companies buy cattle ranches and orange groves in the United States and smoothly prepare to reap many of the benefits of the market opening.

The Americans also asked the Japanese to spread their wealth to help ease the Latin American debt problem, but the Japanese are hesitant to do this because it is not clear what's in it for them. It's not their problem. Again, the Americans are mystified. The lesson is that the Japanese do not operate on the basis of giving to or sharing with strangers for no identifiable advantage. They play a different power game. He who has power exercises it for his own advantage. That is fair. "Can

we trust the Japanese?" pondered one Japanese-speaking Western diplomat in Tokyo. "Sure, we can trust them to constantly advance and
defend their narrow interests. As long as you don't expect them to do
anything they're not programmed to do, you'll never be disappointed."

Armed with a deeper, more realistic understanding of Japan, it is
possible to cut through the confusion that has crippled the Americans
in formulating an effective response. Consider a passage by George
Packard, director of the Center for East Asian Studies at Johns Hopkins
University, that appeared in the *Washington Post:*

> The trade problem, which seems so intractable, will recede when both sides
> come to accept the principle of reciprocity in trade and investment. But how
> this is achieved is critically important.
>
> We can bludgeon the Japanese into submission and leave a residue of
> hostility for future generations. Or we can work with elements in Japan who
> seek change, including the new consumers, women, young married couples
> who aspire to better housing and the newly affluent who would be happy
> to work less hard. . . .
>
> The choice should be clear: either the United States and Japan will be
> closer partners, with benefits for the entire world, or they will be angry
> rivals, on a collision course. Not even the most severe of the critics can wish
> for a new collision with Japan.[3]

Although he receives Japanese funding, Packard seemingly argues
from the heart. His article was widely reprinted in Asia, but he makes
several assumptions that don't stand the test of scrutiny. First, the
Japanese in general don't buy the principle of reciprocity, which is a
fancy word for Western-style fairness. The Japanese system is predicated on getting better access to foreign markets than the foreigners are
allowed in Japan. Second, the United States cannot bludgeon Japan. It
has become too powerful. The United States depends on Japan in too
many ways. Even if it were desirable, it is not possible. Third, the forces
who "seek change" of the sort Packard has in mind are a tiny minority
with no real power.

Packard's last paragraph, however, is the most fascinating. He poses
an either/or choice between being closer partners or angry rivals. But,
in fact, there is nothing to prevent the United States from deepening
its partnership with Japan when it makes sense to do so at the same time
that it redresses imbalances in the economic sphere. There is no reason
to be angry about it. It is merely time to calmly recognize that in certain
aspects of U.S.-Japanese relations, the two countries are already rivals
and already in collision. How else to describe the competition between
the two auto industries, the two computer industries, the two banking

industries, the two machine tool industries? Millions of jobs are at stake. Domination of technologies and financial lifelines are up for grabs. Why pretend these battles don't exist?

Why also pretend that conventional policy concepts and instruments have worked? The Americans have been hobbled with fuzzy thinking. The phrases "global economy" and "international economy" suggest to many Americans that the era of national struggle is over. It is testimony to the fundamental idealism of Americans that they can even entertain this notion. But Japan is trying to advance its own national interests while appealing to the Americans to maintain their ideological commitment to free trade and open investment, even as they sink deeper into the hole.

The phrases "interdependence," "codependence," and "partnership" also strike a chord with Americans, who believe that cooperation and sharing can characterize the entire relationship with Japan. The black/white alternative is seen as conflict, and that is unacceptable. But the Japanese have a more sophisticated understanding of interdependence and partnership. While genuinely cooperating in some spheres, they will compete aggressively in others; conflict never has to become total.

Another phrase that is deeply rooted in a Judeo-Christian notion of sharing is "horizontal division of labor." Japan can excel in certain areas; the Americans will excel in others. The Japanese at one point appeared to endorse this notion. But as they geared up for the 1990s, it was clear they no longer did or never genuinely did. Otherwise, they would be content to allow Americans to retain leadership in some fields. Instead, the Japanese drive toward the top of the technological ladder in nearly all fields has been unremitting.

Perhaps the ultimate statement of the American sense of giving and sharing is the attitude toward the sale of U.S. assets to the Japanese. Conventional economic theory assumes that nationality is not important in the ownership of assets because all owners will manage those assets in the same "rational" way. In a balanced, reciprocal system among like-minded players, there may be an element of truth to this. At a more popular level, Americans assume there is plenty to go around, why not let them have it? Isn't it nationalistic, in a bad way, to insist that Americans retain control?

The Japanese model, however, has proven that the people who control the wealth-creation process enjoy the greater fruits. That's one reason Japanese prefectures do not maintain offices in the United States or Europe seeking foreign investment in Japan. They do not want to give up control of assets. The Japanese have recognized that a preoccupation with short-term consumption alone disperses wealth; long-term commitment to controlling the means of production builds it. A Japanese would instinctively understand that assets in his country should be controlled by Japanese. There would be no debate.

The U.S. response to Japan, like that of the British before, was bankrupt in many respects because it failed to understand Japan's different cultural base and economic model. It assumed that relatively simple instruments that the Americans and Europeans had been using among themselves for decades, the equivalent of gentlemen's agreements, would work with Japan. The result was that Americans have only tinkered at the margin without facing up to the nature of Japan's competitive challenge.

The U.S. government assumed that doubling the value of the Japanese currency would prevent the Japanese from maintaining market share in the United States, and would therefore reduce the trade gap. But the Japanese used the dramatic strengthening of their currency and the weakness of the dollar to maintain the trade gap at about the same level, while greatly expanding their position inside the United States itself. This is reminiscent of the debate from an earlier decade in which the Japanese told the Americans that the reason their goods were not selling in Japan was because of American inflation, which made those goods too expensive. Now that American goods are cheap and inflation largely under control, that does not seem to have had much impact on budging the trade imbalance. The Japanese have kept coming whether it was a strong or a weak dollar, whether interest rates were high or low, and whether inflation was high or low. These macroeconomic tools have not worked in addressing U.S.-Japanese trade imbalances.

Other examples of tinkering have been a series of agreements in the automobile, steel, semiconductor, machine tool, television, textile, and other industries. There is much debate about the concept of "managed trade" these days.[4] But it's nothing new: The United States has engaged in precisely that with Japan for many years, and in fact, the trend accelerated during the last years of the Reagan Administration. In almost every case, the Japanese have lived within the letter of the "voluntary restraint agreements" or other market-managing measures while at the same time beating the U.S. industry in question. The cost to the American consumer has been high. So not only does U.S. industry lose, the American consumer does, too.

The reason the Japanese have been able to succeed is that when a trade restraint is put in place, the American industry being protected often relaxes. Rather than using the temporary breathing space to build new plants, achieve Japanese-style efficiency and quality levels, and expand market share, the American industry keeps prices high and funnels profits into bonuses for executives, unrelated acquisitions, or enhanced shareholder earnings and dividends. Washington usually does not follow through and demand an action plan from those being protected. At the same time, pressure from Wall Street for earnings increases remains intense. Meanwhile, the Japanese, rather than acting like a European or American and simply giving up, are able to sell a fixed number or quantity of their products at an artificially high price. They also "sweeten the mix" of their exports by going upscale in terms of quality or design. The Japanese are able to make increased profits while the Americans relax and dissipate their competitive position. In the next phase of this process, the Japanese companies, in many cases, are able to use their profits to build assembly or manufacturing facilities in the United States and continue their drive to expand market share from a greatly enhanced competitive position. Thus they abide by the letter of these agreements, but use them to advance their interests.

At the same time, market-opening measures that the Americans win in Japan often prove pyrrhic. The U.S. government has negotiated agreements with Japan in both construction and the securities industry, for example. In both cases, U.S. companies are given carefully circumscribed pieces of the pie in Japan, while Japanese companies in those industries surge into the United States. Giving Bechtel a toehold in construction divides the U.S. construction industry while it allows Japanese construction companies to do billions of dollars' worth of business in the United States. Allowing Salomon Brothers and Merrill Lynch to slightly penetrate the Japanese securities industry diminishes the pressure from the overall U.S. securities industry but helps Japanese financial institutions achieve major market positions in the United States. The Americans, once again, assumed the Japanese would deal with them in the biblical sense of good faith. This gap between the letter of U.S.-Japanese agreements and the reality of what happens may help explain why someone like Ryutaro Hashimoto, the current finance minister, can appear bitter about all the times that Japan has "given in" whereas an American is concerned that his side keeps losing.

Japan's method of exploiting the open trading system is not rigid or static. Instead, it is a supremely agile system that can read the American style of debate and decision, and respond quickly. As soon as an argument appears in the American marketplace of ideas, long before implementation, the Japanese can start work on devising a response. Japan's rules and processes shift quickly, while the overall goal remains the same. It's more of a psychology, or a mentality, than a formal system. Because the transparency of Japan's decision making is so low, and always will be, they can shift obstacles. If tariffs come under U.S.

attack and must be phased out, testing requirements can be substituted to prevent major penetration. Whatever works. As one Japanese adage about dealing with American trade pressure has it: "Give the outer wall and retreat to the inner wall." Shift the line of defense. Create a moving target. The Americans will never be able to prove it or document it.

If managed trade has not worked in the past, there are three reasons why an old solution would be even less effective today. First is Japan's globality. The concept of applying tariffs or quotas against another country assumes that the country manufactures those goods on its own soil. But Japan has rapidly developed a global manufacturing base, in part for the express purpose of beating any protectionist measures against it. Not only do the Japanese make goods in the United States, Canada, Mexico, and Puerto Rico, they also have manufacturing platforms in Taiwan, Singapore, Malaysia, Thailand, and elsewhere in Asia. So far there is not much evidence that Japan ships goods from its plants in Europe into the U.S. market, but that is a possibility as well.

It is not at all unusual for a company such as Sony to make components for a color television in Japan, Taiwan, or Singapore; ship them to Mexico for subassembly work; and then ship the unfinished product to the United States for the addition of other parts and final assembly work. In other cases, Japanese companies can manufacture their entire product in the United States, from start to finish. Or else they are able to find cracks in the system. Hyster Corporation of Portland, Oregon, for example, has long fought against forklifts made by Komatsu and other Japanese companies, which it insisted were being "dumped" in the United States at below the cost of actually manufacturing them. When Hyster finally persuaded the U.S. government to put an end to Komatsu's ability to import finished forklifts into the United States, Hyster alleged that Komatsu started making components in Indonesia and Turkey and shipped them into the United States for screwdriver-style assembly.

In short, Japan has the wealth to shift production quickly from one country to another. Washington lacks a mechanism for responding to this tactic. Simple protectionism is like building a Maginot Line, as the French once did against the Germans. Such barriers do not work if the opposition can go around them. In the final analysis, the reason the Japanese cannot be "contained" is that they are out of the bottle. They are a global power.

A second reason an effective brand of managed trade is much more difficult to achieve than generally recognized is that American consumers and American companies are so dependent on Japanese finished goods or parts. Traditionally, whenever the U.S. government tries to identify Japanese goods upon which to impose tariffs or penalties, it must find obscure goods that Americans do not need or desire. If the American government were to suddenly take action that doubled the price of a Toyota or else made them unavailable, there would be a fearsome din of protest from American consumers. The consumer's interests come first.

American companies across the United States could also be devastated by Washington's overt action against semiconductors, auto parts, machine tools, and other items. Some companies depend on Japan to manufacture goods with the American brand name on them. Detroit purchases hundreds of thousands of such cars a year, and Detroit would be hurt if Washington suddenly slammed the door on Japanese cars. States with Japanese assembly and manufacturing plants would also fear for the jobs of their people.

Aside from the lack of federal-state coordination, there is a breakdown in the federal government's coordination with industry. If the United States agreed to impose a Voluntary Restraint Agreement or a tariff on a particular Japanese item, it should make sure that the U.S. industry being protected takes advantage of the relief. The industry's goal should be to gird itself for a cold blast of wind two or three years down the road when the barrier is lifted. But this is a peculiarity of American ideology. An American government will impose a barrier or an impediment to Japan, which is clear interference in the marketplace, but it will be unable to reach an understanding with the U.S. industry involved. That suddenly smacks of industrial planning.

In sum, the myriad ways in which consumers, companies, and states depend on Japan severely constrain the U.S. government. If the U.S. government could not make a punitive action stick against Toshiba, a single company, imagine the howls that would erupt against an across-the-board action. "Managed trade works in Japan and it works in Europe," boasted the Japanese diplomat who threatened a depression. "But it doesn't work in the United States." In the current climate, he is correct.

Third, the Japanese are discussing their alternatives if the Americans were to undertake a sudden trade-limiting measure. Some hawks are talking about a "second-strike capability" against the United States and, as we have heard, Japanese diplomats are threatening draconian countermeasures as well. It is unlikely, however, that the Japanese would do anything sudden or dramatic. A sudden pullout of American financial markets would inflict billions of dollars of losses on the Japanese themselves. They would end up with near-worthless pieces of paper called dollars. Japan cannot suddenly halt its agricultural purchases because its own people would be hungry. There are limits on what Japan could do, simply because the two economies and the two peoples are so interdependent. It would be foolish of Japan to inflict some obvious crippling blow on the Americans if 500,000 Japanese citizens are living in U.S. communities. Japan also depends on a climate of smooth international relations far more than does the United States. So a certain amount of tough talk can be dismissed as bluster. Level heads on both sides understand this. Another phrase from the U.S.-Soviet confrontation that has, fortunately or unfortunately, found its way into the lexicon of U.S.-Japanese ties is "mutual assured destruction."

But it's likely, indeed almost certain, that there would be a subtle, long-term response. In view of the variety of dependencies that the United States has on Japan, and the positive benefits that an intelligent American policy could draw from an improved U.S.-Japanese relationship, it would be imprudent for any U.S. government to suddenly impose tariffs or start slamming the doors to trade across the board. Although Americans are right in seeking a redress of the imbalance, using old tools with new names is not the proper response.

Before turning to that response, the air must be cleared. One of the worst stumbling blocks to serious debate about Japan is a kind of cultural schizophrenia that has hobbled Western observers. Westerners exposed to Japan tend to veer wildly from romance and infatuation, to paranoia. It is emotionally difficult to retain both a sense of admiration and at the same time, a healthy case of fear. The result is that most Japan-watchers choose one of two opposing camps. In 1935, for example, one British writer described the intellectual battle between "Japanophiles" and "Japanophobes."[5]

American thinkers and policy planners today are also polarized into two emotionally estranged camps, one sympathetic to Japan and one not. In some cases, the division overlaps the conservative versus the liberal and Republican versus Democratic rivalries, and this polarization shows signs of deepening rather than easing as the use of labels increases. There is precious little middle ground.

As noted, one of the most commonly used labels is "Japan-basher." To be sure, there are Americans who go off the deep end in venting emotional frustration with Japan. When congressmen smash Toshiba boom boxes on the Capitol lawn, or threaten to slam shut America's markets or pull American troops out of Japan, these are self-defeating responses. The same people who make inflammatory statements about "punishing" Japan are often those who lose patience and move to the next headline-generating opportunity. It's an approach that is destined not only to be ineffective but also to deepen Japan's fear that the Americans might do something rash. But in too many cases, the Japanese use the term *Japan-basher* to discredit Americans who have legitimate concerns and grievances. Any criticism, however valid, is dismissed as "bashing."

The terms *unilateralist* and *techno-nationalist* are also used pejoratively. To call someone a unilateralist is to imply that he or she does not believe in broader multilateral organizations such as the GATT, the International Monetary Fund (IMF), the United Nations, and other entities that have been set up at least in part to manage conflict among nations. The implication is that it is unfair and dangerous to seek an improvement in U.S.-Japanese relations through direct two-way contact. A techno-nationalist is someone who believes that the movement of technology across national borders carries some implications for his or her national security or economic well-being. Of course, when one examines the underlying meaning of the terms, it's clear that they don't represent wild-eyed fanaticism. The Japanese themselves have had a clear bilateral focus on the United States and have used their technology to enhance their interests. Other dismissive labels include *xenophobe*, *Japanophobe*, *McCarthyite*, and *Neo-nationalist*.

On the flip side of the label battle, the term *apologist* is particularly stinging when applied to an American trying to explain what he or she regards as a positive aspect of the U.S.-Japanese relationship. For professors, think tank experts, lobbyists, investment bankers, and others who are on Japan's payroll or who depend on Japanese financing, the terms *shadow shoguns* and *cherry blossom crowd* are often applied.

Although some American elites have been too dependent on Japanese funding, the use of these labels is dangerous because they obscure the voices of legitimate experts who have valuable insights. The general American instinct is to shoot from the hip without understanding the pattern of U.S. dependence on Japan and without understanding the benefits that the overall relationship creates. Many of these experts provide a sense of caution and balance, which is particularly important in dealing with Japan. When the Americans have a trade spat with the Europeans, there is a much greater web of personal relationships between business leaders, politicians, academics, and others in place. There is a greater sense of trust and common cultural background, which is more precarious in relations across the Pacific. As the Americans attempt to redefine their relationship with Japan, thereby ushering in one of the most sensitive periods in relations since the war and Occupation, it is essential to proceed carefully. It would be self-defeating to whip up hatred for Japan of the sort that prevailed during World War II.

That's why it's important to find a vocabulary and tone that are widely acceptable without losing sight of the long-term goal. Americans have to get past the pro-Japan, anti-Japan deadlock, reminiscent of the fight between the doves and the hawks during the Vietnam War, when beating the other side seemed more important than identifying broader American interests.

So it is not "bashing" to say that Japan's economic strength demands a U.S. response. Nor is it "apologist" to say that this can be accomplished while preserving the overall relationship.

The challenge is to accept the differences between the two cultures and the two societies in a pragmatic way and quietly go about the business of formulating an effective response to the economic challenge. There does not need to be any hate. Recognizing that Japan *is* different in many respects, and that it intends to remain that way, could lead to an improvement in the atmosphere between the two countries. There's no point making speeches about free trade doctrine, or expressing U.S.-style moral outrage about the lack of reciprocity, transparency, and openness. Even if the Japanese wanted to offer these things, and there is not much evidence that they do, the way their system is structured and the very force of their culture make it highly unlikely. It is naive to assume that name-calling will change it.

One other boil must be lanced: the racism argument. Shintaro Ishihara, the right-wing author of *The Japan That Can Say No,* and some prominent Japanese bureaucrats and politicians have alleged that racism is the dominant, driving force in the effort to improve the economic balance between the two countries. This is nonsense.

Americans are encouraged to be color-blind, which is not to say that discrimination does not exist. But by European or Japanese standards, the United States is a model. Because most Americans are conditioned to the idea of different races, and because they believe strongly in human rights, when the subject of Japan comes up, they often ask: Why are you expressing concern about the Japanese buying this when you're not worried about the Dutch? Is it because the Dutch are white and the Japanese are not? Why is it one thing for the Japanese to buy Columbia Pictures and something else for Australians to buy a piece of Hollywood? Are you being racist?

This question was put to me by a BBC television interviewer following the Rockefeller Center acquisition. My answer was that, sure, some Americans may harbor an element of racism when it comes to Japan. But they are immediately discredited in the marketplace of ideas. Anyone who gets up and says they do not like the Japanese because of racial characteristics is laughed out of school. The point is that there are important, if not critical, issues of economic imbalance and difference of systems, culture, and even ideology that need to be recognized and addressed when dealing with Japan, and these have little to do with race.

The Japanese are also different from the other Asians who live in American communities. Filipinos, Koreans, Indians, Chinese, Vietnamese, and other Asians have settled in the United States for good. To a lesser or greater extent, they are trying to "buy into" the American system, the American way of life. They are different from Japanese who rotate in and out, who don't believe in assimilating into the American dream. Japanese are not refugees or immigrants. As a whole, they do not believe in the American system or in American values.

The Japanese have consistently and emphatically tried to emphasize their differentness, their uniqueness, not only from the white Western world, but from the rest of Asia as well. In view of their own attitudes toward minorities at home and in the United States, it is the height of hypocrisy for a Japanese to accuse Americans of racism for attempting to dig out of their trade hole and better manage the relationship with Japan. "Many would ask whether Japan, with its society fundamentally closed to all outsiders, is not the most racially minded major power in the world today," says historian Ivan Hall at Keio University.[6] By comparison, Americans are astoundingly open and accepting.

It's clear that not only must Japan be treated differently, it is the only way to treat Japan. It has always seemed a little dirty, a little un-American, to talk about beating the Japanese, but it is necessary to concentrate on beating Japan in sectors where we compete while at the same time maintaining and enhancing cooperative sides of the relationship.

The perfect formulation for responding to Japan came from Michael Armacost, the new U.S. ambassador to Japan. Prior to taking up his post, he put it this way: "For years, there has been a cooperative aspect and a competitive aspect of our relationship with Japan. Now we are going to put a little more emphasis on the competitive aspect." There is no divorce, no punishing, no containing.[7]

For a now-now democracy with a short attention span, formulating this response to a smaller but more highly organized society that is clearly focused on long-term objectives is daunting indeed. That is particularly true if the underlying philosophy and sense of mission have to be carefully calibrated to accept and appreciate the good while mitigating the impact of the bad on our own society and economic base.

The good is that U.S.-Japanese cooperation created the underpinning for East Asia's remarkable drive toward prosperity. Indeed, Japan is a force for stability in many places around the world. Dozens of U.S. companies have crucial stakes in the booming Japanese market, and Japan is the largest overseas buyer of American products. Americans have benefited mightily from Japan's commitment to quality and innovation.

In many respects, U.S. ties with Japan in trade and investment, defense, science and technology, and culture are broader and more complex than with any other nation, including the Soviet Union. No one could quarrel with Mansfield's famous remark that the U.S.-Japanese relationship is America's most important bilateral relationship, bar none. But it is a relationship that demands a new balance. As Wendt, chairman of SmithKline Beckman, expressed it: "It's our most important bilateral relationship and we'd damned well better not screw it up. But the status quo is unacceptable."

❖ 20 ❖

Economic Patriotism

If the United States and Japan are engaged in systemic economic confrontations, Americans need a systematic, national strategy for responding. This should be faced squarely. Piecemeal, stopgap efforts by successive U.S. governments to address chronic economic imbalances have been far too superficial.

Many Americans believe the key lies exclusively in Washington's hands. Others believe the fault lies in the hands of American companies themselves. But it is wrong to believe that problems between the United States and Japan can simply be negotiated away without a broader, more cohesive national strategy. Government-to-government negotiations and company-to-company battles are just one piece of the puzzle.

A systematic response means that every point of contact between the two systems should be examined. It starts with Americans who are in daily contact with Japan. Every supplier and every customer, every employee, every joint venture partner, every university researcher, every union leader, and every state and local government that hosts Japanese investment must recognize that they bear a responsibility for taking steps, however small and however long-term, to advance broader American interests, not just their own. A Korean or a German or a Belgian working for an American multinational would feel that way. Americans should feel that way when they work for the Japanese.

A truly effective U.S. response also depends on millions of daily decisions made by individual Americans with no direct exposure to Japan. There is a connection, poorly recognized, between what we buy and our economic security. Some of the dollars we spend on Japanese products come back into our system to buy U.S. assets and build new strength to compete against U.S. companies. The economic chain does not stop when we complete the purchase. There is also a connection between whether we save money individually and as a nation, or whether we slide more deeply into debt to the Japanese, and there is a connection between how we perform at work and our company's competitive position vis-à-vis the Japanese and other foreign powers. Also key is whether the next generation is prepared with the linguistic and technical skills it needs to compete against the Japanese. These millions of decisions make up the sum total of the American system. In short, there is a connection between individual actions and national well-being.

These vital connections, so painfully obvious to any Japanese, or indeed to the people of any industrial nation in Europe or Asia, have been obscured in recent years in the United States. Americans have long assumed their economic infrastructure, including their living standards and better opportunities for their children, was somehow guaranteed. When the United States dominated the world, many Americans could afford the luxury of perceiving economic struggle as distasteful. But that was an aberration, a unique period in U.S. history. Now, a new wave of Japanese and other foreign competition is breaking over us. Very little economic security is guaranteed. Reality has shifted. Thinking must shift with it.

The purpose is not to revive American hegemony. Rather it is to use Japan's money, technology, and skills to revitalize the United States and to enhance its economic security, not undermine it. In so doing, Americans maintain their values and their political integrity, and build the resources to address other internal challenges.

Persuading Americans to do the things they know they should do may require an "ism." "Economic nationalism" is a term that first appeared in the current context during the 1988 presidential campaign when Democratic candidates toyed with it. Although never fully articulated, it seemed to be an attempt to lay the groundwork for old-style protectionist measures against Japan and other export-driven Asian economies such as South Korea. As a result, the concept has come to be seen as antitrade, anti-open, and antiforeign. The term *economic nationalism* also implies a kind of crass mercantilism, even economic aggression. It has these unfortunate connotations because Hitler, among others, used it as a pretext for reaching out to exploit other nations.

But "economic patriotism," another term that was picked up and dropped during the 1988 election, has a different implication. In its fullest sense, it implies love of country, which is healthy, and the defending of that country, rather than the exploitation of others. It stands for continued trade and investment, open borders, and engaging enthusiastically with the Japanese and anyone else prepared to help America in its revitalization.

The heart of economic patriotism is rejecting declinism and the doctrine of defeat. Paul Kennedy, a British historian who wrote the influential *The Rise and Fall of the Great Powers*,[1] made a sophisticated argument: If the United States could reduce its global military commitments and concentrate on repairing its economic infrastructure, it could avoid the traps that Britain and Spain and other has-beens have fallen into. But no matter what the Americans did, they were headed for a *relative* decline in power vis-à-vis other nations. He did not argue that Americans were facing *absolute* decline, which suggests deterioration and decay.

Although Kennedy had a healthy respect for America's regenerative capabilities, his best-selling book triggered a wave of declinism. The word *decline* entered the vocabulary as a given, as inevitable.[2] As popularly communicated, it came to be perceived that the Americans were caught up in a broad historical vise that condemned them to losing industries, to further indebtedness, and to moral, educational, and social decay. This tapped into a decades-old sense that power would inevitably shift from Europe to America to Japan.

Crisscrossing the nation, I have never met an American who likes the vision of absolute decline. Having a plant close in one's town is a devastating experience. It means the slow, agonizing dismemberment of communities and sometimes families. The same can be said of factories that close in central urban areas. The young people move away, and rarely come back. Entire states or city centers depopulate. Relative decline compared with other powers is one thing, but absolute decline is not a pretty picture, some sparkling conversation piece at cocktail parties. It wrecks a way of life. Having a McDonald's open instead of a factory is scant consolation.

It has traditionally been assumed in Washington that a political leader who advocated making the tough decisions to get America's economic act together, and confronted the tough challenges that Japan poses, would take a merciless pounding in the opinion polls. But increasingly there appears to be a broad receptivity to a philosophy that would help Americans defend their way of life, indeed a hunger for such a philosophy. It seems possible to use the enormity of Japan's economic challenge to stimulate a psychological shift in the United

States, to tap into the wellspring of American moral energy.

This moral energy can be impressive when channeled. Consider how Americans have changed their attitudes toward sexuality and the role of women in society, how they have crusaded against smoking, how a group of mothers campaigned and made strides against drunk driving, and how Americans overturned old attitudes toward health, nutrition, and exercise. In each case there were practical considerations, but there were also waves of moral pressure. This same moral energy is aroused when a little girl gets trapped in a well in Texas, when a baseball hero gets nailed for gambling on baseball, when a married presidential candidate plays with a beautiful girlfriend on a yacht, or when an Iranian madman issues death threats. Americans rarely choose to concentrate on economics. But they have done it with American exports, which have surged to levels that surprised all the skeptics. And it was this force that President Carter tried to tap by declaring the energy crisis "the moral equivalent of war."

The United States is the industrial democracy where political and popular movements often have the greatest impact. Americans have the power to shift attitudes, values, and therefore strategies in a way that no other major society does. This is what a class-conscious, supremely self-assured Britain was never able to do. If Americans choose to exercise this power, they can shift the climate of U.S.-Japanese economic confrontation. They can alter the rules of the engagement in a fundamental way. This economic patriotism would not be anti-Japanese, it would be pro-American.

In fact, the process may already have begun, as evidenced in relaxed antitrust enforcement, a growing number of business-business and business-government consortia, and a growing concern about maintaining the U.S. technological base. Deans of business schools are beginning to talk more about creating MBAs who have language skills and know how to make things rather than merely juggle balance sheets. All this is still, however, in an embryonic and endangered stage.

No one can ask Americans to turn the clock back to the 1950s, but it does seem realistic to ask them to think ahead through the 1990s and beyond. Economic patriotism represents an extension of the notion of love of country beyond the old symbols. It is idealism but not altruism. It means finding the intersection between one's own interests and that of another American, between what's good for the individual and the company, and indeed the nation as a whole. Rather than fighting over pieces of a shrinking pie, make the pie grow.

Some people may ask, Isn't patriotism bad? In a perfect world, we would all be internationalists. Isn't this one big global economy? But if some nations persist in single-minded preoccupation with national goals, then it is foolish for others to be soft-headed. Economic nationalism is in the air in Japan. It is the basis upon which they have staged their astonishing rise to world power. A mild form of U.S. economic patriotism might merely balance the relationship.

American economic patriotism does not require new institutions or legislation, just clarity of mind and purpose. Nor does it require harsh language. In fact, the more subtle, the better. Economics becomes a quiet moral struggle. This is a patriotism defined and sharpened at least in part by living in Japan's shadow.

Look at four tenets of economic patriotism and then examine what they might mean in practice.

New Thinking

Economic patriotism can and should be a notion that supersedes the splits between conservatives and liberals, Republicans and Democrats, between right and left. It is conservative to wish to see a marketplace response to Japan wherever possible. It is liberal to believe in actively shaping that response. If it is right-wing Republican to argue for a revitalization in the wealth-creation process, it is left-wing Democratic to urge that new resources are needed to address social challenges.

But all sides must give ground to hammer out a winning philosophy: Competing with Japan means a slight phasing back of the tenet that short-term consumer interests must always, unquestionably, prevail over producer interests, and that short-term shareholder interests must always prevail over stakeholder interests. These are both forms of immediate gratification at everybody else's expense. Other sides, however, have to recognize that government will never again be the conduit for a massive attempt to redistribute income. The private means of production is the key tool for wealth creation. That requires a change in popular attitude toward American business.

When many congressmen and others talk about changing America, their first instinct is to talk about what laws need to be passed. But new laws by themselves would not clean up the decision-making process in Washington. There are always ways to beat any law, which is testimony to the power of greed. The same ethics that created the savings and loan and the HUD scandals are on display in the Japan lobby. What's needed is new thinking, a climate of opinion that shines a bright light into dirty corners.

Likewise, the United States does not need a brand-new governmental agency, a Department of Trade and Industry, that combines Commerce, the U.S. Trade Representative (USTR), and other agencies. The current institutional framework would work just fine if only the players had a common vision and could place national interests over bureaucratic turf wars. It is a question of psychology, a sense of urgency.

There are few laws that could force Americans to work harder and save more, to persuade union leaders and corporate officials to bury short-term differences to recognize a greater long-term good, to deter an investment banker from carving up American assets, or to force a pension fund manager sitting on billions of dollars in cash to look farther into the future than ten minutes. Of course, there are labor laws, tax codes, and financial regulations. But if Americans do not believe in a law, they resist it or circumvent it. Consider the experience of massive resistance to federally imposed fifty-five-mile-per-hour speed limits. The broader challenge is a philosophical and psychological shift. Americans need to understand how their actions fit into a national economic strategy.

Teamwork

Japanese do not compete primarily as individuals. Instead, they compete as members of groups, which are parts of institutions, which are members of larger industrial groups, which are parts of a nation. One irony is that although many individual Japanese men endure grueling working and drinking schedules, they often seem so soft physically. They don't work out, as a rule. Although there are some Japanese elite men who are obviously proud and assertive, the majority do not engage directly and openly in conflict, certainly not with a *gaijin.* No Sylvester Stallones with sweaty headbands. But when the Japanese form larger groups, they are fiercely competitive against outsiders. Together, they can consistently beat the Rambos of the world. It is no contest.

The point is that team play is necessary in responding to Japan. American-style team play does not mean stamping out individualism, nor does it mean mindless submission to the group. In baseball, sometimes players do things individually; other times they support teammates. There is a tension between being a star and being a team player that the American psyche can handle. Aside from sheer physical size and speed, the cultural ability to nurture stars as part of teams is one reason the Americans consistently beat the Japanese at baseball. The Japanese understand the concept of team play in a way that makes it more difficult for individuals to excel. Everyone has to conform. American players who join Japanese teams simply outshine most Japanese players. Japanese salarymen quietly sucking air across their teeth stand around big television sets in shopping arcades in Tokyo watching Americans on Japanese teams hitting home runs and stealing bases. They don't understand it. Why are these Americans better than our players?

But in the economic game, the Americans are not good enough team players. Americans must renew their dedication to the institutions of which they are members. We have allowed the individualistic star tendency to eclipse commitment to teamwork. Americans have to make their institutions work together more effectively as parts of larger teams. The four key players are business, labor, government, and education. At the moment, business is only warming up in the bullpen. Labor is out in left field doing a solo performance. Government is arguing with the umpire, and education is still trying to get its uniform on. They are not even playing the same game.

When it comes right down to it, some American institutions would rather form alliances with the Japanese than with each other. The level of trust has deteriorated to the point that some of the players on what should be the American all-star team would rather play on the other side. The mark of a society that is winning in today's world is one where people have been able to make their institutions work, and work together, and maintain a sense of team identity. The others lose.

Go for Independence

It seems preposterous in the 1990s to make this argument, but it must be made nonetheless: Americans should recognize that independence is a vital national goal. Americans are long past the point where they have to worry about the king's soldiers. The new battlefield is economic. Americans allowed themselves to slide into dependency on OPEC and paid a bitter price for it during the oil shocks. But the more immediate issue is that they are building a pattern of technological and financial dependencies on Japan.

It is essential for Americans to have ever deepening economic ties with the outside world. But having deep economic ties does not have to mean allowing entire industries to disappear, nor does it mean that Americans should willingly cede positions at crucial levels in each industrial "food chain." In other words, if we fear that the American machine tool industry, for example, is about to be wiped out, it should be a national priority to prevent it from happening. We do not insist on total American control, but we do believe in a viable American presence. The concern about technological dependencies and the role of patriotism in responding to them has for the first time begun appearing on the front pages of major newspapers.[3]

The Pentagon, for one, is worried that its defense industrial base already depends too heavily on Japanese electronics. Even IBM, which few would accuse of misty-eyed patriotism, has taken a series of moves to ensure an American presence at each step of the technology food chain: It helped prevent Perkin-Elmer, a maker of semiconductor manufacturing equipment, from falling into Japanese hands, partly through the use of the media. It has drawn in Motorola to help develop a cutting-edge semiconductor chip etching technology. As for the chips themselves, IBM has licensed the technology for making its most powerful memory chip to a medium-size company, Micron Technology Incorporated.[4] All of this is directed against Japanese domination of these links of the technology food chain.

IBM had its own business reasons for all these moves, but it was also clear that IBM feels it is important to maintain technological independence from Japan. In this respect, it found an intersection between IBM's interests and American interests.

Financial independence does not necessarily mean paying back every penny that Americans owe to Japan overnight. For one thing, Americans literally do not have the money. Aside from the government's $500 billion debt to Japan, American individuals and companies have borrowed extensively. American dependence on Japanese capital has become like a drug addiction. The important thing to recognize is that borrowing money is not a free lunch. There is a price to pay.

What is achievable is turning the corner on this debt overload. At the moment, there is no end in sight to the government's runaway need for new Japanese capital. By assembling a fair, balanced package of deficit-reducing measures in Washington, the U.S. government could signal an end to this out-of-control borrowing. Every time the government rushes through a measure to raise the national debt ceiling rather than facing up to what needs to be done, it should give every American a knot in the stomach because it erodes a measure of U.S. sovereignty. Staunching the red ink, even without starting to actually repay capital or interest, would shift the psychology of America's financial dependence.

The other reason to push for managing these dependencies is the earthquake argument. When San Francisco was hit by its earthquake, the Japanese took it very seriously. They could be next, and they have been preparing for it for years. In the worst-case scenario, Tokyo is destroyed. Billions of dollars are needed to reconstruct. Big Japanese banks, securities houses, life insurance companies, and other financial institutions begin moving funds from around the world back to Japan. Japanese companies would probably divert crucial goods, raw materials, and components, at least in some cases, because their Japan-based production might be disrupted. Such a quake would be a tragedy of enormous human proportions and the whole world, certainly the Americans, would want to help any way they could. But one side effect would be a major shock for the United States. The Americans might be left prostrate. This is still an unlikely scenario, but it is one more reason why it is not prudent to slide into deeper dependencies.

Get Smart

What a jolt it is to fly from Japan to the United States. In Japan, they are talking about capital formation, genetic code sequencing, fifth-generation computers, investment strategies for the year 2000, the globalization of Japanese companies, and how to manage Japan's overseas aid program. These subjects are being discussed on radio talk shows, on television talk shows, and in the average newspaper. Of course, a great deal of time and attention is focused on stars, life-styles, and such, and a surprising number of Japanese can be found reading comic books on the subway. But there is a solid commitment at many different levels of the society to studying and understanding new concepts and new issues.

When one arrives back in the United States and turns on the television, one can find a serious news journalist talking about whether men reporters should be allowed into the locker rooms of professional women athletes. After discussing trade and investment friction with a top Japanese bureaucrat or Dietman, it comes as a surprise to see television film of U.S. congressmen arguing over whether they should say the Pledge of Allegiance. And standing in a checkout line at a supermarket where the magazine headlines dwell on aliens, Jackie Kennedy, Hollywood stars, and Siamese twins, it seems clear the United States and Japan are focusing on different kinds of subjects.

Of course, there are many Americans who understand trade, technology, and manufacturing, but not enough and certainly not as many proportionately as Japan has. The scarcity of American engineers is a particularly acute problem. As Americans dreamed about a postindustrial society, the educational system started producing far fewer people who knew how to make things. Part of the American competitive disadvantage vis-à-vis Japan is sheer brain power. It is not so much a question of IQ as it is a willingness to organize one's society to produce people with the skills and expertise needed to manage complex economic and technological interactions with the rest of the world.

One reason for the lack of "human capital" is that in the years following World War II, the flow of investment and trade from the United States to the rest of the world was the dominant force. It was done on the basis of relatively simple American rules. Now it has become more complex as trade and investment into the United States have exploded. That means, at every point of contact, Americans have to be more sophisticated in dealing with the issues of technology transfer, U.S. content, value-added design and engineering functions, executive decision-making models, capital formation, and the like. Since the Japanese are the largest single U.S. economic partner, Americans must also understand more about their history, language, and culture. A nation's intellectual capital is the best guarantee that it can manage its foreign economic relationships to its own advantage.

Advocating a measure of economic patriotism does not mean shunning Japan. It means engaging enthusiastically. Rather than shunning Japan because it is too difficult or too complex, the United States should double the number of Americans living, working, and competing in Japan and double the number of Americans studying Japanese regardless of the short-term cost.

More Americans should travel to Japan. Unfortunately, many Americans would no more think of going to Japan than to the moon. But it can have a salutary effect. When Corning's management recognized it needed to dramatically improve the competitiveness of its plant in Corning, New York, there naturally was some resistance from labor. So Corning put together a delegation of executives and union leaders and sent them to Japan and then to Europe to study how Corning's competitors had organized themselves. This is not industrial espionage. The Japanese are often delighted to show the fruits of their success. But after seeing Japan in particular, executives and union leaders from Corning were able to reach a consensus on the need to act. They understood the enormity of the challenge. Many American companies have found new ideas and new ways of applying technology from having a presence in Japan or sending people there. The short-term cost pales in significance to the long-term benefit.

Americans should be learning everything they can about Japan and taking cameras into Japanese factories and laboratories, just as the Japanese did in the United States in the 1950s. One constant debating point in the American literature about Japan is whether Americans should attempt to adopt Japanese methods, values, and systems. It makes perfect sense to study and absorb the positive aspects of Japan, which in many cases are refinements of things the Japanese have learned in America. At the same time, Americans should reject what they regard as negative models, values, and perceptions. A wholesale adoption of things Japanese is impossible. Selective importation is essential.

In short, we should turn full face to Japan, as Americans have never done since the war. Our population base is twice as big. Our economy is still larger. We have a much broader mix of companies. Surround the Japanese with positive feelings and indulge in the fascination with their culture. Just beat them on the economic playing field. Politely.

Even Americans who work for Japanese companies can be part of that process. Ambassador Armacost uses 300,000 as the number of Americans working for Japanese companies in the United States. This is a very modest estimate based on a count of 200,000 that the U.S. government did in the early 1980s before the explosion of Japanese investment. No one really knows exactly how many Americans are employed by the Japanese, but it is widely accepted that the number will hit one million sometime in the 1990s.

Some of these Americans are taunted by their friends or family members for being "brainwashed." But this is unfair. Americans who work for Japanese companies need not live in private hells. On the line, workers ("associates" at many Japanese companies) should learn how the Japanese have applied the concepts of teamwork, quality control, just-in-time inventory, and all the techniques and attitudes that have made them so successful. Some Ohioans on the line at Honda, for example, are learning how to become engineers. One day, perhaps, they can play a role in spreading that knowledge to American-owned companies.

Likewise, white-collar Americans should make their best effort. Study Japanese. Work harder. Understand the decision-making process. Try to guide the Japanese company into a win-win situation where it makes money at the same time it fully abides by the letter and spirit of American laws and values. If, after three or four years, the company has not given such an American a genuine decision-making role, he or she should gift-wrap his expertise and cultural insight and take a hike to join a U.S. competitor.

Suppliers who meet Japanese standards and then provide products meeting those standards to other American customers are helping the whole American industry compete. Joint venture partners who extract capital and technology from the Japanese as part of a win-win strategy, while preserving their independence, are contributing to a broader good.

Customers who avoid becoming too dependent on Japanese suppliers, by maintaining multiple sourcing, are following a prudent course of independence at the same time offering the possibility that another American could get a fair crack at the business. In short, the Japanese should be drawn in more deeply, but on U.S. terms. In so doing, Americans can build their expertise and skills.

Economically patriotic Americans who do not have direct contact with Japanese companies can also vote with their dollars. You are what you eat, it is often said. You are also what you buy.

After returning from overseas, my wife and I were confronted with the need to buy a car after not owning one for several years. Lee Iacocca's autobiography seemed to be evidence that if there were one company that had stared into the abyss and therefore gotten the fundamentals right, it would be Chrysler. We bought a 1985 Dodge Lancer. For a while I was proud of my car. Then at 28,000 miles, the head gasket blew. The engine had broken.

I put as much water in the radiator as I could and limped off to the Chrysler dealer near my home in suburban New York, steam beginning to pour out of the hood. I arrived at the Chrysler dealership only to discover that it had sold out. It had become a Honda Acura dealership. I was forced to top off the radiator with more water and head for Yonkers, like a latter-day Joad, to the next Chrysler dealership.

Despite my 5-50 warranty, the repair cost hundreds of dollars because I had a $100 deductible, some related work was not covered by the warranty, and I had to pay to rent a car for a week. Overall, we have invested more money in the car than I would care to admit.

As the end of four years' worth of payments approached, my wife started saying, "Let's buy a Japanese car." I adopted a strategy of passive resistance. Wait her out. And besides, I was confused. Owning this Chrysler had been an unacceptable experience. Lee Iacocca evidently agreed that the car was a lemon because his company stopped making Lancers altogether. But I still wanted an American car.

One Fourth of July we went to an elegant outdoor picnic where people were talking about their cars. "Lots of smart, sophisticated people buy Japanese cars," my wife told me later, resuming the offensive. "They don't give you any trouble. So okay? It's the smart thing to do."

Hmph. I didn't think it was smart. Maintaining an American auto industry was important. At least two U.S. auto companies have to survive and prosper. I refused to believe that all American cars would be as troublesome as my Chrysler.

Finally, after a long-running guerrilla conflict, I talked my wife into agreeing that the next purchase would be a Ford Taurus or a Mercury

Sable. We could drive one of these proudly. Some parts may have been sourced offshore, but the car is mostly American-made. If the Ford proves to be a lemon, I will give the outer wall and retreat to the inner wall again.

It was the same when our fifteen-year-old Sanyo television broke. We could buy any kind of television we wanted, as long as it was a Zenith. Zenith is the last major American manufacturer of consumer electronics. I realized its pattern of procuring parts in Asia and assembling them in the United States was similar to what a Japanese company would do. But though a Zenith set is not 100 percent American, it was important that a company managed and owned by Americans stay in the business. One reason is that in the battle over high-definition television (HDTV), Zenith has an HDTV technology and could emerge as the American standard-bearer. If Zenith goes belly-up, it reduces the chances that Americans will be able to commercialize HDTV technology. It would be the Japanese or Europeans instead. In view of what was at stake, the choice of a Zenith was clear.

In other cases, I have exercised *gaman*, discipline. I do not need a digital whatchamacallit or a laser thingamajig. My dinosaurlike Japanese stereo gear is all of ten years old, but it still emits the right sounds. When I had to put new speakers into my speaker cabinet, I looked to see where they were made: Huntington, Indiana.

Being an economic patriot and choosing to exercise a measure of discretion in purchase decisions does not imply a revulsion for all things Japanese. I have a Sharp VCR and I realize my Apple computer has many Toshiba parts. I have a Japanese point-and-shoot camera and a Sony radio I carry with me on trips. In some areas, there is no U.S. competition.

In the July 1989 Harris poll, Americans were asked if they would put their dollars where their mouths were. If products made in Japan and the United States were equal in quality, would you be willing to pay more for the product made in the United States? It was surprising that 66 percent said yes, 28 percent said no. There is a gap between saying something and doing it, of course. Americans still prefer Japanese autos, as suggested by the fact that identical cars made at Toyota-GM in California and Mitsubishi-Chrysler in Illinois sell better under Japanese nameplates than under American nameplates. But at least Americans are becoming aware that the origin of the product is an issue.

There are other ways to exercise *gaman*. If a consumer does buy something Japanese, he or she could make sure another major purchase is American. Or say you had concluded that you must buy a Japanese car. It boils down to a choice between a Toyota and a Honda. Price, modeling, and all that is the same. Then add a new level of inquiry: Where was it made? If in the United States, what is the U.S. content? Engine made in America? What about the transmission? If a few hundred thousand Americans began asking questions like these in dealer showrooms, it would be the single most powerful lever to persuade Japanese auto manufacturers to transfer more sophisticated functions to U.S. soil. In general, each American should conduct an audit of what he buys and where it's from. There should be a commonsense balance.

American quality in general has made rapid strides over the past decade; the consumer's message has gotten through to most manufacturers, and continues to get through. Although the Japanese have kept improving as well, some Japanese products have some quality problems of their own and even Japanese cars have undergone recalls. Certainly the Japanese no longer enjoy the same overwhelming cost and price advantages they once did. But some American consumers will not even consider buying an American auto or television or computer. Having been stung once, they find it hard to unlearn the notion that all American products are bad. But it is an American's responsibility to at least consider a U.S. alternative. No nation can survive as a major economic power if its people eschew the products they themselves make.

Suggesting that Americans vote with their dollars is not radical, not some 1930s-style economic embargo or boycott. In fact, this is what the Japanese themselves are advocating. The Japanese are attacking American "overconsumption." This is one of the issues that the Japanese government has identified as part of the Structural Impediments Initiative (SII). The Japanese government is urging the American government to persuade Americans to buy fewer Japanese goods as a means of redressing the trade deficit. This is a noble cause indeed.

Economic patriotism is not Pollyannaish. It's not likely that millions of Americans will have sudden conversions on the road to Damascus. There are always going to be investment bankers who would eat their young for a deal and lobbyists who sell their souls to the top bidder. Another major challenge is overcoming cultural and racial differences in an ever more multiracial society. Knitting together the trust and idealism will be more difficult than it was when the United States was an overwhelmingly WASP-dominated society. But there is a real-world incentive for doing so: Those who can find "intersection" strategies stand a far better chance of surviving and indeed enhancing their life positions. Others who attempt to stand alone face the prospect of being ground down into irrelevance.

What's needed is a quiet, steady response. If Americans took only tiny steps toward this vision this year, and more tiny steps next year, the effect would be dramatic. Millions of tiny steps add up to movement. It does not have to be all at once and it does not ever have to be 100 percent. Because the United States is bigger and more richly endowed, even fractional shifts in the climate of opinion and action toward Japan would have major impact.

Advocating economic patriotism in dealing with Japan is an attempt to recognize and accept how Japan is different and respond to that with mild, tangible, level-headed steps. It is a call to restore a sense of balance to the relationship, which has become too unbalanced and is therefore subject to more dangerous eruptions.

Japanese do not object at all to a competitive response. In fact, they themselves promote it. Indeed, many Japanese urge the Americans to wake up. Why don't you respond? Why don't you regain your confidence? What happened to America? Economic patriotism is the kind of talk the Japanese understand and respect. When you ask someone like Sony's Akio Morita about Japan-bashing, the word *childish* keeps emerging. What he objects to is overly demonstrative displays of emotionalism. Economic patriotism is not childish. It is the U.S. response to the Japanese power game.

Isn't it hypocrisy to talk about beating Japan in economic competition while believing that other aspects of the relationship can be preserved, if not enhanced? Not at all. The game is played on many different levels. We need to contain multiple levels within ourselves and within our system. At one level, we retain all that distinguishes us as Americans. We operate by certain principles among ourselves and those who seek refuge on our shores. But we recognize that the Japanese are different. We cooperate with them in guaranteeing security and political stability throughout Asia and other parts of the world and we cooperate in maintaining a world trading and financial system. At the same time, we concentrate on beating them as thoroughly and as consistently as possible on the competitive side of the relationship. Doing that, however, will require a government that is also economically patriotic.

❖ 21 ❖

Industrial Policy Gridlock

The subject of industrial policy has been one of the most important debates taking place in Washington, but it has been superficial, disjointed, ideological, and therefore disappointingly unproductive. In the debate's simplest form, one person says, "I think we need an industrial policy." Then someone else says, "Oh, industrial policy. That means you think we can pick the winners and the losers." That's often the end of the conversation. It's ideological gridlock.

The fact of the matter is that the United States already has an industrial policy, and has already been picking winners and losers. Partly as a result of government funding of NASA, we have a strong aerospace sector. Because of a huge Pentagon budget, we have had a strong defense-related industry. The government also spends untold billions for agricultural support, so we have had one of the strongest agricultural sectors in the world. The enormous flow of government funds into institutions such as MIT and Cal Tech means the United States has the finest university research laboratories in the world. None of this was by accident.

But because this industrial policy shortchanges other sectors of the economy, the government has also been picking losers. The fact that the government is such a big borrower, combined with a paucity of domestic savings, helps keep interest rates higher than they should be. Hence the industrial policy is an expensive-money policy. Either American companies find that capital is scarce, or else they can borrow at higher rates, which encourages them to borrow only if they have a sure bet that will pay off quickly. Expensive money discourages long-term risk-taking, which is a key to success.

Our industrial policy encourages investors to get in and out of the stock market quickly. There is little bias in the capital gains rules to say that short-term investments are penalized and longer-term investments are rewarded. The tax system, which is at the heart of any nation's industrial policy, rewards short-term thinking that maximizes returns to shareholders while ignoring broader stakeholder, and national, interests. This encourages financial wheeling and dealing, even in sensitive areas like airlines and network and cable television, where companies that should serve a public good are often stripped, leveraged, and hocked, not necessarily in that order.

Many major government decisions have competitive implications. Tax laws regarding whether U.S. multinationals are rewarded for investing in the United States or abroad have a dramatic effect, as do the tax rules governing the money that companies earn from exporting. Other important measures are energy policy, auto pollution controls, antitrust policy, antibribery laws, and economic sanctions against, inter alia, the Soviet bloc, South Africa, Cuba, Iran, Vietnam, China, Nicaragua, Panama, and others. Restrictions on the sale of American technology goods to Communist countries, however justifiable on national security grounds, have been important in limiting the international sales of American high-tech companies. Time and time again, the U.S. government reaches decisions that place a premium on domestic interests or strategic interests at the expense of long-term U.S. competitiveness. In short, the U.S. government, knowingly or unknowingly, helps set the entire framework. "What people in the Administration haven't seen is that the U.S. has an industrial policy," says Congressman Don Ritter, a Republican from Pennsylvania. "It is simply a witless one."[1]

Despite the current battle about industrial policy vis-à-vis Japan, the Reagan and Bush Administrations have already taken specific ad hoc decisions to help shape the winners and the losers. One case was when the Reagan Administration told MIT not to buy a Japanese supercomputer. This was interference in the marketplace and a clear attempt to bolster Cray. In another instance, the Federal Communications Commission (FCC) decided to require that a new HDTV technology be compatible with existing televisions and transmission equipment. The net effect was to block the Japanese technology, temporarily at least.

But there is little consistency. Washington is at war with itself on the issue. Despite clear evidence that the Americans already have an industrial policy, some more orthodox members of the Republican Administration still argue that any such policy is bad. It is a fight between the true believers in free markets and congressmen, both Democrats and Republicans, and other members of the Administration, such as Commerce Secretary Robert Mosbacher, who feel some greater governmental role is necessary to help American companies compete against Japan. Although the word *Japan* is not often mentioned, that is what the debate is really about.

Debating whether the United States should have an industrial policy, however, is not the point. The real debate should be over *what kind* of industrial policy we will have and what kind of government involvement works, not whether the government should be involved in the economy. The government cannot escape being involved. It is a Reaganesque myth to think that government can divorce itself from a national economy. The emerging debate over the "peace dividend"— whether dollars that were being spent on the military budget can be redirected elsewhere—is a case in point. This will be a governmental exercise involving decisions on how to redeploy billions of dollars. It will be a major industrial policy decision.

There are many signs of ferment regarding national industrial policy in technology fields, but they are still at the margin. Under the National Cooperative Research Act of 1984, private sector companies have announced plans to form 140 joint R&D ventures in traditional high-tech fields such as computers, semiconductors, and fiber, as well as areas like biotechnology.[2] The Justice and Commerce departments want to extend and improve this concept, and there are several bills before Congress that would do that. At least one bill proposed by the Bush Administration would allow some companies to cooperate in actually making products, not just performing research. All this is a clear example of the U.S. government relaxing its antitrust enforcement so that companies that compete with each other can cooperate at the same time.

The Pentagon, for its part, is supporting Sematech in Austin, Texas, to the modest tune of $100 million a year, and the government also sanctioned efforts to launch U.S. Memories, which would have manufactured semiconductor chips before it was abandoned in January 1990. American makers of semiconductor chips were not able to agree on a cooperative plan to ease their dependence on Japanese memory chips. Despite this failure, another consortium that depends exclusively on corporate contributions is Microelectronics & Computer Technology Corporation. This consortium, also in Texas, is trying to rapidly commercialize its cutting-edge technologies.[3] All these efforts, whether successful or unsuccessful in the short term, represent the breaking of new philosophical ground in America's high-tech businesses. "A decade ago, the idea of major U.S. competitors banding together to mass-produce a crucial part of modern-day manufactured goods would have promptly been branded as collusion," the *Wall Street Journal* noted. "No more."[4]

One other player in this ferment is the Defense Advanced Research Projects Agency (DARPA), which is part of the Pentagon. It has provided small amounts of money to promote the development of certain seed technologies that have military applications as well as commercial applications. For example, it has provided several million dollars to companies developing HDTV monitors.

At the state level, there are far fewer ideological problems about government involvement in the marketplace. Aside from promoting and often subsidizing inward-bound foreign investment, the states have taken the lead in promoting exports from small- and medium-size companies. As the federal government's export-promoting mechanisms at the Commerce Department and Export-Import Bank have been drastically cut back, at least a dozen states have set up programs to provide or subsidize export financing. Several states have programs, often using lottery funds, to encourage smaller businesses to expand in their states or locate there. Iowa has attracted semiconductor makers and San Antonio, Texas, has attracted biotechnology companies through the use of economic development schemes.[5] Other states, such as California and Oregon, have programs to encourage entrepreneurs. In addition, many governors lead delegations of their state's business leaders to foreign countries in pursuit of export contracts.

A particularly fascinating new example of business-business and government-business cooperation is unfolding at Wright-Patterson Air Force Base near Dayton, Ohio.[6] Wright-Patterson has long been the principal research center for the U.S. Air Force. It has worked on developing technologies with military applications, but now, as part of a new consortium called the Ohio Advanced Technology Center, it is making an effort to transfer its technologies as rapidly as possible into civilian commercial use. This could have broader value as the U.S. military undergoes budget cuts and an overall redefining of its mission. AT&T, the Mead Corporation, a paper products company, and Cincinnati Milacron, the machine tool maker, are taking part in the Ohio consortium. Because these companies do not compete with each other, perhaps they can avoid the problems that bedeviled U.S. Memories. There are also many university centers where scientists are trying to forge new intersections with business. The Beckman Institute at the University of Illinois, where scientists are trying to invent machines that work as well and as fast as the human brain, is one. Other examples include the Rensselaer Polytechnic Institute, which has a center for automation, and Carnegie-Mellon's Robotics Institute.[7]

This experimentation in industrial policy at the state level has been unfolding at least since 1958, when North Carolina industrialists, state officials, and university leaders began plotting plans for a Research Triangle. Ezra Vogel, in his 1985 book *Comeback*, which received far less attention than his *Japan as Number One*, argued that North Carolina's success should become a model for the entire nation.[8] Indeed, it was remarkable that a state that once scraped and begged for a few textile companies to relocate from New England was able to develop one of the country's hottest high-tech areas with semiconductors, biotechnology, and other forms of advanced research and manufacturing. It did not happen by accident. The invisible hand did not do it. State, university, and business leaders, mindful of California's Silicon Valley and Boston's Route 128, engineered it.

Since then, Texas has developed a Silicon Plains in the Austin area and Oregon has a Silicon Forest just west of Portland. Minnesota has developed Medical Alley, concentrated in the Minneapolis–St. Paul area, with hundreds of small medical-equipment manufacturers. The presence of universities or medical clinics, such as the Mayo Clinic, was an integral part of these development efforts. A telecommunications corridor has sprung up near Dallas. These states, and others, have consciously targeted industries where they held comparative advantages and built partnerships among business, government, and universities to expand their franchises. Overall, the state governments provide nearly twice as much funding as Washington does to help U.S. manufacturers obtain and use new technologies and improve their productivity, according to the National Governors Association. Of the total $620 million spent on this activity in 1988, the states provided 48 percent of the funding, the federal government provided 26 percent, and industry, universities, and local governments provided the rest. Altogether, at least two hundred organizations ranging from the Michigan Modernization Service to the New Jersey Technology Extension Centers were involved in advising and assisting small and medium-size businesses. These states have become the driving force in setting up research parks, seed capital programs, and technology research centers. In the absence of a strategic economic vision from Washington, the states are trying to take the lead in mounting a response to Japan.[9]

There are potential conflicts of interest in any government-business, university-business, or business-business arrangement, whether at the federal or state level. It would be naive to pretend that cooperation is a panacea. Each of these efforts must be managed with a rigorous, hard-headed approach. One problem is that many companies that are busy competing with each other find it difficult to pool their resources or technology for competitive reasons. If they are winning in the marketplace, they do not want to join forces. In fact, they resent the creation of consortia. This is one problem that helped sink U.S. Memories.

Another risk is that government has a different mentality than business and in general does not understand how products are introduced into the marketplace. So if government becomes too deeply involved, it is a mistake. It is wrong for government to attempt to control the economic process—that is socialism. It is right for government to provide the proper framework by influencing the cost of capital, the development of new technologies, and creating an environment that encourages international trade. There has to be a balance.

Another issue is whether industry is exaggerating the extent of the competition from Japan to win easy government funding. The savings and loan industry certainly raped the government, and therefore the taxpayer. But in the case of high tech, it seems clear that many American companies are in, fact, genuinely outgunned by their Japanese competitors. The news that NEC and Fujitsu have both made one-yen bids for computer projects in Japan is illuminating. Because they are so cash-rich, they are able to give work away in the first stage of a project to win the long-term rewards over a period of several years. Not many American companies can afford that luxury. In other cases, Japanese technology companies are on the brink of leaping entire generations ahead of U.S. rivals, largely on the strength of their capital spending.[10]

Some new collaborative efforts will probably fail, as U.S. Memories did. Others will prove to be wastes of money. But through a process of experimentation, the Americans are learning what kind of consortia, joint R&D projects, and new forms of cooperation work. In Japanese terms, one must plant several seeds before one takes root and blossoms. The early evidence is that business-to-business consortia on a national scale may be the hardest to achieve because of competitive instincts among companies.

Another lesson is that state-level activity, with extensive university involvement and some federal support, is often more successful than efforts coordinated from Washington. There is also relatively little risk to the taxpayer in having the government provide modest amounts of funding, the seed money, to achieve greater national goals. It does not make sense for the government to fully fund these projects. If business is not interested enough to commit its own capital, it's a nonstarter.

Once a technology can be tested and studied, then it is up to business to decide whether to develop and commercialize it. Government cannot do that. In this sense, the government is not "picking winners and losers" but rather providing an infrastructure in which others can.

Even this mild experimentation with new forms of cooperation is being resisted by free-market ideologues in the White House. White House Chief of Staff John H. Sununu, Budget Director Richard G. Darman, and Council of Economic Advisers Chief Michael J. Boskin are attempting to extinguish any attempt to expand or improve the nation's industrial policy toward Japan. They shot down Commerce Secretary Mosbacher's attempt, for example, to expand government funding for HDTV research, and they are trying to reverse the use of Pentagon funding for that purpose. "We just don't believe in picking specific winners and losers," says one White House source, using the same old argument.[11]

Then again in April 1990, Craig I. Fields, the director of DARPA, was eased out of that position and an aide, Michael C. Sekora, resigned because of Administration displeasure. The triggering incident appeared to be a mere $4 million investment that DARPA made in a struggling California company, Gazelle Microcircuits Inc., which is working on developing semiconductors made of gallium arsenide. Although still an imperfect technology, it is widely reckoned that the next major leap in making semiconductors will be to move from silicon to gallium arsenide, which dramatically improves the speed of the circuits. This is obviously a critical technology not only for the Pentagon, but also for the health of the overall U.S. semiconductor industry. By providing seed money, Fields was attempting to prevent the company from having to turn to the Japanese for the capital it needed. But that was unacceptable.

The risk is that more American industries will either get wiped out or fail to keep step with the pace of innovation in Japan. In its most extreme form, conservative economic theory argues that this is not a problem. Milton Friedman, one of the gurus of pure markets, even argues that the United States should unilaterally drop all trade and investment restrictions toward Japan in the full knowledge that Japan plays by a different set of rules. This is the triumph of ideology over the real world.

The real world is that more jobs will be lost and industries destroyed unless there is an American response. The Economic Policy Institute, a nonprofit Washington research organization, argues that the failure of American industry to take part in HDTV and related industries of semiconductors, computers, and video displays could result in a trade

deficit in those industries alone of $225 billion by the year 2010 and
the loss of 2 million jobs.[12] Most Americans would put jobs and technological independence over free-market theory. Billions of federal dollars
are flowing into research institutions across the country, but they are
weighted to support either military research or else theoretical research
that has very little chance of being transformed into practical use in our
lifetimes. Even minor shifts in the flow of federal research dollars
toward commercializing the rich selection of technologies that already
exist in American laboratories could have a major impact. But the high
priests of free-market ideology argue that this would be interfering in
the marketplace.

If Americans can get past this ideological gridlock, there are other
steps they could take to transform a losing industrial policy into a
winning one. It cannot be achieved overnight because Washington has
been steadily abdicating its role in national economic management for
a decade, which is the reason the states have become so active in both
seeking foreign investment and promoting exports. Important elements
of national economic strategy have fallen to the states by default.

But in a climate of greater economic patriotism, the U.S. government,
with fewer Japanese lobbyists in its midst and with lesser dependence
on Japanese capital, could move ahead to develop better coordination
among its own agencies and with the states to respond to specific
Japanese challenges. The ability to use task forces that group representatives from different U.S. agencies ought to be a uniquely flexible tool
for industrial policy. In the absence of presidents who believe in some
form of limited economic coordination, however, the interagency process has become a quagmire. No one is in charge. Federal-state cooperation has also soured as the central government keeps pushing more
costs onto the states and cutting the flow of funds.

In an improved environment, however, if a U.S. company or a U.S.
industry were headed for oblivion against Japanese competition, an
effective industrial policy could involve several elements: The U.S.
government, working with the governor or governors of the states
involved, creates an interagency team that sits down not only with
the companies in trouble but also with their labor unions and their
communities. What went wrong? What needs to be done? In some
cases, there is nothing to be done. It would be difficult, for example,
to argue that America's shoe, watch, camera, or shipbuilding industries should be somehow revived. They are gone, or nearly gone.
Other industries may not be worthy of saving. If the cost of labor or
other global market forces have shifted against an American industry,

and that industry is not vital to national economic security, the goal should be to help the communities, unions, and companies see their way to a new field. The Japanese are masters at making a managed transition from a sunset to a sunrise industry. They do not often pick a fight against overwhelming market forces. From ceramics, a company makes a transition to semiconductor casings. From steel, a company moves to another semiconductor-related area. From cameras, it transposes to precision equipment.

Under no circumstances should any form of U.S. industrial policy amount to a federal bailout. There also is no need for a new bureaucracy. Some advocates of a stronger industrial policy are advocating massive new government-backed funding sources and new governmental departments to administer them. But this is going too far.

Rather, a federal task force could serve as a kind of honest middleman. The executives take pay cuts and lose some perks. Union leaders agree to either wage givebacks or productivity increases. Communities offer tax reductions or improved infrastructures. Shareholders are obliged to accept smaller earnings. If training is needed, universities provide it. Everyone gives up something. This is how it is supposed to work. The government provides a facilitating environment.

If, as a last resort, the troubled company or industry needed protection from Japanese imports for a finite period of time, the stage would be set for effective action. The Japanese company would not be able to merely shift production to the United States or to another country because the states and the federal government would be cooperating to monitor the company's investment response. The American industry would agree to work diligently to take advantage of the breathing space, as motorcycle maker Harley-Davidson did, rather than just coasting. The loopholes would close. Thus, in the best of all possible worlds, trade, investment, and industrial policies are linked.

Hard-headed choices have to be made about when and how to use industrial policy. It does not make a lick of sense, for example, to try to help an industry that does not want to help itself, as was the case with the American steel industry. Nor does it make sense to help a company that has consistently stripped its assets, impoverished its technological base, and taunted its workers for many years. There are all sorts of difficulties in executing a more effective industrial policy. There need to be limits and conditions. There needs to be common sense and balance. A middle path needs to be found. This is what government is for.

It should be emphasized that a more effective industrial policy does not imply a need to create the cozy connections between private business and government that flourish in Japan. This is not mimicking Japan Inc. Americans have a fundamental fear of collusion between business and government. Long before Ralph Nader came along, Dwight Eisenhower was warning of the dangers of a military-industrial complex. An unacceptable form of collusion might come about if senior government officials and private business leaders went to the same universities, played golf together, and intermarried their children. But in view of the depth of mistrust today between business and government in America, there is little chance it could ever go that far. Government and business should never get into bed together, but must they remain strangers?

In some key respects, creating an effective industrial policy is not a question of laws and institutions, but one of finding common philosophical ground. It is a way of thinking that must permeate many different government agencies and many different kinds of decisions.

The power exists to do this, but so far a response has been crippled by ideology. It is simply naive to believe that the American economy is completely wide open with unfettered competition that is somehow guided by Adam Smith's invisible hand. The landscape is littered with dozens of clear-cut attempts by the U.S. government to interfere in the supposedly pure marketplace—some successful, others not. It's not un-American to be pragmatic and shift strategies and mechanisms as conditions warrant. The only thing that is un-American is to consistently get beaten.

❖ 22 ❖

Investment:
Absorb the Benefits

Too many Americans tend to see foreign investment as either black or white. Either foreign investment is good or it is bad. Other Americans are simply confused: They want the employment benefits conferred by Japanese investment, but the polls consistently show that a majority of Americans fear the implications of an expanded Japanese presence. The net result is that the overall American response veers from, on the one hand, fear and paranoia to, on the other hand, an equally unbalanced view that all forms of investment from all nations must be encouraged and allowed without the slightest concern or response.

As we showed in Part Three, Japanese manufacturing investment is based on a model that is different from its U.S. and European counterpart. Japan's investment is surging, and it is destined to become the largest foreign investor in the United States, if it's not already. Overall, investment relations between the United States and Japan are out of balance and are not reciprocal. We have T. Boone Pickens to thank for that recognition, if no one else. In view of the evidence, the American debate about Japanese investment should not be about *whether* to respond but *how* to respond.

It's not a question of stopping Japanese investment altogether. Some members of the pro-Japanese-U.S. intellectual establishment, such as the Blackstone group's Pete Peterson, argue that any response will cause Japanese investment to stop and flow elsewhere. "The cure is worse than the disease," he told me. This is not necessarily true. Even the most rabid critic of Japanese investment would acknowledge that the United States has a desperate need for capital. The world's largest debtor nation should not be slamming the gates to foreign money. Absorbing Japanese capital is absolutely key to American economic revival. The real question is where and how.

The Americans need capital to repair their infrastructure and build their educational system. Businesses need capital to compete, and other social needs beckon. To the extent that Japanese and other foreign capital can be directed toward these goals, it is a win-win situation. But there is little ground for arguing that merely transferring control of CBS Records and Columbia Pictures to Sony, which Peterson pioneered, represents a necessary infusion of Japanese capital. It is difficult to see how this serves any broad American interest.

It is wrong, therefore, to characterize the debate as being between those who are "for" Japanese investment and those who are "against" it. Let us raise the level of the debate. It is a question of what kinds of Japanese investment are desirable and what rules will prevail. Not all Japanese investment is good, not all is bad. Some investment in distribution and retail facilities, for example, merely paves the way for a continued import drive. Investment in municipal bonds, which allows cities to grow and expand, is healthier. Too often, Americans want to leap to conclusions that all Japanese investment is good, or else it is all bad.

The purpose of an intelligent response should be to absorb as many benefits from Japanese investment as other nations have absorbed from our own. If Americans are not able to persuade the Japanese to change the structure of their economy or their protectionist mentality at home, they have far greater power to shape Japanese investment in America. Used properly, this could become a major tool for establishing a more balanced relationship.

As with the often-muddled issue of industrial policy, it is not a question of whether the Americans should create an investment policy toward the Japanese. They already have one. U.S. law, for example, restricts foreign ownership of airlines and shipping. When Fujitsu tried to buy Fairchild Semiconductor, the Commerce Department and the Pentagon made ominous noises and the Japanese company backed down. When Sumitomo paid $500 million for a 12 percent stake in Goldman Sachs, the Federal Reserve demanded that the Japanese have only a nonvoting interest. Conversely, the incentives that the states have provided create a de facto policy of subsidizing Japanese investors to the detriment of established American companies. The United

States does have an investment policy. It is merely disjointed, reactive, and incoherent.

It is curious how little the U.S. government, as an institutional whole, understands about foreign investment in general, much less investment by specific Japanese entities. At least a dozen U.S. agencies collect information, including the Commerce Department, Securities and Exchange Commission, Internal Revenue Service, Treasury Department, and Central Intelligence Agency. Although they gather it, most agencies keep it confidential and there is virtually no attempt to coordinate it. An agency may have one piece of the picture, but a rival agency has another. Partly as a result, Americans are confronted with a hodge-podge of statistics "that only God comprehends and the rest of us struggle with," as one Commerce Department economist complained.[1]

The Bryant Amendment, which has gone through different forms, would currently require foreign investors above a certain size to register with the Commerce Department. There should be little philosophical objection to mere registration. Every major country in the world has more of an infrastructure in place to monitor inward-bound investment than does the United States. But if the Bryant Amendment cannot win passage in the Senate, in the face of heavy lobbying by foreign and U.S.-based multinationals, it seems a first step could be better coordination among U.S. government agencies and a broad improvement in the government's ability to analyze the information that has already been collected. This could be done without a legislative fight.

What might have a negative effect, and what does not make sense to do, is to engage in a massive "screening" of foreign investments or to impose federal performance requirements on them—for the simple reason that it is not practical. Each major investment is a vastly complicated matter in its own right. Look at the complexity of the Mitsubishi group's involvement in automobiles. The United States government would have to set up an entire Mitsubishi desk, over a period of years, to assess the group's local content and sourcing patterns, trade impact, labor relations, management involvement, technology flows, and impact on U.S. industry. Not only would it be a massive investment in paperwork, but the Mitsubishi desk would require inspectors who could visit specific sites to verify the group's statements and help assemble an understanding of how all the pieces fit together. The U.S. government cannot micromanage specific investments. Even attempting to collect comprehensive information across the board would produce an avalanche of paper that could fill the equivalent of another National Archives. Each company would hire the best law firms to complete truckloads of documentation. This is a standard Japanese technique, which has a cross-cultural echo at American law firms: Overwhelm the other guy with information he cannot possibly use.

The best course is to admit Japanese and other foreign investment with a minimum of fuss, and then work to make sure it advances American interests. The laws and mechanisms already exist. There is no need for a big fight in Congress. Thanks to the 1988 trade law, a potentially effective investment body called the Committee on Foreign Investment in the United States (CFIUS) has been strengthened. This is an interagency group chaired by the Treasury Department that includes representatives from the State, Commerce, Defense, and Justice departments, the U.S. Special Trade Representative's office, the Office of Management and Budgets, and the Council of Economic Advisers.

CFIUS is empowered to review any investment that has implications for U.S. "national security." This is a remarkably broad mandate. Upon this body's recommendation, the president has broad discretion to block acquisitions, mergers, and equity stakes. It does not apply to fresh, greenfield investments. CFIUS is already operating and has blocked one Japanese acquisition of an American company that made triggers for nuclear weapons.

Significantly, CFIUS also has the ability to engage in "jawboning." The Japanese call this administrative guidance. It happens when a government official "suggests" that a company do something. CFIUS can, for example, encourage foreign investors to support U.S.-based R&D and to maintain domestic production.[2]

So far, CFIUS, with a staff of only six, has only reviewed defense-related acquisitions. But national security, broadly defined, includes economic security. As those concerns loom larger, it would not necessarily require a new law to quietly expand the body's purview. It should never be taken to the logical extreme of reviewing every investment by every company. As indicated, that is not practical, or desirable. But the point is that the tools are in place to respond to Japanese investment if the U.S. government chooses to exercise them. In view of the nature of Japan's investment practices and the lack of reciprocity, Japanese acquisitions ought to receive special attention. Again, it does not require a law; it is a matter of bureaucratic discretion and political will.

To even pretend to do this effectively, however, the U.S. government would have to reach a new understanding with state governments, which have charged into the lead on the foreign investment issue. Nearly forty states maintain investment and trade promotion offices in Japan, and the emphasis is still more on attracting investment than on stimulating exports from back home. The states also have given the

Japanese investors generous incentives and special treatment in bidding wars, including free driving lessons.[3] California has served as a platform for the entire Japanese banking industry, and as a way station for Japanese companies trying to push into the U.S. market. Few states, in the current environment, are going to support a go-it-alone federal effort to address investment issues with the Japanese. This is a states' rights issue of the highest order, and several have already warned against a response from Washington. "In California, we do not feel the responsibility of controlled foreign investment should lie in the hands of Washington's Congress or Sacramento's legislature," writes Allan Melkesian, director of California's Office of Foreign Investment. He prefers a community-level response, which is patently unworkable.[4]

The lack of cohesiveness between the states and the federal government surprises the Japanese. "You have fifty different foreign economic policies," an economist from the Long-Term Credit Bank once said to me with obvious amazement.

If the states were really going to manage the U.S. investment relationship with Japan, they would require a coordinated response. Theoretically, this could be achieved through the National Governors Association or the National Association of State Development Agencies. At a bare minimum, there should be an exchange of information regionally. The Midwest, Southeast, and West Coast states should harmonize their incentives and their policies. But even this has proven unfeasible. The states are still competing with one another more than they are cooperating. A supra-state response is not practical.

The fact of the matter is that U.S. investment relations with a foreign economic power, with whom there is a major imbalance, should not be exclusively in state hands. A proper response cannot be achieved without federal-state cooperation. But Washington cannot demand that the states simply fall into line. It needs to be more subtle. An ideal first step would be a federal-state meeting. It would not have to involve a president and all fifty governors. It could be handled at the cabinet or subcabinet level and there are only fifteen to twenty states that hold the key. This kind of quiet initiative would never require states to back down on their promises or to "persecute" their investors. Nor does it require a new bureaucracy. It merely begins a dialogue, a sharing of views and information across state lines, and a building of some measure of consensus on how to absorb and shape Japanese investment. Despite all the fuss in Washington about the Bryant Amendment, the states often already possess better-quality information about specific investments than the feds would be able to obtain by themselves. This kind of consultative process is the essence of moderation. It cannot take the form of Washington demanding obedience. It has to be a careful identification or areas where federal and state interests intersect.

The states, if they grow weary of being played against each other for incentives and tax breaks, may one day welcome some loose consultative channels, a federal-state network that allows them to enhance their bargaining positions toward Japanese and other foreign companies. Incentives have cost the states hundreds of millions of dollars, and it is not at all clear in several states that the incentives will be worth it. In some cases, job creation has not been as great as expected. Although states might theoretically impose performance requirements on companies that win incentives, none have dared do it.[5] One reason is if one state did it alone, that state would risk getting frozen out of new investment. If there were a coordinated response, with some level of federal participation, the states would be insulated from possible backlash.

Another reason there needs to be some measure of federal involvement is that the states are not equipped to handle the issue of the *keiretsu.* This is a national-level issue. Nor can states cope with the issue of what happens if the Japanese achieve such a dominant position in an industrial food chain that it threatens U.S. economic security.

It is also the federal government's responsibility to wrestle with the hemorrhaging of technology from federally funded universities, and whether federal research money should support basic research or assist in transferring existing technology into the commercial sector. Another issue that should be addressed, gingerly, is U.S. content. How is it defined? The government does not necessarily have to impose a standard by law, but at the moment there is a gaping hole in U.S. discussion of foreign investment because there is no benchmark other than what the Environmental Protection Agency has established for emission control purposes. It is not at all clear whether U.S. content covers only parts or whether it also includes insurance, marketing, and other soft costs. Nor is it clear whether the use of parts made by transplanted suppliers should count as part of U.S. content. If a Japanese manufacturer brings a third of the value of its components from Japan, obtains another third from Japanese suppliers in the United States, and buys a third from indigenous American suppliers, does that represent a U.S. content of 67 percent or 33 percent? This is not clear. Nor is it clear what the eventual goal is, or what constitutes an acceptable rate of speed in moving toward that goal. A benchmark for all of this, even if not legally binding, would be helpful.

Aside from narrow governmental responses, the broader role for political leaders at all levels should be of an educational nature, encouraging a positive marketplace response to investment of all kinds. Rather than being on bended knee, Americans should understand that they have the right to advance up the management ladder, to be value-added suppliers, to move downstream in selling their raw materials, and to enjoy technology transfer. A better understanding of all the issues inherent in accepting inward-bound investment would lead to a more effective marketplace response.

Ultimately, if a Japanese company or any other foreign investor consistently does not display a positive investment model, then the environment in which it operates should harden. If one company is regularly and consistently identified by suppliers or employees for failing to operate in good faith, or if a company is accused by U.S. industry of dumping, then the federal-state channels are open for an effective response. Aside from CFIUS, the U.S. government has an alphabet-soup collection of agencies like the IRS, EEOC, OSHA, SEC, and FTC that scrutinize American companies on a regular basis. The combination of state and federal probes could tie any company up in paperwork for years.

Americans would never have to force a sale, seize assets, or anything so dramatic. There are more subtle ways to deliver the message. That's the way it works for an American company investing almost anywhere in the world. If you want to make money, you play by our rules. If you don't, you suddenly find yourself bogged down. Americans also have this power. It should be exercised. Politely.

There is cause for a bit of introspection as well. Why do Americans walk away from their own assets? Indeed, why are the people who walk away often called heroes? At the Firestone shareholders' meeting in an elegant Chicago hotel where the company consummated its sale to Bridgestone in 1988, I looked for some sense of drama. Here was a once-great American company being sold off. Did anyone care? After the meeting, there was a group of elderly ladies clustered around Firestone chairman John J. Nevin. Perhaps they were misty-eyed, remembering the old days. No, it turned out; they just wanted to know when they could cash in their shares. Nevin himself had long signaled a desire to get out of the tire business, and he seemed quietly relieved. The only Japanese executive from Bridgestone in the room was surrounded by three-piece suits carrying big legal briefcases. No one in the room was upset. It couldn't be blamed on Bridgestone. I had seen the old Firestone plant in Danville, Kentucky, which had been crippled by bitter management-labor and other problems, indicative of conditions at other Firestone plants. The Japanese had competed with Firestone, but they had not invaded. The Americans simply cashed in and walked away.

The Japanese think, rightly, that Americans are a bit irrational about their fear of Japanese ownership. A common view is that America "foolishly puts its choicest assets on the auction block for quick profit, then blames the buyer for snapping them up."[6] If Americans are so concerned about their economic infrastructure, then fix the root problems: overconsumption of Japanese goods, too much borrowing from the Japanese, poor labor-management relations, and the rest. The net effect of chronic economic imbalances and lack of commitment to remaining competitive is that we put our country up for sale.

All these proposals represent a modest internal realignment. No angry negotiators go and pound on tables in Tokyo. No new laws are passed, or bureaucracies set up. The Americans abide by their international investment treaties. It requires only a sense of economic patriotism and a spirit of consultation and cooperation among Americans. One cannot legislate that.

Those who defend Japanese investment against any form of response often warn in op-ed articles or in speeches that a violent nationalistic reaction is brewing. This is disingenuous. Americans are not extremists. They instinctively reject draconian solutions. They have a keen sense of fairness. They simply want to see some evidence that the issue of Japanese investment is being addressed, which it isn't, in any comprehensive way.

How would Japan respond? Much would depend on how it's done. If there are hostile or emotional outbursts, that would be dangerous. That's the wrong way. But if done calmly and maturely over a period of time, it is fair, and the Japanese would be obliged to accept it. In fact, some Japanese diplomats have said it would be helpful to have a clearer set of national standards on such issues as U.S. content. They would also like to relieve the uncertainty by knowing that a sensible, not irrational, response was in the works.

It is even possible to imagine that the Americans could create new investment opportunities. Japan has a huge capital surplus, like a dam bursting with the pressure of a heavy rain. We have huge capital needs. If a federal-state consortium could be carefully constructed to build a high-speed train or another major infrastructural project such as an airport, and if the project would clearly stimulate American manufacturing know-how, then it might make sense to offer Japan a minority stake. The Japanese get a reasonable, guaranteed profit. We achieve a national goal. Something like this could not be accomplished in an atmosphere of recrimination. The other prospect on the horizon is that the Japanese might offer foreign aid to poor Southern states such as Mississippi, Arkansas, and Louisiana. The governors of these states have requested it, and we should not be too proud to consider it. If Japanese money allows American companies to build projects using American technology that advance long-term American interests, and as a by-product yield a profit to the Japanese, that is to be welcomed. But if Japanese money allows Japanese construction companies to build projects with Japanese or other foreign technology that will merely allow the extraction of American raw materials, that is exploitation, not stimulation.

Japanese investment should not be an ideological or emotional issue. Just because it is big and because it is unfolding on a different model does not mean we have to hate it or fear it, but it does mean that we should redouble the effort to understand it and respond pragmatically. The guiding motto should be, Guard against the negatives and absorb the full benefits.

Although a rethinking of Japan is taking place, and some signs of ferment have appeared on the industrial and investment policy fronts, it is unlikely that there will be a decisive shift in American governmental action until after the 1992 presidential election. Bush's White House seems sufficiently committed to its current mix of trade, industrial, and investment policies that it could prevent or delay the coalescence of a more effective response to Japan. The Democrats have taken a lead on the issue of economic patriotism for now, but there are also Republicans who are hinting at it. Clyde Prestowitz, the former trade negotiator and a Republican, appeals for U.S. government agencies to "hang together" in dealing with Japan. Senator John Heinz from Pennsylvania believes in a governmental response to save America's technological base even though he is a Republican. Other Republicans who have expressed general support for more effective responses to Japan include Senators John Danforth of Missouri and Robert Dole of Kansas.

Whether Democrats win or not in 1992, it would seem that at some point the pendulum will swing back, modestly, from benign neglect of economic fundamentals and cynicism toward a more activist approach. When that happens, Americans should be prepared for the right kind of activism, not the wrong kind. They should understand that American moral energy is one of the strongest tools in the nation's possession. Further, the marketplace of ideas and the economic marketplace are the primary line of defense, not heavy-handed government intervention or smothering new layers of regulation. But it is necessary to shape and guide a marketplace response and that requires a dynamic new policy mix. It will have to be bipartisan to work and it will have to be sustained well into the twenty-first century.

❖ 23 ❖

A Pacific Future

As for Japan, she has risen with simply marvelous rapidity, and she is as formidable from the industrial as from the military standpoint. She is a great civilized nation; though her civilization is in some important respects not like ours. There are some things she can teach us, and some things she can learn from us.

—*Theodore Roosevelt, 1905*

For most of the twentieth century, Americans have pondered the nature of Japan and what it means to the United States. Presidents from Teddy Roosevelt to Ronald Reagan have spoken glowingly about the Pacific era. In recent years, it has become a deeply felt but poorly articulated notion that America's fortunes are bound up with the dynamic people of Japan and Asia in general, and that this will somehow guarantee sustained prosperity for Americans. Less reassuring is the notion that the American Century is ending and the Japanese Century is beginning. This is a discordant variation on the same theme.

It is unquestionably true that the peoples of East Asia possess a unique economic drive. What the American mind finds difficult to grasp is that while this drive offers the prospect of stimulation and rejuvenation, it also poses a direct challenge if Americans fail to respond. The gut-level instinct that "We don't have to do anything differently. The Asians will take care of it" is naive, and, in fact, wrong. If Americans do not understand the new rules of engagement and adapt their thinking appropriately, it will indeed be the end of the American Century. If they can shift gears, they have the power to make a new economic leap, one that could leave much of Western and Eastern Europe behind. Although the apparent breaking up of the Soviet bloc is of profound ideological and emotional gratification to Americans, it offered little immediate prospect of improving America's own economic well-being aside from diminishing the need for devoting massive resources to defense. Overall, the Soviet Union and its erstwhile allies lacked the resources, markets, infrastructure, and skills to generate wealth for most American companies in the foreseeable future. Western Europe was still, naturally, a major economic partner, but the more important frontier lay in the other direction—in East Asia. It was there that wealth and growth prospects far greater than Eastern Europe's beckoned.

For years, one could speak of East Asia in generic terms. There was broad uniformity and overlap in growth prospects for several different nations. Japan, South Korea, Taiwan, Singapore and other countries in the region seemed to be moving in step. But by 1990, it was clear that Japan towered over all others. China and the Philippines were locked in a protracted political struggle. China's problems cast a shadow over Hong Kong, and Indochina was still engaged in military struggle. Korea's takeoff had been muted by labor and political strife. There were good growth prospects in Singapore, Malaysia, and Thailand, and cash-rich Taiwan was on track, both economically and politically, but they represented only a pale shadow of Japan's power. The Japanese faced no significant competitive challenge from other Asian trading states.

In short, the key to achieving an American vision in which Asian economic dynamism stimulates rather than overwhelms, centers increasingly on Japan. There can be no glowing Pacific future unless the Americans come to grips with the challenges and opportunities that Japan presents. Success offers the prospect of invigoration. Failure threatens a loss of ability to control the economic destiny of the United States, not to mention a slow erosion of values held dear and a long-term decline of political integrity.

The first step is to understand who the Japanese are and how their power game is played. As their system has produced staggering wealth, the Japanese have become increasingly open about acknowledging differences of culture, perception, and economic model. Some specialists have even suggested that Japan's is a different form of capitalism, which they call Asian developmental capitalism.

It is equally important to understand that the Japanese do not desire to "change" in the sense Americans have in mind. The Recruit and Uno scandals of 1989 did not represent a wholesale adoption of Western values regarding political bribery and sexual infidelity. Political and bureaucratic elites quickly reconsolidated power following Socialist Party gains in the July elections. Amid a growing sense of confidence and national emergence, the Japanese as a whole were more interested in implanting their values and their systems around the world than in being shaped by a troubled United States. In a word, they did not want to catch what they called "the American disease."

To recognize how the Japanese are different is not to condemn them. This impulse should be resisted. Americans must rise above the good/bad, yes/no mentality to reach a point where they neither hate Japan nor love it, but simply respect it. This is perhaps the hardest part of all—striking this emotional balance. Having done this, we can find it possible to understand that there can be areas of genuine cooperation at the same time that we are engaged in systematic confrontations. Every contact is a point of both cooperation and confrontation. The conflict is not going to "end" one day. It is forever. Hopefully, the cooperation will never end either.

A second step is for Americans to understand how Japan's economic challenge forces us to become more pragmatic in applying old ideas, such as the ideal of pure competition. A certain measure of competition is healthy. It drives Americans to educate themselves better, strive for greater quality, and continue innovating.

But it is foolish to take a commitment to competition to the extreme of allowing entire American industries to be wiped out, or else weakened so seriously that they are scarcely viable. It was one thing in the 1970s or early 1980s—it did not matter as much then. But in the 1990s, some of the industries at risk may be vital for long-term economic security, and this is different.

So, too, must "free trade" and "open investment" be understood as ideals, not rigid formulae. They may exist in some fields, in relations with some like-minded countries, but they certainly cannot be applied across the board with all countries. The philosophical goal should be a middle ground in which there is a degree of competition, a healthy dose of free trade, and as much open investment as possible.

The notion that there must be pure competition, total free trade, and completely open investment with all countries at all times is not grounded in an understanding of how international business works, certainly not in Japan or Asia. Throughout the world's fastest-growing region, there is extensive governmental involvement, clear-cut protection of industries, government-directed targeting of export markets, careful limits on inward-bound investment, extensive use of what Americans consider bribery, and all sorts of competition-limiting devices such as cartels, monopolies, and rigged bidding. One reason the Japanese have been so successful is that they have pragmatically used whatever mechanism works to achieve national economic goals. When one model is no longer effective, they move gracefully to the next. It is not a question of ideology. It is a question of what works.

A third step is to recognize that trade diplomacy can only be a modest piece of the response to Japan. For starters, Japan's politicians are not truly in command, even less so than American politicians. At the bureaucratic negotiating level, Americans tend to produce political appointees with little Japan-savvy and put them up against veteran bureaucrats, the elite of their society, who have been trained and honed for years. The two systems are out of step in this respect.

But an equally important point is that U.S.-style moral pressure and moral outrage are not effective, and will never be effective, in persuading Japan to act or change. Japan is never going to "give away" more than it has to. It's not in the Japanese character to give in the way that is being asked of them. The reason they have not moved to redress the trade imbalance over the course of two decades is because they have not felt compelled to. They perceive that it is in their interest to continue running trade surpluses with the United States. It is naive to think they are going to negotiate this away. If we get a bigger share of their market, we are going to have to earn it by their rules. They have that power. The sooner we recognize the power game for what it is, the better.

The key to responding is to develop positions of genuine power. When the Chinese and Japanese negotiate with each other, what happens at the bargaining table is only a tiny piece of a broader process of testing strengths and intentions. Both sides are consummate bargainers and every time they sit down, whether over a steel plant or a trade treaty, they have an idea of the other's complete political and economic strengths. The breadth of the relationship is often on the table, not just a single issue.

When an American negotiator threatens to curb Japan's access to the U.S. market, the Japanese understand that this is hollow. Not only do they have channels and access in Washington far over the hapless negotiator's head, but they know how dependent the U.S. government is on Japanese capital. And they know that any sincere effort to limit Japan's access to the U.S. market would be shouted down by consumers, companies, and states.

That means the U.S. government must concentrate on narrowing its dependencies on Japan and establishing greater political cohesiveness, both within Washington and with the states, before it can obtain credibility in Tokyo. But most important is encouraging a marketplace response. It is a weakness of the American system, like the Chinese, that we are so pluralistic and fragmented. But it can also be a strength: When Americans make up their minds, when the marketplace of ideas shifts even slightly, it becomes a powerful, long-term force. Even a mild dose of economic patriotism would represent a logic of power that Japan would understand and respect. It is pudding-headed to think that sheer moral force can sway Japan.

*   *   *

There may be an old America at risk, but there is also one that is remarkably vital and that defines itself, at least in part, on its ability to compete with or sell to Japan.

Throughout this sector of the American economy, managers, workers, and communities have never forgotten or else have learned anew the lessons of improved labor-management relations, total commitment to quality, just-in-time delivery and inventory control, and the need for continued technological innovation. They have adopted long-term strategies, entered into deeper relationships with their suppliers, and flattened out their management hierarchies. Entire layers of management have been eliminated at an enormous human cost. They have resisted the wave of leveraged buyouts (LBOs) and stock market games that history will recall as a burst of Pompeii-like indulgence.

In many cases, American companies had to do these things to survive, and clearly imitated their Japanese competitors. "The Japanese have shown us their way is better," Cummins Engine's Henry Schnacht once told fellow CEOs.[1] Cummins, headquartered in Columbus, Indiana, redesigned its entire manufacturing process to compete against cheaper Japanese diesel engines.

Some of the lessons about how to compete, of course, have never been forgotten. Many represent the best America had to offer in the first place. The Japanese simply refined or improved upon these principles. Whatever the precise origin, it is possible to see how the stimulus of Japanese competition and the fruit of Japanese sales have turned some American companies into world-beaters.

Some companies under $250 million in annual sales are doing well in Japan by identifying narrow niches where the Japanese do not or cannot compete. It is impressive to visit the sprawling factory of Marvin Windows in Warroad, Minnesota, six miles south of the Canadian border, and see shipping containers loaded with windows headed for Japan. Marvin takes advantage of a natural resource—wood—and a huge economy of scale to make something the Japanese cannot match at the price. Cybex in Ronkonkoma, New York, makes Nautilus-like exercise and medical diagnostic equipment, another niche area the Japanese have not entered in force. Japan is Cybex's biggest export market. Sequent Computer Systems of Beaverton, Oregon, has a cutting-edge technology in parallel processing computers and it is enjoying major increases in sales to Japan. These companies use American resources, American life-style innovations, and American technology to crack the Japanese market with exports.[2]

A slightly larger tier of emerging multinationals, nicknamed mininationals, both sell and manufacture in Japan. Jim Morgan at Applied

Materials in Santa Clara, California; Fred Krehbiel at Molex in Lisle, Illinois; Bill Madar at Nordson in Westlake, Ohio; and Maurice Hardy at Pall Corporation in Glen Cove, New York, are narrowly focused on semiconductor materials, electrical connectors, industrial equipment, and filters, respectively. But they do what they do better than anyone else and they understand that they need to be in Japan, as well as other places, if they are to remain competitive at home. "You have to attack the market where you think your competition is coming from," says Morgan.[3] Even larger are McDonald's, Federal Express, Microsoft, and similar companies that are successfully penetrating the Japanese market.

Some major American manufacturers simply drew the line against Japanese imports into the United States and fought back. Cummins is one, but others include Harley-Davidson, Black & Decker, Caterpillar, and Xerox. In all these cases, the American companies had to strip down and dramatically improve their competitive level. This was painful, but each of them has done it, and they are winning against their Japanese competitors, at least for now. In Harley's case, the company was aided by four years of tariff protection against four Japanese competitors, a successful but little noticed example of President Reagan's industrial policy. These have been legendary battles, which Wall Street often did not support. Companies that draw the line receive criticism from Wall Street analysts that they are not increasing the earnings to shareholders fast enough. The Japanese competitors do not have this problem.

There is also a tier of major American multinationals that are quite successful in Japan, such as Corning, Coca-Cola, Dow Chemical, Hewlett-Packard, IBM, Merck, Motorola, and Procter & Gamble. All have global operations, but Japan is an area of strength for them. Many have older investment positions—for example, Coca-Cola, whose product arrived, literally, on the Occupation jeeps. Corning is impressive because of its ability to manage its joint-venture strategy with the Japanese. Motorola fights tooth and nail for each step forward it takes in pagers or cellular telephones. Japan has emerged as a major money-maker for companies such as these. Coca-Cola, for example, makes more money in Japan and the Pacific than it does in the United States.

Taken together, these different kinds of companies give the lie to the old sop that Americans cannot make things, that they do not want or cannot figure out how to sell to Japan, and that they are not willing to invest in Japan. When Sony's Akio Morita stands up and says that American companies can only think ten minutes ahead, he is referring only to the losers, not the winners. The gloom-and-doom message may apply to certain companies in autos, auto parts, machine tools, semi-conductors, steel, tires, and other fields, but it is not across the board. The United States can compete against Japan when it chooses to.

This competitive potential toward Japan could be enhanced if the influx of foreign capital, skills, technologies, and people now washing into America is managed and absorbed properly. One characteristic that foreigners often find impressive about the United States is that we have the capacity to allow entire industries and regions to suffer while we build new industries and new prosperity elsewhere. It is more than a boom-and-bust cycle. Rather, the United States is such a vast continental power that one can find signs of decay and despair in one location, but signs of vitality in others. One of the sources of vitality is the current wave of internationalization.

A French investment official, Henri Triebel, captured this best. Triebel, now returned to France, was based in New York and crisscrossed the United States looking for American companies who would invest in France. In so doing, he obtained an excellent grasp of not only specific U.S. corporations, but also some of the underlying strengths of the U.S. economy. In this respect, in our occasional lunches, he reminded me of a latter-day De Tocqueville, who saw things more clearly than many Americans.

Triebel spent time in Silicon Valley and came back from one trip amazed. "I went to several high-tech factories where the top tier of managers, the people with MBAs, were Americans. Then the scientists and the engineers, the people with the Ph.D.s, were Asians. Then the workers were Latin. This is amazing. This could never happen in Europe." Triebel was impressed by the competitive clout that could be mustered by mixing the best managers, with the best scientists and engineers, with the best, cheapest labor. Among major industrial powers, the ability to absorb and mix people in this way is distinctively American. The director of Minnesota's export finance program is an Indian. A German runs an innovative export financing program in Portland, Oregon. The head of the New York–New Jersey Port Authority's export promotion agency is of Lebanese origin. The chief executive officers of major American companies, including Dow, Coke, Merck, and Heinz, are either foreign-born or first-generation immigrants, which would be inconceivable in Japan or Germany. Many foreigners run companies that are developing the U.S. technological base and exporting their products.

As it restructures away from consumer demand to export-driven production, the United States will generate the wealth that it needs to dig out of its trade and fiscal deficits. It is significant that the United

States in 1989 displaced West Germany as the world's largest exporter.[4] The U.S. export boom is one of the single most impressive indications of the vitality that remains in the U.S. economy. American companies of all sizes are contributing to this, as are foreign companies that have invested in the United States. In corporate parlance, the United States has become the world's preeminent manufacturing "platform."

The world-is-ending psychology that some Americans display is not justified in U.S. economic relations with Europe, Latin America, Canada, or the vast majority of Asia. It is only Japan that possesses the power and the ambition to overwhelm industry after industry. True, there are certain companies and certain countries in Europe that are more competitive than others, but none of them, not even Germany, pose the same across-the-board challenge that Japan does.

That is why if we can face up to the Japanese and meet them consistently, our ability to maintain and improve our standard of living will be enhanced. We will have been stimulated, not colonized. This is the essence of what the Pacific century should mean.

Doing that does not imply a rejection of American values. We have shifted economic gears before in our history. From colonialism, we moved to a closed protectionist model for many decades. Following World War II, we were prophets of total openness. Different phases of economic growth require different mixes of policies.

Far from rejecting traditional values, defending and enhancing the American economic base would allow the maintenance and expansion of many ideals that Americans hold dear. It is like a small town that depends on a factory. If all the men have good jobs, they own their homes and raise their children well. The town can afford to maintain the roads, and residents can afford to give money to charity and devote attention to social causes. But if the factory closes, all that is at risk.

America as a whole requires a solid economic underpinning to promote its ideals of a liberal society, one in which disparate peoples are blended together, in which women have expanded life opportunities. A wide-open marketplace of ideas, a vital and effective system of governance, and a measure of economic diversity and openness are other ideals. If Americans trade away financial, technological, and overall economic control, they also trade away part of their continued ability to shape their society. Facing Japan's challenge means growing up, maturing as a nation. We can still have our wide-eyed entrepreneurs and our technological cowboys, but we recognize a need for longer-term consistent strategies predicated on in-depth knowledge of other cultures and other systems.

The world is undergoing the most rapid period of economic and political change since World War II, and this change affects how Americans must interact with other peoples. Japan's economic strength is dramatically greater than it was forty-five years ago, and it is only natural that the Americans adjust their model accordingly. It is a long-term agenda. The greed and short-sightedness of the 1980s is, by necessity, giving way to sober reflection about shaping the American system to compete in a world that the United States no longer dominates through sheer force of arms. Economic patriotism must supplement old-fashioned patriotism, which was limited to security and ideology.

Americans are not interested in reestablishing world hegemony. Japan is a global power and will remain so. The lingering psychology of a patron-client relationship with Japan must be smashed. The Japanese are equals. If anything, Americans are underdogs in many areas of competition. That means we have to understand the reality of today's Japan, rather than trying to use out-of-date tools and models. By better understanding Japan's power game and by managing ourselves better, we can improve the balance of the U.S.-Japanese relationship, the pillar of a Pacific future.

Appendix A
What the Japanese Think of America

Overall, the U.S. Gets Low Marks

How much admiration and fondness do you have for each of the following—a great deal, a fair amount, not very much, or none at all?

	A Great Deal	A Fair Amount	Not Very Much	None at All	Not Sure
America as a nation	9%	33%	41%	13%	4%
America's economic success	6%	29%	40%	16%	9%
The American people	7%	25%	45%	18%	5%

Japanese Trade Barriers Hurt the U.S.

While Japanese companies do better selling products in America, American companies have had trouble selling their products in Japan. Do you think these troubles are or are not the result of . . . ?

	Are Result of	Are Not Result of	Not Sure
American products not being as good quality as Japanese products	54%	30%	16%
American products being too expensive	30%	51%	19%
Japan imposing unfair barriers to imports from America	55%	23%	22%
American companies not trying hard enough	52%	32%	16%

SOURCE: Poll of 1,000 adults conducted in Japan, November 10–14 [1989] for *Business Week* by Louis Harris & Associates Inc. Results should be accurate to within four percentage points. Reprinted from the December 18, 1989, issue of *Business Week* by special permission, copyright © 1989 by McGraw-Hill, Inc.

The Japanese Want Trade and Marketing Reforms

Now, do you favor or oppose the Japanese government taking any of these measures to improve trade relations with America?

	Favor	Oppose	Not Sure
Requiring that a certain amount of American products be allowed in Japan	45%	33%	22%
Reforming Japan's distribution system	64%	12%	24%
Removing the ban on imported rice	39%	48%	13%

America's Racial Mix Is Seen as a Big Failing

Now, please choose from this list which you think are the two or three reasons for America's economic problems.

Poor education system	15%
Too many different minorities	42%
Lazy work force	35%
Incompetent management	11%
Too interested in short-term returns	25%
Insensitivity to foreign markets	29%
None	7%
Not sure	18%

A Split on Closer Japanese Ties with Moscow

If relations with America worsen, should Japan work harder to improve relations with the Soviet Union or not?

Should work harder to improve relations	41%
Should not	40%
Not sure	19%

Bullying Japan on Trade Isn't Cricket . . .

If you had to say, do you think America is trying to unfairly pressure Japan on trade issues or not?

Trying to unfairly pressure	57%
Not trying	27%
Not sure	16%

. . . But Then, Japan Could Loosen Up a Bit

Would you like to see Japan just refuse to make any further trade concessions to America, or do you think Japan could be more flexible on trade with America?

Refuse to make further trade concessions	21%
Japan could be more flexible on trade	62%
Not sure	17%

America's Troubles Are Fixable

Do you think America has begun a process of irreversible social and economic decline, or don't you think that is happening?

Irreversible process of decline	21%
Not happening	51%
Not sure	28%

Japan May Assume America's Mantle

How much do you agree with the statement that eventually Japan will take America's place as the world's leading economic and political power?

Agree strongly	6%
Agree somewhat	37%
Disagree somewhat	23%
Disagree strongly	12%
Not sure	22%

Japan's Technology Gives It an Edge in the U.S.

If you had to say, do you think America's growing dependence on Japanese technology gives Japan more clout in its dealings with America, or not?

Gives Japan more clout	55%
Doesn't give Japan more clout	18%
Not sure	27%

Tokyo Should Rely Less on the U.S. for Defense

In the future, do you think that Japan should rely less on America for its national defense, or don't you think that way?

Think Japan should rely less on America	52%
Don't think Japan should rely less on America	31%
Not sure	17%

Appendix B

What Americans
Think of Japan Inc.

Japan Envy

How much admiration do you have for . . . ?

	A Great Deal	Some	Not Very Much	None at All	Not Sure
Japan as a nation	25%	48%	15%	9%	3%
Japan's economic success	49%	29%	12%	7%	3%
The Japanese people	32%	48%	10%	6%	4%

Feeling Unbalanced About Trade

This year, the Japanese will sell $55 billion more in products to the U.S. than the U.S. will sell to Japan. How serious do you feel it is that Japan is selling so much more to the U.S. than the U.S. is selling to Japan—very serious, somewhat serious, not very serious, or not serious at all?

Very serious	69%
Somewhat serious	23%
Not very serious	4%
Not serious at all	2%
Not sure	2%

SOURCE: Poll of 1,250 adults conducted July 7–11 [1989] for *Business Week* by Louis Harris & Associates Inc. Results should be accurate to within three percentage points. Reprinted from the August 7, 1989, issue of *Business Week* by special permission, copyright © 1989 by McGraw-Hill, Inc.

Pointing the Finger at Tokyo

While Japanese companies do better selling products in the U.S., American companies have had trouble selling their products in Japan. Do you think these troubles are or are not the result of . . . ?

	Are Result of	Aren't Result of	Not Sure
U.S. products not being as good as Japanese products	38%	59%	3%
U.S. products being too expensive	57%	40%	3%
Japan imposing unfair barriers to imports from the U.S.	68%	20%	12%

Calling for a Crackdown

Here are some measures that the U.S. might take to make the Japanese markets more receptive to this country's products. For each, tell me if you favor or oppose that measure.

	Favor	Oppose	Not Sure
Require that a certain amount of U.S. products be allowed into Japan	79%	19%	2%
Impose higher tariffs on Japanese products coming into this country	61%	35%	4%
Put a limit on the amount of Japanese goods allowed into this country	69%	29%	2%
Restrict the outflow of technology from the U.S. to Japan	59%	37%	4%

A Question of Quality

If you were in the market for a major purchase, and you had a choice between a product made in Japan or one made in the U.S. by an American company, which do you think would be a better quality product—the one made in Japan or the one made in the U.S.?

One made in Japan	32%
One made in U.S.	45%
Both equal	4%
Depends on product	16%
Not sure	3%

Buying American

Now, suppose the products made in Japan and the U.S. were equal in quality. Would you be willing to pay more for the product made in the U.S. or not?

Would pay more for U.S. product	66%
Would not	28%
Depends on how much more	6%
Not sure	0%

Move Over, Soviets

If you had to say, which do you now think is a more serious threat to the future of this country—the military threat from the Soviet Union or the economic threat from Japan?

The military threat from the Soviet Union	22%
The economic threat from Japan	68%
No difference	5%
Not sure	5%

Notes

Part One

THE POWER SOCIETY

1. Change, No Change?

1. Thomas F. Millard, *Democracy and the Eastern Question* (New York: The Century Co., 1919).

2. Stanley K. Hornbeck, *Contemporary Politics in the Far East* (New York: Appleton and Company, 1916).

3. Sir George Sansom, "Liberalism in Japan," *Foreign Affairs* 19, 3 (April 1941): 551–52.

4. Edwin O. Reischauer and Albert M. Craig, *Japan: Tradition and Transformation* (Boston: Houghton Mifflin, 1973; reprinted by Charles E. Tuttle, Tokyo, 1978), pp. 295–96.

5. Ezra Vogel, *Japan as Number One: Lessons for America* (Cambridge, Mass.: Harvard University Press, 1979; New York: Harper/Colophon Books, 1980).

6. Andrew Tanzer, "Land of the Rising Billionaires," *Forbes*, July 27, 1987, pp. 66–80.

7. Elisabeth Rubinfien, "Japanese Charter *QE2* for 65 Days But Keep It Docked," *Wall Street Journal*, June 5, 1989, p. 1.

8. Ruth Benedict, *The Chrysanthemum and the Sword* (New York: New American Library, 1946), p. 302.

2. The Difficult Culture

1. Benedict, *The Chrysanthemum and the Sword*, p. 47.

2. Takie Sugiyama Lebra, *Japanese Patterns of Behavior* (Honolulu: University of Hawaii Press, 1976) p. 68.

3. Jared Taylor, *Shadows of the Rising Sun* (New York: William Morrow, 1983) p. 47.

4. Robert Whiting, *You Gotta Have Wa: When Two Cultures Collide on the Baseball Diamond* (New York: Macmillan, 1989). See also *The Chrysanthemum and the Bat* (New York: Dodd, Mead, 1977).

3. Women in a Man's World

1. Sally Solo, "Japan's Rising Women," *Fortune,* International Edition, June 19, 1989.

2. Urban Lehner and Kathryn Graven, "Quiet Revolution: Japanese Women Rise in Their Workplaces, Challenging Tradition," *Wall Street Journal,* September 6, 1989, p. 1.

3. Claudia Wallis, "Women Face the 90s," *Time,* December 4, 1989, pp. 80–89.

4. See Shizuko Ohshima and Carolyn Francis, *Japan Through the Eyes of Women Migrant Workers* (Tokyo: Japan Woman's Christian Temperance Union, 1989).

5. Taylor, *Shadows of the Rising Sun,* p. 195.

6. Elizabeth Ehrlich, "The Mommy Track," *Business Week,* March 20, 1989, pp. 126–34; and Wallis, "Women Face the 90s."

7. Claudia H. Deutsch, "Saying No to the 'Mommy Track,' " *New York Times,* January 28, 1990, Sec. 3, p. 29.

8. Yuri Kageyama, "Women Politicians Divided by Party," *Japan Times,* September 26, 1989, p. 3.

4. Hitting the Wall

1. See George DeVos and Hiroshi Wagatsuma, *Japan's Invisible Race: Caste in Culture and Personality* (Berkeley: University of California Press, 1966).

2. Merry White, *The Japanese Overseas: Can They Go Home Again?* (New York: Free Press, 1988) p. 13.

3. Taylor, *Shadows of the Rising Sun,* p. 62.

4. Michael Weiner, *The Origins of the Korean Community in Japan: 1919–1923* (Atlantic Highlands, N.J.: Humanities Press International, Inc., 1989).

5. "Foreign Workers Feared, Poll Finds," *Japan Times,* July 23, 1989, p. 4.

6. Neil Gross and Ted Holden, "A New Mecca for Third World Workers," *Business Week International,* November 28, 1988. See also Susumu Awanohara, "Open the Door Some More?," *Far Eastern Economic Review,* September 4, 1986.

7. Karl Schoenberger, "Issue of Japanese Racism Grows with Immigration," *Los Angeles Times,* January 1, 1990, p. A1.

8. Gregory Clark, *The Japanese Tribe: Origins of a Nation's Uniqueness* (Tokyo: Saimaru Press, 1977).

5. The Japanese Prism

1. D. Eleanor Westney, *Imitation and Innovation: The Transfer of Western Organizational Patterns to Meiji Japan* (Cambridge, Mass.: Harvard University Press, 1987) p. 5.

2. Edwin O. Reischauer, *The Japanese Today: Change and Continuity* (Tokyo: Charles E. Tuttle, 1988) p. 395.

3. Ayako Doi, " 'America Bashing' a Worrisome Trend Seeping into Many Sectors of Japan," *Japan Times*, July 18, 1989, p. 18.

4. Barbara Buell, "Japan Just Can't Believe It's a Superstar," *Business Week*, July 13, 1987. p. 64.

5. Robert Neff, "Japan's Hardening View of America," *Business Week*, December 18, 1989, pp. 62–64.

6. Lebra *Japanese Patterns of Behavior*, p. 255.

Part Two
SCANDAL

6. The Kingdom

1. "High Technology Gateway," *Business Week*, August 9, 1982, pp. 40–44.

2. "Recruit's Biggest Victim," *Asahi Evening News*, March 13, 1989, p. 5.

3. *Business Week*, August 9, 1982. Ibid.

4. Ian Rodger, "Powerbroker Behind the Japanese Political Throne," *Financial Times*, August 3, 1989, p. 6.

7. The Challengers

1. Hiroji Shimoda, *Recruit—The Study of New Groupism* (Tokyo: Mainichi Shimbun Sha, 1989), p. 105. From Japanese.

2. *Business Week* interview, mostly unpublished.

3. Takao Toshikawa, *Money Connections and People Connections of the NTT Fight* (Tokyo: Ipec Publishing, 1989) p. 25. From Japanese.

4. *Nihon Keizai Shimbun*, July 8, 1982.

5. Hajime Takano and Takao Toshikawa, *Deep Analysis—The Whole Structure of the Recruit Scandal* (Tokyo: Ipec Publishing, 1989), pp. 42–43. From Japanese.

6. *1983 Current Biography* (New York: The H. W. Wilson Co.).

7. Shinichi Sano, *Artificial People from the Showa Era* (Bungei Shunju Publishers, 1989). From Japanese. Showa refers to the reign of the emperor whom Americans knew as Hirohito.

8. K. Taya, "Recruit," *Tokyo Business Today*, June 1987, pp. 41–44.

9. Shimoda, *Recruit*, pp. 59–62, 101.

10. *Mainichi Daily*, December 15, 1988.

11. Takano and Toshikawa, p. 15.

12. Benedict, *The Chrysanthemum and the Sword*, p. 95.

8. The Attack

1. Toshikawa, *Money Connections*, pp. 24, 43.

2. Ibid. p. 40.

3. Ibid. pp. 46–47.

4. *Mainichi Daily*, November 5, 1988.

5. *Japan Times*, March 12, 1989.

6. *Business Week*, "The Doors of NTT Begin to Creak Open," May 4, 1981, pp. 67.

7. Christopher J. Chipello, "Japan Industry Fears Tie-Up by NTT, IBM," *Asian Wall Street Journal*, October 3, 1985, p. 1.

8. Hiroji Shimoda, "The Secret Maneuvering of the Shinto Machine," *Sapio*, July 27, 1989, p. 37. From Japanese.

9. Hiroji Shimoda, "President Reagan Was Satisfied," *Sapio*, July 13, 1989, p.37. From Japanese.

10. Ibid.

9. Tripping on a Small Stone

1. Shimoda, "President Reagan Was Satisfied," p. 37.

2. "Construction Minister Criticizes Money Problem, Opposition Party," *Asahi Shimbun*, April 4, 1989, p. 2. From Japanese.

3. Steven R. Weisman, "So Who's Digging Up All That Scandal in Tokyo?," *New York Times*, May 1, 1989.

4. Karel van Wolferen, *The Enigma of Japanese Power* (New York: Knopf, 1989), p. 143.

5. See David E. Kaplan and Alec Dubro, *Yakuza: The Explosive Account of Japan's Criminal Underworld* (Reading, Mass: Addison-Wesley, 1986).

6. David E. Sanger, "The Samurai's Suicide: Alarm Bell for Japan?," *New York Times*, May 19, 1989, p. A6.

7. *Asahi Evening News*, "Recruit's Biggest Victim," March 13, 1989, p. 5.

8. Weisman, "So Who's Digging."

9. Van Wolferen, *Enigma of Japanese Power*, pp. 98–99.

10. The Uno Affairs

1. "Ten Years with Prime Minister Uno: A Lover Reveals Her Story," *Shincho Weekly*, June 29, 1989.

2. Bill Powell, "The Rising Daughters," *Newsweek*, July 10, 1989, pp. 6–9.

3. Elisabeth Rubinfien, "Sex Scandal Rocking Japan's Premier Shows Traditional Attitudes Changing," *Wall Street Journal*, June 20, 1989, p. A14.

4. "Uno's Wife Apologizes for Geisha Controversy," *Asahi Evening News*, July 20, 1989.

11. Socialists: A Flash in the Pan

1. Gerald L. Curtis, *The Japanese Way of Politics* (New York: Columbia University Press, 1988) pp. 117–56.

2. Ibid., p. 124.

3. "Final Upper House Election Returns," *Asahi Evening News*, July 25, 1989, p. 1.

4. "Japan's Next Revolution," *Economist*, July 29, 1989, p. 15.

5. Barry Hillenbrand, "Woman of the Hour," *Time International*, August 7, 1989, p. 8.

6. Max Lerner, "What Fell in Japan?," *Japan Times*, August 2, 1989, p. 17.

7. As quoted by Takashi Kawauchi, "Mixed Reaction in U.S. Over Emergence of JSP," *Mainichi Daily*, August 1, 1989, p. 1.

8. Charles Wolf, Jr., "If Japan's Socialists Gain," *New York Times*, November 18, 1989, op-ed.

9. Carla Rapoport, "Who Runs Japan?," *Fortune*, August 28, 1989, pp. 113–14.

10. Yuri Kageyama, "JSP May Disappoint Women," *Japan Times*, September 1989, p. 2.

11. Charles Smith, "A House Divided," *Far Eastern Economic Review*, September 21, 1989, p. 12.

12. Konosuke Kuwabara, "Socialist-Led Government Increasingly Unlikely," *Japan Economic Journal*, October 28, 1989, p. 32.

13. Kent E. Calder, *Crisis and Compensation: Public Policy and Political Stability in Japan, 1949–1986* (Princeton: Princeton University Press, 1988).

14. Steven R. Weisman, "For Women and for Socialists, It's Always Uphill, *New York Times*, December 15, 1989, p. A4.

15. Chalmers Johnson, "Their Behavior, Our Policy," *National Interest*, Fall 1989, p. 17.

16. NTT foreign press luncheon, October 1989, Tokyo.

17. Ian Rodger, "Powerbroker Behind the Japanese Political Throne," *Financial Times*, August 3, 1989, p. 12.

18. "Maglev to Levitate Kanemaru's Wallet," *Tokyo Insider*, September 20, 1988, pp. 7–8.

Part Three

INTO THE FUTURE

12. The Political System Rolls On

1. Steven R. Weisman, "Despite Year of Scandal, 'Money Politics' Seems as Strong as Ever in Japan," *New York Times*, January 29, 1990, p. A6.

2. Ian Rodger, "Japan's Money-Driven Election Gets into Top Gear," *Financial Times*, February 16, 1990, p. 4.

3. Koichiro Sakai, "LDP Wrests Control of Donations from Factions," *Japan Economic Journal*, February 3, 1990, p. 3.

4. Kenji Suzuki, "The Increasing Number of Second-Generation Diet Members," *Economist*, June 3, 1989. From Japanese.

5. Ted Holden, "Real Reform in Japan? Don't Hold Your Breath," *Business Week*, May 29, 1989, p. 51.

6. Weisman, "Despite Year of Scandal."

7. See Francis R. Valeo and Charles E. Morrison, *The Japanese Diet and the U.S. Congress* (Boulder, Colo.: Westview Press, 1983).

8. Conversation with author, July 1989.

9. Van Wolferen, *Enigma of Japanese Power*, pp. 84, 111.

13. Nationalistic Drift?

1. Mikio Sumiya, "Easy Prey for Neonationalists," *Japan Times*, October 10, 1989, opinion page.

2. Arthur Schlesinger, Jr., "Our Problem Is Not Japan or Germany," *Wall Street Journal*, December 22, 1989, p. A6.

3. Neff, "Japan's Hardening View of America."

4. See, for example, Edward Behr, *Hirohito: Behind the Myth* (New York: Villard Books, 1989).

5. Seiichi Hirai, "Education Minister Endorses Rules to Restore Sense of National Identity," *Japan Times*, August 19, 1989, p. 3.

6. Masayuki Takagi, "The Japanese Right Wing," *Japan Quarterly*, July–September 1989.

7. Kaplan and Dubro, *Yakuza.* pp. 71–99.

8. Masayuki Takagi, *The Right Wing: Its Activities and Groups* (Tokyo: Doyo Bijyutsu Sha, 1989).

9. Shintaro Ishihara, *Chuo Koron*, July 1989. pp. 184–99. From Japanese.

14. Economic Lift-off

1. Kenneth S. Courtis, "Japan: The Momentum Accelerates," *Intro Japan*, Spring 1989.

2. Yoichi Masuzoe, "Containing the Problem," *Journal of Japanese Trade & Industry*, no. 5 (1989), p. 26.

3. Bill Emmott, *The Sun Also Sets: The Limits to Japan's Economic Power* (New York: Times Books, 1989) pp. 239–56.

4. Morgan Guaranty Trust Company, "Japan: The World's Leading Foreign Investor," *World Financial Markets/1989*, Issue 4.

5. Andrew Tanzer, "How Do You Shut the Darn Thing Off?," *Forbes*, November 13, 1989, p. 38.

6. James B. Treece, "Shaking Up Detroit," *Business Week*, August 14, 1989, p. 74.

7. Sally Solo, "Japan's New Cars," *Fortune*, December 4, 1989, pp. 82–86.

8. Jacob M. Schlesinger, "Japanese Chip Companies Brush Off U.S. Challenge and Forge Further Ahead," *Wall Street Journal*, July 24, 1989, p. A10.

9. Andrew Pollack, "In the Trenches of the Chip Wars," *New York Times*, July 2, 1989, p. F1.

10. Robert Hof and Neil Gross, "Silicon Valley Is Watching Its Worst Nightmare Unfold," *Business Week*, September 4, 1989, p. 63.

11. Geoff Lewis, "Computers: Japan Comes On Strong," *Business Week*, October 23, 1989, p. 104.

12. William M. Bulkeley, "Sensitive Area: Long a U.S. Province, Supercomputer Market Feels a Japanese Threat," *Wall Street Journal*, May 24, 1989, p. 1.

13. "Japan's Commercial Aircraft Industry," Japan Economic Institute, September 1, 1989.

14. Henry F. Myers, "Japan's Huge Banks: How Serious a Threat?," *Wall Street Journal*, September 4, 1989, p. 1.

15. Daniel Burstein, *Yen! Japan's New Financial Empire and Its Threat to America* (New York: Simon and Schuster, 1988).

16. Tanzer, "How Do You Shut the Darn Thing Off?," p. 39.

17. Ted Holden, "Japan Is Like a Kid in a Candy Store—A Rich Kid," *Business Week*, December 4, 1989, p. 50.

18. "Inside Japan's M & A," *Business Tokyo*, November 1989, p. 18.

19. Fumio Okamoto, "Bulging Coffers Drive Investors Overseas," *Japan Economic Journal*, November 11, 1989, p. 1.

15. Going Global: Values

1. R. Murphy, "Japan and the World—Power Without Purpose: The Crisis of Japan's Global Financial Dominance," *Harvard Business Review*, March–April 1989.

2. Jean-Jacques Servan-Schreiber, *The American Challenge* (New York: Atheneum, 1968).

3. William J. Lederer and Eugene Burdick, *The Ugly American* (New York: W. W. Norton & Co., 1958).

4. See Stephen S. Cohen and John Zysman, *Manufacturing Matters: The Myth of the Post-Industrial Economy* (New York: Basic Books, 1987).

5. Susan Chira, "Two Papers Quote Japanese Leader on Abilities of Minorities in U.S.," *New York Times*, September 24, 1986, p. 12.

6. *Business Week* luncheon, New York, December 1989.

7. Robert E. Cole and Donald R. Deskins, Jr., "Racial Factors in Site Location and Employment Patterns of Japanese Auto Firms in America," *California Management Review* (University of California, Berkeley), Fall 1988.

8. Michele Galen and Leah J. Nathans, "White People, Black People, Not Wanted Here?" *Business Week*, July 10, 1989, p. 31. See also Stephen Labaton, "Bias Rulings Aid Japan's U.S. Units," *New York Times*, June 19, 1989, p. D2.

9. Conversation with author, September 1989.

10. Jonathan Peterson, "Americans as 'Watched' Executives," *Los Angeles Times*, July 11, 1988, p. 1. See also Jim Schacter and Nancy Yoshihara, "Bosses from Japan Bring Alien Habits," *Los Angeles Times*, July 10, 1988, p. 1.

11. Vladimir Pucik, et al., "Management Culture and the Effectiveness of Local Executives in Japanese-Owned U.S. Corporations," University of Michigan. October 1989.

16. Going Global: Exporting a Keiretsu

1. William J. Holstein, James B. Treece, and Neil Gross, "Why Mitsubishi Is Right at Home in Illinois," *Business Week*, May 30, 1988, p. 45.

2. "Mitsubishi: A Japanese Giant's Plans for Growth in the U.S.," *Business Week*, July 20, 1981.

3. Masami Iida, "Interlocking Firms Lock Out Foes," *Japan Economic Journal*, June 17, 1989, pp. 1–5. See also Japan Economic Institute, "Keiretsu and Other Large Corporate Groups in Japan," January 12, 1990.

4. Johnson, "Their Behavior, Our Policy," pp. 23–24.

17. Is Japanese Investment Created Equal?

1. "The Quiet Billions Uncle Sam Can't Track," *Fortune*, December 22, 1986, p. 55.

2. Norman J. Glickman and Douglas P. Woodward, *The New Competitors: How Foreign Investors Are Changing the U.S. Economy* (New York: Basic Books, 1989).

3. Sandra D. Atchison, "Head 'Em Up, Move 'Em Out—to Japan," *Business Week*, August 21, 1989, p. 52. See also Barbara Buell, et al., "A New Taste for U.S. Food Companies," *Business Week*, June 20, 1988, pp. 18–19.

4. Lawrence Krause, remarks at Japan Society conference, New York, September 16, 1988.

5. Unpublished interview with Neil Gross, *Business Week*, Tokyo, February 1989.

6. Steve Salerno, "Making a Big Deal of Gen-Probe," *California Business*, February 1990, p. 46.

7. Edward O. Welles, "The Tokyo Connection," *Inc.*, February 1990, p. 52.

8. David E. Sanger, "U.S. Parts, Japanese Computer," *New York Times*, September 7, 1988, p. D1.

9. Martin Tolchin, "A Debate over Access to American Research," *New York Times*, December 17, 1989, p. E4.

10. Leslie Helm, Alice Z. Cuneo, and Dean Foust, "On the Campus: Fat Endowments and Growing Clout," *Business Week*, July 11, 1988, p. 72.

11. Mordechai E. Kreinin, "How Closed Is Japan's Market? Additional Evidence," *World Economy* 11, no. 4 (December 1988): 529–41.

12. Ron Napier, " 'Made in Japan'—Japanese Foreign Direct Investment and Export Prospects," *Salomon Brothers Market Analysis*, August 24, 1988.

13. Larry Armstrong, "Toyota's Fast Lane," *Business Week*, November 4, 1985, pp. 40–46.

14. Linda M. Spencer, "American Assets: An Examination of Foreign Investment in the U.S.," Congressional Economic Leadership Institute, July 1988.

15. David E. Sanger, "Worried About Reaction in U.S., Japanese Assess Investment Policy," *New York Times*, November 24, 1989, p. A1.

18. Managing the Americans

1. See Clyde V. Prestowitz, Jr., *Trading Places: How We Allowed Japan to Take the Lead* (New York: Basic Books, 1988).

2. William J. Holstein, et al., "Japan's Influence in America," *Business Week*, July 11, 1988, pp. 64–75.

3. Unpublished *Business Week* interview, May 1988.

4. Pat Choate, *Agents of Influence* (New York: Knopf, 1990).

5. Steven J. Dryden, Neil Gross, and William J. Holstein, "How Toshiba Is Beating American Sanctions," *Business Week*, September 14, 1987, p. 58.

6. Clyde H. Farnsworth, "Japan's Loud Voice in Washington," *New York Times*, December 10, 1989, p. F6.

7. Martin Tolchin, "Foreign Investment in U.S. Mutes Trade Debate," *New York Times*, February 8, 1987.

8. Martin Tolchin, "Did Japanese Lobbyists Scuttle Top Appointment?," *New York Times*, March 4, 1988.

9. Robert Pear, "Diplomats at Japan's Embassy Worry About Anti-Tokyo Sentiment in U.S.," *New York Times*, November 24, 1989, p. A12.

10. Steven Dryden and Douglas Harbecht, "When Japan's Lobbyists Talk, Washington Doesn't Just Listen," *Business Week*, July, 1988, pp. 67–68.

11. Edward T. Pound and David Rogers, "Savvy Lobbyists Gain Clout in Washington for Foreign Clients," *Wall Street Journal*, July 14, 1986, p. 1.

12. Holstein et al., "Japan's Influence in America."

13. David Wessel, "Consultant's Link to Japan Chafes Several Lawmakers," *Wall Street Journal*, December 14, 1989, p. A24.

14. John B. Judis, "The Japanese Megaphone," *The New Republic*, January 22, 1990, p. 20.

15. Jerry Buckley, "Japan Moves In," *U.S. News & World Report*, May 9, 1988, p. 48.

16. William J. Holstein, "Japan Is Winning Friends in the Rust Belt," *Business Week*, October 19, 1987, p. 54.

17. Martin Tolchin and Susan Tolchin, *Buying into America: How Foreign Money Is Changing the Face of Our Nation* (New York: Times Books, 1988), pp. 113–14.

18. Kenichi Ohmae, "Use Economic Power as Defense Against Japan-Bashing," *Nihon Keizai Shimbun*, October 24, 1988, p. 1.

19. William J. Holstein, "Japan in America," *Business Week*, July 14, 1986, p. 44.

20. Thomas E. Ricks, "Task Force's Brady Says Japanese Sales of U.S. Bonds Touched Off Oct. 19 Crash," *Wall Street Journal*, April 22, 1988, p. 18.

21. This calculation is by Jan VanDenBerg at Merrill Lynch Japan. Of the total $1.6 trillion in foreign government debt that Japanese public and private institutions own, an estimated 30.8 percent, or $492.8 billion, is the U.S. government's.

22. Transcript, *New York Times*, February 22, 1989, p. 16.

23. Schlesinger, "Our Problem."

24. Felix Rohatyn, "America's Economic Dependence," *Foreign Affairs*, 1988/89, America & The World issue, p. 53.

25. Bruce Stokes, "Who's Standing Tall?," *National Journal*, October 21, 1989, pp. 2568–73.

Part Four

THE AMERICAN RESPONSE

19. Rethinking Japan

1. Robert Neff, Paul Magnusson, and William J. Holstein, "Rethinking Japan," *Business Week*, August 7, 1989.

2. Interview with author.

3. As quoted in *Japan Times*, October 13, 1989.

4. James Fallows, "Getting Along with Japan," *The Atlantic Monthly*, December 1989, p. 53.

5. Capt. Malcolm D. Kennedy, *The Problem of Japan* (London: Nisbet & Co. Ltd., 1935).

6. Amy Borrus, "The Book That's Creating a Firestorm," *Business Week*, October 23, 1989, pp. 78–80.

7. Remarks made at a luncheon sponsored by the Businessmen's Council for International Understanding, New York, March 29, 1989.

20. Economic Patriotism

1. Paul Kennedy, *The Rise and Fall of the Great Powers* (New York: Random House, 1987).

2. Nicholas Wade, "The Ascent of Books on Decline of U.S.," *New York Times*, April 10, 1988, p. E9.

3. Andrew Pollack, "The Challenge of Keeping U.S. Technology at Home," *New York Times*, December 10, 1989, p. A1.

4. Andrew Pollack, "IBM Chip Is Licensed to Micron," *New York Times*, November 9, 1989, p. D1.

21. *Industrial Policy Gridlock*

1. John Carey and Otis Port, "Will the White House Torpedo America Inc.?," *Business Week*, November 27, 1989, p. 80.
2. Larry Liebert, "Top Antitrust Enforcer Backs Joint-Production Deals," *San Francisco Chronicle*, September 20, 1989, p. C2.
3. Christopher J. Chipello, "More Competitors Turn to Cooperation," *Wall Street Journal*, June 23, 1989, p. B1.
4. Udayan Gupta, "Home-Grown Businesses Help Revive Local Economies," *Wall Street Journal*, January 4, 1990, p. B2.
5. Kevin Kelly, "A High-Tech Think Tank Thinks Big Bucks," *Business Week*, September 25, 1989, p. 222.
6. Doug McInnis, "Industry Group Formed to Exploit Technology Developed by Military," *New York Times*, January 1, 1990, p. 36.
7. Joel Dreyfuss, "Getting High Tech Back on Track," *Fortune*, January 1, 1990, pp. 74–77.
8. Ezra Vogel, *Comeback* (New York: Simon & Schuster, 1985), pp. 240–62.
9. "Promoting Technological Excellence: The Role of State and Federal Extension Activities," National Governors' Association, November 1989.
10. Richard Brandt, et al., "The Future of Silicon Valley," *Business Week*, February 5, 1990, p. 54.
11. Carey and Port, "Will the White House Torpedo America Inc.?"
12. Andrew Pollack, "Studies Ask Electronics Aid by U.S.," *New York Times*, November 21, 1989, p. D1.

22. *Investment: Absorb the Benefits*

1. Jaclyn Fierman, "The Selling Off of America," *Fortune*, December 22, 1986, p. 45.
2. Leah J. Nathans, "Meet Wall Street's New Bugaboo: CFIUS," *Business Week*, June 12, 1989, pp. 90–91.
3. Bill Powell, "War Between the States," *Newsweek*, May 30, 1988, pp. 44–45.
4. Allan Melkesian, "Foreign Investment Should Serve Community," *Japan Economic Journal*, November 25, 1989, p. 9.
5. Glickman and Woodward, *The New Competitors*, pp. 251–54.
6. Sanger, "Worried About Reaction in U.S."

23. *A Pacific Future*

1. Remarks at International Industrial Conference, San Francisco, September 18–20, 1989.

2. William J. Holstein, "The Small Guys Score Big Overseas," *Business Week,* February 27, 1989, pp. 94–96.

3. William J. Holstein, "Going Global," Business Week Corporate Elite. October 20, 1989, pp. 9–18.

4. Burton Bollag, "GATT Chief Sees U.S. Export Lead," *New York Times,* December 12, 1989, p. D9.

Index

327